Windows 10 Superguide

By Matthew A. Buxton

All rights reserved. No part of this publication may be reproduced, stored in a retrieval system, or transmitted in any form or by any means, electronic, mechanical, photocopying, recording or otherwise, without the prior written permission of the publisher.

The materials contained in this book are provided for general information purposes only and do not constitute legal or other professional advice on any subject matter. Top-Windows-Tutorials / ACEL Systems does not accept any responsibility for any loss which may arise from reliance on the information provided in this product.

While the information provided has been carefully reviewed, no guarantee is given that the information in this product is correct, complete, and/or up-to-date.

Windows and Windows 10 are registered trademarks of Microsoft corporation. This publication is not affiliated with or endorsed by Microsoft corporation.

About the Author

Matthew A. Buxton holds a degree in computer studies and has several years experience working in programming and technical support. He is the author and webmaster of the popular Windows website Top-Windows-Tutorials.com as well as two sites for videogamers, Videogameperfection.com and Play-Old-PC-Games.com. He is also the co-author of WeLoveCalis.com, a fantastic new guide to this Turkish coastal town. His previous books and training courses, the Windows 7 Superguide and the Windows 8 Superguide, are used by individuals, businesses, schools and colleges around the world to help teach Windows to computer users of all experience levels. The Windows 8 Superguide is the highest rated independently published Windows 8 book on Amazon.com. Matthew also writes about video games on blogs and forums and is a passionate game player across several different formats.

He currently works as a self employed webmaster, computer consultant and Wordpress developer. You can contact him by visiting his websites at, http://www.top-windows-tutorials.com or http://www.acelsystems.co.uk

on Facebook at https://en-gb.facebook.com/top.windows.tutorials

or on Twitter at https://twitter.com/TopWindowsTuts

Authors Acknowledgements

First and foremost, I'd like to thank my family, especially my mother whose tireless dedication to proof reading and checking has made this book into the professional document that it is.

Secondly, I'd like to thank the team behind the Wordpress.com website software. Not only are all our websites built on Wordpress now, but the Windows desktop version of this guide is too. Wordpress has dramatically reduced our workload and made publishing rich content sites a breeze.

Once again I would also like to thank Seniornet New Zealand for helping to fund the writing of this book and for their input and suggestions. We hope you find this course as useful as the Windows 7 and 8 Superguides were.

Thank you also to my girlfriend Rachel Mcneill for the cover design and also for her patience during the long months of writing and developing the guide.

Finally, I want to thank you, for purchasing my book and (hopefully!) visiting my websites. I sincerely hope you will find the material easy to understand and that it helps you get the best out of your Windows 10 computer, whatever size and shape it might come in!

Table of Contents

Foreword..**13**
Introduction..**14**
Chapter 1 – The Beginning..**17**
Before You Begin...**18**
    What is Windows 10?..18
    What happened to Windows 9?...18
    Do I need Windows 10?..18
    Choosing the right version..18
        32-bit or 64-bit?...20
    Taking the plunge...21
        Choosing a new computer with Windows 10 installed.......................21
    Upgrading an existing computer...23
        Is my old PC capable of running Windows 10?..................................23
        Upgrading from Windows 7 or 8..23
        What if the upgrade process fails?...31
        Upgrading from Windows Vista or Windows XP...............................32
    Final thoughts on installing and upgrading...32
Lesson 1 – Starting your new Windows 10 PC.......................................**33**
    1.1 – Initial personalisations..33
    1.2 – Choosing a Microsoft or a local account.......................................37
Lesson 2 – Diving into the Desktop..**39**
    2.1 – Logging in..39
    2.2 – Desktop elements...40
    2.3 – Search bar and Task view button...42
    2.4 – Notification area..43
Lesson 3 – The new Start Menu..**45**
    3.1 – Opening the Start menu...45
    3.2 – Areas on the Start menu..46
    3.3 – All apps...47
    3.4 – Locking, signing out and powering down.....................................48
Lesson 4 – Basic Searching...**51**
    4.1 – Search settings and turning Cortana off..51
    4.2 – Performing a search...54
    4.3 – My stuff...55
Lesson 5 – Windows in Windows 10..**59**
    5.1 – A Windows 10 desktop window..59
    5.2 – Moving and resizing..60
    5.3 – Ways to work with windows...60
Lesson 6 – Virtual Desktops..**64**
    6.1 – What are virtual desktops?...64

6.2 – Creating a virtual desktop...64
6.3 – Moving programs between virtual desktops.....................................66
6.4 – Closing a virtual desktop..68

Chapter 2 – Windows 10 on Tablets..70
Lesson 7 – Touch Gestures...71
7.1 – Taps..71
    7.1.1 – Double tap..71
    7.1.2 – Tap and hold..71
    7.1.3 – Dragging..73
7.2 – Swipe...73
    7.2.1 – Swipe in...73
7.3 – Pinch..74

Lesson 8 - Tablet Mode and the New Start Screen...............................75
8.1 - Turning on Tablet mode..75
8.2 - Start screen..76
8.3 - Using Trusted Windows Store apps...77
8.4 – Desktop apps in Tablet mode..77
8.5 – Taskbar differences..78

Lesson 9 – Touch Multitasking...80
9.1 – Task View..80
9.2 – Touch multitasking...81
9.3 - Resizing apps...83

Lesson 10 – Tweaking Windows 10 for Touch..85
10.1 - Making screen elements bigger...85
10.2 – Hiding the taskbar..86
10.3 - Metro Commander – A File Explorer alternative........................88

Chapter 3 – Exploring Files and Folders...90
Lesson 11 – Exploring File Explorer...91
11.1 – Your personal folders...91
11.2 – The individual elements of a File Explorer window....................94
11.3 – Introducing the ribbon...96
11.4 – Breadcrumbs...96
11.5 – Folder views..97

Lesson 12 – Advanced File Explorer Techniques................................104
12.1 – Delving into details view...104
12.2 – Preview pane..105
12.3 – Details pane..106
12.4 - Sort and group by options..108
12.5 – Check boxes, extensions and hidden items...............................110
12.6 – Navigation pane...111

Lesson 13 – Working With Files and Folders.......................................112
13.1 – Working with folders...112
13.2 – Making your own folders..113
13.3 – The context menu in File Explorer...114
13.4 – Send to..115

13.5 – Cut, copy and paste..116
  13.6 – When file names collide...118
  13.7 – Renaming or deleting files and folders..................................119
Lesson 14 – Multiple Files and Folders..121
  14.1 – Dragging and dropping...121
  14.2 – File name collisions revisited...121
  14.3 – Desktop Snap and multiple File Explorer windows................125
  14.4 – Working with multiple files at once..128
  14.5 – Keyboard short cuts and other ways of working with multiple files.............129
Chapter 4 – Deeper into Folders...131
Lesson 15 – Libraries...132
  15.1 – Activating libraries..132
  15.2 – Working with libraries..133
  15.3 – Sorting data in libraries..139
  15.4 – Pictures library...141
  15.5 – Open file/folder location...142
Lesson 16 – Folder Properties..144
  16.1 – Accessing folder properties...144
  16.2 – Customise tab..148
  16.3 – Folder pictures and folder icons...149
Lesson 17 – Folder Options...152
  17.1 – Folder options window..152
  17.2 – General folder options..153
  17.3 – View tab..154
  17.4 – Hidden files and folders..158
  17.5 – Hide extensions for known file types...................................162
Lesson 18 – Recycle Bin..166
  18.1 – Into the Recycle Bin...166
  18.2 – Sending files to the Recycle Bin...169
  18.3 – Files that are not sent to the Recycle Bin............................169
  18.4 – Recycle Bin folders..171
  18.5 – Recycle Bin Properties..171
Lesson 19 – This PC...175
  19.1 – Inside This PC...175
  19.2 – Personal folders...177
  19.3 – Devices and drives..177
    19.3.1 – Hidden drives..180
  19.4 – Network Locations..181
  19.5 – Other devices...181
Lesson 20 – More About the Taskbar...183
  20.1 – Jump lists and the taskbar..183
  20.2 – Moving the taskbar..184
  20.3 – Adding toolbars to the taskbar...185
  20.4 – Other taskbar customisations..186
  20.5 – Multi-monitor support...189

Lesson 21 – Notification Area...191
21.1 – The new notification area versus the old.................................191
21.2 – Customising the notification area..192
Lesson 22 – Search Is Everywhere..197
22.1 – Tags and other metadata...197
22.2 – Indexing options..199
22.3 – Tips for searching in Windows 10..204
Lesson 23 – Cortana..207
23.1 - Activating Cortana..207
23.2 - Cortana and privacy...212
23.3 - Typing a query..212
23.4 - Talking to Cortana...215
23.5 - Cortana's notebook...218
23.6 – Reminders...220
23.7 – Other things Cortana can do..222
23.8 - Troubleshooting Cortana..222
Lesson 24 – Mail and Calendar..224
24.1 – Getting started with Windows 10 Mail..................................224
24.2 – The Inbox..228
24.3 – Replying and composing..230
24.4 – E-mail attachments and inserts..232
24.5 – Adding new accounts..233
24.6 – Moving messages...234
24.7 – Introducing Calendar...234
Lesson 25 – People..237
25.1 – Adding an account..237
25.2 – Browsing the People app...239
25.3 – Adding and amending contacts..240
25.4 – Linking contacts..242
25.5 - Adding other accounts...244
Lesson 26 – Photos...245
26.1 – Browsing photos...246
26.2 – Viewing photos...246
26.3 – Editing and enhancing images..249
Lesson 27 – Groove Music...253
27.1 – Getting your groove on..254
27.2 – Browsing and playing your music..256
27.3 – Playlists...259
27.4 – Online features...261
27.5 – Adding music from other folders...261
Lesson 28 – Film and TV..262
28.1 – Using the Film & TV app..263
28.2 – Browsing and playing your media.......................................265
28.3 – Buying media online..267
28.4 – Adding video from other folders..267

Lesson 29 – News, Weather and Info Apps..268
  29.1 – News app..268
  29.2 – Information app buttons...270
  29.3 – Other News app features...270
  29.4 – Weather app...271
Lesson 30 – Maps...**274**
  30.1 – Navigating maps...275
  30.2 - Route planning and navigation..276
  30.3 - Favourites..279
  30.4 - 3D Cities..281
Lesson 31 – Store..**283**
  31.1 – What are Trusted Windows Store apps?...................................283
  31.2 - Browsing the store..283
  31.3 – Downloading and installing a new app....................................287
  31.4 – Account menu...289
Lesson 32 – OneDrive..**291**
  32.1 – Setting up OneDrive...291
  32.2 – OneDrive Fetch..296
  32.3 – OneDrive in File Explorer...296
  32.4 – OneDrive on the web..299
  32.5 – Managing OneDrive Settings..301
Chapter 7 – Securing Your PC and Your Data................................**304**
Lesson 33 – Planning a Backup Strategy......................................**305**
  33.1 – Backup methodologies..305
  33.2 – Do you have operating system recovery media?.......................306
  33.3 – Where to backup..306
  33.4 – A note about storing your backups...310
Lesson 34 – Configuring File History backup................................**311**
  34.1 – Choosing a File History drive...311
  34.2 – Starting the backup..313
  34.3 – Advanced settings..314
Lesson 35 – Restoring Files from File History...............................**316**
  35.1 – Restoring a file..316
  35.2 – Other ways of working with File History..................................320
  35.3 – Limitations of File History...321
Lesson 36 – Creating System Repair Media..................................**323**
  36.1 – System repair USB device...323
Lesson 37 – Creating and Modifying User Accounts.....................**329**
  37.1 – Adding a user..329
  37.2 – Microsoft accounts vs local accounts......................................333
  37.3 – Adding a Microsoft account...334
  37.4 – Standard users and Administrators...335
  37.5 – Creating local accounts...337
  37.6 – Running as a standard user...337
  37.7 – Microsoft accounts and sign-on options..................................338

Lesson 38 – User Account Controls..340
    38.1 – Halt! Who goes there?...340
    38.2 – User Account Controls to the rescue................................341
    38.3 – Changing User Account Control settings..........................342
    38.4 – User Account Controls and standard accounts................344

Lesson 39 – Family Safety...346
    39.1 – Family Safety requirements and initial setup......................346
    39.2 – Activating a child account..349
    39.3 – Family safety settings..350

Lesson 40 – Updating your PC..358
    40.1 – Manually checking for updates...358
    40.2 – Advanced update options..361

Lesson 41 – Privacy Options...365
    41.1 – Accessing privacy options...365
    41.2 – General privacy settings...366
    41.3 – Location privacy settings..368
    41.4 – Camera and Microphone..371
    41.5 – Speech, inking and typing...371
    41.6 – Account Info privacy options...373
    41.7 – Contacts, Calendar, Messaging and Radios.....................374
    41.8 – Other devices...374
    41.9 – Feedback and diagnostics..376
    41.10 – Background apps...376
    41.11 – Desktop software and privacy.......................................376

Lesson 42 – Windows Firewall..377
    42.1 – About the Windows 10 firewall...377
    42.2 – Changing firewall settings..380
    42.3 – Windows Firewall with Advanced Security.......................381
    42.4 – Third party firewalls..382

Lesson 43 – Windows Defender..384
    43.1 – What is antivirus software?..384
    43.2 – Starting Windows Defender...384
    43.3 – Windows Defender Options...386
    43.4 – Manually scanning your computer...................................388
    43.5 – Automatic scanning..391
    43.6 – Third party antivirus packages...392

Chapter 8 – Your PC Your Way..394
Lesson 44 – Customising the Mouse....................................395
    44.1 – Left handed use and other button options.......................396
    44.2 – Pointers and pointer options...397
    44.3 – Mouse wheel options...399

Lesson 45 – Customising Start..401
    45.1 – Resizing the Start menu..401
    45.2 – Adding and removing tiles...402
    45.3 – Resizing and grouping tiles..404

45.4 – Further Start menu customisations	405
45.5 – Start colour and appearance	408
45.6 – Touch screen differences	409

Lesson 46 – Action Centre and Notifications 411
- 46.1 – Notifications 411
- 46.2 – Quick access buttons 413
- 46.3 – Notification options 415
- 46.4 – Notification sounds 417

Lesson 47 – Installing new Desktop Software 420
- 47.1 – Choosing software 420
- 47.2 – Free software versus paid 422
- 47.3 – Starting installation from optical media 422
- 47.4 – Installation examples 423

Lesson 48 – Legacy Software and Compatibility 428
- 48.1 – Windows 10 - 64-bit edition 428
- 48.2 – Using compatibility options 429
- 48.3 – My software still won't run 434

Lesson 49 – Desktop Backgrounds 436
- 49.1 – Getting started with desktop backgrounds 436
- 49.2 – Using your own pictures on the desktop 437
- 49.3 – Picture positioning options 438
- 49.4 – Slideshow backgrounds 438
- 49.5 – Desktop backgrounds from the internet 440
- 49.6 – Colour settings 441

Lesson 50 – Customising the Lock Screen 443
- 50.1 – Lock screen pictures 443
- 50.2 – Lock screen app settings 444

Lesson 51 – Devices and Printers 447
- 51.1 – Delving into Devices and Printers 447
- 51.2 – Using Devices and Printers 450

Chapter 9 – Networking and the Internet 451

Lesson 52 – Choosing an ISP and Getting Connected 452
- 52.1 – Types of internet connection 452
- 52.2 – Choosing an ISP 453
- 52.3 – Types of internet hardware 453
- 52.4 – Connecting it all up 454

Lesson 53 – The Microsoft Edge Browser 459
- 53.1 – Starting Microsoft Edge 459
- 53.2 – Your first Microsoft Edge session 460

Lesson 54 – Microsoft Edge Part 2 463
- 54.1 – Tabs 464
- 54.2 – Favourites 464
- 54.3 – Advanced Microsoft Edge options 468
- 54.4 – Download manager 471

Lesson 55 – Homegroups..**474**
    55.1 – Creating a homegroup..474
    55.2 – Restricting access to files or folders..477
    55.3 – Joining an existing homegroup...479
    55.4 – Browsing a homegroup..481
    55.5 – Renaming computers..482

Chapter 10 – Windows Media Player...**485**
Lesson 56 – Introducing Windows Media Player 12.........................**486**
    56.1 – Running Media Player for the first time....................................486
    56.2 – Playing video..488
    56.3 – The media library..490

Lesson 57 – Ripping CDs..**491**
    57.1 – Setting ripping options..491
    57.2 – Ripping a CD..493
    57.3 – Copy protection options..496

Lesson 58 – Wrapping up Media Player..**499**
    58.1 – Browsing libraries..499
    58.2 – Viewing pictures...502

Chapter 11 – Troubleshooting and Maintenance.....................**504**
Lesson 59 – Uninstalling Software..**505**
    59.1 – Uninstalling Windows Store software......................................505
    59.2 – Uninstalling desktop software..506

Lesson 60 – The Disk Cleanup Utility..**508**
    60.1 – Starting a disk cleanup..508
    60.2 – Choosing cleaning options..508

Lesson 61 – Disk Defragmentation..**511**
    61.1 – The Optimise Drives window..511
    61.2 – Setting a schedule..513
    61.3 – Manual defragmentation..514

Lesson 62 – System Restore...**516**
    62.1 – Enabling System Restore..516
    62.2 – Creating your own system restore point.................................518
    62.3 – Choosing a restore point..520
    62.3 – Restoring from a restore point...521
    62.4 – Undoing a System Restore...522

Lesson 63 – Reset your PC..**524**
    63.1 – Beginning a system reset...524
    63.2 – Reset options..525
    63.3 – Finalising and resetting..528

Lesson 64 – Task Manager..**531**
    64.1 – Starting the Task Manager...531
    64.2 – Managing tasks...533
    64.3 – Processes..534
    64.4 – Other Task Manager tabs...535

64.5 – Running a program from the Task Manager 540
Chapter 12 – And Finally 541
Popular Windows Software 542
    65.1 – Software recommendations 542
    E-mail 542
    Games 542
    Image and photograph editing 542
    Instant messaging, video and voice chat 543
    Music and Multimedia 543
    Music creation 544
    Online safety 544
    Password Management 545
    Social networking 545
    Web browsing 546
    Word processing and office 546
Appendix – Using Touch PCs 547

Foreword

The launch of a new version of Windows is always an exciting time for anyone who enjoys new technology. Windows 10 is no exception to that of course, but it feels a little sad to be saying goodbye to Windows 8 already. Many people see Windows 8 as a failure, but as anyone who read our Windows 8 Superguide knows, Windows 8 is far from the unusable, confusing mess that many critics make it out to be. With a few tweaks, Windows 8 was easily the best version of Windows there has ever been (until now of course!). It's really disappointing that more people didn't take the time to learn how to get the most out of Windows 8, as its new tiles combined with its traditional desktop made perfect sense for computers like the Microsoft Surface and other high end tablets and convertibles. Contrary to what many people still believe, it's faster boot times, enhanced security and great multi-monitor support made it a perfect fit for traditional computer systems too, even if it wasn't always a particularly compelling upgrade from Windows 7.

Windows 10 may seem on the surface (no pun intended) to be a simple re-branding of Windows 8. The Start screen now turns into a Start menu when you're not using a touch-screen PC. Metro or Tile-based apps (now known as "Trusted Windows Store" apps) run in windows rather than forced full screen. Indeed, all these enhancements were already available to Windows 8 users as third-party add-ons.

What is new in Windows 10 is Microsoft's approach. Still easily the dominant desktop/laptop computer operating system, Microsoft is lagging behind its competitors Apple and Google on both tablets and smartphones. To bridge this gap, Microsoft's goal is one Windows that works across all devices. That goes for software too. Software like the new Microsoft Edge browser is designed to work on desktop and tablet. Theoretically this is great for developers, of course, as it means they can write their software once and deploy it anywhere, but will this approach work? Given that working with a keyboard and mouse is so much different to working with a touch screen, it seems like there will always have to be a compromise one way or another, it just remains to be seen if this will be an acceptable compromise in many cases.

However Windows 10 evolves over its life, the OS is ready for all your modern computing needs. With features like Cortana and the new notification area, Windows 10 works more intelligently across all of your devices. Features like the up-coming DirectX 12 make the operating system into a multimedia and gaming powerhouse and with decades worth of Windows software already fully compatible, there's virtually no computing task a Windows 10 PC can't lend itself to.

Introduction

Welcome to our newest Top-Windows-Tutorials.com Superguide. Windows 10 has been growing and evolving as we wrote this guide and will no doubt continue to do so. Using Windows 10 puts you right at the cutting edge of computing technology, but that doesn't mean things need to be difficult. Thousands of users across the world (just like you!) have benefited from our other Superguides. We sincerely hope that this latest guide will help you not only get to grips with Windows 10 but become more productive with the new operating system and most importantly enjoy using your computer. While Windows 10 is certainly a lot more familiar for Windows veterans compared to Windows 8, there's still a lot that has changed. No matter if your new, or what version of Windows you're migrating from, we hope this guide will help you get more out of Windows 10.

About this book (physical and e-book edition)

The Windows 10 Superguide is designed as a complete training course, this includes video content as well as an e-book. Physical copies of this e-book are also available, as well as e-book copies for devices such as the Amazon Kindle. We originally started offering these additional services at the request of our customers, with the Windows 7 Superguide. With the Windows 10 Superguide, the physical and e-book editions will launch at (or around) the same time as the full training course. We understand some people prefer to have a traditional reference book, while others prefer a full video course. To find out more about all the ways you can get the Windows 10 Superguide, visit this page on our website:-

http://www.top-windows-tutorials.com/windows-10-superguide/

Prerequisites

Apart from a desire to learn about Windows 10, there are a few things you should have before you start this course.

You should know some basic computer skills, such as how to turn your machine on. Knowing how to operate a keyboard and mouse is also very useful. Windows 10 is designed to work both with touch and with keyboard and mouse input. This guide was written to cater for both touch screen and keyboard and mouse users. If you plan to use a touch enabled PC, Chapter 2 in the guide deals with the differences you will encounter when running Windows 10 in Tablet mode.

Remember that Microsoft themselves provide plenty of additional help for Windows 10. Check out their Windows 10 support pages here:-
http://windows.microsoft.com/en-gb/windows-10/support

If you are not familiar with using Windows or desktop operating systems of any kind, you may want to see Microsoft's guide to using menus, buttons, bars and boxes. You can access this guide on the internet here:-
http://windows.microsoft.com/en-gb/windows/using-menus-buttons-bars-boxes#1TC=windows-7

Access to a Windows 10 machine, while not absolutely essential, is also extremely helpful for practising your skills. Remember that if you are a home/private user you can upgrade any Windows 7 or 8 (or 8.1) machine to Windows 10 for free (at least for the first year from Windows 10's release). For a quick tutorial on how to do this, see "Upgrading from Windows 7 or 8" near the end of the "Before you Begin" section.

Conventions used in this book

We have aimed to keep this book free of jargon and technical terms wherever possible. One convention we did decide on is regarding the use of the mouse. This book is written assuming a right handed mouse configuration. When we instruct you to click on an item, we are talking about clicking with the primary mouse button. When we talk about right-clicking, we mean the secondary mouse button. We did consider using different terminology, such as "alt click" or something similar, but nothing was as clear as simply using "click" and "right click". We hope left handed users will forgive us this bias. If you're a touch screen user, see the appendix at the end of the book which explains how to "right click" with a finger!

Remember we're based in the UK, which means we spell certain words differently to those of you who live in the USA. Compared to the US, we spell "Center" as "Centre", "Color" as "Colour", "Customize" as "Customise" and "Favorites" as "Favourites". Check marks (as in, check the box or check off an item on your list) are usually called "ticks" here in the UK, in case you were confused. Our books have always sold well in the USA so we hope these minor regional differences aren't too annoying for our US customers!

How to use this book

Windows 10 is a versatile operating system and we realise that some of the information we present in the guide won't be relevant to all of you. If a specific lesson might not be relevant to you we will usually say so at the start of the lesson. Feel free to complete the lesson anyway, of course, as it's all good practise.

We cover touch screen gestures and differences in Chapter 2. If you aren't using a touch screen PC and don't plan on ever using one, you can skip out Chapter 2 entirely.

If you don't already have your Windows 10 PC connected to the internet, you might want to complete at least lessons 1 to 5, then lessons 7 to 10 if you have a touch screen, then skip ahead to lesson 52 to get connected. Many of the Windows apps we discuss in Chapter 6, for instance, either depend on an internet connection or work much better when one is available.

Finally if you find our File Explorer tutorials to be too daunting, it's okay to skip ahead to more fun topics such as the apps we cover in Chapter 6. Come back later when you've had a break or practised your skills.

Chapter 1 – The Beginning

It is time to start your journey. A whole new, exciting modern operating system holds so many possibilities for you and your PC. Windows has always been about versatility and with Windows 10 that goes even further. Now Windows 10 can be at home on your desktop PC, your laptop, on a tablet or on a touch screen anywhere. Windows 10 may even eventually power the next generation of smartphones. Never before have there been so many exciting ways to interact with your Windows PC!

Before You Begin

After much anticipation and one of the biggest public beta tests in the history of computing, Windows 10 is finally available to the public. With the desktop firmly back in focus and the Start menu making a triumphant return, Windows 10 seeks to win back those who shunned Windows 8.

What is Windows 10?

Windows 10 is still the same Windows operating system that users around the world know and love. The traditional desktop is still available and virtually all the software designed for Windows 7 and 8 is fully compatible. Many users regard Windows 10 as the best of Windows 7 and 8 in one package.

What happened to Windows 9?

With Windows 10, Microsoft decided they needed a clean break from the bad publicity of Windows 8. Rather than go to Windows 9, which consumers might assume was a simple upgrading of Windows 8, they decided to skip Windows 9 entirely and so that is how we've ended up with Windows 10 already.

Do I need Windows 10?

If you are reading this guide then we will assume that you have already downloaded Windows 10 or you are strongly considering an upgrade. If you are planning to purchase a new Windows PC, you should absolutely make sure that it ships with Windows 10 already installed. If you are planning to upgrade your existing computer, things can be a little more complicated but we will discuss the options later.

Choosing the right version

Buying Windows 10, either pre-installed or as an upgrade to an existing PC, might not be as straightforward as you think. There are a total of six different versions of Windows 10 available and most come in 32-bit and 64-bit versions, but more on those later. For home users, the correct choice is usually the standard Windows 10 Home edition, but we'll take a look now at each version of the operating system and describe what it offers.

Windows 10 Home:- This standard version of Windows 10 is designed for the home user and therefore sacrifices some of the advanced features available in the pro version, such as Bitlocker encryption. As with Windows 7 and 8, home versions, computers running this version of Windows 10 cannot join a corporate "domain" network.

Windows 10 Mobile:- This version of the OS is designed for mobile devices like smartphones and small tablets. This version can run only the "Trusted Windows Store" apps. It is similar to the Windows RT version that was available with Windows 8. It is not anticipated that this version will be available to purchase separately from a device.

Windows 10 Professional:- This version includes all the features of the standard edition as well as several features targeted at enthusiasts and business users. Windows 10 Professional users can join a domain based network (common in businesses around the world), as well as use advanced features like Bitlocker and virtual hard disks. We do not cover these features in this guide.

Windows 10 Enterprise:- Similar to Windows 10 professional, but available only to Microsoft's corporate customers and registered software developers. The Enterprise edition has the same features as the Professional edition and can also run prototype/development builds of Trusted Windows Store applications. Normally these applications can only be downloaded and run from the Windows store.

Windows 10 Education:- This is similar to the Enterprise build but available at a discount to educational institutions such as schools, colleges and universities.

Windows 10 Mobile Enterprise:- Like Windows 10 Mobile but tailored for big businesses wanting to outfit a fleet of smartphones or tablets for their employees to use in the field. This version is not readily available to the general public.

If you're still confused as to which version you need, then chances are that the standard Windows 10 Home is the right version for you. The Enterprise and Education editions are not widely available to the public and if the extra features that come with the Professional edition sounded like another language to you then it is unlikely you will ever need them. If you do, it is possible to upgrade through Windows Anytime Upgrade, as long as you have an internet connection and a means of electronic payment such as a credit card. Be warned though, the prices for Anytime Upgrade are not always as economical as simply buying the correct version of Windows in the first place.

That just leaves the mobile edition of the OS. If you're considering a device running Windows 10 Mobile, remember that it cannot run regular desktop apps, it can only run the so-called "Trusted Windows Store" apps that are available in the Windows store. If this doesn't concern you, Windows 10 Mobile powered devices can offer excellent value and portability.

32-bit or 64-bit?

When discussing this subject, it is easy for technical authors such as myself to begin reminiscing about our childhoods and the amount of memory and storage space the early computers of the time had. I decided I would spare you that this time and get to the point. 64-bit versions of Windows can access more memory than their 32-bit counterparts, but the 32-bit versions tend to have better overall compatibility especially with older hardware and software. The 32-bit versions of Windows 10 can access a maximum of 4 gigabytes of RAM. RAM is the primary storage area on your computer that Windows uses for programs and data that it is currently working on. It is not the same as the hard drive which is used to store programs and data that are not currently being used. If you're confused, we will discuss these terms in more detail later, when we talk about choosing a computer for Windows 10 or upgrading an existing machine.

The 64-bit versions of Windows 10 can access either 128gb on the standard edition or up to a whopping 512 gigabytes on the Professional edition. Again, I want to tell you how many hundreds of times more capacity that is than the first hard drive I owned, but I wont.

Now, 4 Gigabytes of memory might seem like a lot and for many users it will be adequate. 4 gigabytes must have sounded like a lot when the first 32-bit versions of Windows were developed, but by today's standards it's quite modest. For instance Windows PCs have the most cutting edge games in the world and many of these games will benefit from machines with large amounts of RAM. It is important to note that this maximum memory allocation includes memory on your graphics card too. Were you to purchase a high end graphics card for gaming, with 1 gigabyte of memory, the most system RAM you could then use with a 32-bit version of Windows would be 3 gigabytes. With graphics cards now shipping with 4 gigabytes or more memory and with top-spec gaming motherboards giving the option of attaching two or more graphics cards at once, enthusiasts should always go 64-bit to get the most out of their machines. Even regular users should probably choose the 64-bit version of Windows 10 unless they have a particular piece of old software that isn't compatible.

Some IT experts believed that Microsoft would actually drop the 32 bit version of Windows 10 and go 64 bit only. However, this hasn't happened. For very low-end machines, the 32 bit version of Windows is actually a tiny bit more memory efficient, so it still makes sense in a small number of cases.

Just like Windows 8, the retail editions of Windows 10 will ship with both 32-bit and 64-bit versions in the same box. However, you can't switch between versions without either reinstalling your operating system or configuring some kind of dual booting system.

Taking the plunge

So, you have decided on which edition of Windows 10 to purchase, how do you go about getting it? Before you tear off to the store with your shopping list, let's look at a couple of options.

Choosing a new computer with Windows 10 installed

Buying a computer with Windows 10 pre-installed is the easiest way to get the operating system. The hard part is done and you can get right on with discovering your new PC. Which PC you choose is largely down to your personal tastes and requirements. Do your homework, look for reviews on the internet if possible and think carefully before parting with your cash. Here are a few pointers to look out for when buying a Windows 10 PC.

Memory:– Windows 10 requires 1 gigabyte of computer memory (2 gigabytes for the 64-bit version). Memory is usually shortened to RAM, it can also be referred to as "primary storage". RAM is where the computer stores programs and data it is currently working on, this is different to the hard disk or drive which is generally only fast enough to store programs and data you are not currently using. One gigabyte of memory is just about adequate for regular computing tasks such as surfing the internet, word-processing or writing e-mails. If you work with lots of programs at once, or you do more demanding tasks on your computer such as gaming, you may want to go for a machine with 2 or more gigabytes of memory. Memory can easily be upgraded in most computers, though some ultra-portable laptops and tablets may be more difficult or impossible to upgrade.

Hard Drive Capacity:– Your hard disk drive is used to store all the programs and data you keep on your PC. Hard drive sizes are measured in gigabytes too, but they are considerably larger than memory or RAM capacities. Windows 10 requires 16 gigabytes of hard drive space (20 gigabytes for the 64 bit version) all to itself. The remaining space is filled up with any other programs you install and any files you create yourself or download from the internet. If you have a large collection of multimedia files, you will want to make sure to purchase a machine with an equally large hard drive. Don't forget that hard drives are prone to sudden, random failures. Always keep a backup of your data if it is important, we discuss backup and the Windows 10 backup utility in Chapter 7.

Hard Drive Type:- There are two types of hard drive available to consumers, solid state and magnetic. Solid state drives or SSD's are extremely fast and can give your computer a noticeable speed boost. However, they have a much less attractive cost to capacity ratio when compared to traditional, magnetic media hard drives. In a desktop PC or larger laptop, you may be able to choose an SSD for Windows and a second, traditional magnetic media drive for secondary storage. In a smaller form factor PC where weight is an issue, you will usually be limited to choosing one or the other.

Graphics Card/processor:– The graphics card, graphics chip or GPU (graphical processing unit) in the computer you buy is often overlooked by consumers when shopping for a new computer. You should make sure to check that the graphics card in the machine is capable of running DirectX 9 and WDDM 1.0 or higher. If you plan to play the latest games on your machine, you will need a PC with a more powerful GPU. Be sure to budget for this and check the requirements for the games you want to play to make sure your new PC matches up.

Internet connection:- Remember that to use the Windows Store app and many of the features of Windows 10 we demonstrate, you will need some kind of internet connection. Typically new PCs come with wired and wireless connections. We discuss types of internet connection in lesson 52. If you aren't planning to connect to the internet, you can still buy and use desktop software from various retailers, but you won't be able to buy any of the new Trusted Windows Store software as this is only available online through the Windows store.

All shapes and sizes:– Modern PCs come in all kinds of different shapes and sizes, from tiny ultra-portables to huge, powerful desktops and this has never been more true than with Windows 10 machines. Again, the machine you choose comes down to personal taste and requirements. As a general rule, desktop computers have better upgrade options, larger displays and give more "bang for the buck" in terms of performance. Laptop, netbook (very small laptops, sometimes called ultra portables) and tablet PCs can, obviously, be transported and used almost anywhere. That could be up and down the country as you travel on business or up and down the house and garden as you work and play at home. Laptops and ultra-portables also take up less space but might not be quite so suited to heavy computing work as desktop PCs are and the smaller the PC gets the less powerful it is likely to be. Tablets can be great for reading or watching a movie, but not so great for when you want to get some work done. Many Windows 10 tablets have docking stations that turn them into mini-laptops, making them very flexible devices indeed.

Should I consider a Windows 10 Mobile machine?

Remember that if you are considering a machine that runs Windows 10 Mobile edition, it will not be compatible with any desktop software. Windows 10 Mobile machines will only run software available from the Windows store. This includes versions of some popular desktop apps such as Office. Don't write off Windows 10 Mobile altogether, although it has this significant drawback, Windows 10 tablets are lighter and cheaper than the machines that run the regular version of Windows. Remember too, that software you buy on your Microsoft account will work on any other Windows 10 machines you have access to, as long as you can sign into them using your Microsoft account. For instance, you could have a heavyweight, super powerful notebook PC for business and a lighter Windows 10 Mobile machine for those weekends away. Both these machines would have access to your Windows store purchases. Finally, of course, Windows 10 Mobile will eventually run on mobile phones and these phones are guaranteed to work brilliantly together with any Windows 10 PC you might own.

Upgrading an existing computer

Windows 10 is a compelling upgrade for many existing computers too, especially considering that for most Windows 7 and 8 users, the upgrade is entirely free. If you're still running Windows Vista or even Windows XP, upgrading to Windows 10 is not free, but it will unlock a slew of new features and particularly for those die-hard Windows XP users, make your PC much more secure too.

Is my old PC capable of running Windows 10?

Windows 10 requires a 1 gigahertz processor and 1 gigabyte of RAM (2 gigabytes for the 64-bit version). You will also need at least a DirectX 9 graphics device. The system requirements are actually exactly the same as for Windows 8, so if you already have Windows 8, you're good to go. If you are not running Windows 8, the easiest way to see if your computer meets these requirements is to use the Windows 8.1 Upgrade Assistant. It's likely that Microsoft will launch a dedicated Windows 10 upgrade assistant tool in the near future, but since the system requirements are exactly the same, the Windows 8.1 version will work just fine too. To obtain this tool, visit the page here:- http://windows.microsoft.com/en-gb/windows-8/upgrade-assistant-download-online-faq

Now, click on "Download Windows 8.1 Upgrade Assistant". You should now see a download link for the Upgrade Assistant. Run the Upgrade Assistant to evaluate your current PC and see if it meets the requirements for installing Windows 10.

Upgrading from Windows 7 or 8

To use the free upgrade offer on a Windows 7 or 8 PC, you must be a home (non-corporate or education) user running a genuine copy of Windows 7 or Windows 8. Home, professional and ultimate editions are eligible. Note that you can't upgrade from 32 bit to 64 bit Windows using this process, if you are running 32 bit Windows 7 or 8, you will always receive 32 bit Windows 10.

To get started, check the notification area (that's the area with the small icons in the bottom right hand corner) for the Windows 10 upgrade icon. Figure A shows this icon on a typical Windows 8 PC.

Figure A – The Windows 10 update icon in the notification area

Double click on the Windows 10 update icon and the window shown in figure B1 will then appear.

Figure B1 – Starting the upgrade process

Now you need to "reserve your free upgrade", so click on the box in this window. If you're lucky, you may find the upgrade tool skips right ahead to figure B5. For the rest of us, the window shown in figure B2 will then appear.

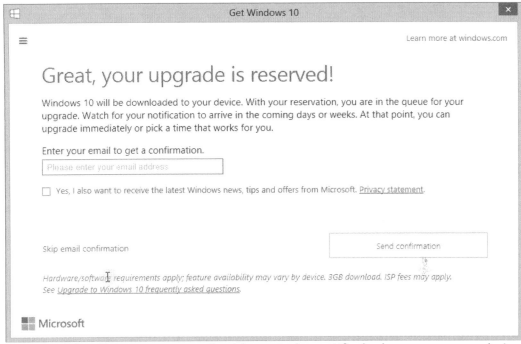

Figure B2 – Enter your e-mail address to be notified when your upgrade is ready

The upgrade is now reserved. The upgrade tool will also offer to e-mail us when the upgrade is ready. Enter your e-mail address to receive your confirmation and then click on "Send confirmation", or simply click on "Skip email confirmation". The window shown in figure B3 will then appear.

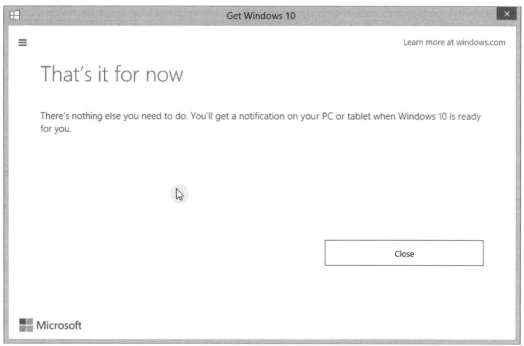

Figure B3 – Be prepared to wait a few days for your upgrade if you see this window

Unfortunately, you now need to wait. At the time of writing this waiting period was usually a couple of days. Keep your computer on as much as possible as Microsoft may begin the download in the background. Once the upgrade is ready, you will receive a notification e-mail and also see the notification on your desktop, as shown in figure B4.

Figure B4 – Your upgrade is ready

Click on the notification shown in figure B4 and the window shown in figure B5 will then appear.

Figure B5 – We're finally downloading Windows 10!

When you see the window shown in figure B5, Windows 10 is actually downloading to your computer. Again, we need to wait until this process has finished. You can click on "View download progress" to watch the progress bar slowly advance in Windows update. When the download is finally done, the window shown in figure B6 will be displayed.

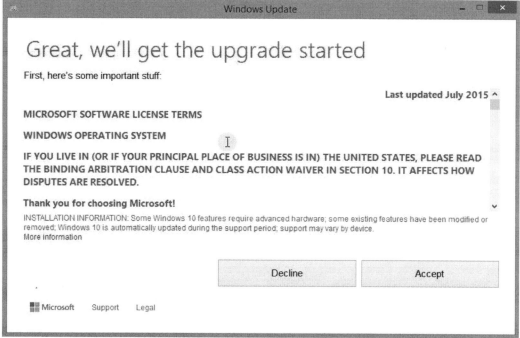

Figure B6 – Finally we are ready to install Windows 10

Click on "Accept" to accept the Windows 10 end user license agreement (EULA). The upgrade assistant will then give you the option of scheduling your update for later or starting it now. Click on "Start the upgrade now" to begin. Your computer will restart as soon as you click on this button, so make sure you have saved all of your work.

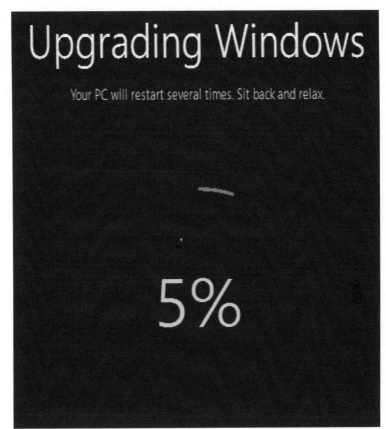

Figure B7 – Sit back and relax while Windows 10 installs

You now simply need to wait for the upgrade process to complete. This can take a while, so go and make a cup of tea or coffee, if you like, then come back later. When the process is complete, there are a few Windows 10 specific settings you need to configure. Figure B8 shows the first prompt that will appear.

Figure B8 – Logging into your newly upgraded machine

Start by entering your password to log back into your newly upgraded machine. Your password is the same as before you upgraded. Type it in here then press enter or click on "Next".

Windows will then offer you the choice of "Use Express settings" or "Customise settings" (see lesson 1, figure 1.3 for a screen shot). For simplicity, new users should choose "Use Express settings". All settings can be changed later once you're more comfortable working with your PC. If you want to know exactly what express settings will configure, click on the "Learn more" link near the bottom of the screen. We only cover the express settings in this guide, but we do show you how to change some of those settings later. Click on "Use Express settings". The options shown in figure B9 will then be displayed.

Figure B9 – Do you want to try out these new apps?

Microsoft have bundled a number of apps with Windows 10 that they are keen for you to try. On this screen, the upgrade assistant is asking for your permission to change several of your default apps. If you normally open websites using the Google Chrome browser, for example, then clicking "Next" here will change that so the default is the new Microsoft Edge browser. Of course you can change back later if you decide that you don't want to use Microsoft Edge.

If you'd rather stick to your current defaults, you will need to click on "Let me choose my default apps" and then select your preferred default applications. Otherwise click on "Next" to give the new Windows 10 apps a trial run.

Once you click on "Next", the process is complete. Windows will set up your new Windows 10 user account. This normally only takes a minute or two. When this process is complete, you will find yourself on the new Windows 10 desktop and you can proceed right to lesson 2 in the guide.

What if the upgrade process fails?

Unfortunately, at the time of going to press a large number of users were struggling to complete this upgrade process. The free Windows 10 upgrade process has failed on a number of our machines here at TWT HQ. If the upgrade does fail on your machine, your first port of call is Microsoft's support page here:-

http://windows.microsoft.com/en-us/windows-10/upgrade-install-errors-windows-10

You may also want to check our Windows 10 tutorial pages:-

http://www.top-windows-tutorials.com/win10

for details of any workarounds we found for our troublesome systems.

Finally, if you still can't upgrade, you might want to consult a local IT professional or computer workshop.

Upgrading from Windows Vista or Windows XP

Upgrading a Windows XP or Vista computer to Windows 10 is a little more tricky. Care must be taken to backup all your data and you will have to reinstall all of your programs once you have finished upgrading your operating system. Note that unlike Windows 7 and 8 users, there is no free upgrade offer for users running Windows Vista, XP or earlier versions of Windows.

Final thoughts on installing and upgrading

We did consider an in-depth guide to installation and upgrading to Windows 10 in in this guide. However, we decided that it was beyond the scope of a book aimed at beginners and that most people would simply be using the free upgrade download provided by Microsoft. We would want to cover dual booting (installing two or more operating systems at once) and various other options to really cover the subject in the kind of detail that Superguide readers would expect. If you want to upgrade your existing computer to Windows 10 and you cannot use the Microsoft free upgrade, discuss the options with a local IT professional or computer workshop. They will be able to asses all your upgrade options.

Lesson 1 – Starting your new Windows 10 PC

Even starting a Windows 10 PC can cause some surprises. In this lesson we will take a look at what happens when you first power on a factory fresh Windows 10 machine. Don't worry if you've already gone over these steps, there is nothing here that you can do wrong or can't change later.

1.1 – Initial personalisations

The very first thing to do on your Windows 10 PC is choose your language, time zone and location settings. Figure 1.1 shows these settings.

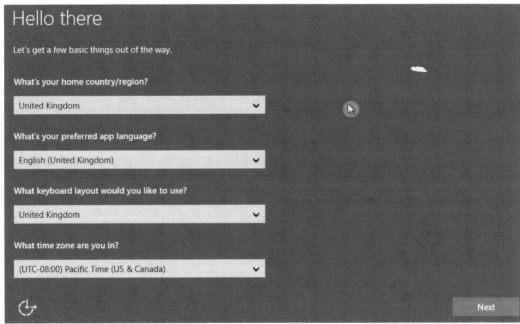

Figure 1.1 – Choose your regional and language settings

To change any values, click (or tap) the boxes and then select from the list that appears. To scroll through values with your finger, use a swipe (see lesson 7.2). To navigate with your mouse, you can drag the scroll control or click the arrows. Click or tap on "Next" when you are done. The screen shown in figure 1.2 will then appear.

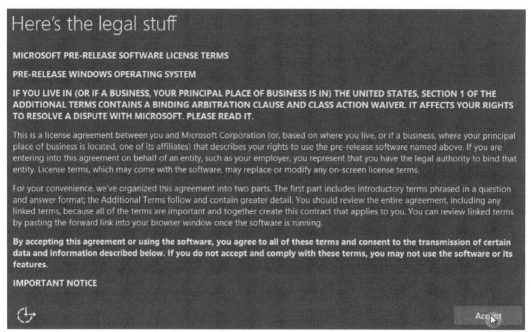

Figure 1.2 – Accepting the license agreement

To use Windows 10 you must agree to this license agreement. If you need to review it, simply scroll down the text. Click or tap on "Accept" when you are done. The screen shown in figure 1.3 will then appear.

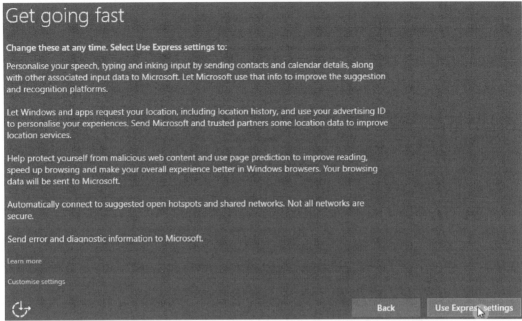

Figure 1.3 – Choosing options and reviewing privacy policies

The screen shown in figure 1.3 will offer the choice of "Use Express settings" or "Customise settings". For simplicity, new users should choose "Use Express settings". All settings can be changed later once you're more comfortable working with your PC. If you want to know exactly what express settings will configure, click on the "Learn more" link near the bottom of the screen. We only cover the express settings in this guide, but we do show you how to change some of those settings later. Click on "Use Express settings". If you're using Windows 10 Professional or Enterprise, you will see the screen shown in figure 1.4. Otherwise, you will skip directly to the screen shown in figure 1.5.

![Who owns this PC? screen]

Figure 1.4 – Who owns your PC?

If your PC is owned by your employer, school or college, you should probably check with them before setting it up. Otherwise, click on "I own it" and then click "Next". The screen shown in figure 1.5 will then appear.

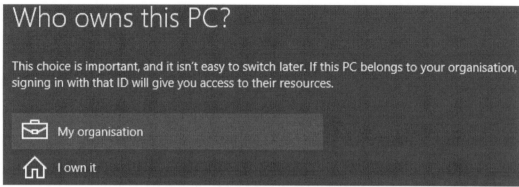

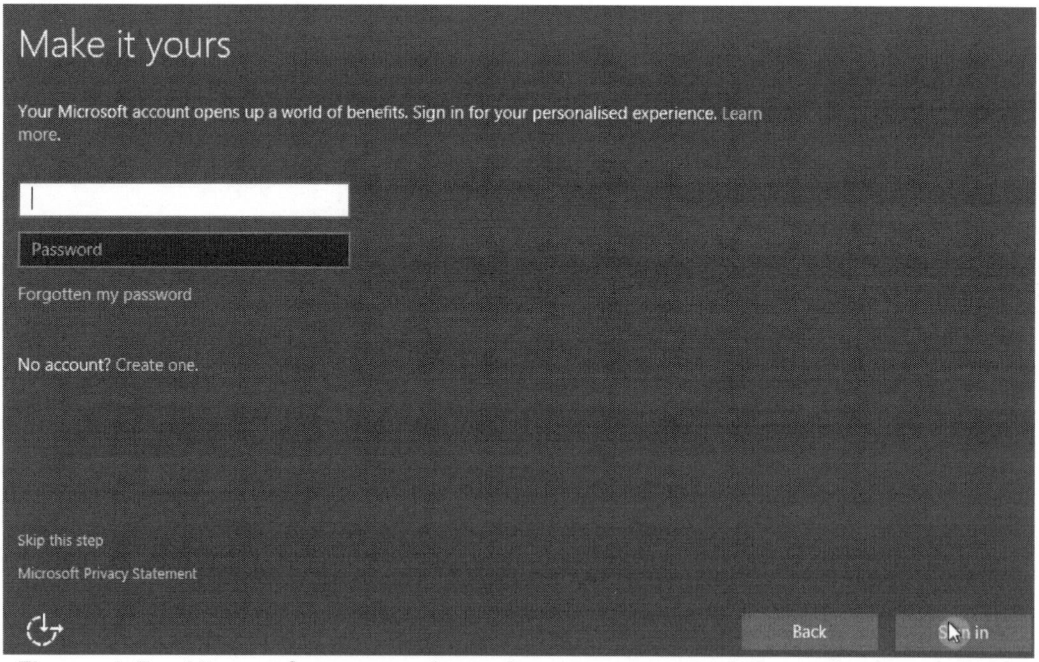

Figure 1.5 – Microsoft are very keen for you to use a Microsoft account with Windows 10, but you don't have to

1.2 – Choosing a Microsoft or a local account

The setup process now presents you with an important choice. You can sign in to your PC using a Microsoft account or you can use a regular Windows account.

What is the difference between each type of account and why was this change introduced? Microsoft are keen for users to sign in with a Microsoft account. When you do this, settings will be synchronised between all the PCs you own and you will be automatically signed into the Windows store. This can be very convenient of course. You might already have a Microsoft account and not even be aware of it. If you use Hotmail or Outlook.com, your log in for these services is your Microsoft account. The same log in is used for OneDrive and Xbox Live too. If you don't have a Microsoft account, you can sign up for one at this point too, by clicking "Create one".

Why might you want to use a regular Windows account instead? You may consider that linking all of your Microsoft services like this to be a security risk. Malware designed to steal Windows log in credentials has appeared in the past and now that Windows credentials can be linked to online accounts too, they become even more valuable. Although Microsoft take steps to mitigate accounts being stolen, as we've seen in the media there's always that danger. Personally, I prefer to keep my Microsoft password in a password manager and use a standard log in for my PC, this means I can use a much longer password than I could normally remember for my Microsoft account. In Windows 10 you can log into your PC and Microsoft account by using a PIN. This PIN is only valid for the PC you're currently using and helps keep your real Microsoft password more secure. The PIN however, can only consist of numbers and not letters, so you may not consider it good enough security for a laptop you carry with you on the road, for instance. We cover password managers briefly in the last chapter and we look at Microsoft accounts in more detail in lesson 37.

The other reason you might not want to log in with a Microsoft account is if you have a home network setup. Perhaps you or a technician or family member has configured devices like media streamers or network attached storage (NAS) boxes in your home. In this setup, these devices may be protected with user names and passwords that prevent certain family members from accessing each others files. In this case, you might want to continue using a regular, old fashioned Windows account rather than reconfiguring all of your network to accept new user names and passwords.

The choice of which type of account you use is entirely up to you. You can add new accounts of both types later, or even switch an old style account to use a Microsoft account or vice versa. Even logging in without a Microsoft account, you can still access features like the Windows store, you will simply be prompted to enter Microsoft account credentials when you access the store. A small number of features such as Cortana, that we cover in lesson 23, are only available if you log in with a Microsoft account.

For this example we will create a local account. Microsoft accounts require an active internet connection the first time you use them, so it's usually a good idea to create a local account first just to get up and running with your PC. If you do want to create a Microsoft account now, go to lesson 37.3 to see how the process is slightly different. Otherwise, click on "Skip this step" and the screen shown in figure 1.6 will appear.

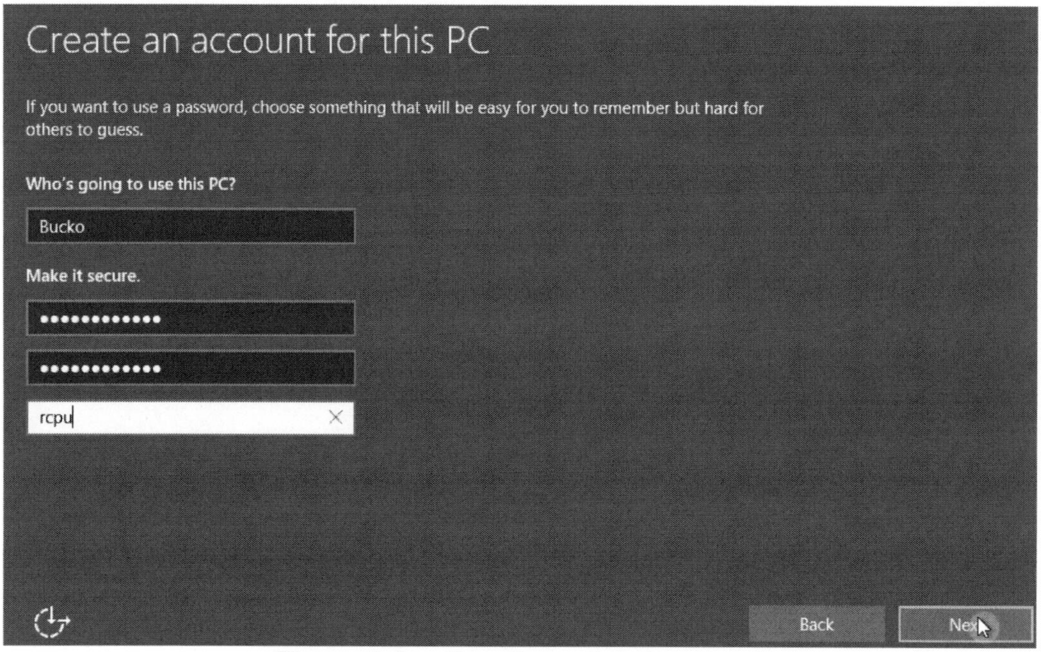

Figure 1.6 – Creating a local account

Fill out a user name, password and password hint for your local account. These details will then be stored locally on your PC. Remember that the password hint can be seen by anyone who has access to this PC, so don't make the hint too obvious. Click on "Next" when you are done.

Once you are done configuring your account, Windows will prepare it. When the configuration is complete, the desktop will appear. You've now set up your new Windows 10 PC and you can proceed to the next lesson.

Lesson 2 – Diving into the Desktop

It's time for a quick tour of the Windows 10 desktop. The desktop has changed a little, but it should still be at least somewhat familiar to those of you who have used Windows before.

2.1 – Logging in

When you power on your Windows 10 PC, you will need to log into the machine. This works slightly differently to Windows 7 and previous versions of Windows. Initially, you will see the Lock screen. Figure 2.1 shows a typical Lock screen, though as you will see in lesson 50 you can actually customise it to display any picture you want to.

Figure 2.1 – The Windows 10 Lock screen

To unlock your PC, either click once with the mouse or swipe your finger upwards. The Lock screen will then disappear, revealing the log in screen shown in figure 2.2.

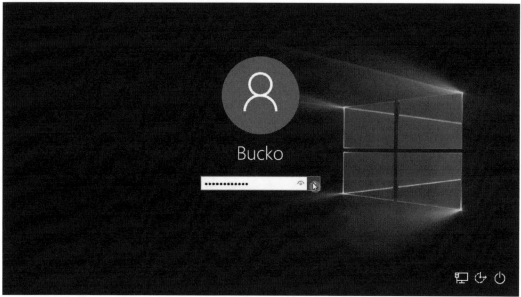

Figure 2.2 – Once the Lock screen has been dismissed, you can log in

Enter your password into the text entry box shown in figure 2.2. If you are using a touch screen, tap on the password box with your finger and the on-screen keyboard will appear. Press enter or click the right-pointing arrow once you have entered your password. You will then be logged into the PC. What happens next depends on what kind of PC you are running. If Windows does not detect a touch screen, you will be taken directly to the desktop. The desktop is where most users who have keyboard and mouse equipped systems will spend most of their time.

If Windows does detect a touch screen and no keyboard and mouse, it should switch you directly into Tablet PC mode. Tablet PC mode changes the Start menu into a full-screen Start screen and makes some other changes to make working with touch only systems more manageable. To find out more about Tablet PC mode and how to toggle between modes, see lesson 8.

2.2 – Desktop elements

Since we are starting the guide looking at Windows 10 on a traditional desktop or laptop computer, we will now take a look at the elements of the Windows 10 desktop. Figure 2.3 illustrates these elements.

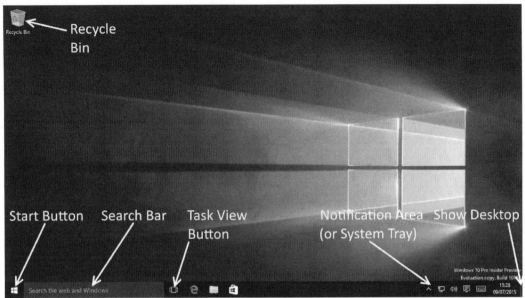

Figure 2.3 – The standard Windows 10 desktop

Figure 2.3 shows the standard Windows 10 desktop you will see on a clean (new) installation of the operating system. We will now go over the basic elements shown in the picture.

Start button:- In Windows 10 both the Start button and the Start menu make a welcome return. To open the Start menu from the desktop, simply click on the Start button. Alternatively, press the Windows key to access the Start menu, or press the Windows button on your device (if present).

Taskbar:- The area at the bottom to the left of the notification area is called the taskbar. The taskbar works just like it did in Windows 7 and 8, but a little differently to both Windows XP and Windows Vista. On the bottom left of the screen you may have noticed some icons. If you are familiar with Windows Vista or earlier versions of Windows you will know that the taskbar is where you can see programs that are already running. Since you can see some icons here already, you might be wondering why there appear to be programs already running. Well, these programs are not actually running at all. Unlike earlier versions of Windows, programs can be "pinned" on the taskbar. This means that they will stay on the taskbar for easy access even when they are not running. By default we get the Microsoft Edge web browser, File Explorer and the Windows Store.

It is important to understand that icons on the taskbar do not necessarily represent programs that are running. You can click on the icons pinned to the taskbar to start a program running. When a program is running, it will have a line underneath its taskbar icon, see figure 2.4 for an example.

Figure 2.4 – Microsoft Edge running on the taskbar, next to File Explorer and Windows Store which are "pinned" but not running

If you hover your mouse pointer over a running taskbar icon, Windows will show you a preview window.

Figure 2.5 – Hover your mouse pointer over a program running on the taskbar to see a preview of the window

You can click on the preview window to go directly to the application.

2.3 – Search bar and Task view button

Search bar:- Searching in Windows 10 has gone through several improvements. You can now search directly from the taskbar by using the search bar. Click on the search bar and then enter your query, this will search your PC and the web. If you don't see the full search bar, click the magnifying glass icon to open it. We cover basic searching in lesson 4.

Task view button:- You can click or tap the Task view button to see all your running programs and quickly switch to them. This icon also gives you access to the virtual desktops feature that we cover in lesson 6.

2.4 – Notification area

Notification Area or System Tray:- The official Microsoft name for this part of the desktop is the notification area, but lots of users refer to it as the System Tray. The notification area works the same in Windows 10 as it did in Windows 8. To see your notification area icons, you click the small up pointing arrow. See figure 2.6 for more details.

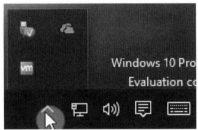

Figure 2.6 – The notification area/System Tray is opened with a click on this small arrow icon

If you are not sure what the notification area is for, do not worry, we cover it in more detail in lesson 21.

To the right of the arrow icon highlighted in figure 2.6, there are four other icons. These icons are also counted as part of the notification area, though you might think otherwise at first glance. The first icon (furthest left) is the network icon, this can be used for connecting quickly to networks, both wired and wireless. We cover connecting to networks in lesson 52.4. Then there's the volume icon, a quick click of this accesses a sliding control which can adjust the volume level for all sounds on your computer.

The next icon is the Action Centre icon. The Action Centre is where you can view notifications that you missed and also change various settings. We cover it in detail in lesson 46.

Finally, the last icon (which may not appear on all PCs) calls up the on-screen keyboard. Useful if you are using a touch-only machine.

Date and time:- To the right of the notification area (see figure 2.3) is the date and time display. This is self explanatory. You can click on the date and time display down here to adjust your computers clock if it is not showing the correct time.

Show Desktop button:- Clicking in the very bottom right hand corner of the Windows 10 desktop will activate the Show Desktop button. This button hides all of your open windows so that you can see the desktop. Clicking it again will reveal the windows again.

Recycle Bin:- This lonely looking icon in the top left hand corner of the desktop is the Recycle Bin. Files and folders you delete are (usually!) placed in this folder before being removed entirely. We cover this in more detail in lesson 18.

Note:- The picture in the background on our desktop is called the desktop background or wallpaper. This picture can be changed to any image you like and we show you how in lesson 49. Many of our videos and lessons were compiled using pre-release versions of Windows 10 and the standard desktop background may change for the release version. Because of this, don't be alarmed if your desktop background looks different.

If you have never used Windows before, you might be confused as to what all these different components do. This lesson was really to give you an overview of the desktop components and not what they do, so move along to the next lesson where we look at how the Start menu works on a Windows 10 PC.

Lesson 3 – The new Start Menu

Back by popular demand, the Start menu in Windows 10 replaces the Start screen as seen in Windows 8, at least for desktop users. In this lesson we will introduce the new Start menu and show you how to use it.

3.1 – Opening the Start menu

To open the Start menu at any time, simply click on the Start button in the bottom left hand corner of the screen. You can also press either of the Windows logo keys on your keyboard or press the Windows button on your device, if it has one. Figure 3.1 shows the Start menu open on a typical Windows 10 PC.

Figure 3.1 – The Windows 10 Start menu

The Windows 10 Start menu is a hybrid of the old Windows 7 Start menu and the Windows 8 Start screen. Anything you could do from the old Windows 8

Start screen or the Windows 7 Start menu you can also do here. To launch an app, just click or tap on its icon or tile once.

3.2 – Areas on the Start menu

The new Start menu is made up of several areas. We've numbered each area in the picture below and we will discuss each section.

Figure 3.2 – Start menu areas

Area 1 - Most used programs – This is where your most frequently run programs will be placed. Some of these programs may have an arrow next to them. By clicking on this arrow you open the programs "jump list". This usually opens a list of files that this app has recently opened. You can then click on any item in this list to open the file in the app directly.

Area 2 – Recently added apps – Any apps that you recently installed, either from the Windows store or through the desktop will appear here.

Area 3 – Common tasks – Shortcuts to commonly performed tasks can be seen here. You can open File Explorer (see Chapter 3), change computer settings or power down or restart your PC. We'll cover power options later in the lesson.

Area 4 – All Apps – The all apps section allows you to browse all the applications on your PC in alphabetical order. We will look at this in more detail later in the lesson.

Area 5 – Tiles – The live tiles shown on the right of the Start menu should be familiar to Windows 8 users. Each tile on the Start menu represents a program. In figures 3.1 and 3.2 we can see a tile in the second column from the left with a picture on it and the words "Alton Towers and Thorpe Park close". This is the News tile and the picture and headline relates to the roller coaster accident that was sadly in the news at the time the picture was taken. The pictures and information on the tiles are constantly changing, unlike traditional icons that usually remain static.

You can pin other applications and add more tiles to this section too. We show you how in lesson 45.2. If you have more tiles than will fit on the Start menu, a scroll bar will appear on the right allowing you to scroll down to see more tiles.

Many tiles on the Start menu can show information. As you work with Windows 10 the Start menu will "come alive". For instance, pictures from your Pictures library will appear on the Pictures tile, music recommendations may appear on the Music tile.

Area 6 – User account functions – Go to this section to log out or switch user. We will look at that in more detail later in the lesson.

3.3 – All apps

If a program isn't listed anywhere on the basic Start menu, as seen in figures 3.1 and 3.2, you can find it under "All apps" (section 4 in figure 3.2). To open the All apps section you need to click on it just once. This is like opening the "All programs" section on the Windows 7 Start menu, or the All apps page on the Windows 8 Start screen. Figure 3.3 shows the Start menu with the All apps section open.

Figure 3.3 – All apps on the Windows 10 Start menu

Rather than a custom sorting order, as with Windows 7 and earlier versions of Windows, All apps view lets you browse your applications alphabetically. Use the scroll bar at the side (the one under the mouse pointer in figure 3.3) to scroll down the list. When you're done working with All apps view, click on "Back".

As an alternative to trawling through the All apps view, you can use the "Search the web and Windows" bar that's next to the Start button and we will cover that in some detail in lesson 4.

3.4 – Locking, signing out and powering down

You can lock, sign out and shut down your PC from the Start menu too.

To lock or sign out of your PC, click on the user account functions icon (area 6 in figure 3.2). The options shown in figure 3.4 will then appear.

Figure 3.4 – User account functions

Usually you would lock your PC if you were coming back to it in a moment, or sign out if you wanted to pass the machine to another user (we cover user accounts in lesson 37). Below the sign out option you can see "Matthew Buxton". This is another user account that exists on this PC. By clicking on another account here you can switch directly to it.

To shut down or restart your PC, click on the "Power" option in the common tasks area (area 3 in figure 3.2). The options shown in figure 3.5 will then appear.

Figure 3.5 – Power options

Selecting "Sleep" will put the PC into a low-power standby mode. Windows will save the status of your currently open applications and allow you to resume them later. Sleep is useful for those times when you need to step away from your computer but you know that you will need to come back and work some more an hour or two later. Waking the PC from sleep mode is much faster than starting it from cold, but sleep mode still consumes some power. It is advisable to save anything you are working on before using sleep mode.

Selecting Shut down or Restart will, as you probably guessed, either shut down the PC entirely or restart it. Sometimes it is necessary to restart your computer after installing new software, for instance. If there are Windows updates pending, you will see the option "Update and restart" in place of just "Restart".

That covers the basics of using the Start menu to work with your Windows 10 PC. If you're used to previous versions of Windows you will probably have noticed that Search is now part of the taskbar. Fear not as we will be looking at how you can search a Windows 10 PC in the next lesson.

Lesson 4 – Basic Searching

Learning to search your Windows 10 PC is an important skill. After all, few of us will be able to remember where everything is on the Start menu, or in our documents folders. In Windows 10, rather than searching from the Start screen or Start menu, there's a search bar at the bottom left of the screen on the taskbar near the Start button, labelled "Search the Web and Windows". From here, you can search your PC and also summon Microsoft's digital assistant Cortana. We'll be covering Cortana in lesson 23, so we will focus just on basic searching for this lesson.

4.1 – Search settings and turning Cortana off

Since we're focusing on basic search in this lesson, we need to make sure Cortana is switched off. To do this, click on the "Search the web and Windows" toolbar. This will open a menu, as shown in figure 4.1.

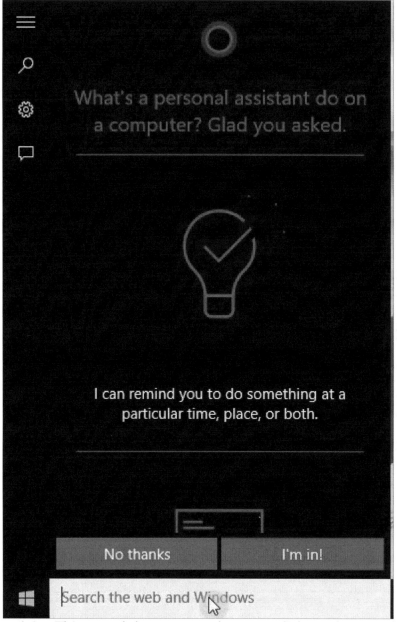

Figure 4.1 – This search box opens when you click on the search bar

On the left of the box there are four icons running down the side of the box. Click on the third one down, that is supposed to resemble a gear or cog. This will access the search settings options, as shown in figure 4.2.

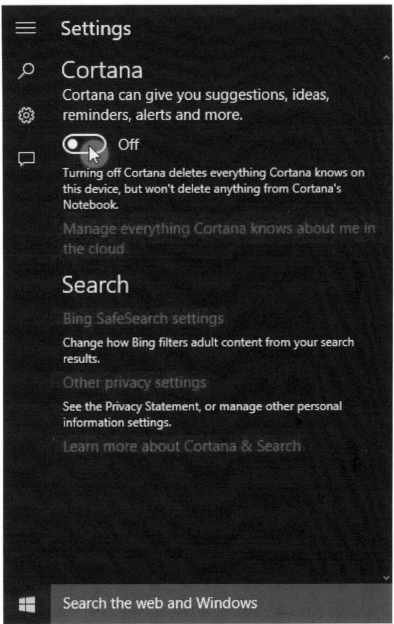

Figure 4.2 – Search options

To turn Cortana off, simply make sure the "Cortana" setting is set to "Off". The other options available here relate to privacy settings for searching the web. We will be covering those in lesson 41.

4.2 – Performing a search

Searching a Windows 10 PC is easy, simply type the search query into the search bar. Figure 4.3 shows a search for "weather".

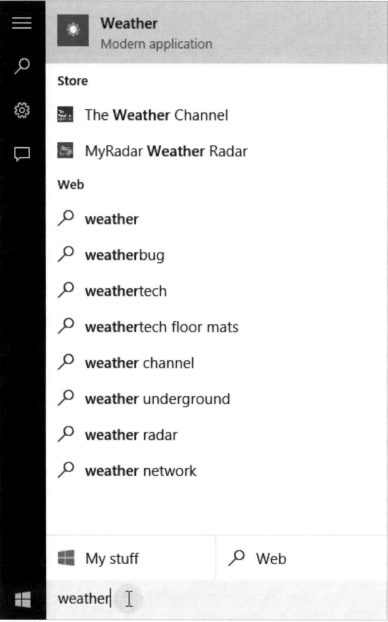

Figure 4.3 – Searching for "weather"

At the top of the search results, Windows has found the Weather app on our PC. Below that, there are results from the Windows store. Below that, we can perform a web search for the queries Windows has suggested. As you can see, search in Windows 10 is highly streamlined and very convenient. As well as finding apps, Windows can also find files too, so you can use the search bar to search for music, picture or video files on your PC or in your OneDrive (we cover OneDrive in lesson 32). In figure 4.4 below, the user has searched for "Butterfly" (just the top part of the search box is shown).

Figure 4.4 – Finding a picture file with Windows 10 search

Since this user had a picture file with the word "Butterfly" in it, Windows found the file and presented it in the search results. To open a picture that Windows finds like this, you only need to click or tap on it. In the picture, the user has right-clicked on the file which presents the option "Open file location". This would open a File Explorer window at the location of the file on the computer. File Explorer allows you to copy, move and organise your files. We cover File Explorer extensively in Chapters 3 and 4.

4.3 – My stuff

If you have a large number of files to search on your Windows 10 PC, you may find that the quick search results that Windows brings back aren't adequate to locate your file. In this case you can use the "My stuff" button, as seen in figure 4.3. In figure 4.5, the user has searched for "People" and then clicked the "My stuff" button.

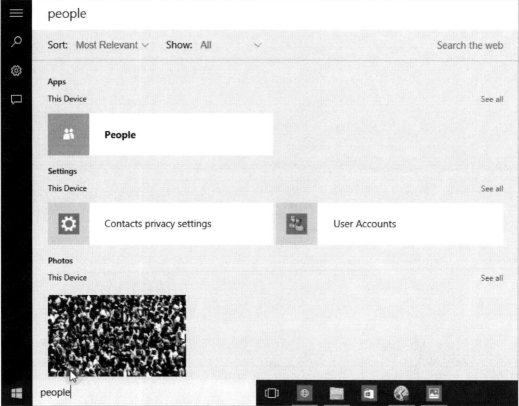

Figure 4.5 – Searching for "People" using the My stuff feature

Using the My stuff feature, you can search through different categories and quickly see results. Notice in figure 4.5, Windows has located the People app, a photograph called "People" and some PC settings that affect people who use the computer.

By clicking on the "Show" menu, we can narrow down the search results by selecting a file type to show. Figure 4.6 shows this menu.

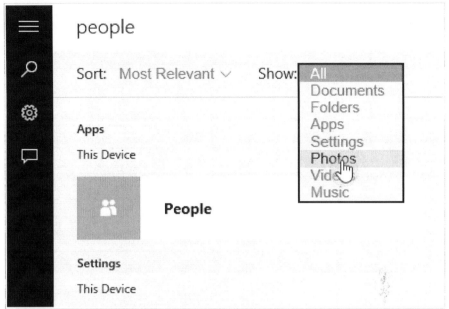

Figure 4.6 – Selecting file types to narrow down search results

Figure 4.7 shows the "My stuff" search results after selecting "Photos".

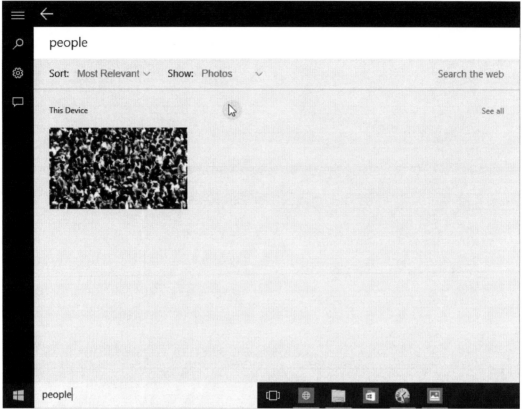

Figure 4.7 – The filtered search results

As you can probably appreciate, being able to filter searches like this can help you quickly narrow down the results and is very useful especially for computers that contain large file collections.

That covers the basics of searching your Windows 10 PC. In lesson 22 we will be looking at other ways you can search your Windows 10 PC. In lesson 23 we take a look at how the digital assistant Cortana can help you with searches and related tasks.

Lesson 5 – Windows in Windows 10

As you might imagine, windows are an important concept to master in Windows 10. Virtually every program you run on the Windows 10 desktop will create a window of some kind, the only exception being certain game and multimedia titles which take over the whole screen. Windows 10 comes with the same handy features for managing windows that Windows 7 introduced, as well as some great new features to make working with windows even more convenient.

5.1 – A Windows 10 desktop window

The majority of desktop windows you will work with in Windows 10 have a common set of controls at the top. Take a look at figure 5.1.

Figure 5.1 – Common window elements

At the top left of the window is the programs icon (which you will see on the taskbar when the program is running). Some Trusted Windows Store apps have a clickable menu here (represented by three horizontal lines) or a back button. The name of the window (which is usually the programs name) is shown next to the icon. Directly below that, many desktop programs have menus which can be accessed by clicking on them. In figure 5.1 you may be able to make out "File", "Edit", "Format", "View" and "Help".

On the top right of the window we have the common window controls. Clicking Minimise hides the window and shrinks the application down to the taskbar. Unlike Windows Vista and earlier versions of Windows, items on the taskbar are now represented by icons. To restore the window again, click on the programs icon on the taskbar.

Clicking Close will close down the application completely.

The middle button (labelled Restore/Maximise in figure 5.1) changes depending on what state the window is in. When a window is maximised, that is, sized to fill all the available space on your monitor, this button is called "Restore". Clicking on Restore will make the window slightly smaller. Why would you want to do this?, simply because it makes it easier to resize and move the window, as we will see in a moment.

If the window is not maximised then clicking on the middle button will maximise it, expanding it to fill up all available space on your desktop.

5.2 – Moving and resizing

When a window is not maximised, it is easy to move and resize it. To move a window, simply click with your left mouse button on the title bar and hold your left mouse button down (or press with your finger on a touch screen). Now, drag the window to wherever you want it. When the window is in place, let go of your mouse button.

To resize a window, firstly move your mouse pointer to the edge of the window. When the pointer is in the correct place, it will turn into two oppositely pointing arrows. Click your left mouse button and hold it down, then drag with the mouse and let go. Your window will now snap to the new size. You can resize from any side, and from the corners too, which allows you to adjust the width and height at the same time. Figure 5.2 shows a mouse pointer ready to resize a window.

Figure 5.2 – When your mouse pointer looks like two arrows, you are ready to resize your window

5.3 – Ways to work with windows

Windows 7 introduced some great new tools to make working with Windows easier and more productive and Windows 10 builds on these tools. As you start becoming more confident with the desktop, you will start working with more and more open windows at once. The following features can help you manage and organise your desktop windows.

Desktop Peek:- In lesson 2, we touched on how the taskbar had been overhauled for Windows 7. Instead of window names, as seen in Windows Vista and earlier versions, we now get icons. When a program opens multiple windows, the icons stack on top of each other. To help you find the correct window, you can use Desktop Peek. Hover your mouse pointer over icons on the taskbar and you will see a preview of their window. Figure 5.3 illustrates this.

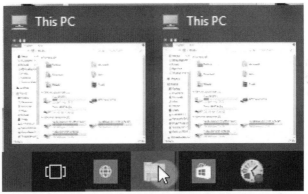

Figure 5.3 – Using Desktop Peek to preview windows from the taskbar

Hover your mouse pointer over one of the previews and Windows will turn all the other windows on the desktop transparent, allowing you to focus on the window you are previewing. To open or select one of the windows you are peeking at, simply click on the preview with your mouse.

Desktop Snap:- If you are used to working with multiple windows, you will know that windows can often become cluttered on your desktop. Windows 10 gives you a great tool to help with this called Desktop Snap. This feature was in Windows 7 and 8 too, but has been improved further in Windows 10. Take any window and then move it off the edge of your screen on either side. When you have moved it far enough you will then see a transparent frame appear. Let go of the mouse button now and the window will snap to exactly half of the screen width.

After you have snapped the Window to one half of the screen, Windows 10 will show you a list of all your other open windows in the other half of the screen, as shown in figure 5.4.

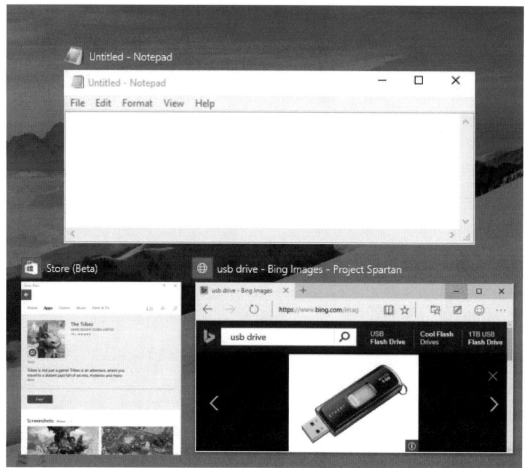

Figure 5.4 – Choosing another window to snap

If you click on one of these preview windows, Windows 10 will immediately snap this window to the opposite side of the screen. If you don't want to snap another window opposite, simply click anywhere else on the desktop.

In Windows 10 it is also possible to snap windows to a quarter of the screen instead of half. To do that, simply drag the window to any of the four corners of the screen. Keep dragging until the transparent frame appears and then let go. This is sometimes called "Corner Snap".

Desktop Shake:- Shake is a feature introduced in Windows 7, possibly born out of frustration. If you are working with a desktop with a lot of open windows, all piled on top of one another in a chaotic fashion, simply grab the window you want to work with from the chaos and then by holding down your mouse button (just like when you move a window) shake it quite vigorously. Now the other windows on your desktop are minimised and you will be left with just the window you were shaking. You can also shake the window again to reverse the effect.

So, hopefully you will have discovered that working with windows on the Windows 10 desktop is easy and dare we say even fun? With the new improved Desktop Snap and the virtual desktops feature we cover in the next lesson, we're sure you will agree that Windows 10 has the most powerful and easy to use Windows desktop ever.

Lesson 6 – Virtual Desktops

In this lesson we will take a look at a new feature on the Windows 10 desktop called "Virtual Desktops". Virtual desktops let you create multiple different desktops, each with their own windows. If you are a heavy multi-tasker and need to work on several projects at once, you may find virtual desktops help keep your windows more organised.

Note:– Virtual desktops are not available when running in Tablet mode.

6.1 – What are virtual desktops?

Virtual desktops are a way of expanding your desktop space without buying a new, bigger monitor or adding secondary monitors to your PC. Imagine for instance that you are working on two projects. The first project is on the web, perhaps a blog or website and requires you to work in your web browser and maybe a text editor. The second project is a manuscript you are working on in your word processor. You want to keep all those web browser windows from distracting you when you work on your manuscript, but you need to switch back at a moments notice when your boss tells you to work on the company website.

In a situation like this, you could create a new virtual desktop for your word processor, to keep it separate from your web browser and other windows. You could then organise your web browser windows on one desktop and leave them set up exactly how you wanted them while you worked with your word processor over on the other desktop.

Virtual desktops are a completely optional feature. If you find them too confusing then don't worry, there's no need to use them if you don't want to.

6.2 – Creating a virtual desktop

To create a new virtual desktop, first click the Task view button on the taskbar (or swipe your finger in from the left of the screen on a touch-screen) and then click the "New desktop" button on the Task view screen. Figure 6.1 shows the location of these buttons.

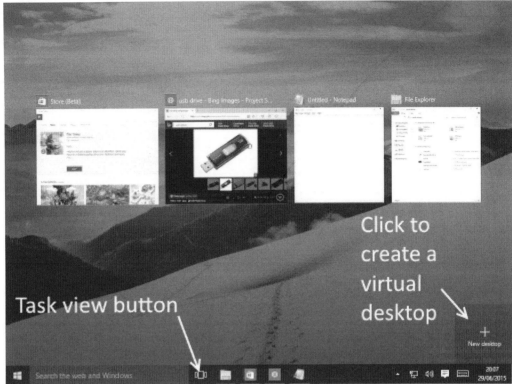
Figure 6.1 – Creating a new virtual desktop

Once you click on the New desktop button, the new desktop is created immediately. Windows will now show all your active desktops, just like in figure 6.2.

Figure 6.2 – Selecting a virtual desktop to work with

Click on the preview of the desktop to switch to it. When you switch to the new desktop, it will appear as if all your running programs have closed. These programs are still running, just not on this desktop, so you will not be able to interact with them until you switch back to the other desktop.

On your newly created desktop you can open any Windows application and start using it. When you need to switch back to your other desktop, simply click on the Task view button again. You can then create another virtual desktop or simply click on the one you want to work with. You can also hover your mouse pointer over the desktops preview icon to peek at all the windows open on that particular virtual desktop.

6.3 – Moving programs between virtual desktops

It is possible to move programs between virtual desktops. To do so, first click on the Task view button again. Now, find the virtual desktop which contains the program you want to work with. Remember, when in Task view you can hover your mouse pointer over the virtual desktop to preview all the open windows on that desktop. Figure 6.3 shows the sequence you need to follow.

Figure 6.3 – Moving apps between virtual desktops

With Task view open, locate the preview window of the program you want to move, right click on it and choose "Move to". You will then be able to select another desktop from the menu shown. Figure 6.4 shows an example of moving Notepad to another desktop.

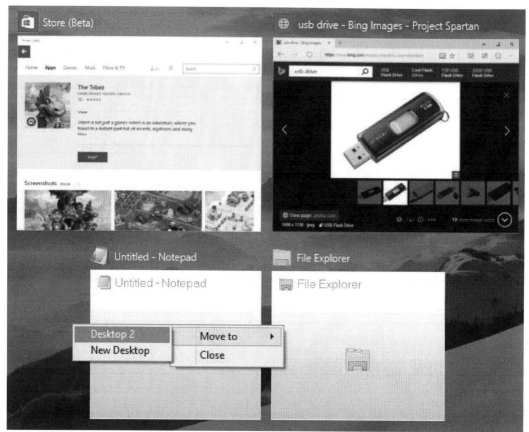

Figure 6.4 – Using Task view to move apps between virtual desktops

6.4 – Closing a virtual desktop

To close a virtual desktop when you are done working with it, open Task view again and then move your mouse pointer to the top right hand corner of the desktops preview icon. A close icon will then appear, figure 6.5 shows an example of this.

Figure 6.5 – About to close virtual desktop "Desktop 2"

Click on the red cross to close the chosen desktop. Any programs that were running on the virtual desktop you just closed will not be closed themselves, they will simply be moved to another desktop.

That concludes this lesson on virtual desktops. If you are the kind of user that likes to run a lot of programs at once, you may find virtual desktops an ideal feature for reducing desktop clutter. Give them a try yourself and see if they fit in with your workflow.

Chapter 2 – Windows 10 on Tablets

Like Windows 8, Windows 10 is designed to work on a wide variety of devices. In this chapter we'll take a look at how the operating system behaves differently on machines with touch screens but without keyboards and mice and get you up and running quickly on your tablet device.

Lesson 7 – Touch Gestures

To get the most out of your super powerful Windows 10 tablet or touch screen device, you need to learn a few basic gestures that you can perform with your fingers. In this lesson we'll take you through all the gestures you need to know to get started working, playing and enjoying your Windows 10 tablet.

To work with a touch screen, use gentle presses, taps and swipes. Do not apply excessive pressure, particularly when performing gestures like flicks or tap and hold/drag, remember that you do not need to press on hard.

Note:- Touch screens vary in capabilities, if you buy a new Windows 10 machine with a touch screen, all the gestures discussed here will work correctly. If you are upgrading an older machine, such as a Windows 7 tablet PC, then the capabilities may be more limited.

7.1 – Taps

A tap is a quick press and release of the touch screen. Touch your finger to the touch screen and immediately remove it again, just like you might tap someone on the shoulder.

7.1.1 – Double tap

Sometimes you will need to double tap, in that case perform two taps in quick succession. For instance in File Explorer you single tap on a folder to select it and double tap on a folder to open it. Tapping is the equivalent of clicking with the mouse on a traditional Windows system.

7.1.2 – Tap and hold

Tap and hold is where you tap the screen but keep your finger held rather than removing it immediately. This gesture is used in a variety of places. In desktop apps, tap and hold is used in place of right clicks. Tap and hold on the app until a box appears around your finger and then let go. This will perform a right click. Figure 7.1 shows this gesture being performed.

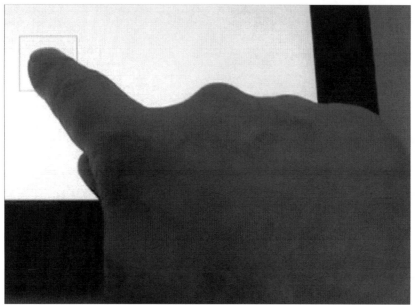

Figure 7.1 – Performing a tap and hold in a desktop app

In figure 7.1, the user has pressed his finger to the screen and held it there until the box appeared. Now all that remains is to remove his finger from the touch screen and this will perform a tap and hold, which is the equivalent of right clicking in desktop apps.

Tap and hold is used on the Start screen too. You can tap and hold your finger on a tile to move it. Press your finger gently to the tile you want to move and keep it held down for a moment. Now, you can move your finger (keeping it in contact with the touch screen) to move the tile.

Figure 7.2 – Using tap and hold to drag a tile

7.1.3 – Dragging

If the guide tells you to "Drag" a tile or other element, you first perform a tap and hold. Then, keeping your finger in contact with the screen you move or drag the tile or other element to the desired place. Dragging can be performed with a mouse too, typically you click and hold the mouse button and then move the mouse to perform a drag.

7.2 – Swipe

The swipe gesture means moving your finger quickly across the screen in a gentle flicking motion. Swipes are used throughout Windows 10 to browse through content. They are used on the Start screen to browse through tiles and in Microsoft Edge or other web browsers to browse through content.

Swipes can be vertical or horizontal. On the Start screen for instance, you swipe up and down to scroll through your tiles. In a web browser you might swipe up and down or left and right to view web page content.

7.2.1 – Swipe in

Windows uses the swipe in gesture quite frequently. Swiping in from the right hand edge of the screen for instance will open the Action Centre. Swipe in works exactly like a normal swipe, but you should start the gesture from the outside of the screen. For instance, to swipe in from the right, touch your finger gently just outside of the screen area on the right of your tablet or touch screen, then move your finger to the left over the screen.

7.3 – Pinch

The pinch gesture is usually used for zooming, it's often (though not always) the equivalent of using the mouse wheel on a computer mouse while holding down the control key on the keyboard. To pinch, you place two fingers on the screen and then either move them apart (typically to zoom in) or move them together (typically to zoom out). Figure 7.3 shows a user performing a pinch gesture.

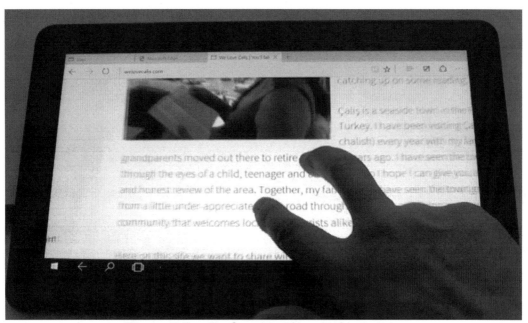

Figure 7.3 – Performing the pinch gesture

If you find that you have moved your fingers as far as they will physically go and you still need to zoom or pinch the screen some more, simply lift your hand from the screen, reset your digits and then perform the gesture again.

You now know all the gestures you need for getting around your Windows 10 touch-screen PC. You will have plenty of chance to practise these gestures in the next few lessons. Refer to Appendix – Using Touch PCs at the end of the book for a quick reminder on touch gestures and their mouse equivalents.

Lesson 8 - Tablet Mode and the New Start Screen

Twenty years ago, a Windows computer meant a box on a desk with a monitor. Today, a Windows machine can be anything from a towering behemoth with several monitors to a tiny tablet that fits comfortably in your hand. In the past, Windows machines were a little clunky to use when stripped of their keyboard and mouse. Windows 10 hopes to address that problem with its dedicated Tablet mode, which we will be looking at in this lesson.

8.1 - Turning on Tablet mode

If you have a touch screen PC you can turn Tablet mode on or off at any time. To do so, first swipe your finger in from the right of the screen to open the Action Centre. Then, simply tap the Tablet mode button. Figure 8.1 shows the Action Centre buttons with the Tablet mode button highlighted. Tablet mode is off if the button is grey and on if it is any other colour.

Figure 8.1 – Tap here to turn on Tablet mode

Once you turn Tablet mode on, the Start menu becomes a full screen Start screen and will open automatically. Figure 8.2 shows the Windows 10 Start screen.

Figure 8.2 – Start screen

In Tablet mode, all applications run full screen by default and the taskbar behaves slightly differently. Unlike in Windows 8, the desktop pretty much goes away entirely, though you can still run desktop apps as we will see later in the lesson.

8.2 - Start screen

Figure 8.2 shows a typical Start screen in tablet PC mode. To navigate the Start screen in Windows 10, you flick vertically, rather than horizontally like in Windows 8. Figure 8.2 also shows the following elements.

Expand button:– Opens the left hand part of the Start screen. The part that is always visible on the Start menu.

Power button:– Power down, restart or sleep your PC by tapping here.

All apps:– Accesses the "All apps" section of the Start screen, see lesson 3.3 for details of how this works.

Back button:– This is actually part of the taskbar and allows you to navigate back from an app or page in an app. We will cover this in more detail in a moment.

To open any app from the Start screen, just tap on its tile or icon once. If your app doesn't appear on the Start screen, you can use the magnifying glass to open the search bar and search for it.

8.3 - Using Trusted Windows Store apps

The Trusted Windows Store apps tend to work best with touch screen PCs and are usually optimised for touch. Figure 8.3 shows the Weather app running in Tablet mode.

Figure 8.3 – Weather app running in Tablet mode

Notice the app opens in a full screen rather than a window, but otherwise works exactly the same as it does when running in desktop mode. We take a more detailed look at the Weather app in lesson 29.4.

To navigate back to the Start screen press the Start button on the taskbar or press the Windows button on your device, usually this is located just above or below the screen. You can then launch another app or go back to the app you just came from by tapping its tile again.

8.4 – Desktop apps in Tablet mode

In Tablet mode, desktop apps will open maximised (their biggest possible size). Figure 8.4 shows File Explorer running in Tablet mode.

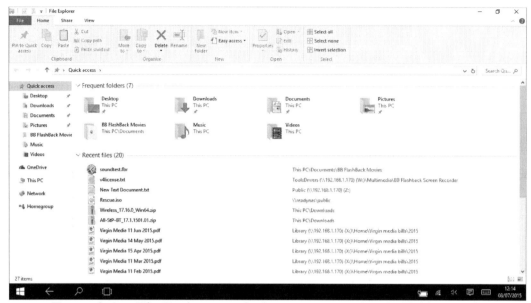

Figure 8.4 – File Explorer, a desktop app, running in Tablet mode

Despite running full screen, Desktop apps may still be rather fiddly to use without a keyboard and mouse. If you try to "Restore" the window down, using the techniques discussed in lesson 5.2, nothing happens. Resizing windows and apps works differently in Tablet mode and we will cover how to do this in lesson 9.3.

8.5 – Taskbar differences

When running in Tablet mode the taskbar has a number of key differences. Firstly, there's a back button added to the right of the Start button (see figure 8.2). The back button takes you back to the previous page. For example, if you launched the Weather app and tapped on the maps icon, tapping the back button now would take you back to the main weather screen. If you tapped it again, you would go back to the Start screen.

You may have noticed that the search bar has also disappeared. Fortunately that's only a minor difference from desktop mode. To open the search simply tap on the magnifying glass icon to the right of the back button. Search then works in exactly the same way as in desktop mode. See lesson 4, Basic Searching, to learn more about these techniques.

You may also have noticed that when running in Tablet mode, Windows does not place icons for running apps on the taskbar. This behaviour can be changed if desired. To do so, search for "hide app icons" and then tap on the result that appears at the top. The window shown in figure 8.5 will then appear.

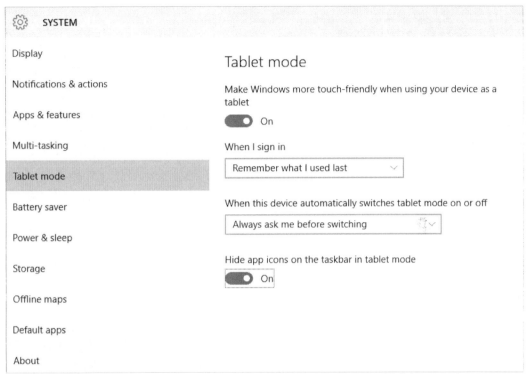

Figure 8.5 – Restoring or disabling app icons in Tablet mode

This setting allows the app icons on the taskbar to be re-enabled in Tablet mode so that they appear just like in desktop mode. Of course this is entirely up to you. On a tablet with a larger screen you may find it useful for quickly switching between apps.

That concludes our tour of Tablet mode. Windows 10 tablets are super powerful, easily more powerful than competing Android or Apple devices and are therefore ideal for anyone who demands more flexibility from their device.

Lesson 9 – Touch Multitasking

Windows has always been about multitasking and productivity and even on touch only devices that's still the case. Working with multiple apps works slightly differently when Windows 10 is in Tablet mode. In this lesson we will see how Windows handles multitasking on a touch device.

9.1 – Task View

In the last lesson we told you that you can switch between apps by first opening one app and then pressing the Start button, or the Windows button on your device and going back to the Start screen. This is the simplest way to work with apps on your device and is similar to how most popular touch-based operating systems work.

There is another way to switch between apps that you may find very convenient when you become more proficient with your tablet and that is to use Task view. Task view shows all your currently running apps. There are two ways to access Task view. Firstly, you can tap the Task view button on the taskbar, as seen in figure 2.3. Secondly, you can swipe your finger in from the left of the screen. Figure 9.1 shows Task view open on a PC in Tablet mode.

Figure 9.1 - Tablet PC Task view

Using Task view is faster than going back to the Start screen. To switch to any app shown in Task view, just tap on it. You can also use the back button on the taskbar to jump directly to the previously used app.

You can also close apps from the Task view by tapping the cross icon in the top right hand corner of the apps picture. The close button for Microsoft Edge is circled in figure 9.1. If an app won't close when you tap its close button in Task view, it may need your attention. Tap on it and check that it is not notifying you to save your work before you close it, for instance.

9.2 – Touch multitasking

Just like in Windows 8, we can work with multiple apps on a touch screen device. To do this, swipe your finger down from the top of the screen, keeping it held to the screen. The currently running app will then shrink down and follow your finger. Figure 9.2 shows an example of this.

Figure 9.2 – Moving an app in Tablet mode

If you move (drag) the app right to the bottom of the screen now, you will close it. If you want to multitask with the app, drag it instead to the left or right of the screen. A dividing bar will appear in the middle of the screen when you have moved the app far enough. Take your finger off the screen now and the app will snap to the side of the screen. Windows will then open Task view on the other side of the screen. Figure 9.3 illustrates this.

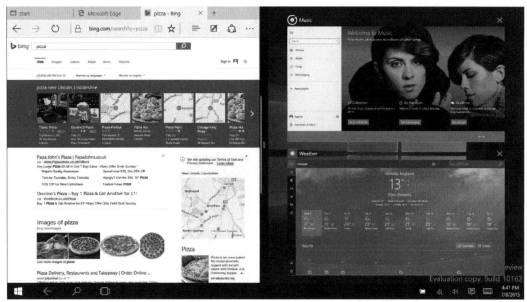

Figure 9.3 – Selecting an app to multitask with

To open an app in the opposite side of the screen, simply tap on the other app you want to work with. Figure 9.4 shows Microsoft Edge and the Music App (Groove Music) running side by side.

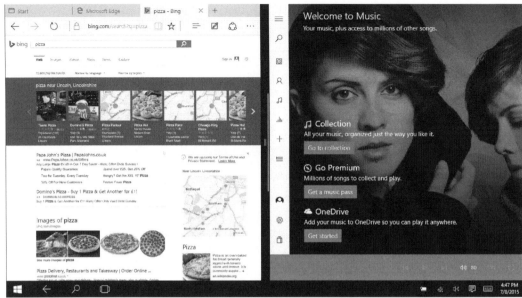

Figure 9.4 – Using two apps at once

9.3 - Resizing apps

When you use Task view to multitask two apps together, they will usually take up exactly half of the screen each when you first set them out. In some instances you might want to resize one of the apps. One typical situation where you might want to do this is using the Groove Music app. If you were working or surfing on the web and wanted some tunes while you worked, you can shrink the Groove Music app down so that it is only a quarter of the screen. At this size, the app still lets you change tracks and pause your music, while the rest of the screen can be used for your browser or other apps.

To resize an app, you need to drag the dividing bar by tapping and holding your finger on it. The bar is a little small so catching it with your finger might take a couple of tries. Once you have hold of the bar you can resize your app. Keep your finger on the screen and drag the bar to the left or right. Your app will then resize itself. Let go of the screen once your app is the desired size. If it disappears from the screen entirely while you are resizing, you have resized it too far. Drag the bar back again and the app will re-appear. If you shrink an app down too far and then let go of the screen, it will disappear from your screen but won't be closed and you can still access it in Task view. Figure 9.5 shows the Groove Music app running quarter screen size next to the Microsoft Edge web browser. Make sure you set up your play lists (see lesson 27.3) before resizing it like this.

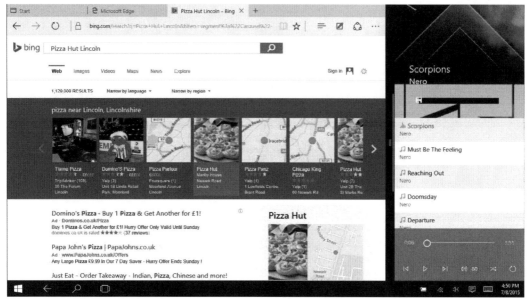

Figure 9.5 – Some apps can work at different screen sizes

That's all you need to know to work with multiple apps in Tablet mode. For all the criticism Windows 8 got, it's powerful multitasking capabilities, which Windows 10 builds on, are more advanced than any other tablet PC operating system on the market and Microsoft's competitors are scrambling to catch up with this awesome feature.

Lesson 10 – Tweaking Windows 10 for Touch

With Windows 10, Microsoft are trying to make an operating system that is instantly familiar for both desktop PC users and users on tablet PCs or touch screens. This is quite a challenge, as these two methods of interacting with your PC are quite different. In some ways, when using Windows 10 on a tablet PC it can feel like a step backwards compared to Windows 8. In this lesson we will look at several tweaks and changes you can make to optimise the operating system for tablet PCs.

10.1 - Making screen elements bigger

Our biggest criticism of Windows 10 in Tablet mode, especially on smaller tablets, is that many of the icons are too small to accurately tap with your finger. If you find this to be a problem you could see if your device supports a stylus pen. This can make working with desktop apps like File Explorer much easier. A stylus also gives finer, pin-point control than a finger and may make working with certain games and apps easier.

Your other choice is to make certain elements on your screen bigger. To do this, swipe your finger in from the right of the screen to open the Action Centre. Now, tap on the "All settings" button. The settings window should then appear. From the main settings screen, tap on "System". Finally, make sure "Display" is selected. Figure 10.1 shows the correct window.

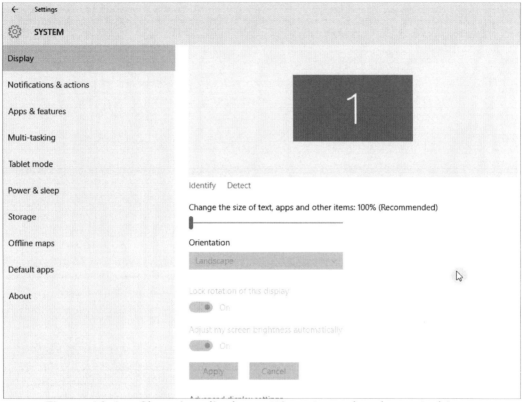

Figure 10.1 – Changing display settings to make elements bigger

Notice the control "Change the size of text, apps and other items". On some PCs the control is set to 100% and cannot be changed, but on many machines you will be able to change this control. Drag it to the right to make text and other elements on your screen bigger. Tap on "Apply" when you are done. You will need to sign out now and then sign back in again so that Windows can change all the visual elements.

10.2 – Hiding the taskbar

If you're migrating from Windows 8 you've probably noticed the taskbar stays on the screen permanently in Windows 10, even in Tablet mode. If you're using a smaller tablet this may be taking up valuable screen space. However, there is a solution but this setting isn't very easy to find if you don't know about it. Start by going back to the Start screen and use the search button to search for "taskbar and navigation", then tap the icon that appears at the top of the search results. The window shown in figure 10.2 will then appear.

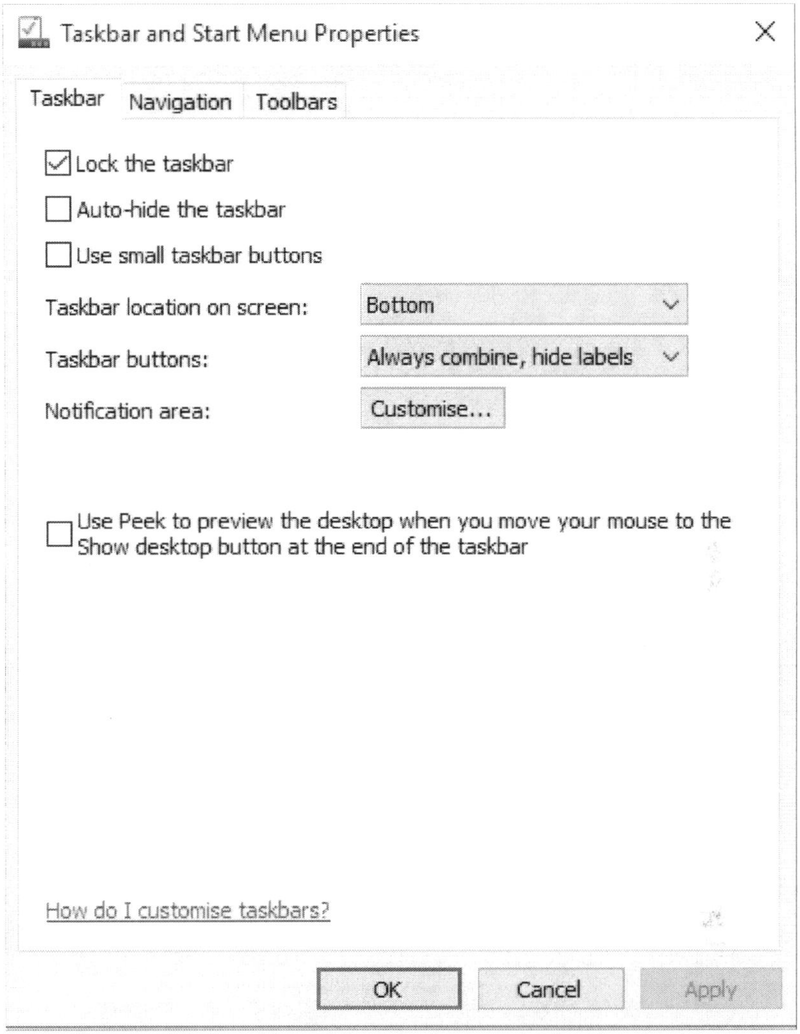

Figure 10.2 – Use this window to hide the taskbar

Unfortunately this particular window is not optimised for touch use. Carefully tap on "Auto-hide the taskbar" so that a tick/check mark appears in the box, then tap on "OK". The taskbar will then disappear from your screen (except when using the Start screen), freeing up valuable space. You can get it back at any time simply by swiping up from the bottom of the screen. It is a mystery why Microsoft didn't make this setting more obvious and accessible to touch screen users.

10.3 - Metro Commander – A File Explorer alternative

Throughout Chapters 3 and 4 of this Superguide you will be working with File Explorer. File Explorer is the app you use to manipulate and organise all the files and folders on your PC. While File Explorer can be used on a touch screen, it's hardly optimal and tapping some of its smaller icons is very fiddly. For the times you do need to use it you could simply attach a USB mouse and work on your tablet at your desk. Many Windows tablets include docking stations or clip-on keyboards that make them into fully featured laptop replacements. If this isn't possible there is another alternative. In the Windows store (see lesson 31) you can download a program called "Metro Commander". Metro Commander is a File Explorer replacement that's fully touch-optimised. Figure 10.3 shows Metro Commander running on a Windows 10 tablet.

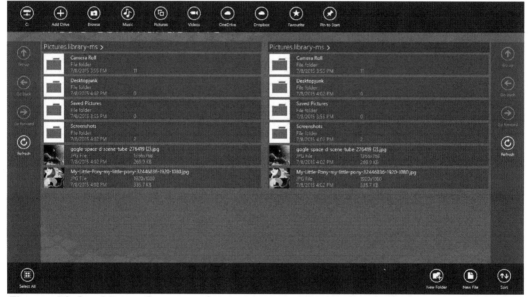

Figure 10.3 – Metro Commander is a great File Explorer alternative for touch

At the time of going to press, Windows 10 was still in pre-release and Metro Commander isn't optimised for it yet. Even so, using it on a touch screen is much more comfortable than trying to use File Explorer.

When working with Metro Commander, one side of the app is the source directory and the other side the destination. If you don't understand these concepts yet don't worry, we will cover them in detail in Chapter 3.

One of the tasks we carry out in Chapter 3 (lesson 13.2) is making a new folder and copying files. You might want to make a new folder for your favourite desktop backgrounds images for example. In Metro Commander you swipe in from the top of the screen to reveal the toolbars, then tap on the side you want to work with and then tap the "New Folder" button at the bottom.

Copying files is much easier too. You simply select the files you want to copy with a flick of your finger. Then, on the opposite side, open the folder you want to copy them to and then just tap the copy button that then appears.

We're not going to go into Metro Commander in any more detail for this guide, but its certainly an app worth trying if you find File Explorer too fiddly and hopefully it will be updated for Windows 10 shortly after the operating system is released.

That concludes this lesson on optimising your Windows 10 operating system for your tablet PC and concludes this chapter on Windows 10 on touch screens. If you already own a touch device, hopefully this material will help you get more out of it. If you don't, maybe the information here has inspired you to try or buy one for yourself.

Chapter 3 – Exploring Files and Folders

Data is organised in a Windows 10 PC as files and folders. Learning how to navigate around files and folders is a key skill for any Windows user. In this chapter we will be working with File Explorer and manipulating files and folders on our PC.

Lesson 11 – Exploring File Explorer

Computers run programs that manipulate information. In our ultra connected internet age, desktop and laptop computers in homes crunch through data and information at a rate that would have humbled the supercomputers of the past. Never before has it been easier and quicker to manipulate your pictures, videos and music files. In the next few lessons, we will show you how you can work with files and folders. The program you will be using to do this is called File Explorer. File Explorer was known as Windows Explorer in previous versions of Windows. It was upgraded with a new interface in Windows 8 and has had a few tweaks in Windows 10 too. Once mastered, File Explorer makes working with files as easy as organising a filing cabinet, easier in fact, since it does all the lifting and refiling for you!

11.1 – Your personal folders

Your personal folder contains four sub-folders by default. The folders are "Documents", "Music", "Pictures" and "Videos". You can access these folders from File Explorer or from the search bar. To access your Documents folder, for instance, search for "documents" and click the first icon that appears in the results. You can also start File Explorer from the taskbar and then click on the "Documents" icon in the window. Your Documents folder will then be open in File Explorer and will look something like figure 11.1.

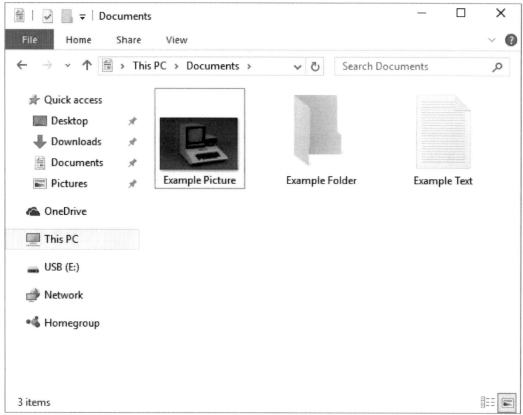

Figure 11.1 – A users Documents folder open in File Explorer

On a clean installation of Windows 10, the Documents folder will be empty. The items shown in figure 11.1 have been added just as an example.

In the left of the File Explorer window, we can jump quickly to several folders. Figure 11.2 shows the left hand column (or Navigation pane to give it its correct name) in more detail.

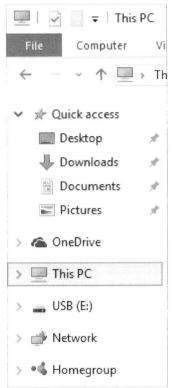

Figure 11.2 – The Navigation pane

Using the Navigation pane in File Explorer, we can jump to several folders. At the top of the list, the "Quick access" section gives us access to several folders including the Downloads folder, where files that you download from the web are stored. You can customise which folders appear in Quick access by right clicking on any folder you work with in File Explorer and choosing "Pin to Quick access".

Underneath the Quick access section we can see OneDrive. OneDrive is a cloud (online) storage service that is available to all Windows 10 users, we cover it in detail in lesson 32.

You can also jump directly to Homegroup and Network, which take you to resources on the network you're currently connected to, if they are available.

Notice the small arrows (>) next to the icons in the Navigation pane. These appear when you hover your mouse pointer over the Navigation pane. You can click these arrows to expand that particular location. For instance, clicking on the arrow next to "This PC" will show you the folders or locations that are available directly from "This PC". Figure 11.3 illustrates this.

Figure 11.3 – Expanding out "This PC" in the Navigation pane

The contents you will see under "This PC" will vary depending on what drives you have in your PC and what compatible devices there are on your network. We cover "This PC" in more detail in lesson 19.

To open folders in the Navigation pane, single click on them. File Explorer will then open the folder and show the contents in the main area on the right. To open files or folders in the main working area of File Explorer, we double click on them. So to see the contents of the folder "Example Folder" shown in figure 11.1 for example, we would double click on it.

11.2 – The individual elements of a File Explorer window

Figure 11.4 shows the basic controls from the top of a typical File Explorer window.

Figure 11.4 – Elements of a File Explorer window

Back/forward navigation controls:- As you browse through folders, you can use the back button (the arrow pointing to the left) to go back to the folder you were previously viewing. Similarly, the forward button (the arrow pointing to the right) will take you forward again.

Parent directory:- This control was new in Windows 8, if you can't make it out easily in the picture, it just looks like an up-pointing arrow. The button will take you to the parent directory, so for instance if you were in the "Videos" folder inside the "Documents" folder, clicking this arrow would take you back up to Documents.

Address bar:- The Address bar shows the address of the file on your computer. This is often referred to as the file path. Expert users can even type the address or path of a file directly into the address bar.

Search tool:- If you need to search through the contents of a folder, enter your search query here. Note that searching like this will only search through the contents of the current folder and its sub-folders, not through the entire computer.

Context sensitive ribbon:- The new ribbon replaces the toolbar in the new File Explorer. Tabs appear at the very top of the window as you work with files and folders in File Explorer. These tabs will change based on the content you are working with. Figure 11.5 shows an example of the tab that will appear when working with music in your music folder.

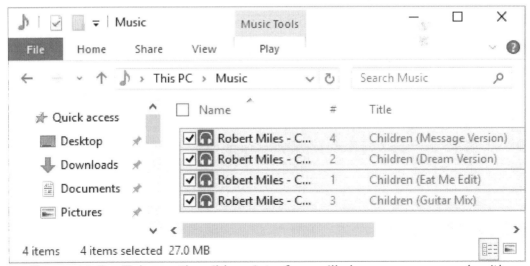

Figure 11.5 – Tabs on the ribbon interface will change as you work with different content

11.3 – Introducing the ribbon

In figure 11.5 the ribbon interface was hidden, but by clicking the tabs at the top of the window at any time you can open the ribbon. Figure 11.6 shows what happens when the "Music Tools/Play" tab is clicked.

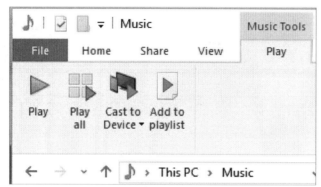

Figure 11.6 – The music tools ribbon

From the Music Tools ribbon you can play all music in the current folder. By clicking once on a media file, the option to play the currently selected file will become available. You can always access the different categories on the ribbon by using the individual tabs too. For instance we can see "File", "Home", Share" etc in figure 11.6. We will be seeing more of the ribbon in later lessons. Remember that at any point you can use the minimise/maximise ribbon control near the top right of the Explorer window to show or hide the ribbon. Figure 11.7 shows this control.

Figure 11.7 – The minimise/maximise ribbon control is circled

11.4 – Breadcrumbs

If you want to find your way back along a path, then leaving a trail of breadcrumbs might work, provided there's nothing around to eat them. Since birds and other animals don't eat digital breadcrumbs, you can rely on them for finding your way back down the path and off in other directions. To use breadcrumbs, click on the > shaped icons on the address bar. Take a look at figure 11.8, it shows an example of using the breadcrumbs feature to navigate around the personal folders.

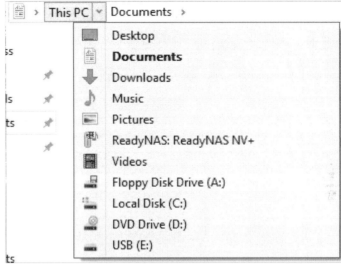

Figure 11.8 – Using breadcrumbs to navigate around folders in the path

In figure 11.8 we have opened the breadcrumbs menu at "This PC". The menu is showing us all the other folders we could navigate to from there. Rather than having to navigate back to the folder we can simply use the breadcrumbs here to quickly jump off to somewhere else.

Breadcrumbs are an advanced user feature so don't worry if you don't quite understand them yet. Do not be afraid to experiment for yourself, it is not possible to break anything playing with this feature.

11.5 – Folder views

Computers view all data as strings of binary numbers, but people are much more visual than that. Fortunately, there are several ways we can represent content in File Explorer. To change viewing mode, click on the "View" tab. This will open the ribbon and allow you to choose a viewing mode. Refer to figure 11.9 for a list of all the different folder view modes.

Figure 11.9 – Folder viewing modes available on the ribbon under the "View" tab

So what do all those viewing options do? Take a look at the following pictures for an example. These screen shots were taken from within a picture folder, other content will look different, of course.

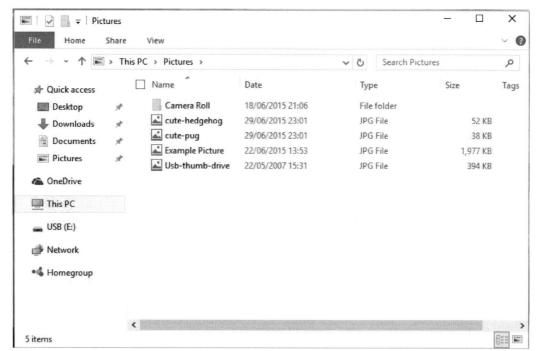

Figure 11.10.1 – Details view, the power users favourite

Details view is used most often when working with large numbers of files. You can easily see important information such as file types and sizes. We will be looking at details view in more detail in the next lesson.

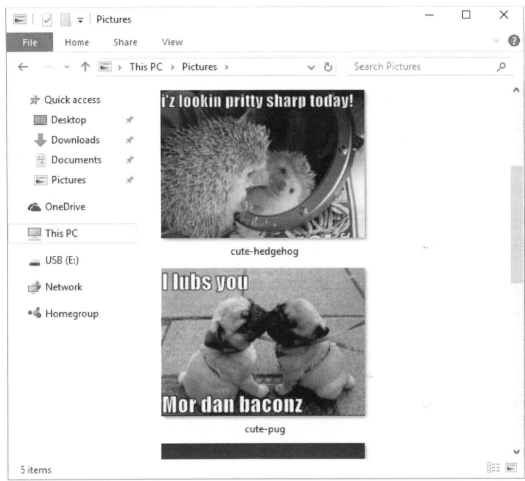

Figure 11.10.2 – Extra large icons view

An icon is a visual representation of a file or folder on your computer. In File Explorer, we can choose four different sizes of icon. Picture files will display as a thumbnail preview as seen in figure 11.10.2 if the icon size is large enough.

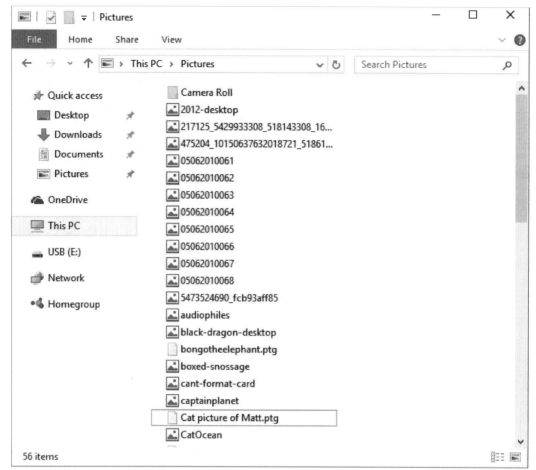

Figure 11.10.3 – Small icons view

In small icons view, the icons become too small to show a thumbnail picture preview and so simply revert to this small representation of a picture. Small icons view and list view, which we look at next, are very similar. You can only see the difference between these views when you have a folder with several files, hence the screen shots here are from a more crowded Windows 10 picture folder.

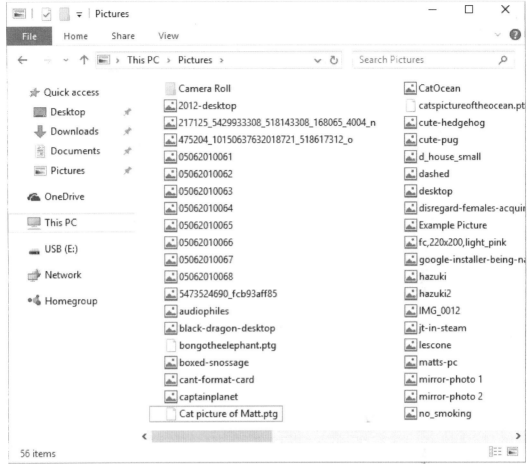
Figure 11.10.4 – List view

List view is similar to small icons view but lays things out slightly differently.

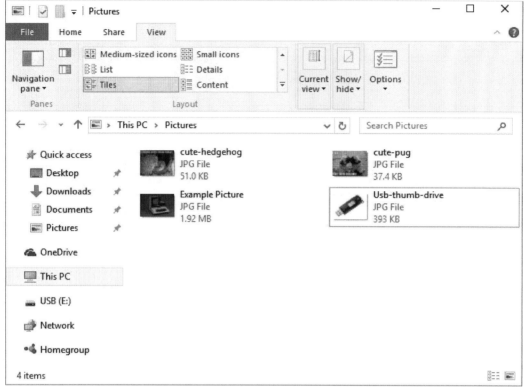

Figure 11.10.5 – Tiles view

Tiles view is similar to medium icons view except some information about the file is placed on the right next to the icon.

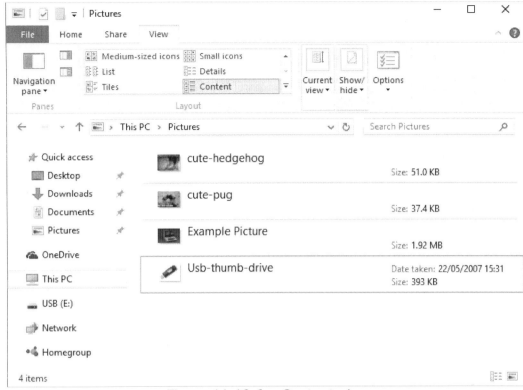

Figure 11.10.6 – Content view

Content view aims to strike a balance between details view and icon view. Files are arranged in a list with their file sizes shown on the right.

That concludes this extensive introduction to File Explorer. You should now be reasonably confident navigating between folders on your PC. If not, be sure to practise all the techniques we showed in this lesson and learn at your own pace.

Lesson 12 – Advanced File Explorer Techniques

Continuing our tour of File Explorer, in this lesson we will look at some more techniques for viewing and managing files on your computer.

12.1 – Delving into details view

Recall how in lesson 11.5 we showed you the different folder views. Back then we said that details view was the view that power users used the most. Details view lets you find out all kinds of information about files on your computer. Figure 12.1 shows a folder open in details view in File Explorer.

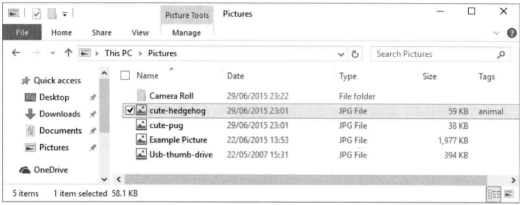

Figure 12.1 – Details view

In figure 12.1, we can see the date that the files were modified, the size of the files in kilobytes (KB) and any tags that are applied (we cover tags in a moment). Right clicking on a column heading in details view enables us to add a new column, figure 12.2 demonstrates this.

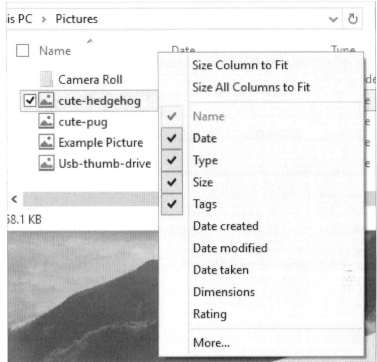

Figure 12.2 – Customising details view by adding more columns of information

After right clicking on a column heading, adding or removing new columns is just a matter of clicking on them from the menu. By clicking on "More..." at the bottom of the menu you can choose from hundreds of different types of meta-data (data about data). Not all metadata is relevant to all kinds of files, for example a picture of your back garden isn't usually going to have an "Album Artist" and your favourite music file is unlikely to have "Dimensions", at least not the kind that can be measured in inches or centimetres.

You can also sort your list of files by any of the columns you currently have displayed in details view. Simply click on the column to sort by that criteria, click again on the same column to reverse the sorting order (i.e. change from sorting from high to low or A to Z to low to high or Z to A).

12.2 – Preview pane

When you want to open a file in File Explorer, you double click on it. If you are sifting through a lot of files at once however, you might find it more convenient to use the Preview pane. To enable or disable the Preview pane, first click on the View tab on the ribbon. Figure 12.3 shows the Preview pane opened, the icon circled is the icon you will need to click to open the Preview pane.

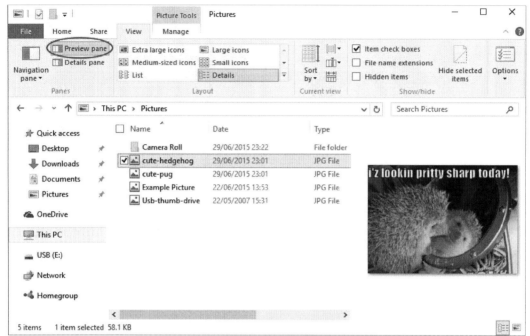

Figure 12.3 – A File Explorer window with the Preview pane enabled. Notice how the selected file appears in the preview on the right

12.3 – Details pane

The Details pane can be activated by clicking the icon below "Preview pane". The Details pane gives us a huge amount of information about the currently selected file. Figure 12.4 shows an example of the Details pane.

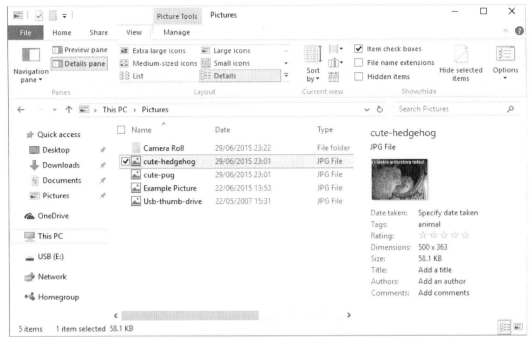

Figure 12.4 – Viewing the Details pane

Not only can you view these details using the Details pane, you can edit some of them too. Click on the text next to "Tags", "Title" or "Authors" for instance, to edit that information. By adding tags to your pictures, you can more easily find them when you search for them. For instance, if we tagged the hedgehog picture with the "Animal" tag, it would show up when we searched on the taskbar for "Animal". We cover searching in more detail in lesson 22.

The types of metadata that are displayed when you click on a file actually depend on what kind of file you are viewing. In figure 12.5 we can see the Details pane for a PNG picture file.

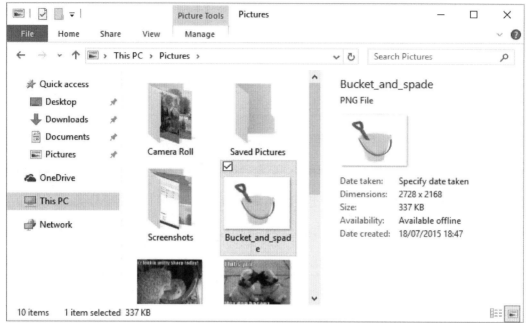

Figure 12.5 – Details for a PNG picture file are different to a JPG picture file

Notice that although the file shown in figure 12.5 is still a picture file, it's a different type of picture file and unfortunately this type of image doesn't support tags and other metadata.

12.4 - Sort and group by options

File Explorer also has extensive options for sorting and grouping your data. On the View tab on the ribbon, there are two buttons that control how your data is sorted. Figure 12.6 shows these buttons.

Figure 12.6 – Sort by and Group By buttons on the ribbon

The Sort by button performs the same operation as clicking on a column heading, that is, it lets you sort your files by any of the currently visible columns. The group by button will change the File Explorer window by grouping all your files into convenient clusters. Figure 12.7 shows a pictures folder with the files grouped by name.

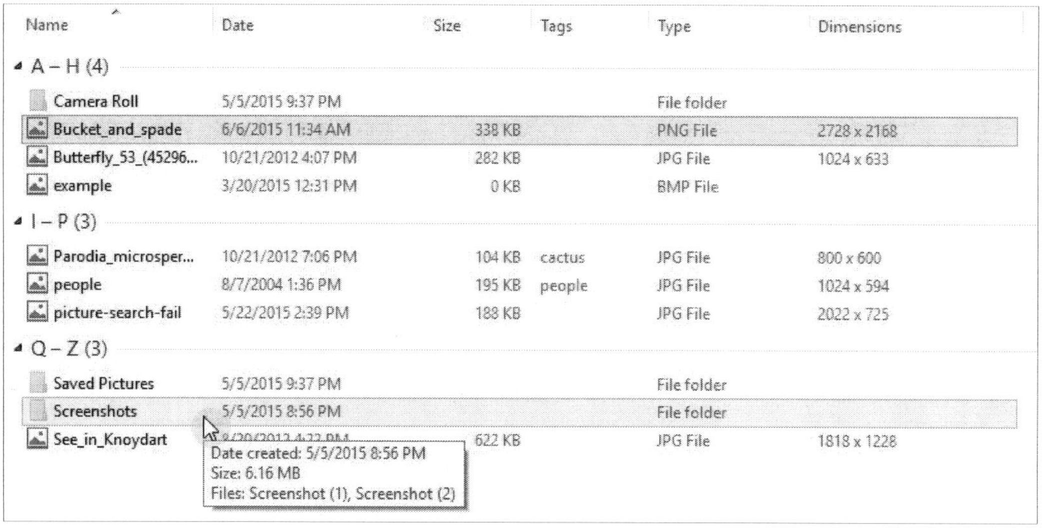

Figure 12.7 – Files in a folder grouped by name

Grouping your files by a certain criteria can make sifting through larger folders much more manageable.

12.5 – Check boxes, extensions and hidden items

There's one last part of the View tab on the ribbon that we will be covering in this lesson. Figure 12.8 shows these particular options.

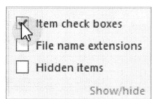

Figure 12.8 – Turning on Item check boxes

By turning on Item check boxes, Windows will place a small square box either over the file or folder icon (with medium or large icon viewing mode) or to the left of the icon (in any other viewing mode). These check boxes make it easier to select and deselect multiple files. Particularly when working with File Explorer using a stylus or your finger, being able to tap a check box like this is much easier than calling up the on-screen keyboard to press the control or alt keys. We cover working with multiple files in lesson 14.

The file name extensions option allows you to quickly show or hide the file name extension on a file name. File name extensions are three or more letters at the end of a file name. We cover file name extensions in lesson 17.5.

Finally, the hidden items option lets you show files and folders that are normally hidden. We discuss this in detail in lesson 17.4.

12.6 – Navigation pane

The Navigation pane is the list of items on the left hand side of the File Explorer window. You can see it clearly in figure 12.5 for instance. You can also toggle the Navigation pane off or on from the View tab on the ribbon. There are several useful functions you can carry out on the Navigation pane.

At the very top of the pane are the Quick access folders and locations. If you find you are often using the same folder, you can pin it to the Quick access section. Right click on the folder in the File Explorer window and choose "Pin to Quick access". To unpin a file or folder from Quick access, just right click on it in the Quick access section and choose "Unpin from Quick access".

Below that is the OneDrive icon that takes you to your OneDrive online or Cloud storage, when configured. We cover OneDrive in lesson 32.

The other short-cuts in the Navigation pane will take you to various places which we will be covering in later lessons. The Homegroup folders are shared folders on your network. Homegroups are covered in lesson 55. There are also short-cuts to "This PC" (previously known as "Computer"), which lets you explore all the drives attached to your local computer (we cover that in lesson 19) and if your computer is on a network, the network short-cut will let you browse available network storage locations.

As you have seen, there are lots of ways to work with your data in Windows 10. Don't feel you have to learn and master every possible way to display your data, experiment and use the views that work best for you and the way you work. As with most things in computing, the best way to learn is by trying for yourself, so don't be afraid to have a go.

Lesson 13 – Working With Files and Folders

In this lesson we will be building on some of the skills we developed in the previous lesson by taking a more detailed look at folders and files. For those of you who have used Windows before, much of the material here may be familiar. If this is your first time using Windows then, as always, we encourage you to learn at your own pace and experiment when reviewing the material presented here.

13.1 – Working with folders

We have seen several folders in the last few lessons that Windows 10 places on your computer by default. You are not limited to these folders however and creating new folders of your own is really easy. Figure 13.1 shows File Explorer open at a users personal folder.

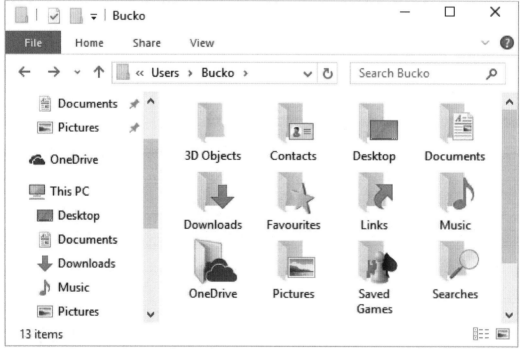

Figure 13.1 – File Explorer open on a users personal folder

Although the folders you can see in the picture are named "Documents" "Music", "Videos" and so on, you can still copy any kind of information into these folders and that holds true for all folders on a Windows PC. Opening any folder is as simple as double clicking on it.

13.2 – Making your own folders

Just like with a real world filing cabinet, you can create your own folders inside your computer too. Unlike a typical office filing cabinet however, on your Windows 10 PC you can create a new folder wherever you like (except in protected locations such as operating system folders). You can nest new folders inside another folder, and folders inside these folders too. In fact you can nest folders almost without limits. You can create a new folder in several ways. One way is to open the "Home" tab on the ribbon and then click "New Folder". Figure 13.2 shows an example of this, the New folder button is circled.

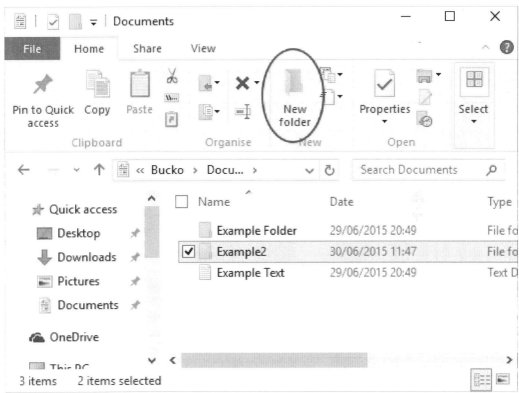

Figure 13.2 – Creating a new folder using the ribbon

Once you click the New Folder button, the new folder will appear instantly, all you need to do is type in a name for the folder using the keyboard. If you don't have a physical keyboard attached, Windows will open the on-screen keyboard for you.

You can also create new folders by opening the context menu (with a right click) and choosing New→Folder. We'll look at the context menu in a moment.

Creating folders is great for organising files on your computer. You can create sub-folders for different projects, different events that you photographed or filmed perhaps, different albums or artists in your music collection or any way you choose.

13.3 – The context menu in File Explorer

Just like in previous versions of Windows, it is a good idea to get used to using the context menu. The context menu is very handy when working with files. To open the context menu in File Explorer, simply right click on a file or folder (see the Appendix – Using touch gestures at the end of the book if you are using a touch only machine). Figure 13.3 shows the resulting menu.

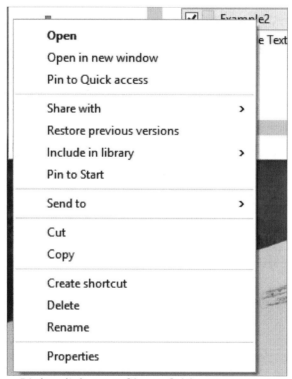

Figure 13.3 – Right click on a file or folder to open a context menu containing some common tasks

Context menus vary slightly between machines, and new software that you install may add extra options to the menu. Most of the options you can see in figure 13.3 will be covered in later lessons. In this lesson we will show you some of the most common tasks you can perform with files and folders from the context menu. Notice you can also pin a folder to the Start menu from here, by using the "Pin to Start" option. Very useful if you want to add a commonly used folder to your Start menu.

13.4 – Send to

Hovering your mouse pointer over the "Send to" option opens up another sub-menu. Figure 13.4 shows this menu.

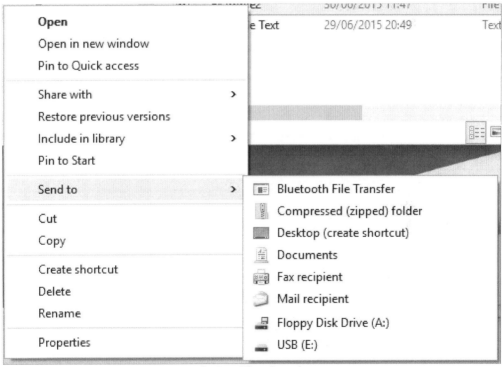

Figure 13.4 – The Send to menu

From this menu we can send the file or folder to various places or programs on our PC. What do each of these options do? We will take a look at each one now.

Bluetooth File Transfer:- Sends the file or folder to another device via Bluetooth. This is suitable for transferring smaller files and folders only and requires a Bluetooth radio in your PC and in the receiving device. This option will not appear if your PC does not have Bluetooth.

Compressed (zipped) folder:- This option creates a zip file with the files and folders we currently have selected. You can think of a zipped folder as being a compressed collection of files and folders. If you have dozens of files you want to transport across the internet, compressing them into a zipped folder can make them much easier to manage. Note that sending files or folders to a compressed (zipped) folder will not damage them in any way, nor will it remove them from their original locations. Accessing files inside a compressed or zipped folder is slower than accessing them in a normal folder.

Desktop (create shortcut):- This creates a shortcut to the file or folder on the desktop. The shortcut icon will appear on the same area as the Recycle Bin icon.

Documents:- Sends the currently selected file or folder to the Documents folder. If the file or folder is already in the Documents folder, it will create a copy.

Fax recipient:- Sends the currently selected document or folder to the Fax machine. This option will only work correctly if you have configured your Fax or Fax/Modem correctly. See the documentation that accompanied your hardware for more information.

Mail recipient:- Sends the currently selected files or folders to your e-mail program where they can then be forwarded across the internet to friends or associates. Avoid sending excessive or large files through e-mail as this may cause problems with many popular e-mail services.

Floppy Disk Drive:- If your computer still has an old fashioned floppy disk drive, choosing this option will copy the files (space permitting) to the floppy disk in drive A. It is a little surprising to see the venerable floppy disk still featured on the Send to menu in these days of gigabyte sized USB drives physically no bigger than your thumb!

The other options on the menu will send the file to the various drives or apps on your PC. Of course, your PC will certainly have different drives to ours and so the remaining options will be different.

13.5 – Cut, copy and paste

Directly below the Send to options on the context menu are the Cut and Copy options. Mastering the art of cut, copy and paste is one of the best things you can do to make yourself more productive on your Windows PC.

Cut is used for moving files or folders, whereas copy is used (unsurprisingly) to copy them. Take a look at figure 13.5.

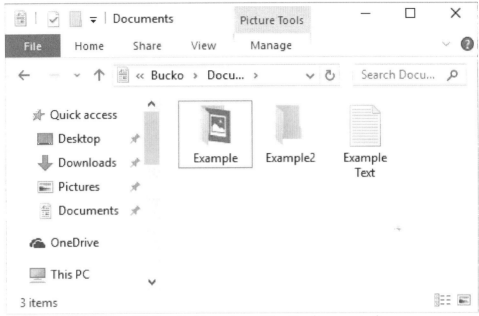

Figure 13.5 – Folders in a File Explorer window

If you wanted to move the folder named "example2", shown in figure 13.5 so that it was nested inside the folder named "example", you could do this by using the context menu. Right click on the "example2" folder and choose "Cut" from the context menu. Now, open the folder you want to move the file or folder into, in this case the folder called "example". Now right click on an empty space in the File Explorer window and choose "Paste" from the context menu. The "example2" folder will then appear. If we had chosen "Copy" instead of "Cut" then the folder would not have been removed from its original location.

The Cut, Copy and Paste functions are also available on the ribbon under the "Home" tab. Furthermore, you can use the Control (Ctrl) and C keyboard shortcut for copy and the Control and V keyboard shortcut for paste.

You can also move files and folders by dragging them. Dragging is done by clicking with your left mouse button on an icon and then holding down your left button. Now, as you move your mouse the icon will move too. You can now simply drop the icon wherever you want it. We explore this in more detail in lesson 14.1.

13.6 – When file names collide

Windows needs to tell files apart just the same as you do, so you cannot have two files with the same name in the same folder.

If you try and put a file with the same name as an existing one into the same folder, Windows will show you information about both files and ask you to confirm that you want to replace the original file.

If you try and put a folder with the same name as an existing one into the same folder, the contents of the folders will be merged. Any files which exist inside both folders will be overwritten. If a file is in the source folder but not in the destination folder, it will be moved to the destination. If a file is in the destination folder but not the source folder, it will be left alone. Figure 13.7 shows two folders. Notice how there's a file called "File3" in both folders.

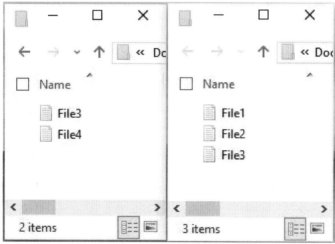

Figure 13.7 – Two folders prior to being merged

Now, consider figure 13.8, here the contents of the two folders have been merged together.

Figure 13.8 – The merged contents of two folders, shading has been added to File3 for illustration purposes

In the example illustrated, File1 and File2 are unchanged. File3 (coloured red or shaded darker in figure 13.8) was overwritten, because it existed in both the source and the destination folders. File4 was moved in from its original location, because it existed in the source folder but NOT in the destination. We will explore file name collisions more in lesson 14.2.

13.7 – Renaming or deleting files and folders

Renaming any type of file or folder can be done easily from the context menu. Simply right click on the file or folder you want to work with then choose "Rename" from the context menu. Now, type a new name and press Enter. If you prefer, you can select the file and click "Rename" from the Home tab on the ribbon too, both methods work exactly the same.

Eventually you will want to remove a file or folder from your PC. You can do this easily from the context menu, simply right click on a file and choose "Delete". Files and folders that are deleted are usually (but not always) sent to the Recycle Bin. You should see the Recycle Bin on your desktop, you can open it with a double click. To take a file out of the Recycle Bin, right click on it and choose "Restore". We take a more detailed look at the Recycle Bin in lesson 18.

You can also delete files or folders by clicking on them once and then clicking the Delete button on the Home tab of the ribbon or by pressing the Delete key on your keyboard.

That concludes this lesson. By now you are becoming quite competent at working with files and folders on your PC, the next lesson will show you some advanced techniques for dealing with large numbers of files. Remember, practise makes perfect so don't be afraid to try out the techniques we have reviewed here.

Lesson 14 – Multiple Files and Folders

In the last lesson, we saw how to use the context menu or the ribbon to copy and move files on our hard drive. In this lesson, we will review and build on those skills as we work with multiple files.

14.1 – Dragging and dropping

This is a somewhat difficult concept to explain with just words and pictures. You can move, or drag an icon by clicking on it with your left mouse button, then, keeping your mouse button held down, move your mouse. The file or folder will now follow your mouse cursor. It's then just a matter of dragging the file or folder to wherever you want it and then letting go of the mouse button. Figure 14.1 shows an example of a folder being dragged into another folder.

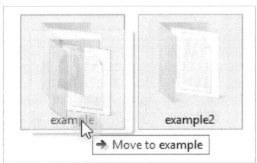

Figure 14.1 – Dragging a folder into another folder will move it

14.2 – File name collisions revisited

We already learned that we can't have two files or folders with the same name in the same folder. If there is a file name collision when copying or moving a file, you will see the window shown in figure 14.2.

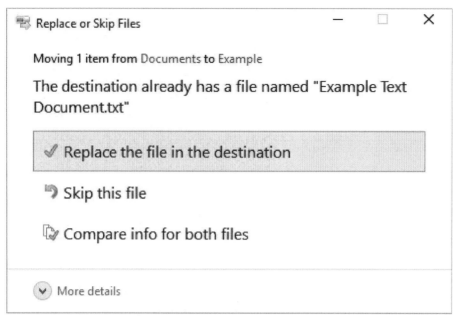

Figure 14.2 – Windows needs your permission to replace this file

The choice is pretty easy here, click on "Replace the file" to overwrite the conflicting file or "Skip this file" to leave the files as they are. If you click on "Compare info for both files" you can check things like date stamps to help you decide which file to keep.

If there is a file name collision during a folder merge, you will then see the window shown in figure 14.3.

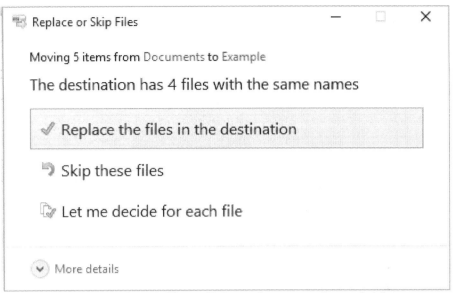

Figure 14.3 – A file collision when merging a folder

You now have the option to "Let me decide for each file". Figure 14.4 shows what happens if you choose this option.

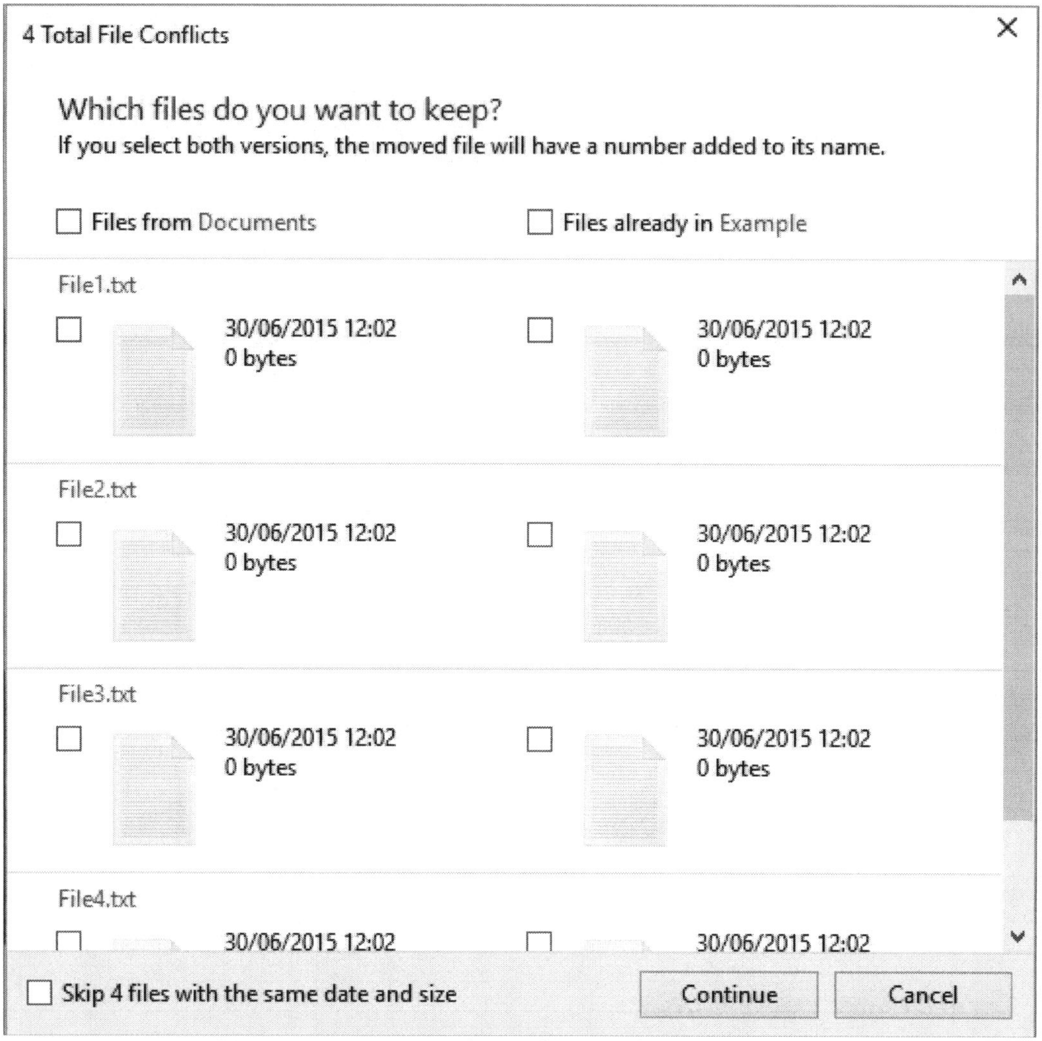

Figure 14.4 – Resolving file conflicts manually

Files in the source directory are shown on the left, while files in the destination directory are shown on the right. Windows gives us information about when the file was last modified, you can use this information to determine which is the most recent copy of a document. Tick or check the files you want to keep. If you choose to keep both conflicting files, then the file in the source directory will have a number automatically appended to its file name. This renaming by numbering enables you to keep both versions of a file if you are unsure which is the correct one.

14.3 – Desktop Snap and multiple File Explorer windows

It is possible to drag and drop files between File Explorer windows. A neat way of setting this up is to use Snap. When working, copying and moving files between two folders, you can use Snap to size their File Explorer windows to exactly half the screen width. To do this, first make sure you have two File Explorer windows open. If you need to open a new File Explorer window, right click on the folder you want to work with and choose "Open in new window". Figure 14.5 shows this.

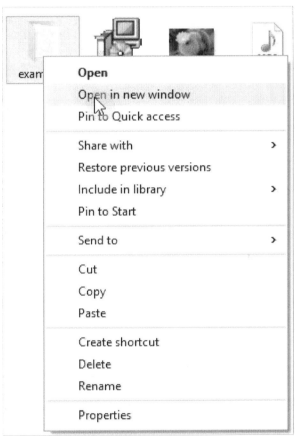

Figure 14.5 – Right click on a folder and choose "Open in new window" to open up a whole new File Explorer window

Now, drag one of the Explorer windows to the edge of the screen until a transparent frame appears (remember, to drag a window you click and hold on its title bar as you move your mouse). See figure 14.6 for an example.

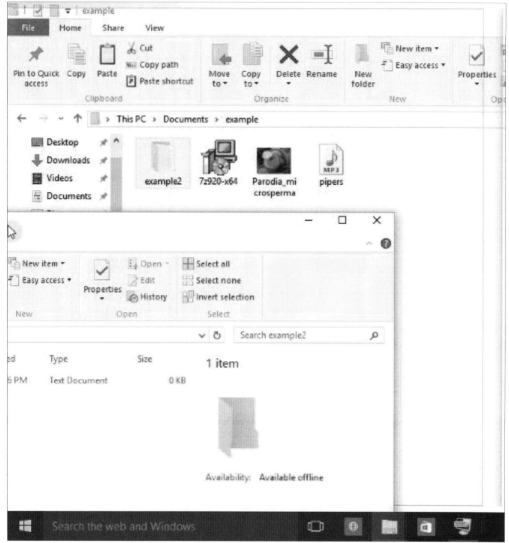

Figure 14.6 – Using Snap to resize a File Explorer window, wait for the transparent box to appear before letting go of the mouse button

Once you have snapped one window to one side of the screen, Windows 10 will open a list of windows in the other half of the screen. Simply select the second File Explorer window that you want to work with. The window will then appear on the other half of the screen. Figure 14.7 shows a screen shot of a desktop configured like this.

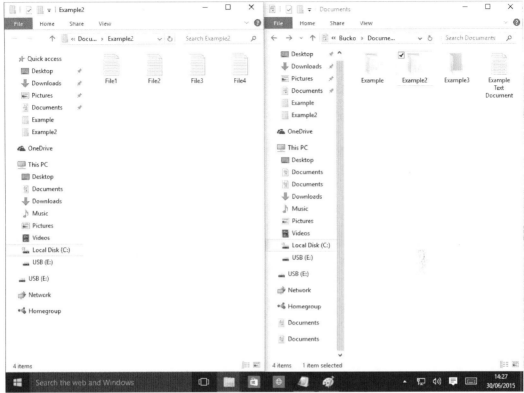

Figure 14.7 – Two File Explorer windows 'Snapped' to the sides of the screen

With your windows configured like this, it is easy to drag and drop files between them (of course, the windows could be sized or positioned however you like, but this configuration is particularly convenient for working with two folders at once).

To move files between the two folders, all you need to do is drag the file across from one window to the other. Files can be moved back in exactly the same way.

Remember when using this technique that dragging a file from one window to another can either move or copy the file, depending on the storage device you are working with. Files are moved if you drag them between two folders on the same storage device. If you drag a file or folder from one storage device to another, the files are copied instead.

To demonstrate this, consider an external USB stick/thumb drive. USB stick drives (also known as thumb drives or pen drives) are portable storage devices which can be attached to the common USB connectors on most modern computers. They are very useful for transporting files to and from work, school or college, for example. When we drag a file from our computers hard drive onto a device like this, it is copied, rather than moved. Why is this? It is not usually worth making lots of copies of a file over the same drive since it just wastes space. When you are working with a removable drive on the other hand, perhaps for backup or transporting files, it would not be a good idea to remove the originals from your computer, especially considering how easy it is to lose a USB stick drive!

14.4 – *Working with multiple files at once*

So far we have been working with individual files and folders, but what if we wanted to copy or move dozens of files at once? Fortunately for us, we do not have to do them one at a time. There are several ways we can select more than one file or folder at once. One of the easiest ways is to lasso them. To do this, click in an empty space in the File Explorer window and hold down your mouse button, just like you do when you drag an icon or window. You will see a square start to appear, Figure 14.8 illustrates this.

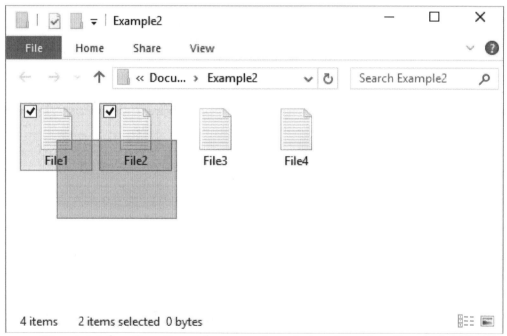

Figure 14.8 – Creating a lasso rectangle by dragging the mouse

Drag the lasso rectangle over the files you want to select and then let go. Now all of the files that were within the boundary of the lasso will be selected.

14.5 – Keyboard short cuts and other ways of working with multiple files

There are also some handy keyboard short cuts for selecting multiple files.

The Shift keys (sometimes represented as a small up pointing arrow) are located at the far right and far left of the second row of keys from the bottom on a standard keyboard. Using Shift, you can select a range of files from a list. For example, to select File1, File2 and File3 in figure 14.8, first click on "File1", then hold down shift and click on "File3".

The Control or Ctrl keys are located at the far right and far left of the bottom row of keys on a standard keyboard. This key can be used to select and deselect individual files. Simply hold down Control while you click on files and folders to individually select and deselect them. Any files you click while holding down Control will stay selected once you let go of the key.

You can also use the Home tab on the ribbon to select multiple files and folders. The file selection tools are on the far right of the Home tab. Figure 14.9 shows the options that are available.

Figure 14.9 – File and folder selection tools on the ribbon

By turning on the "Item check boxes" option on the View tab of the ribbon (see lesson 12.5) you can also select multiple files and folders simply by ticking or checking them. In figure 14.8 you can see the item check boxes are turned on, notice in the top left hand corner of File1 and File2 there is a check or tick mark. This check box may appear to the left of the file in other viewing modes.

When you have multiple files selected, you can work with them just like you do with an individual file. That means you can use the context menu or the ribbon to Cut, Copy or Send to, or you can drag and drop them. When working with a large number of files, selecting several at once is a huge time-saver, so be sure to practise and master this technique.

That concludes this lesson and is the end of this chapter. Now you have a solid understanding of how to manipulate files on your computer. In the next lesson we look at Libraries, a file organisation feature that was introduced in Windows 7 and improved even further for Windows 8 and Windows 10.

Chapter 4 – Deeper into Folders

In this chapter we will continue to build your Windows 10 desktop skills by looking at some advanced folder and file operations. You have come a long way since the start of the course and you are rapidly turning into a Windows 10 expert! Remember, review the material at your own pace. As we delve into these more complex subjects you might find you need to refresh your memory from earlier chapters. Learning to use an operating system well is not a race, so take your time.

Lesson 15 – Libraries

Modern computer users are storing more and more information on their machines. Digital cameras have made it super easy to take thousands of pictures. The internet has made it cheap and easy to purchase huge music collections and even video collections too. Libraries were introduced in Windows 7 to help manage users rapidly expanding file collections. Power users will often rave about libraries, but regular users frequently find them confusing. In Windows 10, the libraries have been hidden away, meaning that regular users may rarely encounter them. If you only have one hard drive on your PC, then you can skip this lesson if you like. Otherwise, read on for some handy tips for organising bigger media collections.

15.1 – Activating libraries

If you want to use libraries in Windows 10, you will need to enable them in the Navigation pane. To do this, open a File Explorer window and click on the View tab, then click on the Options button on the right of the ribbon. A Folder Options window will then appear. Select the "View" tab and then scroll down in the "Advanced Settings" section until you get right to the bottom. The window should look like the one shown in figure 15.1.

Figure 15.1 – Restoring libraries to the Navigation pane

Make sure the "Show libraries" option is selected and then click on "OK". You will now be able to see a shortcut to your libraries in the Navigation pane.

15.2 – Working with libraries

When you access a library in File Explorer, or anywhere in Windows, it appears just like a regular folder. This is probably why beginners often find the concept to be confusing. Libraries can, in fact, show data from several locations on your computer. This can be useful on machines with two or more hard drives. On a machine like this, media files may be spread over different hard drives and in different folders. If you want to browse all your photographs or music together, you can put them in the same library even if they are not in the same folder. Figure 15.2 shows a Music library on a Windows 10 machine. The user has already added some music files to his computer and this can be seen in the example.

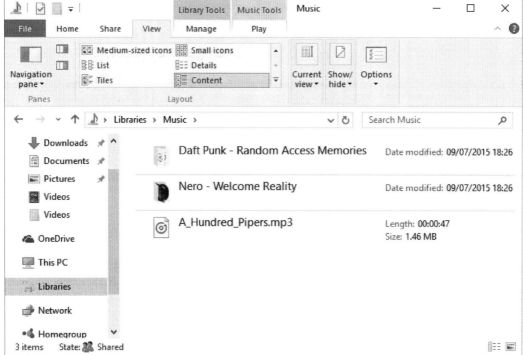

Figure 15.2 – File Explorer in a Music library on a Windows 10 machine

In Windows 10, libraries only contain one location by default. In Windows 8 and Windows 7, there were two locations for each of the libraries. For the Music library, this would be the users own music folder and the public music folder. If you have upgraded to Windows 10 from Windows 7, then your libraries should still include those two locations.

Note that if you have set up OneDrive (see lesson 32) your OneDrive folders will be included in the libraries automatically.

To see which locations are included in a library, click on the Library Tools tab on the ribbon, then click on "Manage Library".

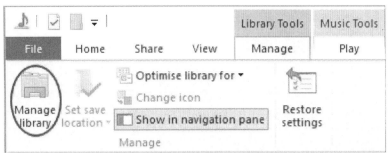

Figure 15.3 – Use the ribbon under "Library Tools" to access the Manage library button

The window shown in figure 15.4 will then open.

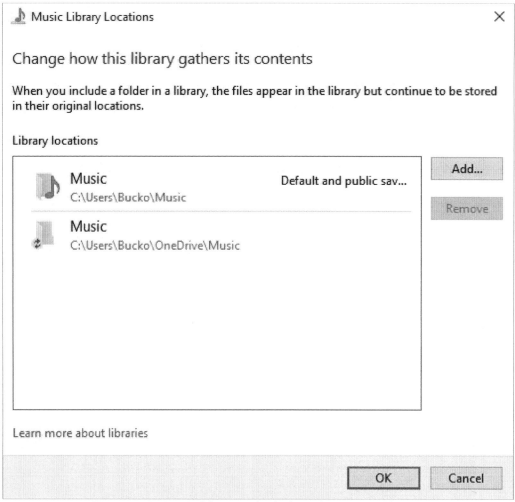

Figure 15.4 – Folders included in the Music library

In figure 15.4 we can see that the library contains two folders. To add a location, click on the "Add…" button. You can then browse to any folder on any storage location on your PC (well, almost any location, there are some exceptions that we will discuss in a moment). When you have located the folder you want to include in your library, click on "Include folder". Figure 15.5 shows a Music library with content added from a secondary hard drive.

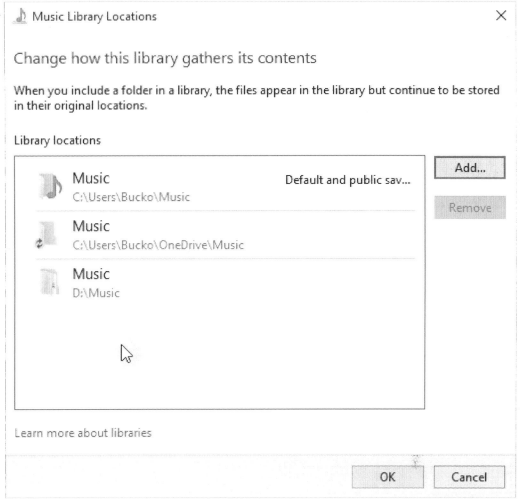

Figure 15.5 – A Music library with an extra location added

Now, when the user browses to their Music library, they will in actual fact be getting a combined view of the "Music" folder at 'C:\Users\Bucko\Music', the OneDrive music folder at 'C:\Users\Bucko\OneDrive\Music' and the folder at 'D:\Music'. So in effect the library will show the content in all three of these folders. If you're not sure what that means, you can take a refresher on file paths in our prerequisite skills section, either on your Superguide DVD/Download or in the PC basics section on Top-Windows-Tutorials.com.

Figure 15.6 shows the newly configured library open in File Explorer.

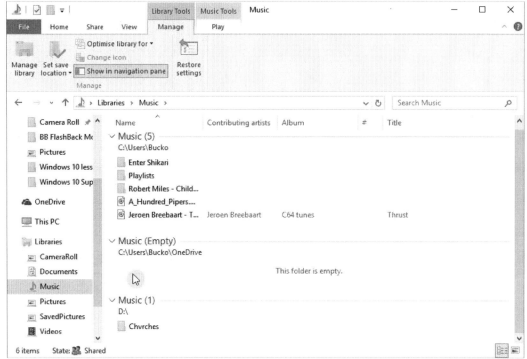

Figure 15.6 – Browsing a library with three locations included in File Explorer

Music folders you add to your music library like this will also be available instantly in the music libraries in the Groove Music app and in Windows Media Player.

Notice in figure 15.5 that the top folder is marked as the "Default and public save location". What does this mean? Since we can work with our libraries like any other folder, if we were to copy or move a file into this library from somewhere else, the file would actually be placed into the My Music folder, since that is the "Default save location".

The idea of the public save location was to make it easier for users to share files. Public sections of a library can be accessed by all users of the PC, while the regular private sections are only accessible to the user who is currently logged in. Public save locations are rarely used now and Microsoft may phase them out entirely in the future.

You can change the default and public save locations easily. Simply open the Manage library window (figure 15.5) and then right click on a folder in the list. A menu will then appear with the option to set the public or default save locations to this folder.

You can add several more locations to your libraries if you want to. As well as folders on local hard drives, it is possible to add network storage locations or even a removable hard drive. As mentioned earlier, there are some restrictions on what kind of locations can be added to libraries. Unfortunately, USB thumb or stick drives are not supported and you can only add network locations that are indexed and available off-line (this basically means their contents are mirrored on your computers hard drive). For more information about what files and folders can be included, open the Manage Library window again (figure 15.5) and click on the "Learn more about libraries" link at the bottom of the window. A help and support page will then open, from here, click "What types of locations are supported in libraries?".

15.3 – Sorting data in libraries

When working with libraries in File Explorer, they behave almost exactly the same as regular folders. Figure 15.6 shows a Music library with several folders added to it. Notice that the File Explorer window shown in figure 15.6 is showing us the path to the folders included in the library (C:\Users\Bucko and D:\). To view your libraries like this, you will need to use the "Group by" button on the View tab of the ribbon. We discussed the Group By options briefly in lesson 12.4. Figure 15.7 demonstrates this button.

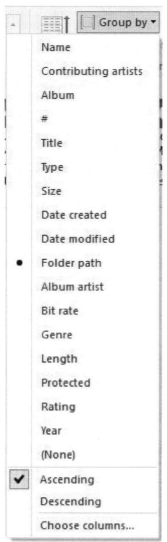

Figure 15.7 – Choosing a different grouping for a library folder

You can also use the "Sort by" button, which is to the left of the "Group by" button to sort the files different ways. If you don't see these buttons, try making your File Explorer window wider using the window sizing techniques we covered in lesson 5.2. Windows 10 gives you dozens of ways to view the data in your libraries and folders, there are far too many possibilities for us to cover here, so experiment and find the views that work best for you.

15.4 – Pictures library

The Pictures library behaves in much the same way as the Music library. Figure 15.8 shows a typical Pictures library.

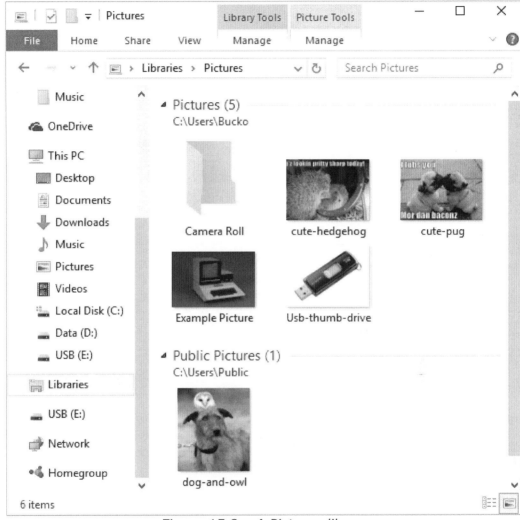

Figure 15.8 – A Pictures library

The Pictures library shown in figure 15.8 has two locations, the users personal pictures folder and the public pictures folder. This was the default configuration for libraries in Windows 7 and 8. If you don't have a public folder in any of your libraries, you can add it again easily if you want to.

Simply open the Manage library window (figure 15.3/15.4) then add a new location (by clicking the Add... button) and browse to C:\Users\Public. There you will find several folders named "Public Documents", "Public Pictures" etc. Simply add the appropriate one to your library and you're all set. Remember you can set the default and public save locations by right clicking on any location in the Manage library window.

Just like with the Music library, data in the Pictures library can be sorted by using the Group by and Sort by controls on the ribbon. Of course, we can also use the folder views, Preview pane and Details pane with all our libraries just like we did with regular folders in lesson 12.

Any picture folders you add to your Pictures library will also instantly be available in the Pictures app.

15.5 – Open file/folder location

When working with libraries, you can instantly go to the actual file or folder location by using "Open file location" or "Open folder location" on the context menu. Figure 15.9 shows an example of this.

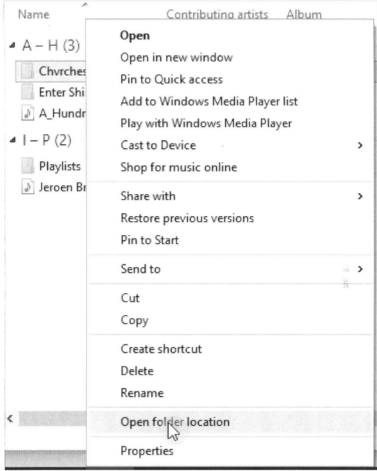

Figure 15.9 – Use this context menu option to jump directly to a folders location on your computer

Certain operations can only be carried out when you open the folders true location in File Explorer and not when viewing the file or folder in library view.

That concludes our lesson on libraries. For those of us with powerful PCs with multiple hard drives, libraries are a great feature of Windows 10 that help keep your files organised and grouped together.

Lesson 16 – Folder Properties

Folders on a Windows 10 machine have unique attributes, or properties associated with them. In this lesson we will delve into these properties and explore some of the attributes we can change.

16.1 – Accessing folder properties

To access the folder properties for any given folder, simply right click on the folder and choose "Properties" from the bottom of the context menu. Figure 16.1 illustrates this.

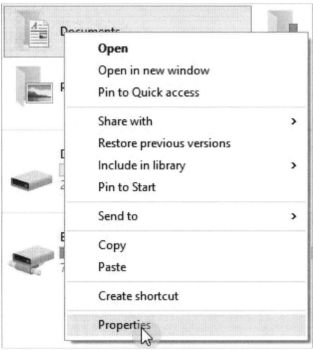

Figure 16.1 – Accessing folder properties

You can also access folder properties by opening the Home tab on the ribbon and clicking on "Properties". Once you do this, you will see the folder Properties window, figure 16.2 shows this window.

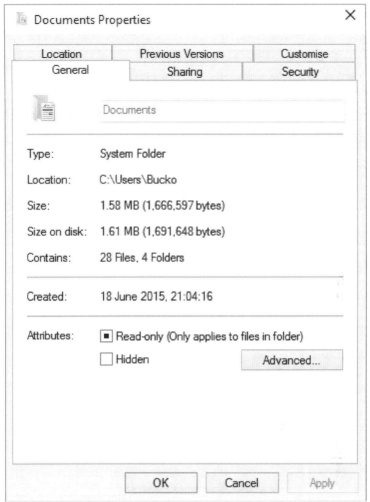

Figure 16.2 – The Properties window for the "Documents" folder

By default the folder Properties window will open on the "General" tab. This tab shows us some general information about the folder, such as the size it takes up and how many files it contains. Notice that we can see values for "Size" and "Size on disk". "Size" refers to the total size of all the files, "Size on disk" is the actual amount of storage space these files take up. Size on disk is always a little bigger due to the way files are stored on a hard drive.

Under "Attributes" at the bottom of the window there is a box labelled "Read-only". If you cannot delete a file or folder then sometimes deselecting this box will help.

Notice the tabs labelled "Sharing" and "Security". These tabs let you set permissions for other users to access your folders either locally or over the network (the local network not the internet). We discuss Homegroups and how to share folders on a home network using Homegroups in lesson 55. Discussing security permissions is an advanced topic that you will probably never have to deal with unless you are a systems administrator. On some systems, these tabs may not appear, so don't be alarmed if you don't see them.

The "Previous Versions" tab works with File History backup to allow you to browse backups of the data stored in the folder. We cover File History in lesson 34.

Special folders such as "Documents", "Pictures" and "Music" have a location tab. That is because these folders are actually links to other folders. See figure 16.3.

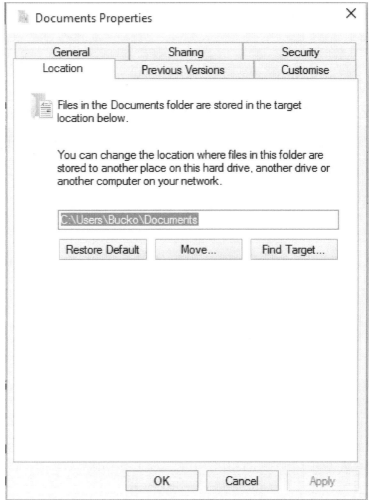
Figure 16.3 – Some special folders are actually links to other folders

In figure 16.3 we can see that actually, the documents folder points to "C:\users\Bucko\Documents". The default location should be suitable for most users, but if necessary it is possible to change the location of your personal folders by clicking on "Move...". This is occasionally useful if you want to move your pictures or music folder to a larger, secondary hard drive for example. However, since certain badly written third party software may have issues with systems that have been reconfigured like this, we would advise against it. If you need to add more storage space to your personal folders, you can always use libraries, as shown in lesson 15.

Regular folders, including folders you create yourself, do not have a Location tab like this on their folder properties window.

16.2 – Customise tab

The bulk of this lesson will focus on the options available in this tab. Note that if you do not see this tab when you open the folder properties window, you are probably working with the folder in a library or a folder that is actually a link, and not from the folders true location. To go to any file or folders true path or location, right click on the file or folder and choose Open file/folder location.

Figure 16.4 shows the folder Properties window open on the Customise tab.

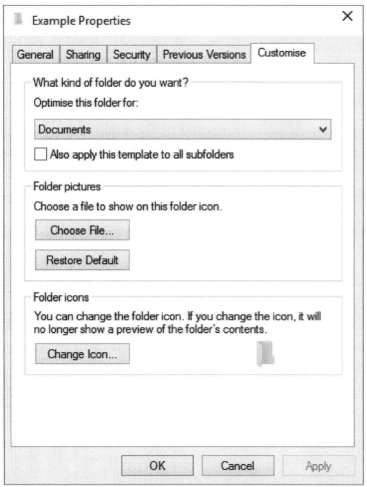

Figure 16.4 – A folder Properties window open on the customise tab

At the top of the window, we are asked "What kind of folder do you want?" Windows 10 knows about several different types of content and the designers of Windows 10 realised that the best way to view pictures in a folder might not necessarily be the best way to view music, for example. Use the drop down box under "Optimise this folder for:" to tell Windows what type of content is stored in the folder. We can choose from "General Items", "Documents", "Pictures", "Music" and "Videos". When you choose one, Windows will open this folder in a viewing mode suitable for that kind of content.

In lesson 11.5 we demonstrated the different folder viewing modes. It is possible to specify what kind of folder view is used for each type of content. For example, you can have large icons view for pictures and details view for documents, we will show you how in the next lesson.

If the box labelled "Also apply this template to all subfolders" is selected, then any folders inside the current folder will also be switched to documents view, or whatever view was selected in the drop down box.

16.3 – Folder pictures and folder icons

In the bottom of the window shown in figure 16.4 is a button labelled "Change Icon...". Using this option we can change the icon for the folder to any icon we choose.

If you don't see this option on your folder, try going to the location tab (see figure 16.3) then clicking on the "Find Target..." button. This should open up a new File Explorer window with your folder in it. Now, right click on the folder and choose "Properties" again. This time you should be able to see the "Change Icon..." option on the Customise tab.

Above that option is the option to change the folder picture. Note that this option isn't available for certain folders (e.g "Documents", "Pictures" etc), but it is available for any folder you create yourself. You can use any picture on your PC as the folder picture. Click on "Choose File" and then browse to your pictures. Choose the picture by clicking on it and then click "Open". Back on the folder properties window, click "Apply". The picture will then be added to the folder in File Explorer. If you don't see the picture right away, click on the Refresh button (the curly shaped arrow next to the address bar in File Explorer).

Figure 16.5 – A folder with a custom picture applied to it

Changing folder icons is also easy. Click on the "Change Icon…" button as shown in figure 16.4. The standard Windows icon library will then appear, this is shown in figure 16.6.

Figure 16.6 – Browsing for an icon

Browse through the icon gallery here and pick out any icon you like, then click "OK". This will return you to the folder Properties window. Click on "Apply". You should now see your new icon in File Explorer, if you do not, click on Refresh. Note that Windows will not allow you to apply folder pictures and/or change icons on certain pre-created folders. If you create the folder yourself however, you can always change the icon or the picture.

If you want to remove your custom icon, simply access the icon gallery and click the "Restore Defaults" button that can be seen in figure 16.6. To remove a custom folder picture, access the Customise tab of the folder Properties window (figure 16.4) and click on "Restore Default" under "Folder pictures".

That concludes this lesson on folder properties. Changing and customising your folders can be useful and fun. Go ahead and experiment for yourself, you can always undo any changes you make by using the "Restore Default" buttons shown previously. In the next lesson we look at advanced folder customisation, don't worry, it's not as hard as it sounds!

Lesson 17 – Folder Options

Since we have been exploring folders in the past few lessons, now might be a good time to look at some advanced folder customisation options.

17.1 – Folder options window

We can access the Folder Options window from any File Explorer window. Open the ribbon and select the View tab, then click on the Options button on the right. Figure 17.1 illustrates this.

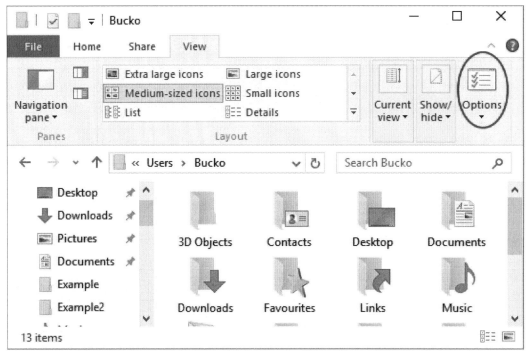

Figure 17.1 – Accessing Folder Options from File Explorer

Figure 17.2 shows the Folder Options window which appears when you click the Options button on the ribbon.

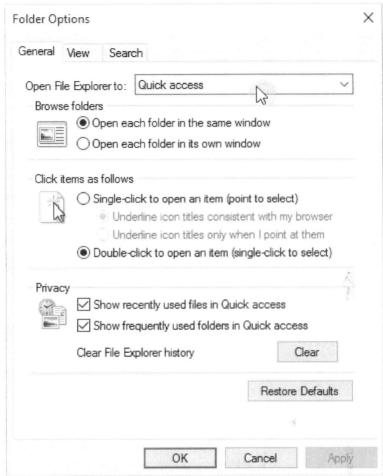

Figure 17.2 – The Folder Options window

17.2 – General folder options

In figure 17.2, there are four categories of options. We will take a look at what each of these options does.

Open File Explorer to:- This option is at the very top of the window. It controls which folder will be displayed when you first launch File Explorer. You can choose between "Quick access", which shows your pinned favourite folders and the folders you accessed most recently, or "This PC", which shows all the storage devices connected to your PC. We cover This PC in lesson 19.

Browse folders:- In lesson 14.3 we demonstrated how to work with multiple File Explorer windows. We opened a new File Explorer window by right clicking on a folder and choosing "Open in new window". By choosing the "Open each folder in its own window" option, you will change the behaviour of File Explorer so that every time you double click on a folder, a new Explorer window will open.

With this option enabled, the desktop can become cluttered very quickly, but some users do prefer to work this way.

Click items as follows:- For users who struggle with the timing on double clicks, these options can be very helpful. Choose "Single click to open an item (point to select)" and now you only need to click once on an icon to open it. This does make dragging icons a little more tricky and you may find you accidentally open them when trying to drag, but a lot of users prefer this method rather than the dratted double click.

In the sub options, "Underline icon titles only when I point at them" is fairly self-explanatory. However, you might be wondering what "Underline icon titles consistent with my browser" means. Basically it means that all icon titles (the text below the icons) will be underlined, just like links are underlined in Microsoft Edge or Internet Explorer.

Privacy:- The privacy options are new for Windows 10 and allow you to control which recently accessed or frequently used files or folders appear in the Quick access section. You can also clear your recent folder browsing history by clicking the "Clear" button here.

Remember, to protect your privacy on your computer, create separate user accounts for everyone that uses the PC. We cover user accounts in lesson 37. We also cover privacy settings in lesson 41.

When changing options in the Folder Options window, don't forget that you can always revert back to the default options by clicking "Restore Defaults" and then clicking on "Apply".

17.3 – View tab

You can access the "View" tab in the Folder Options window by clicking on it once. Figure 17.3 shows the Folder Options window open on the "View" tab.

Figure 17.3 – The "View" tab of the Folder Options window

There are two main sections to this tab, they are "Folder Views" and "Advanced settings".

The Folder Views options contains just two buttons. By clicking "Apply to folders" it is possible to set the current viewing mode across all folders of the same type. What does this mean? Consider this example, File Explorer is viewing a music folder and the viewing mode has been changed to details view (changing folder viewing modes was covered in lesson 11.5). Now, the user opens the Folder Options window (just like we did at the start of the lesson) and then navigates to the View tab. The user wants all the music folders to open up in details view, so he/she clicks the "Apply to Folders" button. From now on, all music folders will be shown in details view whenever they are opened up.

Clicking on the "Reset Folders" button restores all the folders to their default view.

The Advanced Settings in the bottom half of this tab contain all kinds of tweaks and customisations you can do to File Explorer. Rather than try to cover every minor option in excruciating detail, the best way to learn is by experimenting. You cannot damage your computer by changing these options and you can always revert back by clicking on "Restore Defaults".

There are a couple of important options that are found under the advanced options that we do want to look at in detail however.

Navigation pane options – In Windows 7 and 8, these options were present on the General tab, but in Windows 10, the options have moved to the bottom of the Advanced settings list on the View tab. Scroll to the very bottom to find the "Expand to open folder", "Show all folders" and "Show libraries" options.

Recall that the Navigation pane is the left hand column on a File Explorer window. Choosing the "Show all folders" option changes the layout of the Navigation pane so that more icons are displayed. With show all folders selected, you will see the Libraries become stacked under "Desktop" for instance. If you prefer a more compact less cluttered view, keep this option turned off.

The "Automatically expand to current folder" option is best demonstrated with pictures. Figure 17.4 shows a File Explorer window with this option turned **off**.

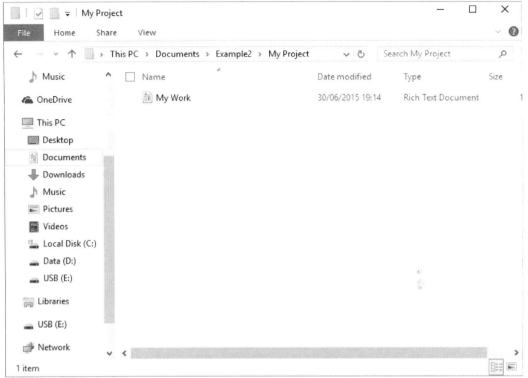

Figure 17.4 – File Explorer window with the "Automatically expand to current folder" option turned off

Notice that although the address bar shows that the current folder is "This PC\Documents\Example2\My Project", the Navigation pane is still pointing at just "Documents". Now, figure 17.5 shows an Explorer window with the "Automatically expand to current folder" option turned on.

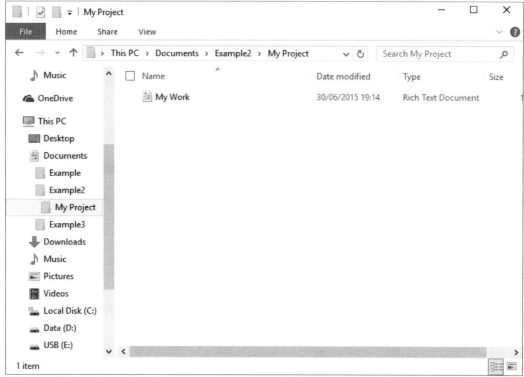

Figure 17.5 - File Explorer window with the "Automatically expand to current folder" option turned on

In figure 17.5 you can see that the Navigation pane now matches the address or path shown in the address bar. With the Automatically expand to current folder option enabled, the Navigation pane will always match the address bar like this.

The last Navigation pane option, "Show libraries", was covered in lesson 15.1.

17.4 – Hidden files and folders

On a Windows 10 computer, there are several folders that are used exclusively by the operating system. These folders contain files that are used by Windows when it loads and when it runs. Because tampering with these files can potentially be disastrous, by default Windows will hide them from view, so you cannot accidentally navigate into them. Occasionally, while troubleshooting your computer or if directed to do so by a technical support representative, you may need to access these folders. Please be careful if you do modify the contents of these folders however! One mistake and you might find your Windows installation starts acting in a very strange manner or even stops working altogether.

In Windows 10, you can also show or hide hidden files and folders from the View tab on the ribbon, figure 17.6 shows the location of this option.

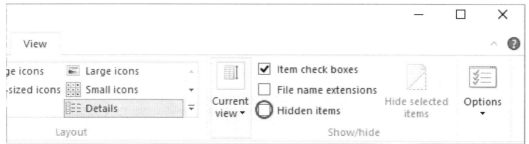

Figure 17.6 – Show or hide hidden items quickly by using this option on the View tab of the ribbon

If you can't see the option to show hidden files on your ribbon, you may need to make your current File Explorer window a little wider.

Figure 17.7 shows the root (top level) folder on a Windows 10 hard drive with the "Show hidden files, folders and drives" option turned **off**.

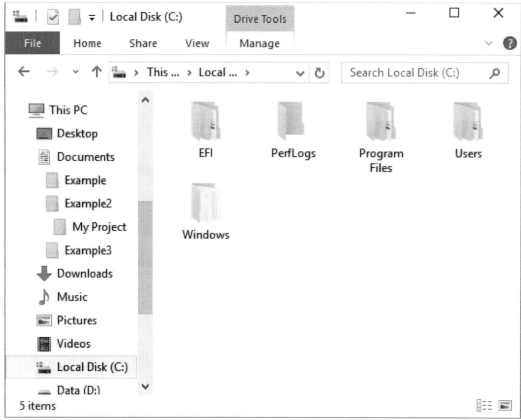

Figure 17.7 – Standard view of the top level directory on a Windows 10 system drive

Figure 17.8 shows the same folder, but with the "Show hidden files, folders and drives" option turned on.

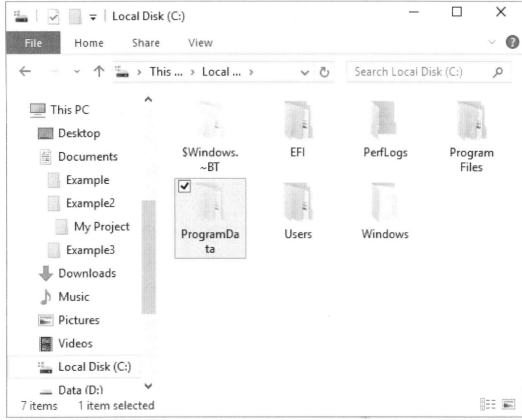

Figure 17.8 – View of the top level directory on a Windows 10 system drive, with the Show hidden files, folders and drives option turned on. Notice the extra ProgramData folder that has appeared

In figure 17.8 we can see an extra folder has appeared (it is highlighted in the picture). You may also have noticed that the folder appears fainter, or ghosted compared to the other folders, to indicate that it is normally hidden. There may be other hidden folders too, depending on your system and installed software.

A related option to "Show hidden files, folders and drives" is "Hide protected operating system files". This option is only available on the View tab of the Folder Options window. If you deselect this option, you will see even more files and folders appear on your computer. Again these are important operating system files that you should never change or tamper with unless you are absolutely certain that you know what you are doing. We recommend leaving these files hidden while working normally with your computer.

17.5 – Hide extensions for known file types

This option causes a lot of confusion and even trips up seasoned Windows users. Most files on a Windows computer have a file extension at the end of their file names. A file extension is a period (dot) character followed by three letters or more (historically file extensions were limited to three characters, but in modern versions of Windows they can be longer). Typical file extensions include ".mp3" for mp3 files, ".avi" for video files and ".jpg" for Jpeg photograph files. By default, Windows hides this information from you, this was probably done to make working with files less confusing for beginners.

Consider figure 17.9. You can see several music files in File Explorer.

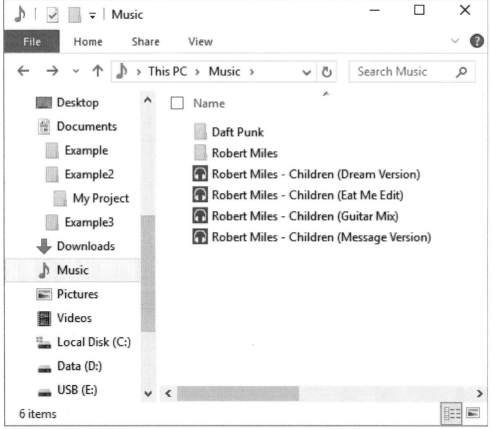

Figure 17.9 – Viewing music files with the "Hide extensions for known file types" option turned on

The top file is called "Robert Miles – Children (Dream Version)". The actual file name of this file is "Robert Miles – Children (Dream Version).mp3" but Windows is hiding the extra file extension information from us. Figure 17.10 shows another File Explorer window with the hide file extensions option turned **on** (the default setting).

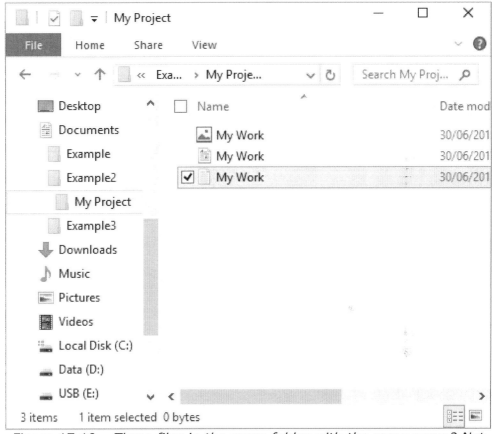

Figure 17.10 – Three files in the same folder with the same name? Not really, the file extensions are different, just Windows is hiding this information from us

The hide file extensions option can be particularly confusing with files of similar names. In figure 17.10 we have three files. "My Work.bmp", "My Work.rtf" and "My Work.txt". With the "Hide extensions for known file types" option turned **on** (the default setting) it appears as if we have three files in the same folder with the same name, something that we already told you is impossible! Figure 17.11 shows the same folder but with the "Hide extensions for known file types" option turned **off**.

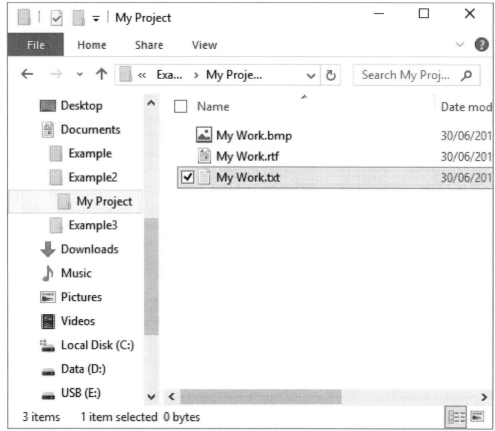

Figure 17.11 – Turning "Hide extensions for known file types" off reveals extra information about a file name

To avoid this kind of confusion, many users turn the "Hide extensions for known file types" option off. If you do turn it off, keep in mind that if you rename a file and accidentally remove its file extension, Windows will not know how to handle that file any more, unless you rename it again and put the file extension back. Even worse, if you remove the file extension and put the wrong one back, Windows may try to open the file with the wrong program.

That concludes this lesson on folder options. We are getting into some advanced Windows 10 operations and hope the information presented here was not too daunting. In the next lesson we will be looking at the Recycle Bin and how Windows handles the files you delete.

Lesson 18 – Recycle Bin

Because it is easy to accidentally delete files and something of a chore to undelete them again, Microsoft introduced the Recycle Bin way back in Windows 95. Now, when you delete files from your PC, they (usually) end up in the Recycle Bin before being removed completely. In this lesson we will explore how the Recycle Bin works and how to recover files that have been sent there.

18.1 – Into the Recycle Bin

The Recycle Bin is, by default, the only icon on your Windows 10 desktop. The icon shown here looks as if it has some crumpled paper inside it. This is to indicate that there are files or folders in the bin. To open the Recycle Bin, we simply double click on it. Figure 18.2 shows the Recycle Bin window.

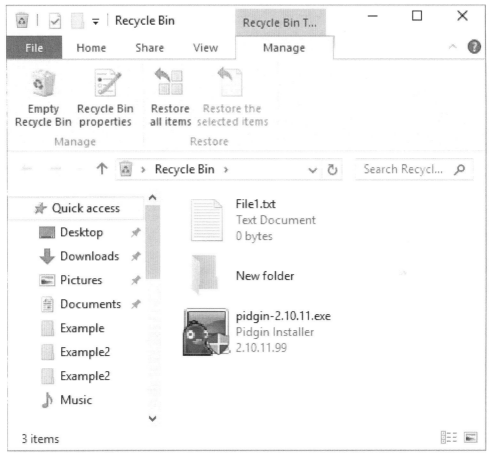

Figure 18.2 – The Recycle Bin opens in a standard File Explorer window

The Recycle Bin opens in a File Explorer window just like any other folder on your PC. The ribbon will automatically change to reflect the special tasks that can be carried out with the Recycle Bin. In figure 18.2, the user has clicked on "Manage" under Recycle Bin Tools on the ribbon. By clicking on "Empty the Recycle Bin", all the items in the window will be permanently deleted. By clicking on "Restore all items", all the items shown are put back into their original folders (i.e. the folders that they were placed in before they were deleted).

Notice that we said the files would be "permanently deleted" when "Empty the Recycle Bin" was clicked. This is not strictly true. There is still the possibility of recovering those files with some kind of undelete utility or data forensics tool kit. Emptying the Recycle Bin does not protect you from this. If you are working with particularly sensitive information you may need to use a third party file shredding utility. These work like their real-world counterparts and make sure that files cannot be recovered once the are removed from your computer.

Naturally, it is possible to work with individual files in the Recycle Bin as well as its entire contents. Turn on the Details pane (from the View tab on the ribbon) and single click on an item in the Recycle Bin and you can see the original file path or address for the file or folder. Clicking on "Restore this item" will move the file back to its original location. See figure 18.3.

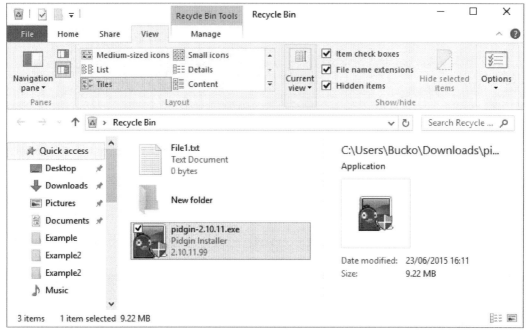

Figure 18.3 – Working with individual files in the Recycle Bin

In figure 18.3, we can see that if we click on "Restore the selected items", the "pidgin-2-10-11.exe" file will be restored to "C:\Users\Bucko\Downloads". This is the address or path of the users downloads folder, so the file would reappear in the downloads folder in this case.

To permanently delete a selected file, right click on it and choose "Delete" from the context menu. This will free up the space on your hard drive that the file was occupying.

18.2 – Sending files to the Recycle Bin

Most files that you delete will initially be sent to the Recycle Bin. Take a look at figure 18.4.

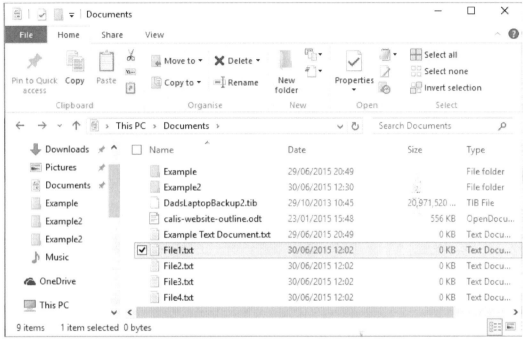

Figure 18.4 – A typical File Explorer window with the Home tab open on the ribbon

There are several ways to send the file "File1.txt" to the Recycle Bin. We can select it and then press the "Delete" key on the keyboard. We can use the Home tab on the ribbon and click "Delete". Alternatively, use the context menu by right clicking on the icon and then choosing "Delete". Whichever method you prefer, they all have the same end result, the file is removed from this folder and placed in the Recycle Bin. Once there, we can click on it and see where it came from and then restore it back to its original location if necessary.

18.3 – Files that are not sent to the Recycle Bin

While most files you delete are initially sent to the Recycle Bin, some are not. In figure 18.4 we can see a large file called "DadsLaptopBackup2.tib". This file is over 20 gigabytes in size. Files this large are normally just too big to fit in the Recycle Bin. We can still remove them by deleting them with any of the methods described previously. However, this time when you attempt to delete the file, the window shown in figure 18.5 will appear.

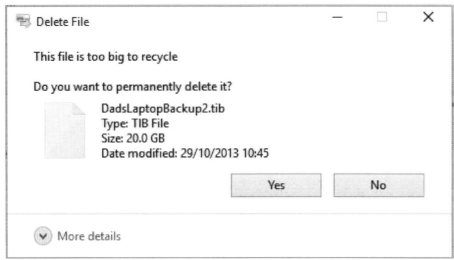

Figure 18.5 – This file is too big to fit in the Recycle Bin

If you click "Yes" then the file will be removed from your computer. Of course, it would still be possible (though somewhat inconvenient) to use special data recovery software to undelete it.

Certain other files are not sent to the Recycle Bin when deleted. One example of this is a file or folder on a network storage device. Depending on the device in question, when you try to delete a file from a network storage device, you may see the window shown in figure 18.6.

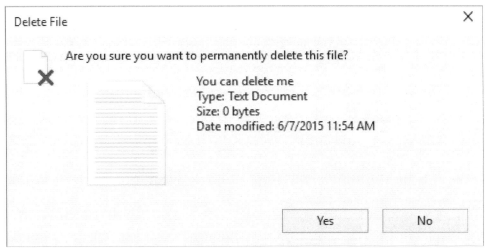

Figure 18.6 – This file on the network will be deleted permanently

Clearly this file isn't too big for the recycle bin, so why will it be permanently deleted? This is because there was no recycle bin folder on this network storage location. To explain exactly what this means, we need to explore some technical information about how the Recycle Bin works.

18.4 – Recycle Bin folders

The Recycle Bin is a little like the library folders in that in actual fact it is an aggregate or combined view of several folders. Each drive on your computer, be it internal or external, can have its own Recycle Bin folder. This folder is normally a hidden folder called "$Recycle.Bin". When you open the Recycle Bin then the folder that opens shows the combined view of all the "$Recycle.Bin" folders on your PC.

If you connect to a storage device, perhaps a network drive or network folder that hasn't had a Recycle Bin configured, then any files that you delete will not be sent to the Recycle Bin, they will just be removed. Windows will warn you that the file will be permanently removed so make sure you pay attention to the messages and be extra careful.

So, with those two important exceptions, all files and folders you delete are sent to your Recycle Bin first. Note that you can also empty the Recycle Bin by right clicking on it and choosing "Empty Recycle Bin".

18.5 – Recycle Bin Properties

There are some advanced Recycle Bin preferences that can be changed by clicking "Recycle Bin properties" from the ribbon or by right clicking on the

Recycle Bin and choosing "Properties". Figure 18.7 shows the Recycle Bin Properties window.

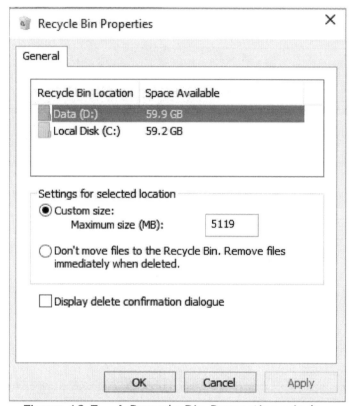

Figure 18.7 – A Recycle Bin Properties window

In the Recycle Bin Properties window there are several settings we can tweak. At the top of the window we can see the Recycle Bin Location. Recall that each drive has a Recycle Bin folder associated with it. From this list you can choose the Recycle Bin to work with. On the machine that figure 18.7 was taken from there were two hard drives and so two recycle bin folders.

Under "Settings for selected location" we can specify a maximum size. Remember the size specified is in megabytes, but the size shown under "Space Available" is in gigabytes. There are one thousand and twenty four (1024) megabytes to a gigabyte, so the maximum size for this Recycle Bin is around the five gigabyte mark. It is possible to increase or decrease that size by entering a new value in the Maximum size (MB): box, although for most users the default size is fine.

Below the Custom Size option is the option to disable the Recycle Bin altogether. If this option is chosen, files are removed immediately when deleted. We do not recommend that beginners enable this option, in fact we don't recommend that anyone does. Having the safety net of the Recycle Bin is always a good idea.

Finally there is an option called "Display delete confirmation dialogue". This option was turned on by default in previous versions of Windows, but Microsoft decided to turn it off by default in Windows 8 and Windows 10. If you select this option then Windows will put up a window asking "Are you sure you want to remove this file?" when you send a file to the Recycle Bin. You may prefer to turn this option on while you get used to your PC, to avoid accidentally sending any files to the Recycle Bin.

When you are done configuring the Recycle Bin Properties, click on "Apply" and then "OK".

That concludes this lesson on the Recycle Bin and this chapter! You are now quite the competent Windows 10 user, give yourself a pat on the back for getting this far. The next chapter focuses on the remaining elements of the desktop.

Chapter 5 – Wrapping Up the Desktop

In this chapter we will wrap up our lessons about the Windows desktop and File Explorer. We'll look at the taskbar, Notification area and dig deeper into searching in Windows 10.

Lesson 19 – This PC

Computer (also known as "My Computer" in Windows XP) was renamed to "This PC" in Windows 8.1, and Windows 10 keeps this new naming convention. From "This PC", you can get access or browse to all of the storage devices attached to your PC. You can open This PC by searching for "This PC" and then clicking the icon that appears or alternatively, click on "This PC" on the Navigation pane of any File Explorer window.

19.1 – Inside This PC

Figure 19.1 shows a typical "This PC" window.

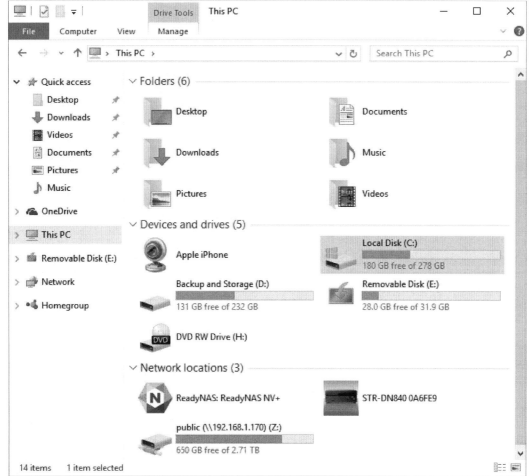

Figure 19.1 – "This PC" Window from a desktop PC with several drives

Figure 19.1 shows a desktop computer with two hard drives, a DVD recorder drive and several other removable drives, as well as several network drives and locations.

19.2 – Personal folders

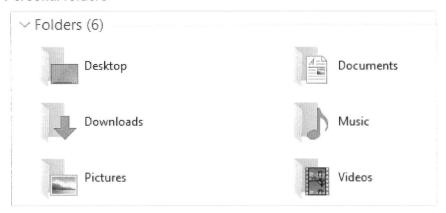

In Windows 10, convenient shortcuts to your personal folders are always available at the top of the "This PC" window. Simply double click on any of the folders to open them in File Explorer.

19.3 – Devices and drives

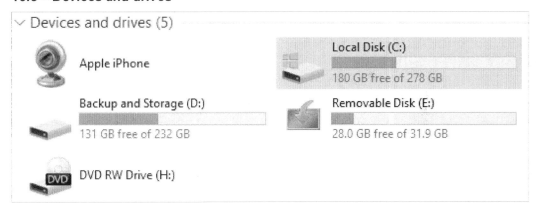

In Windows 10, all storage devices that are attached locally to your PC are shown in the Devices and drives section. This is different to Windows 7 where removable drives were in their own section.

There are several drives attached to the PC we can see in the picture. Every Windows 10 machine will have at least one hard drive. The machine in this example has two hard drives, Local Disk (C:) and Backup and Storage (D:). We can see at a glance how much space is free on each drive by looking at the blue bar or the values below it (C: drive has 180 gigabytes (GB) free out of 278GB, for example). To get some more detailed information about a hard drive, right click on the drives icon and from the context menu choose "Properties", or click once on the drive icon and choose "Properties" from the Computer tab on the ribbon. The drive Properties window will then open, figure 19.4 shows this window.

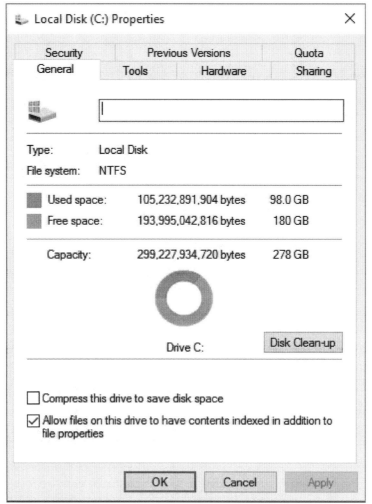

Figure 19.4 – General drive properties

We can see in figure 19.4 a pie chart which represents space on the drive. Next to the chart, the button "Disk Clean-up" will launch the Disk Cleanup tool that we cover in lesson 60. There are also two options below the pie chart.

Compress this drive to save disk space:- When we talk about compressing data in computing it refers to the art of storing information more efficiently so that less space is consumed. By selecting this option to compress the drive, you might gain a little space on your hard drive but adversely it might degrade your computers performance. We recommend leaving this option disabled.

Allow files on this drive to have contents indexed in addition to file properties:- When this option is selected, Windows will add the contents of files such as Word documents into the search index. Then, when you perform a search you can quickly search inside text files too. The only reasons to turn this option off are to improve disk performance on an older computer or to prevent sensitive file information being left in the search index.

There are a few other drives we can see under Devices and drives too. Drive H: is a DVD rewriter drive. Everyone should be familiar with CDs and DVDs, the universally popular format for storing music and videos. If your Windows 10 computer has a DVD rewriter drive, you can use it to play DVD videos (with suitable third-party apps) and also write your files to CD or DVD recordable discs.

Device E: is a portable USB stick drive or thumb drive. These are common portable storage devices that fit in your pocket and store gigabytes of information. Their convenient size, high speed and the widespread adoption of USB ports mean that USB sticks have rendered the old-style floppy disks obsolete.

Figure 19.5 – A SanDisk Cruzer USB stick drive. Actual length is around the length of an adult thumb, so these drives are often referred to as "thumb drives"

Finally, we can also see an Apple iPhone. Many smartphones, media players and similar devices can connect to the PC for backup or to share files. For most devices, it's just a matter of double clicking on the devices icon to browse whatever files are stored on the device. To get the most out of your device, you may need to install additional software or drivers. Furthermore, especially with Apple devices, there may be device imposed restrictions on how much of the internal storage you can access or modify from your PC. Consult the documentation that came with your device for more details.

Windows 10 also includes a new app called the "Phone Companion" that adds new ways for your PC and smartphone to work together. We don't cover Phone Companion in this guide however.

19.3.1 – Hidden drives

By default, Windows 10 will hide removable storage devices that it detects have no media inserted into them. To change this behaviour, access the View tab on the Folder Options window (see lesson 17.3). Now, deselect the option "Hide empty drives". On the PC shown in our example, drives F:, I: and J: are present, but not shown in Devices and drives. These drives are part of a memory card or storage card reader. Memory card readers accept storage cards that are commonly used in cameras, media players and even games consoles. Figure 19.6 shows a typical memory card reader.

Figure 19.6 – A typical memory card reader

Since the memory card reader was empty, Windows hid those drive letters as it would not be possible to access them.

To browse any of the attached drives when working with This PC, simply double click on them. If you double click on an empty drive, Windows will prompt you with "Please insert a disk into Removable Disk". Disk in this context can refer to a storage card too.

19.4 – Network Locations

The last section we can see in figure 19.1 is called "Network Locations". Storage devices here exist on your home network, rather than the public internet. Windows 10 can detect all kinds of network services. The top two icons represent media devices on the same network as the PC. The STR-DN device, for instance, is a home theatre receiver that Windows can stream music content to.

If you use network storage devices for backup or file storage, you can create shortcuts to your most commonly used network locations by mapping a drive letter to them. To do this, choose "Map network drive" from the Computer tab on the ribbon. You can then either enter the network address manually or browse across your network for the correct location. The PC in our example has one such mapped drive (drive Z:), which points to a storage location on the network. When you map a network drive like this, you can access it in most apps as if it were a physical drive attached to your PC.

19.5 – Other devices

What other devices might we find in This PC? Some portable devices, such as media players, personal digital assistants or smartphones install their own special software. These devices then appear below Network Connections in their own category. Usually working with them is as easy as working with other storage devices, but consult the owners manual that came with the hardware for more details.

That concludes our tour of "This PC" in Windows 10. Now you understand how to access storage devices on your PC you will be ready for our tutorials on system backup which we cover in lesson 33.

Lesson 20 – More About the Taskbar

The taskbar has seen some dramatic changes in Windows 10. Back in lesson 2 we went over the basic elements and in this lesson we will look at some advanced features and some personalisation options.

20.1 – Jump lists and the taskbar

Jump lists first appeared in Windows 7 and have persisted to Windows 10 too. On the taskbar they can be used to quickly jump to frequently used tasks in an application. To access the jump list for a program on the taskbar, simply right click on the programs taskbar icon. The program does not need to be running in order to access the jump list, it could simply be pinned. Not all apps support jump lists but one that does is Windows Media Player. We cover Windows Media Player extensively in Chapter 10, but for now we will simply look at its jump list. In figure 20.1, the user has started Windows Media Player and right clicked on its taskbar icon.

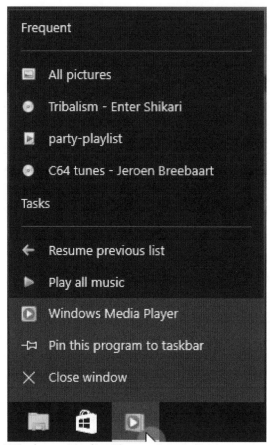

Figure 20.1 – The Windows Media Player jump list, accessed by right clicking on its taskbar icon

The actions you can take from a jump list depend on the program. From Media Player's jump list we can play one of our most frequently played media files. Under "Tasks" we can resume a previous playlist or simply play all our music. Finally, we can pin the program to the taskbar or close it, or simply launch it as normal by selecting "Windows Media Player".

Any program on the taskbar can have its own jump list. For some software the jump list simply includes the most recently opened documents or the most frequently opened files or folders. Programs that are Windows 7, 8 or 10 aware can have their own custom jump lists.

20.2 – Moving the taskbar

There are several customisations we can do with the taskbar, the most simple being moving and resizing it. Before you can move the taskbar, it needs to be unlocked. Right click on the taskbar and deselect the "Lock the taskbar" or "Lock all taskbars" option, as shown in figure 20.2.

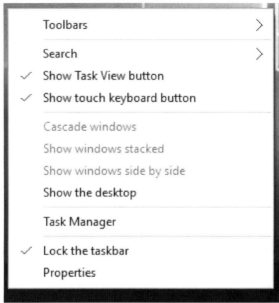

Figure 20.2 – Before the taskbar can be moved or resized it must be unlocked

When the taskbar is unlocked it can be moved to any screen edge. This is done by clicking and holding down the mouse button and then dragging the mouse towards one of the screen edges. The taskbar can also be resized in the same way we resized a window in lesson 5.2 by moving the mouse to the edge of the taskbar and dragging it upwards. A bigger taskbar is often useful on powerful machines with large monitors. When there are lots of programs open at once, a bigger taskbar gets less cluttered.

It is a good idea to lock the taskbar again when you are done moving and/or resizing it. If you do not, you are likely to accidentally move or resize it as you work with your PC.

20.3 – Adding toolbars to the taskbar

There are several optional toolbars that can be added to the taskbar. To add a toolbar, right click on the taskbar and choose "Toolbars". Figure 20.3 shows the available toolbars.

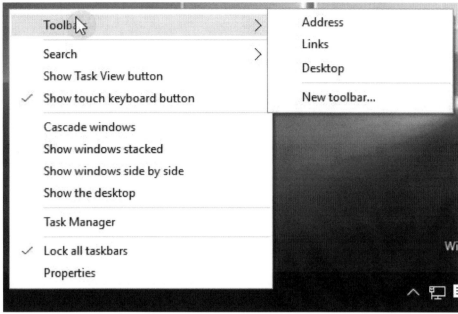

Figure 20.3 – Choosing a toolbar to add to the taskbar

Let's see what each of these toolbars does.

Address:- Enables the user to enter a web address or local address or path directly into the taskbar.

Links:- This toolbar enables you to quickly jump to your favourite internet links. In order for a link to appear here, you need to add it to the Favourites bar in Internet Explorer or Microsoft Edge.

Desktop:- Provides links to common locations on the computer and on the desktop.

New toolbar:- Creates a custom toolbar. Choosing "New toolbar…" opens up a file browser window. Simply browse to any folder on your PC and choose "Select Folder". The content from that folder will then be available to browse from the taskbar.

20.4 – Other taskbar customisations

There are several other customisation options for the taskbar. To access them, right click on the taskbar and choose "Properties". Figure 20.4 shows the resulting window.

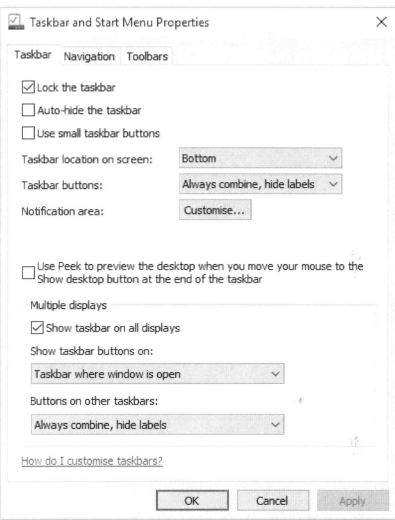

Figure 20.4 – Taskbar and Navigation properties Window

At the top of the Window there are several options. We already covered the "Lock the taskbar" option. "Auto-hide the taskbar" makes the taskbar automatically shrink down out of sight when it is not in use. To reveal it again, move the mouse pointer to the bottom of the screen (or the edge of the screen where the taskbar is positioned), the taskbar will then reappear. This option is useful on smaller monitors where screen space is at a premium. We also discussed this option in lesson 10.2.

Selecting "Use small taskbar buttons" reduces the size of program icons on your taskbar, figure 20.5 shows an example of this.

Figure 20.5– Small icons (top) Vs large icons (bottom) on a Windows 10 taskbar

Using the "Taskbar location on screen:" menu, it is possible to reposition the taskbar automatically, rather than by dragging it.

Below this control is the "Taskbar buttons:" control, figure 20.6 shows the available options.

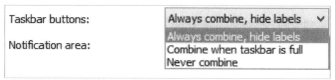

Figure 20.6 – Taskbar button options

Each option will change how the icons are displayed on your taskbar. We will take a detailed look at each option now.

Always combine, hide labels:- This is the default setting you have been using while working through this course. Icons will appear on your taskbar without labels. Windows from the same applications will stack on top of each other.

Combine when taskbar is full:- This makes the taskbar behave more like it did in previous versions of Windows. Icons for programs that are running will be displayed next to a label indicating the window title. Figure 20.7 shows an example of this.

Figure 20.7 – A taskbar set to "Combine when taskbar is full" mode

Never combine:- Works the same as "Combine when taskbar is full", except that as the taskbar fills up, Windows won't combine related windows (e.g. multiple File Explorer windows) into groups.

Finally, it is possible to disable the desktop Peek button (the button at the end of the taskbar that we showed you way back in lesson 2) by deselecting the "Use Peek to preview the desktop" option.

When you are done making changes, be sure to click on "Apply" to make them take effect.

20.5 – Multi-monitor support

Windows 8 brought us some great improvements for multi-monitor users that have also carried over into Windows 10. If you're doing any kind of work on your PC, two or even three monitors can be extremely useful. This book was written on a workstation with no less than three monitors, and the author is a strong advocate of the multi monitor desktop!

In figure 20.4 we can see a section at the bottom of the window called "Multiple displays" (On a PC with just one monitor, this section will be blank). We'll go over the options available in this section of the window now.

First of all, if "Show taskbar on all displays" is selected, then each monitor on your PC will get its own independent taskbar. In previous versions of Windows, there was only ever one taskbar, which users usually placed on their central display.

There are also several options for how the taskbar icons are positioned across your multiple taskbars. Figure 20.8 shows the available options.

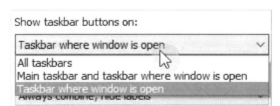

Figure 20.8 – Changing taskbar button options for multiple displays

On a system with three monitors (which we'll call A, B and C) the options would have the following effect.

All taskbars:- A window open on either monitor A, B or C would have a corresponding taskbar icon on all three taskbars/monitors.

Main taskbar and taskbar where window is open:- Assuming monitor B is the main monitor, a window open on monitor A would have an icon on the taskbar on monitor A and on monitor B, but not on monitor C. If the window was on monitor B, it would only have a taskbar icon on monitor B (since monitor B is where the main taskbar is positioned).

Taskbar where window is open:- A window open on monitor A would have a taskbar icon on monitor A's taskbar only.

Below the options for taskbar buttons is the option to change the types of button shown on your secondary taskbars. This works in exactly the same way as with the primary taskbar (see figure 20.6).

That concludes our tour of taskbar customisation. In the next lesson we will take a more detailed look at another component that changed significantly in Windows 7, the notification area or system tray as it is sometimes called.

Lesson 21 – Notification Area

The notification area was significantly overhauled for Windows 7 and these improvements have persisted in Windows 10 too. The notification area is often called the system tray, though the official Microsoft name has always been "notification area". It was introduced as a place for programs which generally ran in the background and did not need a window permanently open. Software such as antivirus packages or automatic backup tools can place small notification icons in this area. From these icons users can see at a glance that the program is running normally, or the program can notify the user that it needs their attention.

21.1 – The new notification area versus the old

As computers became faster and equipped with more memory and other resources, many users started installing all kinds of programs that utilised the notification area. As a result, it became very cluttered. It is not uncommon for systems to have more than twenty of these little icons and it quickly becomes unmanageable.

Figure 21.1 – A cluttered notification area from a Windows XP machine

Windows 7 tackled this problem by redesigning the notification area. The most important or frequently used icons can still be present on the taskbar, while the rest are hidden away in a pop-up menu and only appear if they need your attention. Figure 21.2 shows the Windows 10 notification area.

Figure 21.2 – A Windows 10 notification area showing hidden icons

In figure 21.2 we can see to the right of the mouse pointer, three notification icons that are permanently displayed. The first icon is the network icon, this can be used for connecting quickly to networks, both wired and wireless. The second icon is the volume icon, a quick click of this accesses a sliding control which can adjust the volume level for all sounds on your computer. The final icon that looks a little like a speech bubble opens the Action Centre. We cover this in lesson 46.

In figure 21.2 we can also see that by clicking the arrow icon, we get a pop-up menu showing us some other notification icons that are normally hidden. On this system we can see an icon for safely removing USB and other removable drives (top middle). It is always advisable to use this icon to let Windows know that you are going to remove a device before physically unplugging it.

You can also see a cloud shaped icon for Microsoft OneDrive (middle left). This gives you quick access to your OneDrive folder and various common tasks that you can perform using this cloud storage platform. We cover OneDrive in lesson 32.

There are also several icons for third-party software the user has installed. To access additional settings for any application running in the notification area, simply open the pop-up menu and then click, double click or right click on the programs icon. These actions will access different options depending on the program.

21.2 – Customising the notification area

If you have an application that you access regularly from the notification area, you may want to make it appear permanently like the three default icons. To do this, first right click on the taskbar and choose "Properties". The window shown in figure 21.3 will then appear.

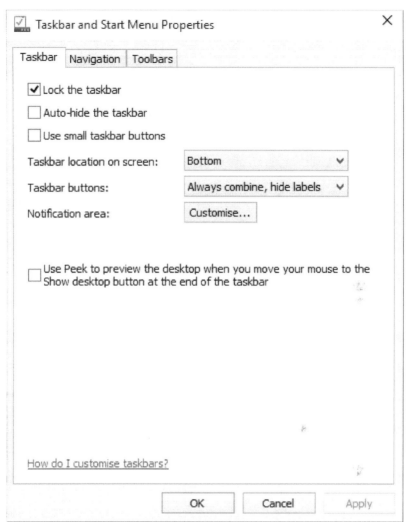

Figure 21.3 – Accessing the customisation options for the notification area

Click on "Customise…" next to "Notification area:" near the middle of the window. The window shown in figure 21.4 will then appear.

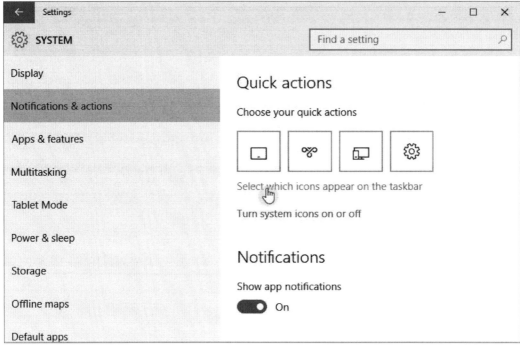

Figure 21.4 – Customisation options for the notification area

The notification area settings have been overhauled in Windows 10. To change the notification area, click on "Select which icons appear on the taskbar". The window shown in figure 21.5 will then appear.

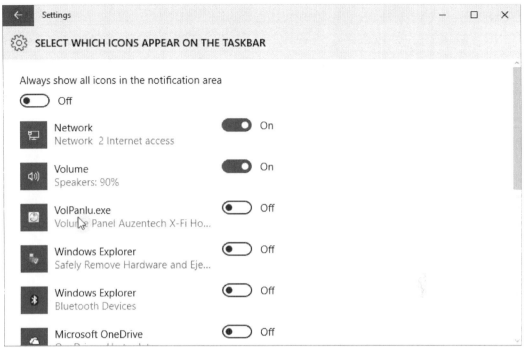

Figure 21.5 – Customising the notification area icons

The list in figure 21.5 shows all the items in the notification area, including the default Windows 10 ones. Notice that "Network" and "Volume" are set to "On", that means they will always be shown on the taskbar. The other icons below are set to "Off", but you can switch any of them to On to show them permanently on the taskbar without needing to open the notification area pop-up.

Finally, right at the top of the window is the option to "Always show all icons in the notification area". This reverts back to the old behaviour (pre Windows 7) described at the start of the lesson. If you don't have many notification area icons you might prefer to do this, but for most of us the new way is a big improvement.

When you're done changing icons in this window, click the back button in the top left hand corner to go back to the window shown in figure 21.4. You can make further customisations to your notification area from here by clicking on "Turn system icons on or off". Figure 21.6 shows the window that then appears.

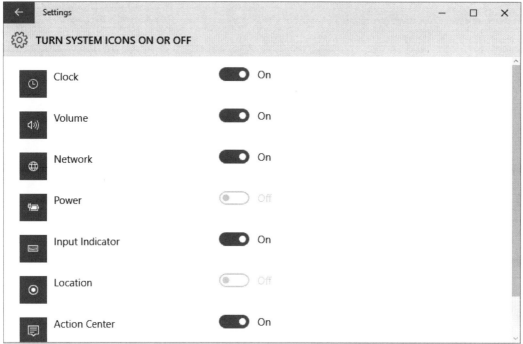

Figure 21.6 – Turning system icons on or off

This window works in exactly the same way as the one we just discussed. Use the toggle controls to turn icons in the notification area on or off. If the PC you were using didn't have any speakers, for instance, you could turn off the volume control icon and save room in the notification area.

That concludes this lesson on the Windows 10 notification area. Don't forget that although the notification area icons are hidden away neatly in Windows 10, they still represent programs that are running and therefore consuming computer resources. If you let too many of these programs run, you will start to slow your computer down, so be careful not to install too many. In the next lesson we will look at the Windows 10 extensive in-built search options.

Lesson 22 – Search Is Everywhere

In Windows 10, as was the case with Windows 7 and 8, search is built into almost everything. In lesson 4 we showed you how to search from the taskbar. It is also possible to search from File Explorer windows and in places such as the Control Panel, as well as from many apps. Basically, anywhere you see a search control, you can search. Windows 10 search is a powerful tool and learning how to use it correctly can make you super productive.

22.1 – Tags and other metadata

Metadata (data about data) enables you to add descriptive information to files to help you find them more quickly. Just like you might add coloured stickers to items you file in a filing cabinet, in Windows you can add tags to your data. Figure 22.1 shows the available metadata for a picture file.

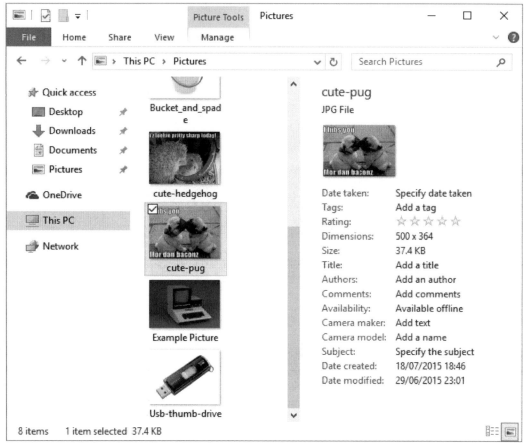

Figure 22.1 – Metadata for the selected image can be seen in the Details pane on the right

In figure 22.1 the user has opened the Details pane and clicked on an image. The metadata for the image is then shown on the right of the File Explorer window. As we explained in lesson 12.3, the types of metadata we can see and/or edit depend on the file itself. For JPG picture files like this, we can specify the date taken, a rating out of five and add tags, as well as edit the title, authors, comments, subject and camera make and model. Tags are probably the most useful types of metadata to add to pictures. To add a tag, click on "Add a tag" and type a descriptive tag for this image, for example "animal", since this is a cute animal image. Press the Enter key to save a tag or press the right arrow key and enter another tag. Tags are separated with semicolons (;). You can add as many tags as you like, just press Enter when you are finished and make sure each tag has a semicolon separating it.

Once you have tagged an image, you can search for it from the search bar, just like we did in lesson 4.2. Any images tagged "garden" for example, would show up if you search for "garden". Use the "My stuff" button to narrow down your search if you don't see the search results you expected, see lesson 4.2 for more information. If you tag all your pictures with descriptive tags, you will be able to locate them much more quickly.

You can use the same techniques to edit metadata for music files too. MP3 format music files don't support tags, but they do have metadata that can contain artist, album and date information, for instance.

22.2 – Indexing options

Windows can find information on your PC more quickly by using a search index. Files that are indexed have a reference to them in a giant search index or catalogue that Windows 10 maintains. In this lesson we will take a look at the indexing options. You can access these options from the Control Panel or more simply by searching for "indexing options" from the search bar and then clicking the icon that appears. Figure 22.2 shows the Indexing Options window.

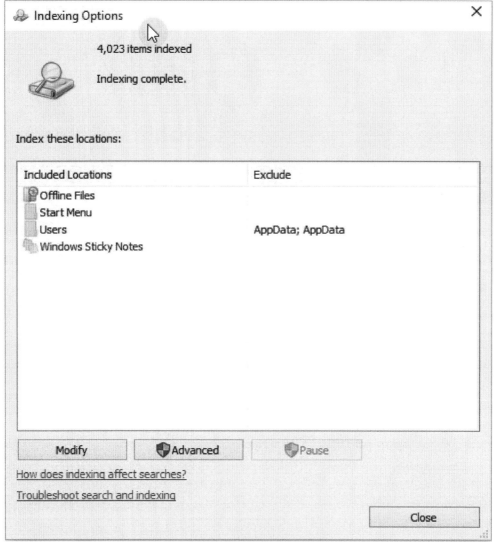

Figure 22.2 – Indexing Options

In figure 22.2 we can see the default indexing options. Under "Included Locations" you can see which places on your computer are added to the index. By clicking "Modify" it is possible to add other locations to the index, although we can only add locations on local drives, not network drives. Any folder you add to your libraries (as in lesson 15) will also automatically be added to the index.

Click on the "Advanced" button to change the advanced options. Figure 22.3

shows the advanced indexing options.

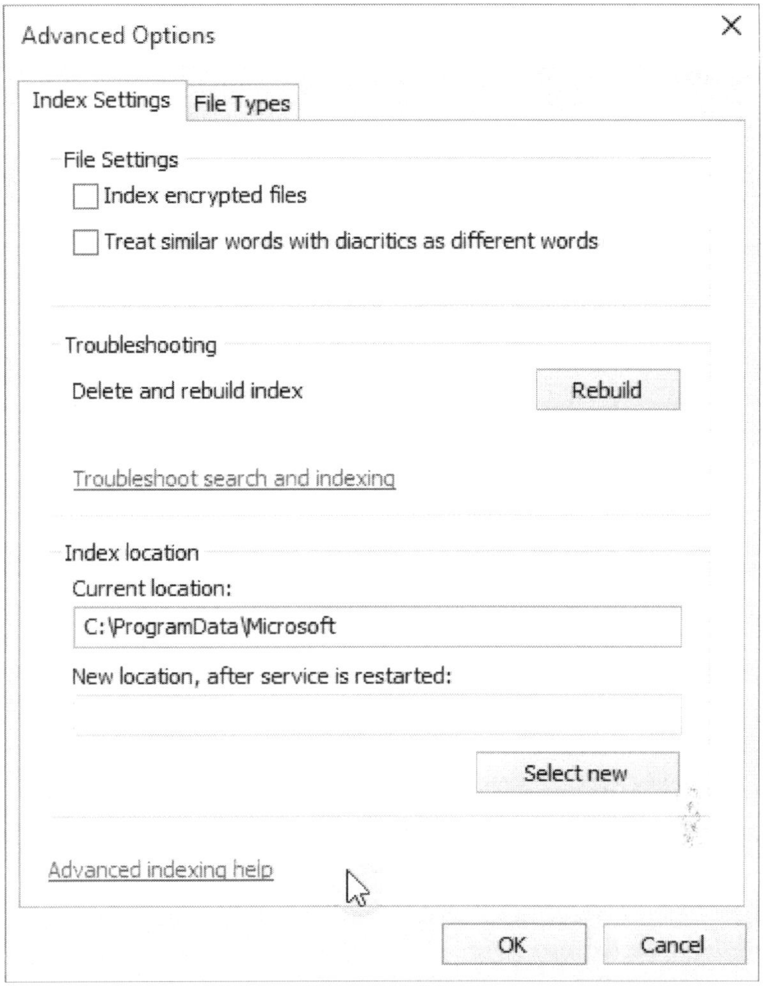

Figure 22.3 – Advanced indexing options

Under "File Settings" we can firstly choose to index encrypted files. This only applies to Windows encrypted files and not, for example, Truecrypt or PGP encrypted files. This option is off by default as it represents a security risk, since the contents of the encrypted file can be stored in the index in an unencrypted state. This option might not be present on all versions of Windows 10 and we do not cover encrypted files or Bitlocker in this course.

The second option under File Settings is "Treat similar words with diacritics as different words". What are diacritics? Diacritics are often called accents (though in actual fact an accent is only one of many different types of diacritic) and the English language doesn't generally use them. In other languages, such as French, they can be applied to letters to change the pronunciation. For example 'é' and 'e' are distinct because of the diacritic on the letter.

If you regularly work with other languages you may wish to turn this option on, but for those of us who work only in English, it can safely stay off.

Under "Troubleshooting" is the option to rebuild the index. If you find yourself searching for files and getting either no results or unexpected results, there is the possibility that the index is corrupt. Click on "Rebuild" to rebuild and repair it. Normally you will not need to do this as Windows is capable of maintaining the index on its own.

Finally, under "Index Location", it is possible to move the index to another drive. If you have a secondary hard drive it may be faster to store the search index separately from the Windows system drive, though for most users the default location is fine.

Clicking on the "File types" tab at the top of the window lists the current file types that are indexed. Figure 22.4 shows this window.

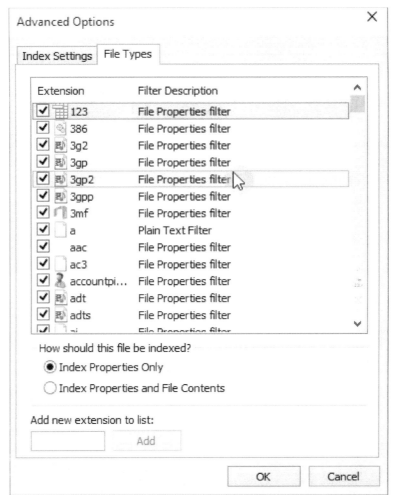
Figure 22.4 – Windows indexes hundreds of different file types

You can see from figure 22.4 that Windows knows about and indexes all kinds of files. For some types of file such as plain text or Microsoft Word documents, Windows will also index the contents of these documents. That means you could search for a word contained in the file itself and Windows would find it for you.

At the bottom of the window you can add your own file types just by typing in the file extension (we covered file extensions in lesson 17.5). If the file does not contain text, you should choose "Index Properties Only" to avoid cluttering up the index with junk data, since Windows isn't clever enough to recognise file contents in picture or sound files just yet.

When you are done changing indexing options, click on "OK".

22.3 – Tips for searching in Windows 10

Not being able to find what you are looking for is frustrating and the nice thing about storing information digitally is that computers can look for things much quicker than we can in the physical world. Having said that, computers are pretty dumb, so be sure to tell yours exactly what you are looking for and where, to avoid frustration. Here are a couple of tips to help with the searching process.

When searching in File Explorer, the search starts from the current location:- If you use the built in search in File Explorer, keep in mind that it does not search your entire computer. For example, if you are in your video folder and you search for a photograph, it is unlikely that the search will find anything (unless you are in the habit of storing photographs in your video folder). The search will only search within the current folder and any sub-folders in that folder.

Searching in File Explorer does search through tags and metadata:- If you want to find a picture you tagged, you can search from the search bar or from File Explorer. This is different to Windows 7 where searching in Windows Explorer would not search through tags.

Use the Search Tools tab on the ribbon:- If you are working in File Explorer and struggling to find a certain file, let Windows know that you are not interested in text files or other types of file by telling it exactly what type of file you want to find. Click on the search box in File Explorer and then use the Search tab on the ribbon to filter files by type or size, figure 22.5 shows an example of this.

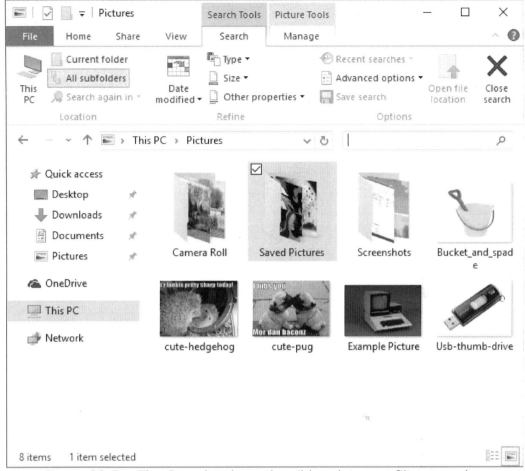

Figure 22.5 – The Search tab on the ribbon lets you filter searches

Be sure to try these techniques for yourself. The Windows 10 search facilities are the most powerful yet. Learn to use them and you will potentially save yourself a lot of time.

That is the end of this lesson and this chapter. You can breathe a sigh of relief as we're done with the desktop and File Explorer for now. In the next chapter we take a look at some of the apps that Microsoft has included with Windows 10.

Chapter 6 – New Windows 10 Apps

Windows 10 comes with several apps for you to use right away. In this chapter we take a look at the best of these apps and show you how to use them. The skills you learn in this chapter will also help you work with the thousands of apps available in the Windows app store.

Lesson 23 – Cortana

Microsoft want Windows 10 to scale to a wide range of devices, from tiny embedded PCs to full blown desktop workstations. We've already seen how you can use either your mouse or a touch screen to work with Windows, but now thanks to Cortana you can use your voice too. While Cortana can't completely control your PC just through your voice commands, she does offer a range of functionality that we will look at in this lesson.

23.1 - Activating Cortana

To activate Cortana you must be signed in with a Microsoft account. Unlike most of the other apps in Windows 10, you cannot sign in separately to Cortana. If you need help setting up a Microsoft account, see lesson 37.

When you are logged in with your Microsoft account you can enable Cortana by clicking on the search bar on the taskbar and then clicking or tapping on the gear icon to open the settings menu. Figure 23.1 shows the menu that will appear.

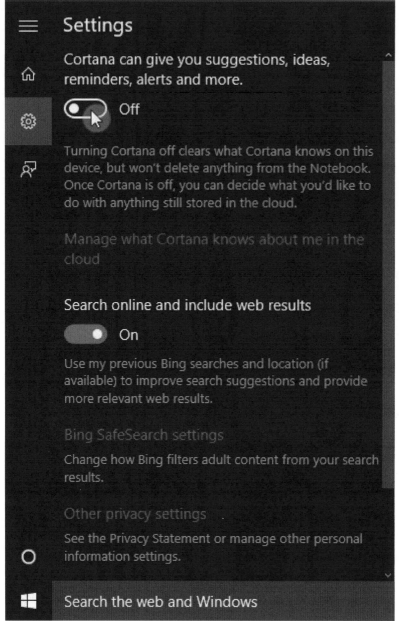

Figure 23.1 – This is the first step to enable Cortana

Once you turn this option on, you will be shown a little introduction to Cortana. Click on "Next". The information shown in figure 23.2 will then appear.

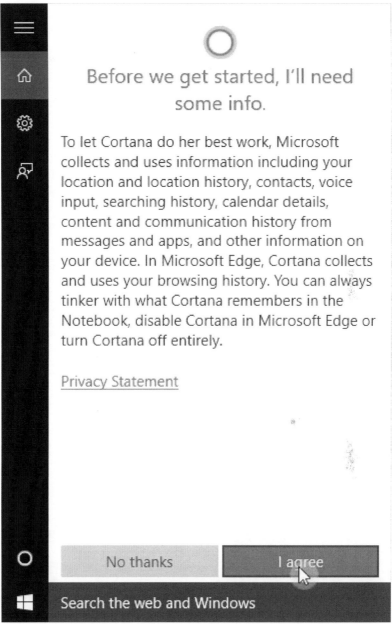

Figure 23.2 – Cortana needs access to certain potentially private data

In order to function, Cortana needs to collect a certain amount of data about you and what you do on your device. If you want to know more about this, skip ahead to section 23.2 – Cortana and privacy. You need to decide if this trade off in privacy is acceptable to you. If it is, click "I agree". You then simply need to tell Cortana what to call you. Type a name or nickname and press enter. If you're familiar with Cortana from the Halo video games, you might be disappointed to know that Windows 10 Cortana doesn't sound anything like Cortana did in those video games.

Once you have agreed to the privacy agreement and entered your name, Cortana is good to go. The program will then open with the "Top Stories" for today, as shown in figure 23.3.

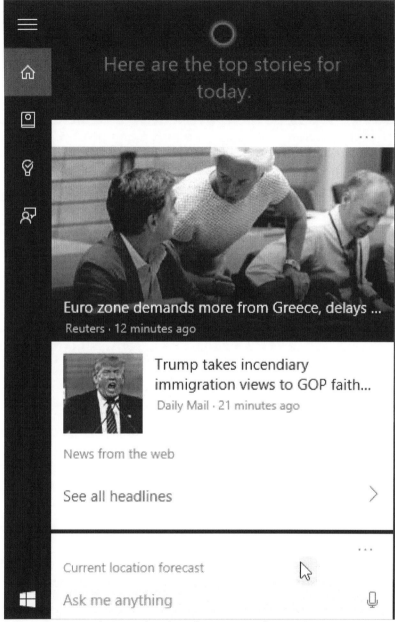

Figure 23.3 – Cortana brings back information from the web tailored to you

As Cortana gets to know you better, it will use the data it collects to better tailor these top stories to your own personal interests.

23.2 - Cortana and privacy

Cortana collects data about how you use your devices, places you visit with your devices and things you search for on the web. Cortana may go through your e-mails looking for appointments for instance, so that it can remind you. The information Cortana collects is stored on the internet in the cloud. This is because Microsoft have designed the service to work across multiple devices, such as your PC, tablet and phone.

All this data that Cortana collects can mount up and paint a pretty vivid picture of your life and how you use your Windows devices. If you want to know the full privacy policy for Cortana, click on the "Privacy statement" link as shown in figure 23.2. You can also turn Cortana off temporarily if you're visiting somewhere you don't want her to know about for instance. Finally, you can manage the stored data and delete it at any time by clicking on the notebook (which we will see later in the lesson) and choosing "Settings" and then "Manage what Cortana knows about me in the cloud".

23.3 - Typing a query

Typing a query is one way you can interact with Cortana. To do this, click on the search bar on the taskbar. When Cortana is activated, the text on the search bar should read "Ask me anything". You can ask Cortana a question about the weather, about traffic, about local restaurants or any topic you like. In figure 23.4 the user has asked "Will it rain today?".

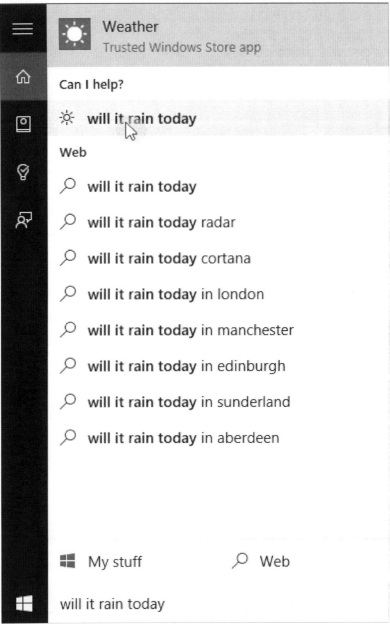

Figure 23.4 – Typing a question to Cortana

If Cortana has an answer to your question, you will see it under "Can I help?". Notice that you can still search your PC normally (as in lesson 4) even when Cortana is activated. To see the answer, simply click or tap on it.

Figure 23.5 shows the resulting answer from Cortana.

23.5 – Cortana can fetch weather data for you

23.4 - Talking to Cortana

Just like on a mobile phone, you can talk to Cortana and ask her questions. Cortana needs a good quality microphone in order to work well with voice recognition. At the moment Cortana always uses the default microphone. If you have more than one microphone attached to your PC (for instance a webcam microphone and a headset microphone) you may need to change the default device. Refer to 23.8 at the end of the lesson where we cover some troubleshooting tips.

In figure 23.5 you can see a small microphone icon in the very bottom right of the window. Click on this icon to dictate to Cortana. If this is the first time you've tried to talk to her, the window shown in figure 23.6 will appear.

Figure 23.6 – Configuring your microphone for Cortana

Click on "Next". Windows will now ask you to dictate a short sentence into the microphone. Once this is done, click on "Finish". Now, try talking to Cortana again, this time she should listen to you.

Speak your question and Cortana will either answer, if she knows the answer, or simply open up Microsoft Edge (or your default web browser) and perform a search. If you dictate your query to Cortana she will speak back to you, whereas if you type you will simply see the result on your screen.

You can also have Cortana respond when you call "hey Cortana". Having this option turned on can be convenient, but it does mean that your devices battery may be drained a tiny bit faster. To turn on this option, click on the search bar and then click the notebook icon on the left. In figures 23.4 and 23.5 the notebook is the second icon from the top. Figure 23.7 shows Cortana's notebook menu.

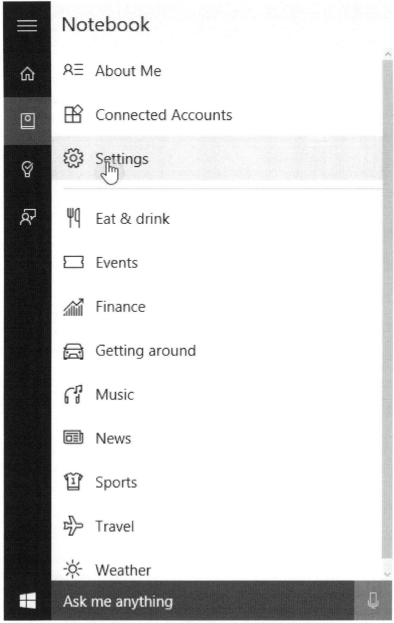

Figure 23.7 – Cortana's notebook menu

Click on "settings". You should then be able to see the "Hey Cortana" option (second from the top). Turn it on to enable the feature.

Now, simply say the words "Hey Cortana" into your microphone. Cortana will respond with a beep. After the beep, simply ask your question.

Figure 23.8– Using the Hey Cortana feature

23.5 - Cortana's notebook

In figure 23.7 we saw Cortana's notebook menu. Notice all the various categories in the notebook. These are categories that the software uses to collect information about you. Cortana might look at your music collection, for instance, to tailor information she gives you about music events or to recommend new music. These recommendations will then appear on the "Top stories" page you saw in figure 23.3. You can also add information to the notebook yourself. For instance, by clicking on "News" and then scrolling to the bottom of the Cortana window, you can see the options to "Add a topic" or "Add a category", as shown in figure 23.9.

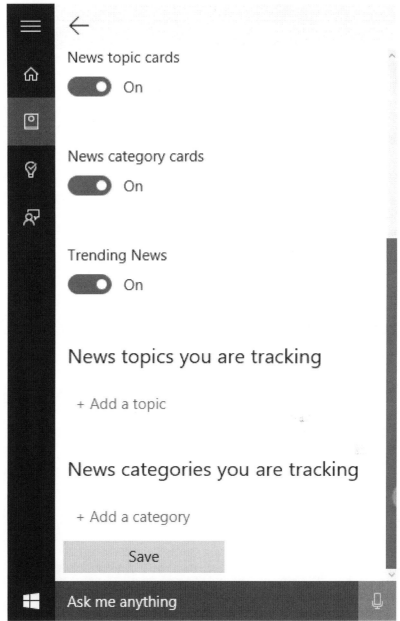

Figure 23.9 – Adding news topics

Click on either "Add a topic" or "Add a category" to tell Cortana about news stories that interest you. You can perform similar customisations in other categories too. There are far too many options for us to cover in the guide, so explore and experiment yourself.

23.6 – Reminders

Reminders are one of the most useful ways you can use Cortana. Simply type or dictate "Remind me to" and then type/say anything you want Cortana to remind you about. For instance you could type "remind me to water the plants". In the search results you should then see "Set a reminder". If you click this result, Cortana will set up the reminder for you, as shown in figure 23.10.

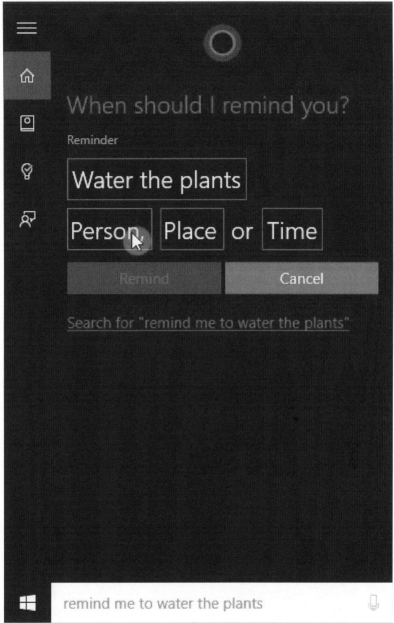

Figure 23.10 – Setting a reminder

Click or tap on the boxes to fill out the details, make sure you set a time and Cortana will remind you about this event without fail (provided your computer is turned on, that is).

23.7 – Other things Cortana can do

Talking to your computer can be a bit of a novelty, at least at first, and there are way more things you can ask Cortana than we can possibly fit into this guide. Here are just a few things it can do.

You can try asking Cortana to tell you a joke, though we can't promise great comedic timing.

You can have Cortana send e-mails, though dictating more than a few lines to it quickly becomes frustrating.

Cortana can play music, though for some reason it's not yet intelligent enough to be able to play a specific artist or track.

Cortana can open apps, simply say "hey Cortana, launch Store" or any other app. Though once you have your app launched, Cortana cannot help you interact with it, so this is of limited use.

23.8 - Troubleshooting Cortana

If Cortana seems to be hearing your voice, but getting lots of words wrong, you should check your language settings. Often PCs in the UK are set accidentally to US language settings, for instance. Rather than go all Hugh Laurie and put on your best American accent, search for "Region and Language" on the search bar then click the "Region & Language settings" icon that appears. Go through each setting on the window that now appears and make sure it is set to English (United Kingdom) or the appropriate setting for wherever you live. Cortana should now understand you much better, spiffing! (nobody in the UK actually says that, for the record).

If you're having trouble getting Cortana to understand you at all, it may simply be that your computers microphone isn't up to the task. If you have more than one audio device, make sure that the microphone you have set as the default device is the one you want to use with Cortana. To check your default audio device, search for "manage audio devices" on the search bar and click the result that appears. A "Sound" window will then pop open. Click on the "Recording" tab, as shown in figure 23.11.

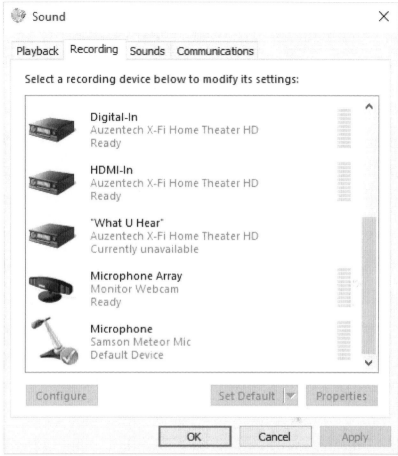
Figure 23.11 - Selecting a default recording device

Now, click on the device you want to use to talk to Cortana and then click on "Set Default". The default device is marked with the green tick or check mark.

Click on "Apply" and then "OK". Now try talking to Cortana again, it should now use your preferred microphone or headset device.

That concludes this lesson on using and interacting with Cortana. Indispensable feature or gimmick? That is for you to decide!

The next lesson will look at the Mail and Calendar apps.

Lesson 24 – Mail and Calendar

E-mail could be considered the oldest of the social networking tools available on the internet today. Pre-dating even the modern internet, e-mail isn't without its problems. Without special software it lacks any kind of security. Furthermore, support for sending files with e-mails is primitive compared to more modern alternatives. Nevertheless, e-mail is still widely used especially in workplaces where social networking sites may be frowned upon. In this lesson we will look at both the Mail and Calendar apps in Windows 10. While you can use both of these apps separately, they are also linked together for convenience.

24.1 – Getting started with Windows 10 Mail

Windows 10 mail works a lot like the Mail app in Windows 8, but with a few changes and improvements. To launch the Mail app, either click on its tile on the Start menu/screen or search for "mail" on the search bar. Figure 24.1 shows the Mail app when opened for the first time.

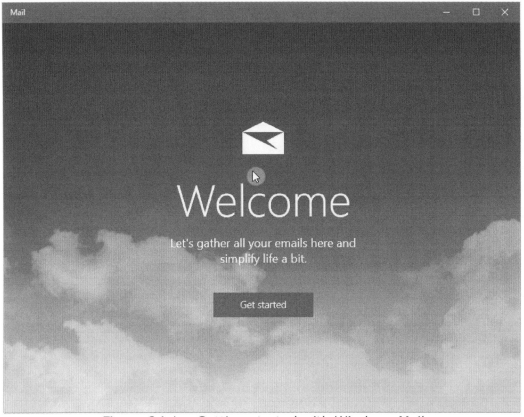

Figure 24.1 – Getting started with Windows Mail

Click on the "Get started" button, and the window shown in figure 24.2 will then appear.

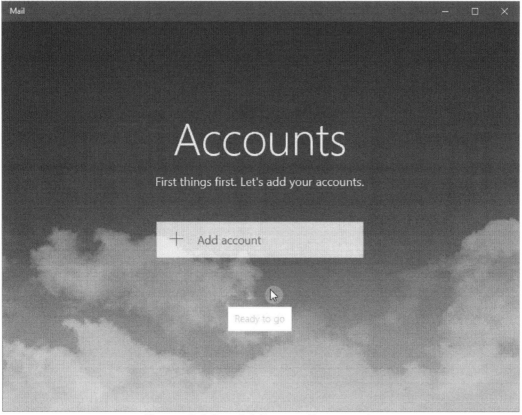

Figure 24.2 – Adding mail accounts

We now need to add some e-mail accounts to the Mail app. If you signed in with a Microsoft account, you should see that your Outlook.com or Hotmail.com account has already been added. Click on "Add account" to get started adding your e-mail account to the program. The window shown in figure 24.3 will then appear.

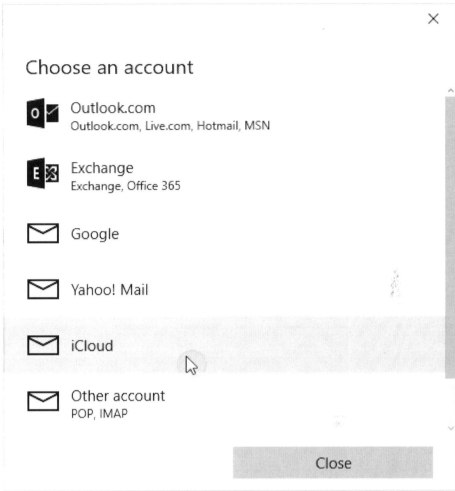

Figure 24.3 – The Mail app supports all kinds of e-mail accounts

The Mail app can add e-mail accounts from popular providers such as Outlook.com, Yahoo! Mail and Google Mail automatically. All you will need in this instance is your e-mail address and account password. If you have a different e-mail account, such as one from your ISP or hosting company (e.g you@yourbusiness.com) you can add this account by clicking on "Other account". In this instance Windows Mail will need some more details from you, such as your IMAP and SMTP server addresses. Your ISP or hosting company should be able to provide this information for you.

If you don't have an e-mail account already, choose the "Outlook.com" option. You will then be able to create one by clicking on the link provided.

Remember, if you have a Microsoft account, that account is also your Outlook.com/Hotmail account too.

As with most of the new apps, if you add your Microsoft account to the Mail app and you are logged in with a local account, the app will offer to convert your user account to a Microsoft account. If you want to skip this step, click on "I'll connect my Microsoft account later."

Once you have successfully added at least one account, you should see the "Ready to go" button appear on the window shown in figure 24.2. Click the button and the window shown in figure 24.4 will appear.

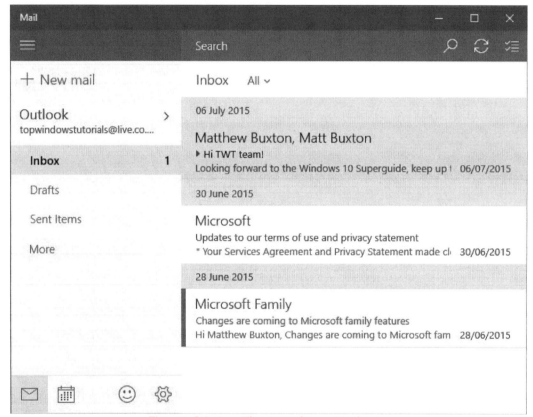

Figure 24.4 – The Windows Mail app

24.2 – The Inbox

In figure 24.4, we can see the various folders in the users Outlook.com account (Inbox, Drafts, Sent Items) on the left. To open the inbox and read messages, simply click or tap on the inbox folder. Since the mail application will open the inbox by default, we can see the contents of the users inbox in figure 24.4.

By default the Mail app will only download a months worth of e-mail from each of your accounts. If you are using your Windows 10 PC on a metered connection, such as a cellular modem, this setting will prevent too much unnecessary data being transferred. You can change this setting by clicking on the gear icon, choosing "Accounts", then the account you want to work with and then clicking "Change mailbox sync settings".

In the example shown in figure 24.4 the user has three e-mails in the inbox folder. Messages are listed in date order with the most recent message listed first. The name of the sender is shown on the first line in big lettering and then below it the subject of the e-mail. For instance, the highlighted message is from "Matthew Buxton" and the subject is "Hi TWT team!". To read a mail, simply click or tap on it. If the window is large enough, the e-mail will then open in the right of the Mail app window. If not, it will open in a new window. Figure 24.5 shows an open e-mail.

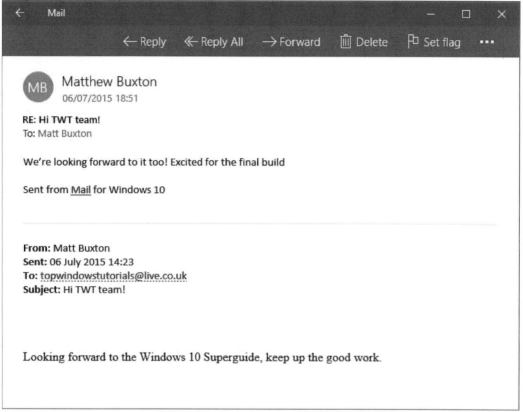

Figure 24.5 – Reading an e-mail

If the whole e-mail doesn't fit on the screen or in the window, you can use the scroll control at the right of the screen, or a swipe of your finger, to scroll down the screen and read the message.

24.3 – Replying and composing

When an e-mail is selected, there are five options the user can click. These options are at the top right of the screen in figure 24.5.

Reply:- Click or tap this option to compose a reply to this e-mail. Remember, some e-mails are sent out by automated delivery systems and typically replies to these e-mails will just be ignored.

Reply All:- If the current e-mail has been sent to multiple recipients, this will reply to everyone who got the e-mail, not just the original sender. Be careful when using this option, chain e-mails like those that send virus hoaxes often get forwarded to thousands of people like this. The original sender then harvests e-mail addresses for spamming.

Forward:- Sends the message to another user. You will be given the option of editing the message before sending it on to another contact.

Delete:- Removes the message from your inbox and stores it in the deleted items folder.

Set flag:- If you need to mark a particular e-mail as important, so as to remind yourself to come back to it later, for instance, use the Set flag button.

When you're done reading an e-mail, click the back button in the top left hand corner of the window to get back to your inbox if necessary (if the Mail app window is big enough, your inbox will still be displayed).

To compose an entirely new message, use the "+ New mail" button located in the top left of the inbox window (figure 24.4). Composing a new message or a reply works in the same way. Figure 24.6 shows a new message being composed.

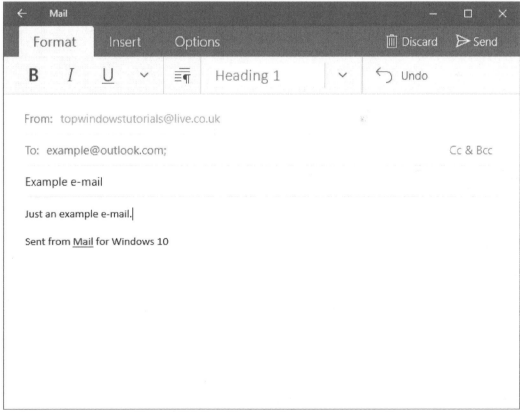

Figure 24.6 – Composing a new e-mail

To send an e-mail, the first thing needed is the recipients e-mail address. If you're composing a reply, this will be filled out automatically. When writing a new e-mail, the recipients address can be typed in manually into the box near the top (in figure 24.6 it has already been entered as example@outlook.com). Alternatively, start typing someone's name and Windows 10 will look them up automatically from the People app. In Windows 10, the People application provides address book type functionality you may have used in other e-mail software. We cover the People application in more detail in lesson 25. You can send an e-mail to multiple people too, just keep typing names into the "To" box.

Notice the link that says "Cc & Bcc". Cc is short for "Carbon copy". This means that anyone you add to this list will also receive the e-mail. "Bcc" is short for "Blind carbon copy". Anyone you add to the Bcc list will also receive the e-mail, but they won't be able to see the e-mail addresses of any other recipient on the Bcc list. This is a great way to protect your friends privacy if you absolutely must send out an e-mail to dozens of your contacts.

Below that line is the subject line. Typically, e-mails include a subject that describes the contents of the message. In figure 24.6, this has been set to "Example e-mail".

Below the subject is the area where you compose your main message. If this is a reply e-mail, this area will contain a copy of the message you are replying to. You can delete this content if you wish, but many users like to refer to it as they compose their reply.

Notice the toolbar at the top of the compose window, above the recipients e-mail address. This toolbar controls formatting for your message. Clicking or tapping the B, I and U icons for instance turns on Bold, Italic or Underline text. There are too many formatting options for us to cover in the guide, so experiment yourself when composing an e-mail.

When you click on the "Options" tab, you can access a spell check feature and if an e-mail is important, you can try marking it as high priority, but many e-mail programs (and users!) simply ignore this.

When you're done composing your message, click on "Send" to send it. Note that while most e-mails are received correctly, there are no guarantees. If your message is important and you don't receive a reply then be sure to send a follow up message or contact the recipient by another means. The e-mail system will sometimes send you a message to notify you if an e-mail account is invalid, but it does not send a message to confirm that an e-mail has been received.

24.4 – E-mail attachments and inserts

It is possible to include pictures and other files with e-mail messages. To do this, click on the "Insert" tab at the top of the compose window. Figure 24.7 shows the options that will be displayed.

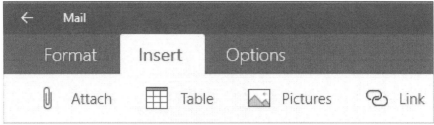

Figure 24.7 – Insert options

The available options work as follows.

Attach:- Attach any file to the e-mail. Clicking this option will allow you to browse to any file in your personal folders or libraries and attach it to the e-mail. See the notes on sending files and pictures before you do this.

Table:- Adds a table (as in time table or periodic table) to the e-mail.

Pictures:- Embeds a picture directly into the e-mail. Clicking this option will allow you to browse to any picture in your personal folders or libraries and embed it into the e-mail. The picture will appear in-line with your text rather than just as an attachment.

Link:- Inserts a link to content anywhere on the internet.

Read this before attaching files or pictures to your e-mail - Attaching or embedding files to e-mails is a highly inefficient way of sending files across the internet. E-mail was never designed with file transfer in mind. Avoid sending any files larger than a couple of megabytes as e-mail attachments. Your recipient may read his or her e-mail on a mobile device, for instance, where e-mail attachments may eat into the devices valuable storage space. Many e-mail gateways across the internet will simply reject messages with larger attachments. To send bigger files, you can use the public folder in your OneDrive. We cover OneDrive in lesson 32.

24.5 – Adding new accounts

If you want to add another account to the Mail application, follow these steps. First of all, navigate back to the inbox. Now, click on the gear icon near the bottom of the window (to the right of the smiley face icon as seen in figure 24.4). Now, choose "Accounts" and then "Add account". Now simply follow the procedure as shown at the start of the lesson to add your new account.

24.6 – Moving messages

There are two ways you can move messages between folders in the Mail app. The first way is by simply dragging them. Click on the message you want to move and hold your mouse button down (or tap and hold with your finger) then simply drag the message to the desired folder. Alternatively, right click on the message (or tap and hold with your finger) to open up the menu shown in figure 24.8.

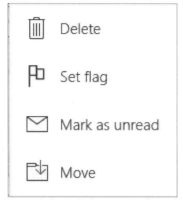

Figure 24.8 – Right click menu for the Mail app

Choose "Move" from this menu and you can then choose the folder to move your e-mail to from another menu. This is often easier than dragging the message if you have a lot of e-mail folders.

24.7 – Introducing Calendar

You can access the Calendar app from within Mail by tapping the calendar icon. It is the second icon from the left at the bottom of the Inbox window, as seen in figure 24.4. You can also launch Calendar directly from the search bar or Start menu.

When you first start the calendar, it will look almost exactly like the Mail app in figure 24.1. The only difference is that the Calendar app has a calendar icon rather than an envelope. Again, you should click on "Get started". This will take you to the add accounts window just like in figure 24.2. If you have added an e-mail account that also supports calendars (such as Outlook.com or Google) this account should already be added to the Calendar app, so simply click on "Ready to go". Figure 24.9 shows the Calendar app open and ready for use.

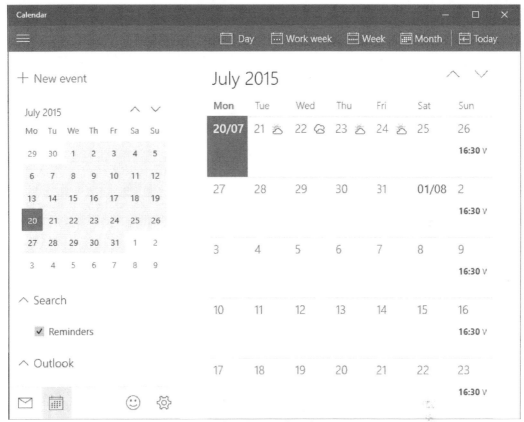

Figure 24.9 – Calendar app

The buttons at the top of the window (Day, Work week etc) allow you to view the calendar over different spans of time. The default view, as shown in figure 24.9, is the month view. Use the up and down pointing arrows near the top right of the window to move back and forward in time and the "Today" button at the top right to automatically jump back to today's date.

Thanks to Cortana, we have a reminder added to our calendar already, to water the plants every Sunday at 16:30. We set this reminder back in lesson 23 and Cortana went ahead and updated the calendar automatically.

Like your e-mail inbox, your calendar is synced through the cloud to your other devices too. If you have multiple calendars, you can toggle them on and off by using the tick/check boxes under "Search" on the left hand side of the window. You can see the "Reminders" calendar is checked and just out of view on the left hand column is the check box for the regular Outlook.com calendar.

To add an event to your calendar, just click or tap on a day. The window shown in figure 24.10 will then appear.

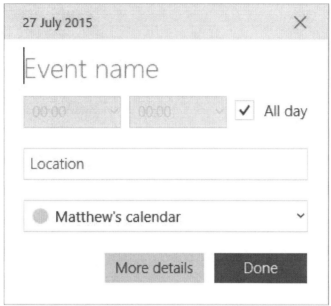

Figure 24.10 – Adding an event to the calendar

Fill out the boxes in the window with the details of your event. To schedule a meeting for instance, you might enter "Important Meeting" as the event name. Deselect "All day" unless the meeting was scheduled for the whole day (heaven forbid), then use the drop-down boxes to select the time. For location you could enter "Office, meeting room 3" for instance. The second drop down box lets you choose which calendar to add the event to. If you have a Google calendar for work and a Live calendar for home, for instance, you'd choose your Google calendar.

Click on "Done" when you have entered all the details. The event will now appear on your calendar.

That concludes our tour of the Windows 10 Mail and Calendar apps. The Mail app is great for touch screen users and works reasonably well for desktop PCs. If you want a powerful e-mail solution tailored to desktop use, check out our Mozilla Thunderbird tutorials on Top-Windows-Tutorials.com.

Lesson 25 – People

Continuing our tour of the apps included with Windows 10, in this lesson we will be focusing on the People app. The People app is where you go to manage all your contacts on your Windows devices. Compared to the fun, social network enabled people app in Windows 8, the Windows 10 people app is a much simpler affair, focused solely on managing your contacts. You can start the People app by clicking on its tile on the Start menu/screen or by searching for "people" from the search bar.

25.1 – Adding an account

Figure 25.1 shows the People app running for the first time on a users account.

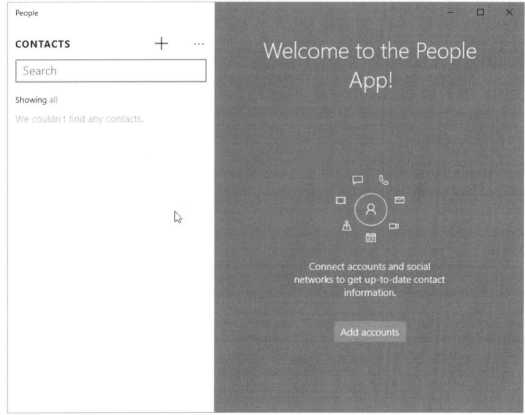

Figure 25.1 – Running the People app for the first time

The first thing to do with the People app is to add an account. If you signed in with a Microsoft account, that account should be added automatically. If not, click on the "Add accounts button" to get started. The window shown in figure 25.2 will then appear.

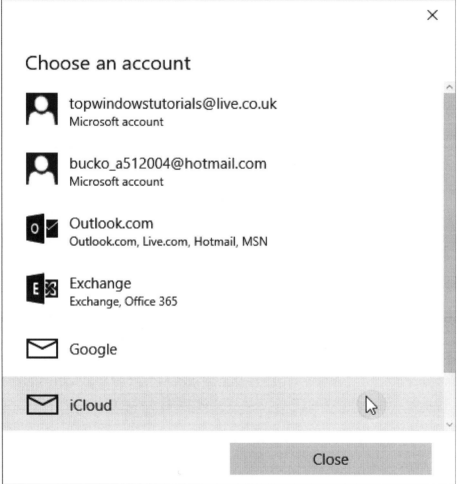

Figure 25.2 – Adding accounts to the People app

If you've already added an account to another app (such as Mail) it should appear on the list here at the top. In the example shown in figure 25.2 you can see two accounts that have been used while making the tutorials. You can also add accounts from several major service providers such as Microsoft

(Outlook.com), Google and iCloud (Apple). Naturally, you will need your log in details and password for any service in order to import your contacts.

Once you have added an account, the People app should fetch your contacts and open its main window. Figure 25.3 shows an example of this.

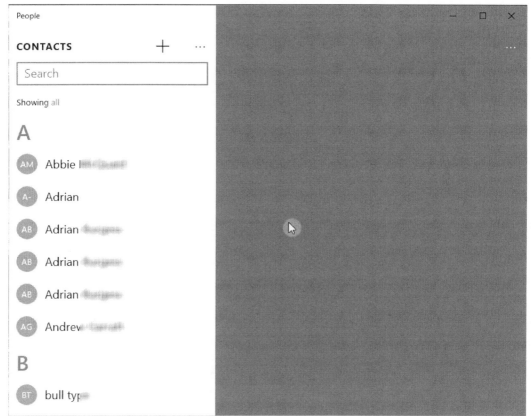

Figure 25.3 – The new People app is much plainer than the old one

25.2 – Browsing the People app

The People app is laid out like a typical address book. You can see names in the left of the program and, by moving your mouse to the white column, a scroll bar will appear allowing you to scroll down the list. On a touch screen, you can scroll through names by swiping with your finger.

You can search for contacts using the search bar at the top. You can also browse by letter. Click on a letter (e.g the big letter A as seen in figure 25.3).

The column will then turn into a list of letters. Simply click or tap the letter you want to browse to.

To view a contacts details, simply click or tap on them from the list.

25.3 – Adding and amending contacts

In the people app you can add, edit and delete information about contacts. Figure 25.4 shows a fictitious contact open in the People app.

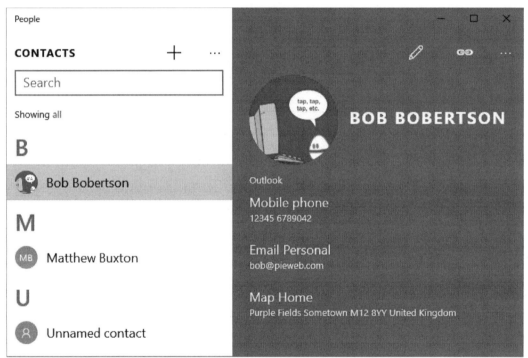

Figure 25.4 – A contact open in the People app

In this example, we can see that we have the contacts mobile phone and e-mail address, as well as a home address. Privacy conscious internet users tend to avoid filling out too much personal information on publicly viewable profiles, so you may need to fill in more personal information like address or phone numbers by editing the contact yourself. This additional information you add will not be viewable on the public internet.

To edit a contact and add or amend any information, click on the pencil icon near the top right of the window. You will then be taken to the edit contact window as shown in figure 25.5.

Figure 25.5 – Editing a contact

At the top of the window is the contacts picture. If you click or tap on this you can choose a new picture from your pictures folder or pictures library.

You can now amend any details for your contact by clicking or tapping in the boxes. Scroll down the window with your mouse (a scrollbar will appear at the right when your mouse pointer clicks on the window) or swipe with your finger to see more information. Click anywhere on a + icon to add additional information such as alternative e-mail addresses or additional phone numbers. When you are done, make sure you click on the save icon (the little floppy disk icon to the left of the cross in the top right of the image).

Of course you can add new contacts too. The new contacts button is at the top of the left column (the area where all your contact names are). It is a large plus shaped icon. The process of adding a new contact is exactly the same as editing an existing one, though of course this time you will need to fill out all details from scratch. If you have multiple accounts linked to your People app, you can also choose which account to save a new contact to while adding them.

25.4 – Linking contacts

In figure 25.3 you can see three separate entries for someone called "Adrian". These contact cards actually belong to the same person. To tidy up the clutter, we can link these accounts together. To get started, click or tap on any of the duplicate contact cards. Near the top right of a contact card there is a chain icon, you can see it in figure 25.4. Click on this to start the linking process. The window shown in figure 25.6 will then appear.

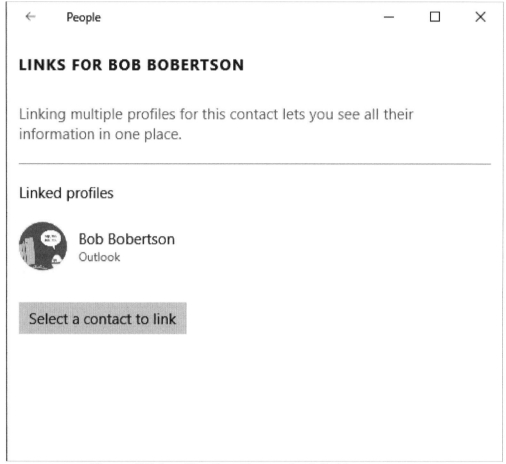

Figure 25.6 – Starting the contact linking process

Click on "Select a contact to link". You can then search for or scroll to a contact card to link together. When you find the contact card you want to link, click or tap on it. The window should then look like the one shown in figure 25.7.

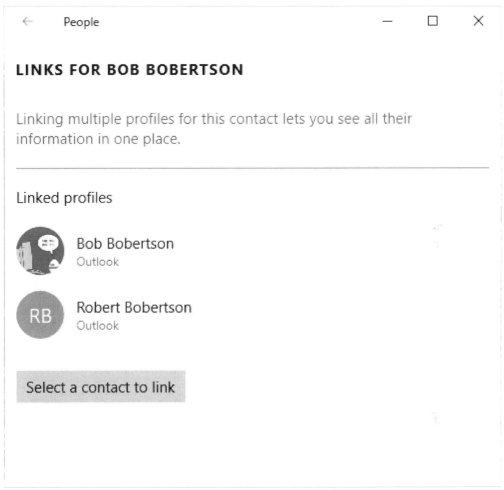

Figure 25.7 – Two contacts linked together

You can link another contact now, if necessary, or just tap the back arrow in the top left of the window to go back to the main People app. You will now only see one entry for Bob Bobertson instead of two, cutting down the clutter in your address book.

If you ever want to unlink a contact, you can click on it once from the Links window (figures 25.6 and 25.7). The People app will then give you the option to unlink the contact again.

25.5 - Adding other accounts

You can add additional accounts to the People app at any time. Click on the "..." icon at the top of the left hand column and choose "Settings". Then click on "Add an account". The process of adding an additional account is exactly the same as adding your first account when you first start the app. Unlike the Windows 8 people app, the Windows 10 version doesn't support Twitter or Facebook at all, so you're limited to importing contacts from popular e-mail services. We're not sure why this functionality was dropped in Windows 10.

That concludes our tour of the People app. In the next lesson we will take a look at the new Photos app.

Lesson 26 – Photos

In this lesson we're going to look at the Photos app. Just like in Windows 8, this app makes it easy to view all your photographs. In Windows 10 you can even do some basic photo editing with the app too. Like other apps, you launch the Photos app from the Start menu/screen or by searching for it on the search bar. Figure 26.1 shows the app running.

Figure 26.1 – Windows 10 Photos app

If you're not signed in with a Microsoft account, the Photos app may prompt you to sign in. If you do sign in, the app will include photos from your

OneDrive account too, if there are any. We cover OneDrive in lesson 32.

26.1 – Browsing photos

The Photos app shows you pictures from your pictures folder and pictures library. On a clean installation of Windows 10, these folders are empty, but we've put some pictures on this PC for demonstration purposes. The Photos app shows all your pictures sorted in date order with the newest first.

You can browse your pictures by scrolling down the window (a scroll bar will appear when you click on the window with your mouse, or use your finger on a touch screen). You can also click on any date to be taken to a sub-menu where you can quickly select another month to jump to.

26.2 – Viewing photos

To view a picture, simply click or tap on it. In figure 26.2, the user has tapped on a picture of a cactus.

Figure 26.2 – Viewing a picture

With the picture selected, we can use the buttons along the top of the window here to perform various actions. The functions of the buttons are detailed below.

 Share – Click or tap this button to share or send the current picture with a compatible app, such as Mail. This works like the Share charm in Windows 8.

 Slideshow – Click this button to start a slideshow. Windows will show your pictures one after the other until you click or tap on a picture.

 Enhance – Click this icon to automatically enhance the lighting of your photograph. Click it again to revert back to the original image if you didn't like the automatic enhancement.

 Edit – Click this button to access a suite of photo editing and enhancement tools. We will cover these tools later in the lesson.

 Rotate – Click this button to rotate your image 90 degrees. Keep clicking it until the image is the desired rotation.

 Delete – Click this button if you no longer want the image. It will be sent to the Recycle Bin (see lesson 18).

 More options – Click this icon to access some additional options. The menu shown in figure 26.3 will appear when you click this icon.

Figure 26.3 – Additional photo options

There are a number of additional options on this menu that are useful when working with a photo or picture. The "Open with" option lets you open the photo in another app, perhaps a more in-depth image editing tool. The Copy option makes a copy of the current photo, useful if you want to make changes but keep the original picture. Print makes a hard copy of the image if you have a suitable printer attached to your PC.

The Set as lock screen and Set as background options let you place the image on the lock screen or background respectively. We cover customising the lock screen in lesson 50 and the desktop background in lesson 49.

Finally, the file information option shows the file name, date modified, size, dimensions and other information about the picture.

26.3 – Editing and enhancing images

Microsoft have added some fun picture editing tools to the Windows 10 Photos app. To access them, click on the edit icon (the one that looks like a pencil). The window shown in figure 26.4 will then appear.

Figure 26.4 – Editing a photo

As you can see in figure 26.4, there are now quite a few neat little tools you can access to edit and enhance your images. These tools won't replace professional photo editing tools like Adobe Photoshop, but they are a good replacement for the old Windows Live Photo Gallery app. Unfortunately, we don't have the space to cover every possible option in this guide, so we will take a look at just a couple of examples.

Clicking on the Filters button causes a number of preview windows to open on the right, as shown in figure 26.5.

Figure 26.5 – Applying filters

Click or tap on one of the previews to apply that filter to the picture. If you don't like any change you make, click the undo arrow at the top of the screen, it's the curly one pointing to the left.

 When you're done working with your image you will need to save it. Usually it's better to click on "save a copy" (the icon shown here).

This keeps your original photo and the one you edited. To manage photos and other files on your PC, see our File Explorer tutorials (Chapters 3 and 4).

Click on the back button when you're done working with your image. If you made any changes the Photo app will prompt you to save first.

Some of the image editing tools work on parts of the image, rather than the whole image. If you click or tap on "Effects" (on the left of the window) and choose "Selective focus" you will see a tool like the one shown in figure 26.6.

Figure 26.6 – Selective focus tool

To use the selective focus tool, you drag it to the part of the image you want to focus on (by clicking or tapping in the middle of the circle) and then set the size of the circle by dragging any of the white dots on the outside. When you are happy with the effect, click on the tick or check mark at the top of the window, or click the cross to the right of it to abandon any changes.

When you're done editing your photo, click the back button in the top left hand corner of the window to go back to the gallery.

That concludes this tutorial on the Photo app. There are lots of other neat features to explore, particularly to do with image editing, so we recommend that you dive right in and explore them yourself. As you can see the Photo app is a quick and fun way of browsing photos on your PC and making some simple changes to them too.

Lesson 27 – Groove Music

The music app in Windows 10 is known as "Groove Music" and replaces the Xbox Music app as seen in Windows 8. Windows 10 actually comes with two music playing apps. Windows Media Player, which we cover later in the guide, is optimised for keyboard and mouse use. The Groove Music app on the other hand is optimised for touch, but works well with keyboard and mouse too. As always, you can start the app by clicking on its tile from the Start menu/screen or searching for it using the search bar. Figure 27.1 shows the Groove Music app running on a standard PC.

Figure 27.1 – Groove Music app in medium size mode

27.1 – Getting your groove on

Groove Music has three sizes that it can work in. We saw its smallest size in lesson 9.3 when we placed it next to our web browser. The size shown in figure 27.1 is the medium size. When you're first working with the app, it's easier to use it in large size, since then each of the buttons on the left gets a label. Figure 27.2 illustrates these labels.

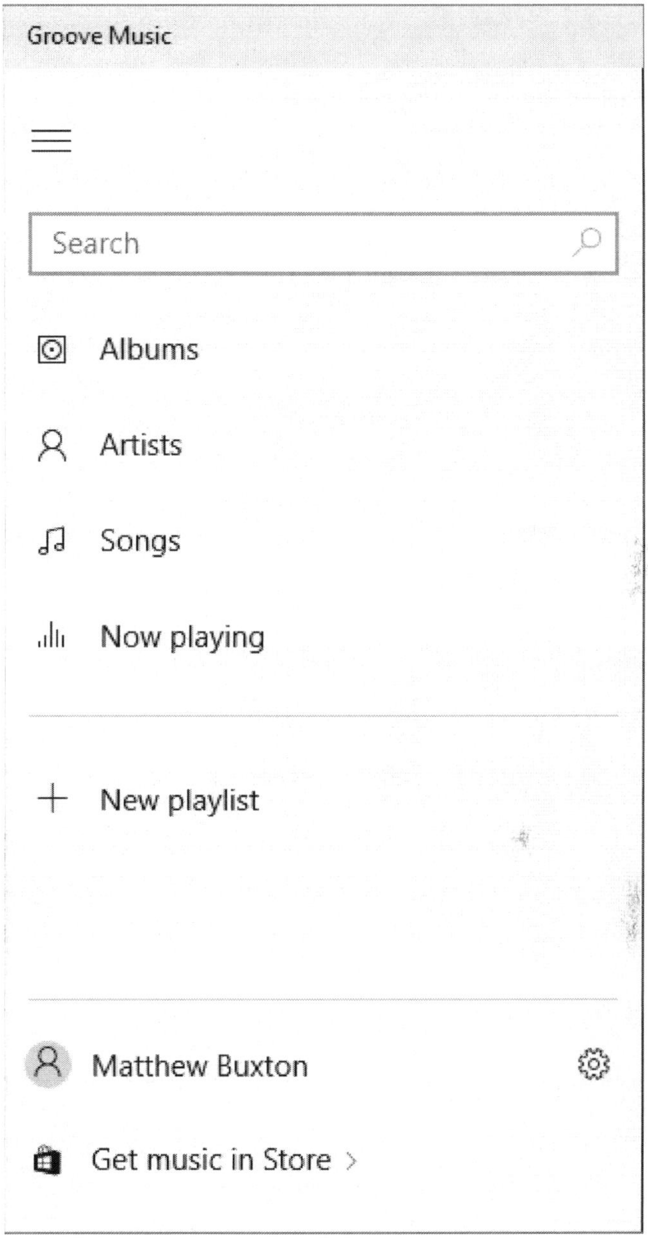

Figure 27.2 – Groove Music app left hand column when running in large mode

If you have a smaller screen on your Windows 10 device you might not be able to access large window mode, in which case you can use the image in figure 27.2 as a reference while you learn to use the program.

27.2 – *Browsing and playing your music*

The top three buttons on the sidebar, "Albums", "Artists" and "Songs", let you browse music on your device sorted by those respective categories. Of course, you can also search your music collection by using the search bar at the top. Unlike Windows 7, Windows 10 doesn't come with any example media, so you will need some of your own in order to explore Groove Music. If you purchased our full Windows 10 Superguide, use the sample media installer included with the guide to install an example music file. Groove Music will detect any music you place in your Music folder or in the Music library.

Figure 27.3 shows the app open in Albums view.

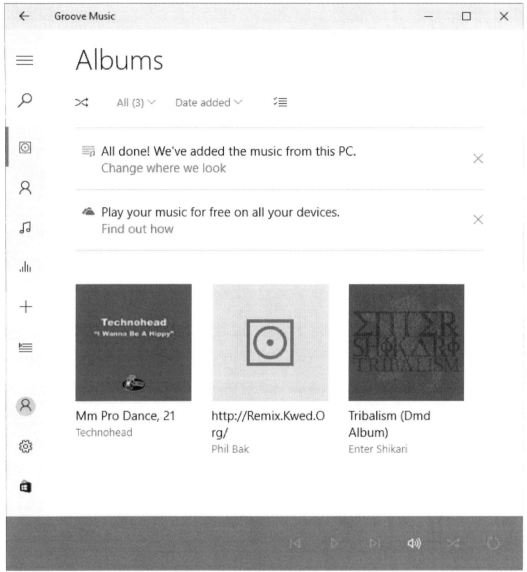

Figure 27.3 – Viewing albums on your PC

To browse a particular album, click or tap on it once. You will then see a list of tracks, figure 27.4 shows an example of this.

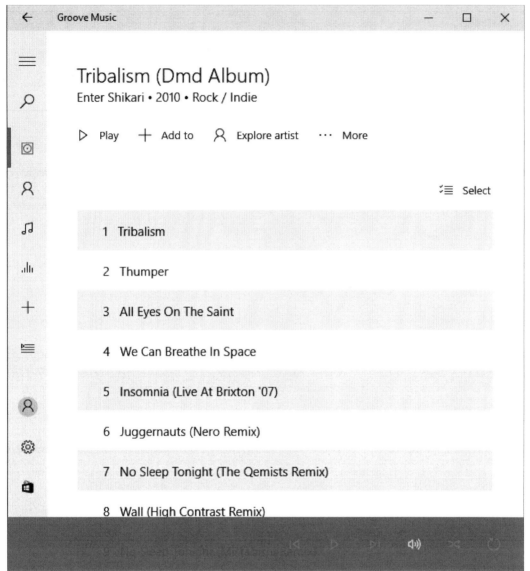

Figure 27.4 – Browsing tracks

To play a track, double click on it, or click or tap it once then click the play button on the control bar at the bottom of the app window. While a track is playing you can use the following buttons to control playback.

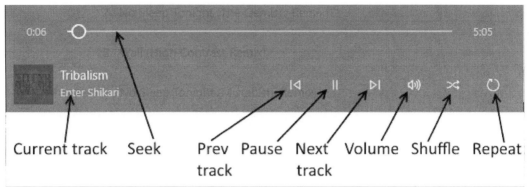

Figure 27.5 – Playback controls

Current Track:- Shows the name and artist of the currently playing track.

Seek:- The bar here lets you jump to a specific point in the track. Click and drag the little round nub to the position in the track you want to hear.

Prev and Next Track:- These buttons jump to the previous and next track in the album or playlist.

Volume:– Tap this button to quickly adjust the playback volume.

Shuffle:– When this button is turned on, it makes the tracks on the current playlist or album play in a random order.

Repeat:- When this button is turned on, the music in the current album or playlist will repeat when it has done playing.

27.3 – Playlists

When you click on an individual track while browsing your music, you will notice a plus (+) icon next to the track. If you click on this icon you will access a menu with two options; "Now playing" and "New playlist". Figure 27.6 shows an example of this.

Figure 27.6 – Accessing the playlist menu

If you access this menu and select "Now playing", the highlighted track would be queued to the current playlist. By using this menu you can quickly queue up songs to play.

By clicking "New playlist", you can create a list of songs from any of the tunes on your PC. Perhaps you are planning a house party or simply want different tunes for different moods or times of the day. When you click on "New playlist", Groove Music will ask you to name the playlist. Type any name you like and the playlist will be saved and the current song added to it. In figure 27.7 the user has created a playlist called "House Party" and browsed to another track in their library and pressed the plus button again.

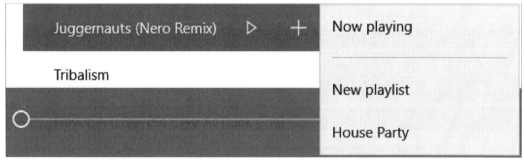

Figure 27.7 – Adding tracks to playlists is easy

Notice now we can add tracks not only to "Now playing" but also to "House Party" too.

When you create a new playlist like this it will appear on the Groove Music main menu (figure 27.2) underneath "New playlist". To play the playlist simply click on it then click the "Play" button.

27.4 – Online features

If you're signed into your PC with a Microsoft account, you will also be signed into the Groove Music app automatically. If not, click on the "Sign In" icon which is second from the bottom on the Groove Music menu (figure 27.2). When signed in, you can access various online features and services. In some countries you can purchase music subscriptions (Groove Music Pass), for instance. You can also click the "Get music in Store" option to browse music in the Windows Store app. We cover the store in lesson 31.

27.5 – Adding music from other folders

By default the Groove Music app will look in your Music folder and library for music. You can add other folders too, including network folders. To do this, click on the Gear icon on the menu (you can see it near the bottom right in figure 27.2). Then, click on "Choose where we look for music". You will then be able to add any folder your PC can see to the Groove Music app.

If the music you want to add is on another hard drive in your PC, then rather than adding it like this we recommend you use libraries and add the additional music folder to your libraries. See lesson 15 for details of how to do this.

That concludes our tour of the Groove Music app. There are some other neat things to discover that we didn't have time to cover here, so as usual, do not be afraid to dive in and experiment.

Lesson 28 – Film and TV

In Windows 10, The Film & TV app replaces the old Xbox Video app as seen in Windows 8. The app can play back your own media files as well as those purchased from the Windows store. The app shares many similarities with Groove Music. Windows Media Player, which we cover later in the guide, can also play video files and is optimised for keyboard and mouse use. Film & TV on the other hand is optimised for touch, but works well with keyboard and mouse too.

To start the app, click on its tile on the Start menu/screen or search for "Film and TV" on the search bar and click the icon that appears. Figure 28.1 shows the Film & TV app running.

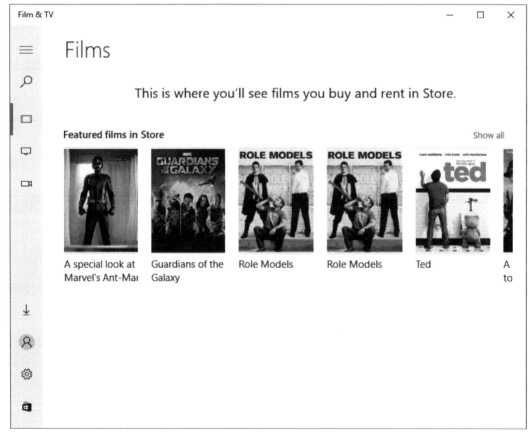

Figure 28.1 – The Film & TV app

28.1 – Using the Film & TV app

Just like the Groove Music app, the Film & TV app has several sizes and when you first start using it, you will probably want to use the largest size since this size conveniently labels all the icons on the left hand side. Figure 28.2 shows the sidebar from the Film & TV app when running in large window size.

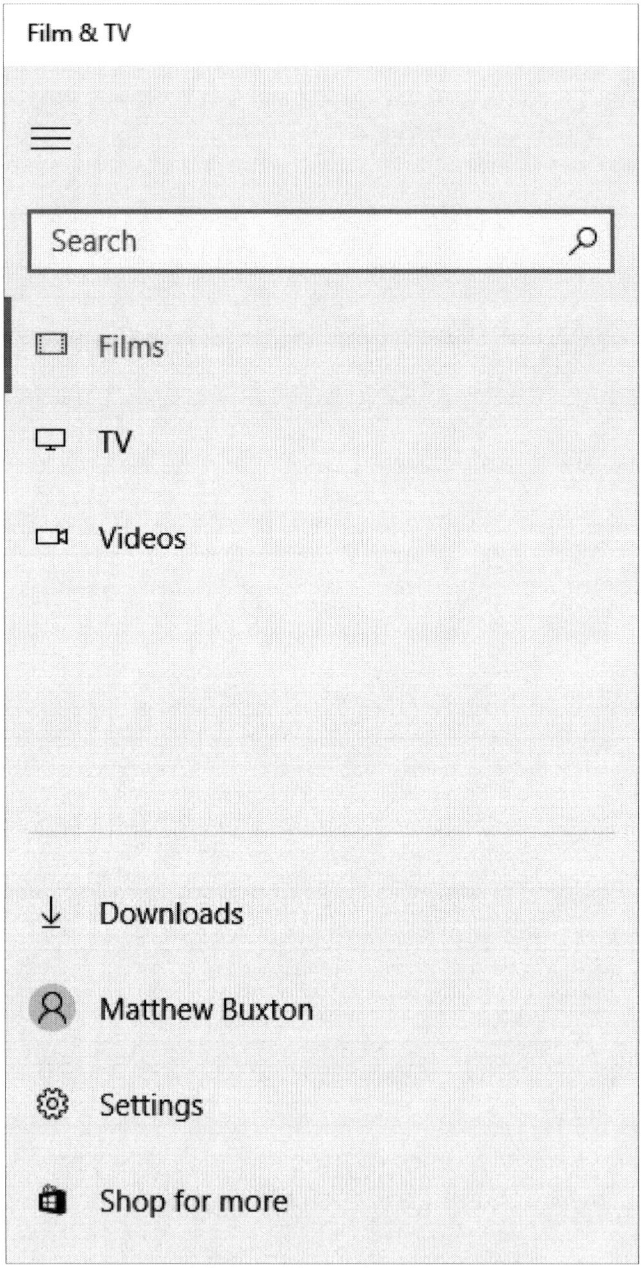

Figure 28.2 – The Film & TV menu

If you have a smaller screen on your Windows 10 device you might not be able to access this mode. In that case you will only see the icons, but not the labels. Use figure 28.2 as a reference while you learn to use the program if you cannot run the program in large screen mode.

28.2 – Browsing and playing your media

There are three main sections to the Film & TV app; "Films", "TV" and "Videos". Films and TV contain content you buy in the Windows store. If you haven't purchased any content yet, these sections will be empty and typically will show you thumbnail images of featured films and television programs from the store that you can buy.

The app can also play your own media files. To do that, click or tap on "Videos". Figure 28.3 shows this section open on a PC with a small number of media files.

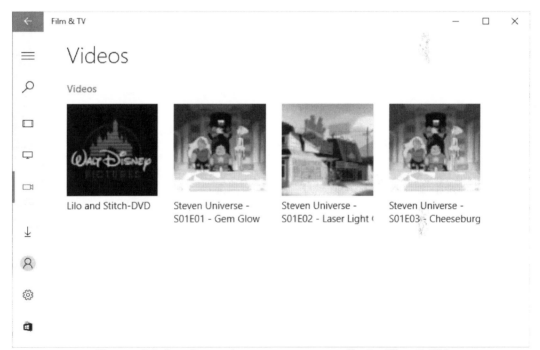

Figure 28.3 – Browsing your own media in Film & TV

Windows 10 doesn't come with any sample media files, so you will need to add some of your own. You may have film and TV of your own, perhaps format shifted from your DVDs. The Film & TV app is not smart enough to know the difference between a media file containing TV content and one containing film content, so all your own videos are lumped together in this section.

To play a video, just click on its thumbnail image once. Figure 28.4 shows the Film & TV app playing back a video file stored in the users Videos folder.

Figure 28.4 – Playing media in Film & TV

The controls for playing media are very similar to the Groove Music app but with a few key differences. The blue bar you can see directly below the video lets you move to different parts of the video. Drag the little round ball left to go back in time or right to go forward.

From left to right, the buttons below the seek control are as follows.

Cast to Device:- If you have a compatible device, like an Xbox One console, on the same network, you can use this button to play your video directly on your console or media streamer. This can often be more convenient than trying to connect your PC to the television.

Aspect Ratio:- Adjusts the dimensions of the currently playing video. Typically older videos were recorded for non-widescreen displays and so may appear stretched when played back on modern monitors or tablets. Click this button to fix that.

Play/Pause:- Toggles the video between play and pause.

Volume:- Tap this button to quickly adjust the playback volume.

Full Screen:- Press this button to enter full screen mode. When you are in full screen mode and the video is not paused, the windows title bar at the top and the playback controls will shrink away, allowing you to watch your content without distractions. To get them back again, move your mouse or touch the touch screen.

Repeat:- When this button is turned on, the currently playing video will repeat when it has done playing.

When you are done viewing a video, click the back button in the top left hand corner of the app to go back to the media library. You will need to leave full screen mode before this control becomes visible.

28.3 – Buying media online

As with the Groove Music app you can use the button near the bottom of the menu (under Downloads) to sign in, if you're not signed in already. Once signed in you can click the "Shop for more" button to buy Film and TV content in the Windows store. We cover the Windows Store app in lesson 31.

28.4 – Adding video from other folders

Just like in the Groove Music app, you can add additional folders to the Film & TV app too. By default the app will look in your Video folder and library for media files. You can add other folders too, including network folders. To do this, click on the Settings icon on the menu (you can see it near the bottom in figure 28.2). Then, click on "Choose where we look for videos". You will then be able to add any folder your PC can see to the Film & TV app.

If the media files you want to add are on another hard drive in your PC, then rather than adding the folder like this we recommend you use libraries and add the additional media directory to your libraries. See lesson 15 for details of how to do this.

That concludes this tour of the Film & TV app. Like the Groove Music app, this app is likely to keep evolving and Microsoft may add new features, so don't be afraid to explore and experiment for yourself.

Lesson 29 – News, Weather and Info Apps

Windows 10 comes with several information apps. These apps collect and aggregate data from the web into a convenient app form, which saves you the hassle of searching and browsing for the information yourself. In this lesson we will take a look at the News and Weather information apps. The aim of this lesson isn't to cover these programs in great detail, more to show what they are and what common features they share, so you can start playing with them and other similar apps yourself.

29.1 – News app

The News app is one of the most useful information apps. You can start it by clicking its tile on the Start menu/screen or by searching for it on the search bar. Figure 29.1 shows the News app.

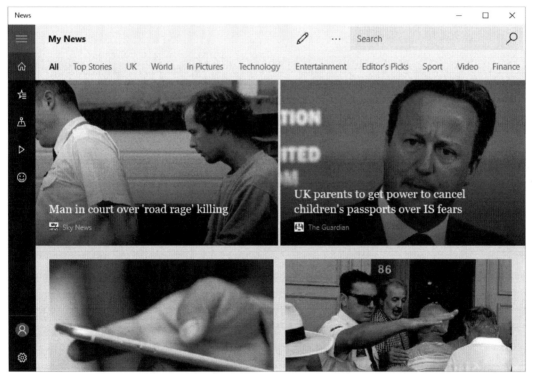

Figure 29.1 – The News app open on its main page

The News app behaves a lot like the other information apps that come with Windows 10. You can search through the news by using the search bar at the top of the apps window. Below the search control, you can pick a category to view news about that particular topic. In figure 29.2, the user has clicked on the "Technology" category.

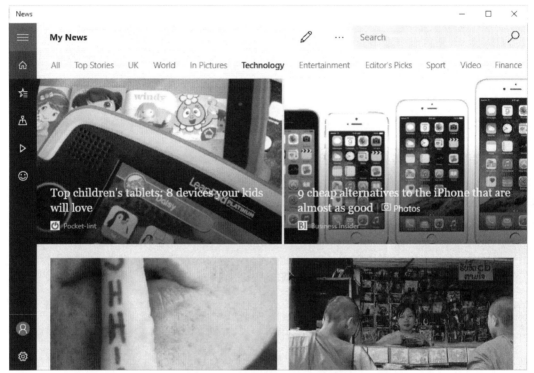

Figure 29.2 – Viewing technology news

When viewing headlines or information in the News app and most other information apps, you scroll vertically, rather than horizontally like in Windows 8. Mouse users will see a scroll control appear when they move their mouse pointer towards the right hand edge of the app window. Touch screen users can simply use a swipe of their finger.

When you find a story you want to read, click or tap on it. You can then scroll through the story in the same way. When you're done and want to go to another story, you either use the back button in the top left hand corner of the app window or, in some apps, you can jump directly to the next story by using the arrow shaped buttons at the middle left and right edges of the app window.

29.2 – Information app buttons

Most information apps have a bank of buttons down the left hand side of the app. You can hover your mouse pointer over these buttons to activate a tool tip that tells you what they do. The star shaped icon, third from the top in the News app, for example, is "Interests". If you click on this button in the News app you can customise which stories appear for you. Figure 29.3 shows an example of this.

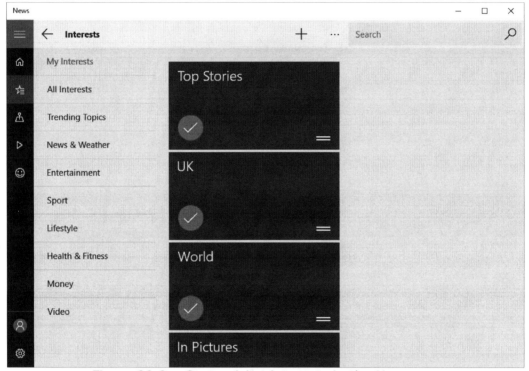

Figure 29.3 – Customising interests in the News app

From this window you can browse the various news categories. If you see a category you are not interested in, click or tap the big green check mark to turn it into a cross. This category of news will now no longer be displayed on your news feed. Obviously, if you see a category you are interested in that isn't checked, you can click or tap to add it to the news feed.

29.3 – Other News app features

The button directly below the Interests button takes you to the local news section. Here, if you have location services turned on, the app will check your location and collect news from local media outlets.

Near the bottom of the column there is the option to sign in (the person shaped icon). If you signed in with a Microsoft account you will already be signed into the News app, otherwise you can click this button to sign in manually. When you are signed in, any news preferences you set in the "Interests" section will be synchronised between any other Windows devices you use.

As you can see the News app is really easy to use. There's nothing that you can do in the News app that you couldn't do just by browsing the news on the world wide web, but having all this information sorted, aggregated and available at your fingertips can be a big time saver.

29.4 – Weather app

The Weather app shares many similarities with the News app. Again the app can be launched from the Start menu/screen or by searching for it. Figure 29.4 shows the Weather app. Note that the first time you start the Weather app, you may need to enter a default location before you see the window shown in figure 29.4.

Figure 29.4 – The Weather app

As you can see, the app is laid out in a very similar way to the News app. There are buttons along the left hand edge that link to different parts of the program. The main forecast is shown in the main program window. By scrolling down the app you can see more details such as an hourly forecast.

Again just like with the News app you can hover the mouse pointer over the icons on the left to reveal a tool tip showing what they do. The places button, the fifth button from the top that is shaped like a star, is quite useful. Click or tap here to add a new place. If you frequently travel between two or more locations you can add and view weather reports for each place.

There is also the sign in option (second button from the bottom) that, just like with the News app, lets you synchronise your preferences between all your Windows devices. Finally, the settings icon at the bottom lets you reconfigure the apps settings, for instance you can change between Fahrenheit and Celsius here.

That concludes our little tour of these information apps. There are other information apps in Windows 10 too, such as Sport and Money and they all work in a similar fashion, so go experiment with them using the skills you learned in this lesson.

Lesson 30 – Maps

The Maps app in Windows 10 is far more advanced than in Windows 8 and now includes full navigation and route planning capabilities. In this lesson we will be taking a tour of the Maps app and demonstrating some of its features. As usual, you can launch the app from the Start menu/screen or by searching for it in the search bar. Figure 30.1 shows the main window of the Maps app. If this is the first time you have run the app, you may need to grant permission for the app to turn on location services.

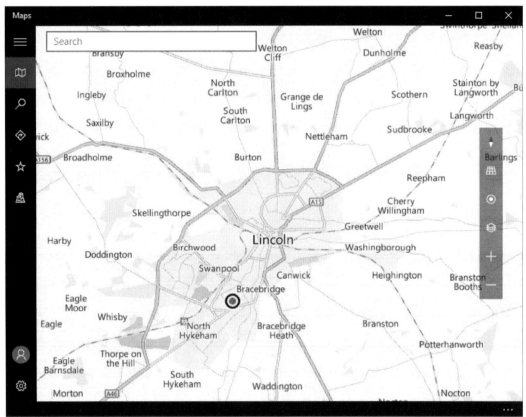

Figure 30.1 – The Maps app

Like several of the new Windows 10 apps, the Maps app has different layouts depending on the size of its window. If you don't see the bank of buttons on the left edge of the app, you may need to make its window slightly wider.

30.1 – Navigating maps

As you can see in Figure 30.1, the Maps app has determined our current location with surprising accuracy, placing it close to the TWT HQ in Lincoln, United Kingdom. To navigate around the map, you drag with your mouse or swipe with your finger in any direction. The bank of buttons on the right hand side perform the following functions.

Rotate map – Click on this button to rotate the map so that North is up (the default rotation). Hover your mouse pointer over the button to reveal two arrow icons. Click these arrows to rotate the map clockwise or counter clockwise.

To rotate the map on a touch screen you need to perform a special gesture that we've not seen before. Start by placing two fingers on the screen as if you were performing the pinch gesture (see lesson 7.3). Make sure to place both fingers at the same time, otherwise Windows may miss-interpret your gesture as a tap and hold and this will cause the map to zoom in. With both fingers on the screen, rather than bringing them together or apart like in a pinch, simply swipe one up or down while keeping the other stationary. If your finger cannot reach any further simply reposition your fingers and perform the gesture again.

Tilt map - Click or tap this button to toggle between a flat, traditional map view (as seen in figure 30.1) and a tilted view that's more often seen in vehicle navigation systems. You can also hover your mouse pointer or tap and hold over the button to access two further buttons that gently increase or decrease the angle of the tilt.

Show Location - Clicking or tapping this button moves the map instantly to your current location, as detected by your devices GPS or through your internet connection.

Zoom in - Zooms into the map. You can also do this on a touch screen by using the pinch gesture (see lesson 7.3) or by tapping and holding on the screen.

Zoom out - Zooms out of the map. You can also do this on a touch screen by using the pinch gesture.

Map views - Allows you to toggle between Aerial and Traffic view on the map. Figure 30.2 shows the map in Aerial view

Figure 30.2 – Aerial view

Aerial view is fun to use while browsing the map and spotting major landmarks. Unfortunately the Maps app does not have a street view feature like the popular Google maps service just yet.

30.2 - Route planning and navigation

The Maps app in Windows 10 works much more like a fully featured GPS navigation system. Smaller tablets in particular make great GPS devices when safely mounted in vehicles.

To get driving directions to a location, first search for it using the search bar on the app. For example, if you wanted to get directions to Manchester, you would start by searching for it. Figure 30.3 shows an example of this.

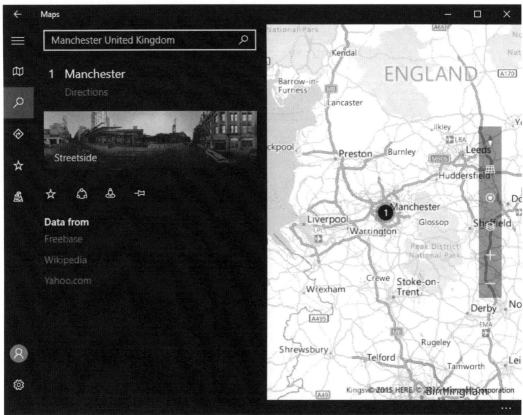

Figure 30.3 – Searching for a location

To get directions, click on the "Directions" link near the top of the window. You will then see the options shown in figure 30.4.

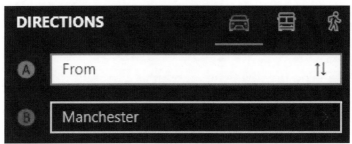

Figure 30.4 – Entering direction information

The three icons at the top of figure 30.4 let you choose between driving, public transport and walking directions. In the box below (labelled A) you enter your starting location. For some reason, there's no easy way to automatically enter your current location here, though you can use either a street address or a postal code/zip code.

Once you have entered all the relevant information, you should see something similar to the information shown in figure 30.5.

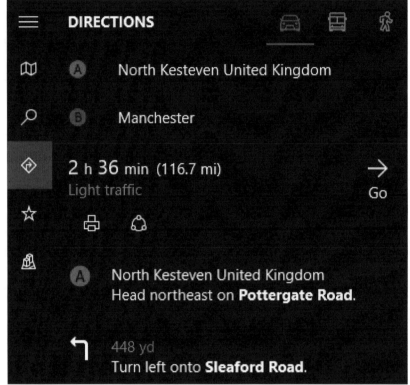

Figure 30.5 – The Maps app is ready to go into navigation mode

By clicking or tapping on "Go", the Maps app will go into navigation mode. Figure 30.6 shows an example of this.

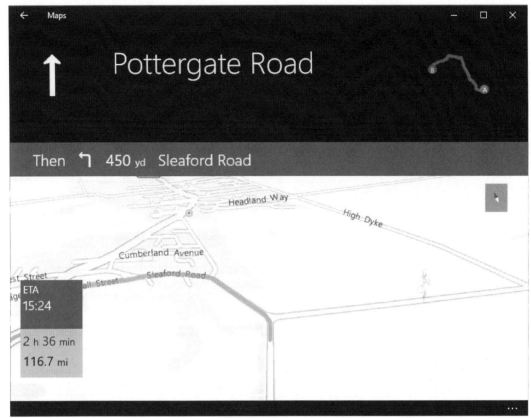

Figure 30.6 – Mapps app in navigation mode

In navigation mode, the Maps app will narrate directions to you turn by turn as you drive. Obviously you will need a device equipped with a GPS and a safe and legal way to mount your device in your car. Be sensible and if in doubt check local road traffic laws, some states in the USA do not allow windscreen mounted GPS devices for instance.

To exit navigation mode, click or tap the arrow on the top left hand corner of the window.

30.3 - Favourites

The Windows 10 Map app also lets you save places as "favourites" so you can quickly find them again. Search for any location using the search tool, then when you find a location you want to save, click or tap on the star icon to make it a favourite. Figure 30.7 shows an example of this.

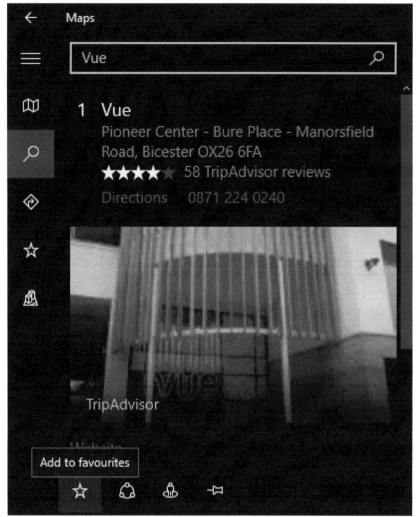

Figure 30.7 – Adding a favourite location

Favourites are synced with your Microsoft account if you are signed in. If you sign into your PC with a Microsoft account you will be signed into the Maps app automatically. If not, you can sign in by clicking the person shaped button. This button is the second one from the bottom on the left hand side of the app window (see figure 30.1).

You can even pin a location to your Start menu if you need to, making it quick and easy to find it again. To do that, simply click or tap the push-pin icon that you can see in figure 30.7.

You can view all your saved favourites at any time by clicking the star-shaped button on the left hand button panel, as shown here.

30.4 - 3D Cities

The 3D Cities feature is a little novelty Microsoft have added to the Maps app. Certain major cities now have a 3D map view that you can use to explore them. Although this is no substitute for a street view feature of course. Click or tap the button shown here, then choose a city. You will be taken to that city on the map, but this time you will get a full 3D view, letting you explore several famous locations. You can scroll around and zoom in and out just like when working with the regular maps. Figure 30.8 shows an example of exploring New York in 3D Cities mode.

Figure 30.8 – 3D Cities view

That concludes our tour of the Maps app. Like all the Windows 10 apps, Maps is likely to continue to evolve once Windows 10 is released, having access to maps and favourite locations on the big screen of your PC and on your Windows phone is an attractive proposition for those of us who travel frequently.

Lesson 31 – Store

In this lesson, we are going to learn about the Store app in Windows 10. Microsoft are very keen for Windows 10 users to try the store and to purchase the so-called "Trusted Windows Store" apps. These apps and games have been pre-approved and vetted by Microsoft and are only available to buy in the Windows store. While Microsoft may be keen to promote their message that using trusted apps makes your PC safer, they also take a cut on each and every app, film, song or game sold in the Windows store too, so they certainly have plenty of motivation to promote its use.

31.1 – What are Trusted Windows Store apps?

Trusted Windows Store apps are apps that have been pre-approved and checked by Microsoft before being allowed in to the Windows store. They can take advantage of special features of Windows 10 such as location services. You can identify Trusted Windows Store apps from their icons. If you search for "News" for instance, Windows will tell you that it is a "Trusted Windows Store app".

Figure 31.1 – Most of the new apps bundled with Windows 10 are Trusted Windows Store apps

Microsoft has struggled to come up with a consistent and non-confusing name for these apps. In Windows 8 they were sometimes referred to as "tile" apps, but of course they now run in a window like regular Windows apps. Microsoft referred to them as "Modern" apps for a while too, but of course there are many modern Windows programs in development that aren't sold through the Windows store. Currently, the name Microsoft has settled on in Windows 10 is "Trusted Windows Store app", which is a bit of a mouthful but at least it is clear.

31.2 - Browsing the store

You can start the Store app by clicking on its tile on the Start menu/screen, or the pinned icon on the taskbar, or by searching for it on the search bar. Figure 31.2 shows the store app running on a desktop PC.

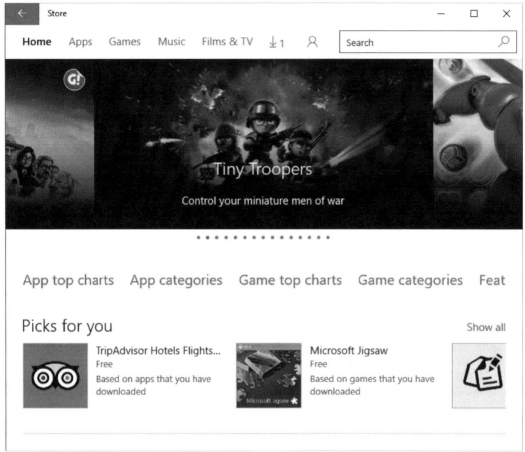

Figure 31.2 – Store app home page

When you first start the store, it will open on the home page as shown in figure 31.2. You can browse here through the most popular apps and see recommendations that Microsoft have picked out for you.

If you have a specific app or game in mind, the quickest way to find it is usually by searching. Type your search query into the box in the top right hand corner and then press enter or click or tap the magnifying glass icon. You will then be taken to a page of search results for your query.

The store is split into several categories. Scrolling down the homepage you will see categories like "Top free apps", "Best rated apps", "Top free games" and "New and rising apps". To see more results under any category, click or tap on the "Show all" link to the right of the category. You can see the "Show all" link for "Picks for you" in figure 31.2, for instance.

When browsing a sub-category, you can quickly narrow your search by selecting any of the options under the "refine" menu on the left. If you don't see this menu, you may need to make the Store window a little wider. Figure 31.3 shows an example of this menu when browsing apps.

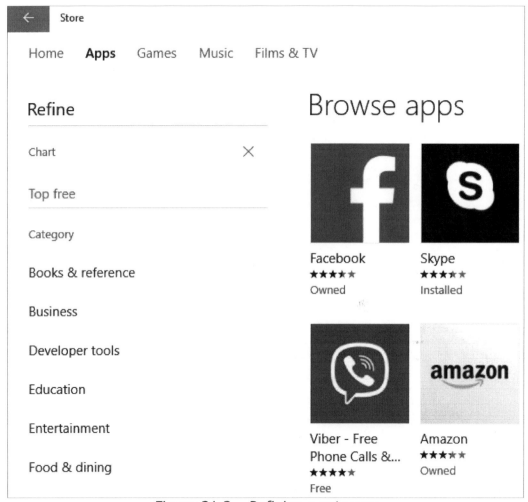

Figure 31.3 – Refining a category

If you were only interested in business apps, for example, you could quickly drill down to them by clicking "Business" on the refine menu.

When you find an app you are interested in, click or tap on it. You will then be taken to a store page for this specific app. Figure 31.4 shows the store page for the game Rayman Jungle Run.

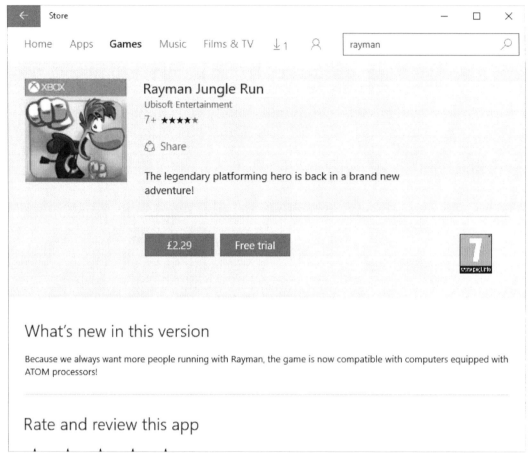

Figure 31.4 – A store page for a game in the Windows store

At the top of this page you can see the price of the app. Many apps are entirely free to download, while some, such as this Rayman Jungle Run game here, have a fee. Some apps or games allow you to download a free trial that gives a small taster of some of the functionality of the app or the game play. You can get this simply by clicking the "Free trial" button.

If you scroll down the store page, you will be able to see reviews and ratings for the app that other users have left. You may also see screen shots and other information, as well as recommendations for similar apps or games.

31.3 – Downloading and installing a new app

If you wanted to buy the Rayman Jungle Run app, you simply need to click on the button labelled with the apps price, in this case £2.29. Of course, you will need some means to pay for it. At this point you will be asked to sign into your Microsoft account if you are not already signed in. Payment can then be made with a credit card or by using a pre-paid top up card that can be purchased from supermarkets and other retailers. Remember that apps you purchase in the store will be available on any other Windows 10 PCs you use, without any additional charges.

Installing a new app through the store is extremely easy. In figure 31.5 the user has browsed to the ever popular Facebook app.

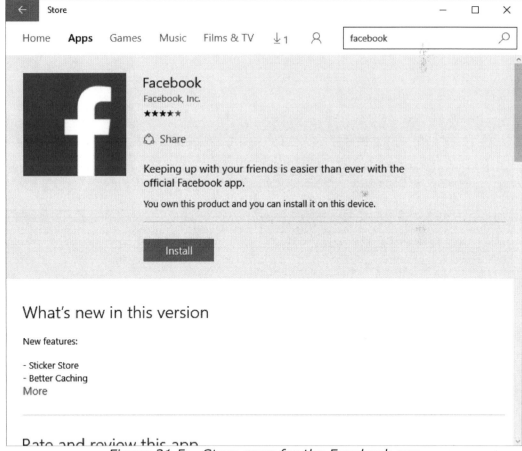

Figure 31.5 – Store page for the Facebook app

The Facebook app is free, so all you need to do is click on "Install". If you're not signed into a Microsoft account, you will be prompted to do so now, even if you are installing an entirely free app, you will still need to be signed in. Like most of the new apps, when you sign into the store while running a local account, you will be given the opportunity to convert your account to a Microsoft account. Click on "I'll connect my Microsoft account later" to skip this step.

Once you are signed in, you may need to click the "Install" button again to start the process. The app is now added to your download list.

Near the top right hand side of the Windows Store window, you should see the downloads icon shown here, with a number 1 next to it. The number next to the icon indicates there is one active download. You can continue to browse the store or do anything else on your PC while the app downloads. To check the status of your download, click on the icon to go to the download manager. Figure 31.6 shows the download manager.

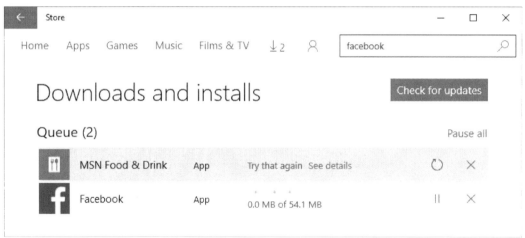

Figure 31.6 – The Windows Store download manager

Once your app has downloaded, you should be able to find it from the search bar on the taskbar and launch it (it will not appear on your Start menu/screen unless you first search for it and then pin it there). Unlike Windows desktop software, there is no further installation process necessary and you can simply start using your new app.

In Windows 10, apps that you download from the store should automatically keep themselves up to date, but you can manually check for app updates too. If you have updates pending or downloading you can view them in the download manager. In figure 31.6 we can see that the Facebook app is downloading, while an update for MSN Food & Drink failed for some reason. We could retry the top download by clicking on the retry button (the curly arrow). You can also use the "Check for updates" button to force the Windows Store app to check immediately for any updates to all your Trusted Windows Store apps. You can also pause or cancel a download by clicking on the pause (II) or cancel (X) buttons available in the download manager.

31.4 – Account menu

The account menu can be accessed in the store by clicking or tapping the icon shown here. This menu contains some options for managing your account and accessing other options in the Windows Store app. Figure 31.7 shows this menu.

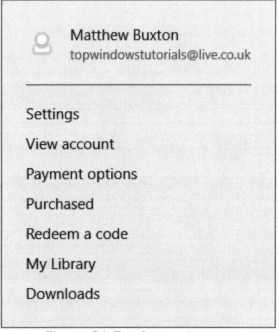

Figure 31.7 – Account menu

We will now briefly go over what each of these options does.

Settings:- Accesses the preferences for the Windows Store app. Here you can turn automatic updates on and off and turn off updating when not on Wi-Fi (or Ethernet/wired) internet connections.

View account:- Takes you to your account management page on the web.

Payment options:- Use this option to manage credit cards and payment options associated with your account.

Purchased:- Shows you a list of apps you have purchased from the Windows store in the past.

Redeem a code:- If you have a pre-paid card, perhaps purchased from a supermarket or other store, you can use this option to redeem it. Simply enter the code as provided on the card to add credit to your Microsoft account. This can be spent in the Windows store or in the store for Windows Phone or Microsoft Xbox too.

My Library:- This section lets you browse through all the apps you bought or downloaded before and download them again if necessary. This can include apps downloaded on another device. Remember, if you buy an app once, you can install it on any device you own without paying again.

Downloads:- When there are no active downloads, the download icon will disappear. In this case, you can access it from this menu option if you need to.

That's all there is to using the Windows Store app. The store contains some great free and paid-for apps and as Windows 10 grows in popularity we expect the range to expand even further. Of course, there's likely to be plenty of desktop software produced for the foreseeable future too. To learn more about the difference between desktop and Trusted Windows Store apps, see lesson 47 – Installing New Desktop Software.

Lesson 32 – OneDrive

Windows 10 features full integration with Microsoft's online storage service OneDrive, previously known as SkyDrive. In this lesson we will take a look at OneDrive in Windows 10 and show you how using this useful cloud storage service has been made extremely easy.

32.1 – Setting up OneDrive

OneDrive is a service which stores your files in the cloud, or in other words, on a server on the internet. This can be useful for backup or for accessing files on other computers or other devices such as mobile phones. In order to access your OneDrive account you will need to be signed in. If you sign into your PC with a Microsoft account, you should automatically be signed into OneDrive too. If not, you can sign in manually. Search for "OneDrive" on the search bar and click on the "OneDrive – Desktop app" icon that then appears. A Microsoft OneDrive window should then appear, as shown in figure 32.1.

Figure 32.1 – Setting up OneDrive

Click on the "Get started" button in the bottom right of the window. The app will then prompt you to sign in with your Microsoft account, so enter your e-mail address and password now, then click "Sign in". You should then see the window shown in figure 32.2.

Figure 32.2 – Choosing your OneDrive folder

The window shown in figure 32.2 explains a little about how OneDrive integration works in Windows 10. As you can see, you can now access your OneDrive folder in File Explorer. Notice the text that says "Your OneDrive folder is here". This folder on your PC will be synchronised with your OneDrive account in the cloud. Any file you place in this folder will be uploaded to your OneDrive. Any file that is uploaded or changed on your OneDrive will be downloaded and changed on your PC in this folder.

If you need to, you can change the location of your OneDrive folder by clicking "Change". You may want to do this if you only have limited space on your C: drive for instance. Click on the "Change" button and browse to any storage location on your PC, or simply leave the folder selection as the default.

Click on "Next" to proceed to the next step. The window shown in figure 32.3 will then appear.

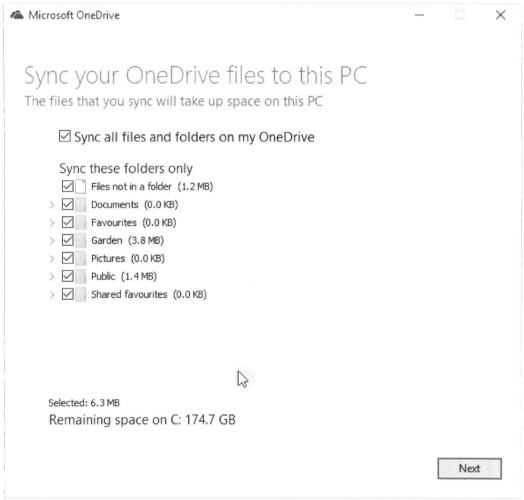

Figure 32.3 – Choosing which folders to synchronise

You now need to decide which folders to synchronise with your OneDrive. Usually, you would simply select all the folders and files shown here, so that your entire OneDrive was available on your PC. If you're using a tablet or other small, portable Windows 10 device and space is at a premium, you may want to deselect some folders here. In the example picture in figure 32.3, there's a mere 5.3 megabytes in the users OneDrive and 174.7 gigabytes of storage on the PC, so in this instance it wouldn't make much sense to select anything but the entire OneDrive contents.

Click on "Next" when you have chosen the files and folders to synchronise. The window shown in figure 32.4 will then appear.

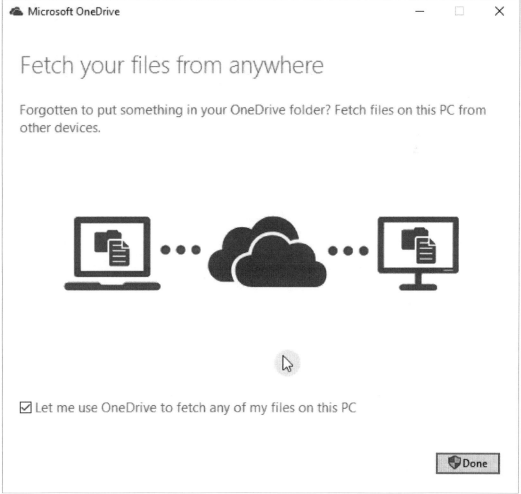

Figure 32.4 – Do you want to turn on OneDrive Fetch?

32.2 – OneDrive Fetch

OneDrive has a feature called "Fetch". If Fetch is turned on, you can access any file or folder on your PC, not just files in your OneDrive folder, through your OneDrive account, as long as your PC is turned on and connected to the internet. For example, you could be at work and signed into OneDrive on your phone when you realise that the crucial Power Point presentation that you need to give was left in your documents folder on your home PC. If you have Fetch turned on (on your home PC) and your home PC was turned on and connected to the internet, it would be possible to go into your OneDrive and fetch that file, saving your bacon.

Of course, turning on OneDrive Fetch could also be a security risk. If you lost your Microsoft account password, an attacker could not only potentially get access to your Microsoft account, but files stored on your PC too. The choice is yours. Once you have decided, click on "Done".

OneDrive setup is now complete. A File Explorer window should now appear, showing you the contents of your OneDrive folder. If you have a large number of files in your folder, they may take a moment or two to download. If you need to change any of these settings later, you can do so from the cloud icon in the notification area. Open the notification area (see lesson 21), right click on the OneDrive cloud icon and choose "Settings".

32.3 – OneDrive in File Explorer

Figure 32.5 shows a OneDrive folder on a typical PC.

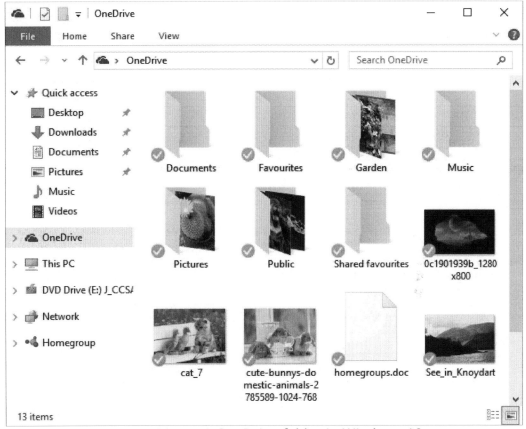

Figure 32.5 – A OneDrive folder in Windows 10

We covered File Explorer extensively in Chapters 3 and 4. Working with a OneDrive folder works exactly the same way as with any other File Explorer folder. The green tick or check marks you can see mean that the file or folder is in-sync with the OneDrive account.

If you copy or move any files into this OneDrive folder (or any of its sub-folders) the files you copy in will automatically upload to your OneDrive. If you change or edit a file in this folder, the changes will automatically upload to your OneDrive too. In figure 32.6, the user has dropped a music file into the Music sub-folder within the OneDrive folder.

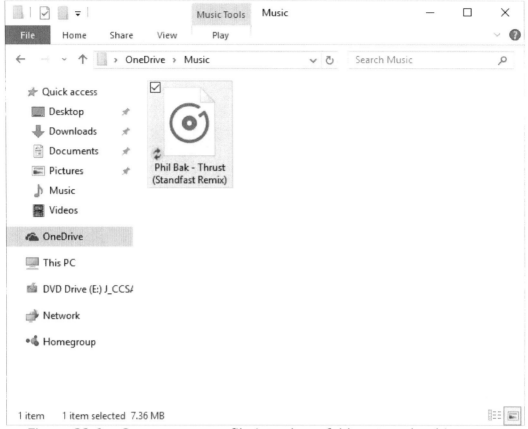

Figure 32.6 – Copy or move a file into these folders to upload it to your OneDrive

Notice the file in figure 32.6 doesn't have a check mark yet, instead the icon shows two arrows. This means that the file is still uploading to your OneDrive. Once it is complete, the arrows will turn into the tick/check mark we see in figure 32.5. Once this check mark appears, the file is available in OneDrive. Not only does this mean the file is backed up, it also means it can be accessed anywhere where you have an internet connection.

Files in OneDrive can also be used with Microsoft's other online services, such as the online version of Office, Office 365. Of course, you can easily access OneDrive files from any of your Windows 10 PCs or even a smartphone with the appropriate OneDrive app. The only downside of course is that files stored in the cloud are more vulnerable to being stolen or accessed by hackers. Of course, Microsoft puts protections in place to help prevent this happening but security breaches continue to happen to companies big and small throughout the world, so keep this in mind before you upload any particularly sensitive data to your OneDrive.

32.4 – OneDrive on the web

You don't even need a special app or a Windows 10 machine to access your OneDrive files, you can simply use any modern web browser. Point your browser to https://**onedrive**.live.com/ or simply search for OneDrive with your favourite search engine. Sign in using your Microsoft account and you will be taken to your OneDrive. Figure 32.7 shows a OneDrive folder open in the Microsoft Edge web browser.

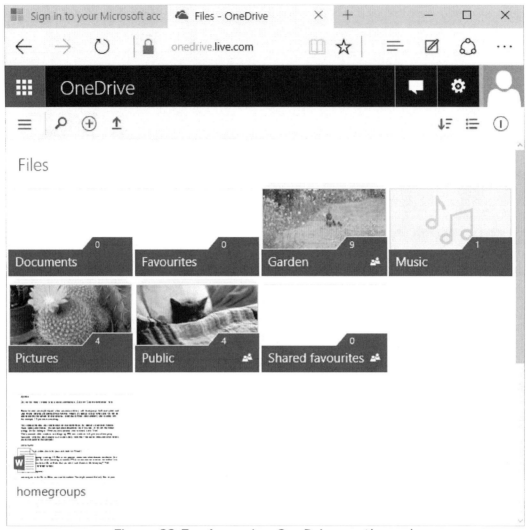

Figure 32.7 – Accessing OneDrive on the web

You can access any of your OneDrive files from the web interface and download them. You can also add new files by clicking the upload button (the up pointing arrow on the top toolbar). Since we all work on multiple devices these days, having access to your files like this is very useful. Rather than carrying around an easy to lose USB stick between home and work, college or school, you could use OneDrive to store your documents and then just access them through the browser.

32.5 – Managing OneDrive Settings

You can manage settings for Onedrive in Windows 10 by using the notification area icon. Open the notification area by clicking the arrow (see lesson 21) then right click on the cloud shaped OneDrive icon. The icon is circled in the picture on the left here.

When you right click this icon, the menu shown in figure 32.9 will then appear.

Figure 32.9 – The OneDrive notification icon menu

If you need more storage space in your OneDrive account, you can click on "Manage storage" here to purchase more space. If any of your files are in conflict, you can click on "View sync problems" to see why.

OneDrive settings can be changed by clicking on "Settings". The settings window is shown in figure 32.10.

Figure 32.10 – OneDrive settings window

On the settings window we can turn the Fetch feature on and off, unlink our OneDrive account altogether or, by going to the "Choose folders" tab, specify which folders we want to synchronise. We covered these options in detail at the start of the lesson, so refer back to lesson 32.1 for a detailed explanation of what they do.

What happened to the OneDrive touch app? Users upgrading from Windows 8 may be wondering where their OneDrive app went. Well, its no longer included with Windows 10. Until recently it was still available in the Windows store, but just as we were going to press it now seems to have been removed.

Microsoft feel that there is no need for a separate OneDrive app now that support is built into the operating system and other apps support OneDrive natively. For instance, the Photos app we covered in lesson 26 will include content from your OneDrive automatically when you are signed in.

That concludes our lesson on OneDrive and this chapter. We hope you have enjoyed exploring some of the free Windows 10 apps and that you now feel confident exploring apps both on your PC and in the Windows store.

Chapter 7 – Securing Your PC and Your Data

If you have been following this course so far, you are probably excited to dive head-first into your new Windows 10 PC and start changing, tweaking and trying all kinds of things. Indeed, we encourage you to do this, it is the best way to learn. Before you start getting too carried away however, it is time to consider security, the security of your computer and your important data.

This chapter firstly tackles the subject of backup. An alarming number of people still do not backup their data at all. Computer hard drives are mechanical devices and will eventually fail through wear and tear. Without a proper backup strategy, any information you have on a hard drive which fails may well be lost forever.

Once we are done backing our system up, we will look at the various security mechanisms in Windows itself. We will show you how to create additional accounts for other family members and how to secure your account against malicious software, using User Account Controls. We also discuss security software including Antivirus software like Windows Defender, the Windows 10 firewall and tell you about the importance of keeping your PC up to date.

Lesson 33 – Planning a Backup Strategy

It is important to remember that files and folders on your PC can vanish into oblivion at any time if you do not have a proper backup strategy. Hard drive failures are the most common hardware fault on modern PCs. While it is more usual for a hard drive to fail when it is old, it is not uncommon for hard drives to fail randomly at any time. This applies to both the old style mechanical hard drives and the newer, solid state or SSD drives too.

In this lesson we will discuss how to plan a backup strategy around the capabilities of the Windows 10 backup utility. If you are planning to use a third party backup solution this lesson might also be useful to you, but it is focused on the backup utility provided with Windows 10.

33.1 – Backup methodologies

Using the Windows 10 backup software is not too complicated but understanding what to backup often is. Luckily Windows 10 backup supports two different kinds of backup, image backup and file history backup. What is the difference between these two options?

Image backup:- This option takes a snapshot of your entire computer, you can think of it like creating a time capsule and putting your current hard drive inside it. When you restore from an image backup, all information (programs and data) on your hard drive reverts to the state it was in when the backup was taken. You can only restore the entire snapshot, you cannot select individual files from an image backup (this is true in Windows 10 backup, though some third party backup solutions do not have this restriction). You can however, restore your computer in the event of a total failure of your computers hard drive or operating system.

File History backup:- This option backs up individual files and folders. It works in the background and monitors changes to your files, creating a new backup whenever a file is changed. If you need to recover a file that has been deleted or changed, you can then go into the file history vault and recover it. File history backup does not backup programs and system files, so cannot be used to restore your operating system in the event of a hard drive failure, for instance.

Consider the information on your computer, we can split it roughly into two categories.

Programs:- These are the things you install and run on your computer, including the actual operating system itself. It also includes word processors, web browsers, games, music players and anything and everything that runs on your computer. Programs change infrequently compared with data.

Data:- This is information that programs work with. It includes word processor documents, spreadsheets, music and video files, digital photographs, saved game positions and anything and everything that the programs you run on your computer work with.

Data is personal to you and usually needs extra protection compared with programs which can usually be reinstalled from their original media or from the internet. Windows 10 File History backup makes it easy to protect your data.

Windows 10 does include image backup too. The feature is called "System Image Backup". It is pretty well hidden, to find it you will need to go to the Control Panel and open the "File History" section under "System and Security". You should then find it in the bottom left hand corner. Windows 10 offers only the bare minimum image backup facilities, we recommend that if you want to create full system images on your PC, you should investigate one of the many third-party backup tools available.

33.2 – Do you have operating system recovery media?

There may come a time when you want to revert your computer back to the state it was in when you first bought it. Perhaps you have clogged your computer up with too much third party software and you just want a clean start, or maybe you are selling your PC and want to make sure that no unlicensed software or personal information remains on it. Windows 10 does give you the option to reset your PC from the Update & Security menu and we look at these options in lesson 63. However, if your PC cannot start, you will need operating system recovery media. This can be a DVD but more commonly these days it is a USB device.

If you purchased your copy of Windows 10 from a store, your operating system recovery DVD is the same DVD you used to install Windows 10 in the first place, so you are covered. If you purchased your computer with Windows 10 pre installed, or upgraded a Windows 7 or 8 machine, you may not have any operating system recovery media. When you buy a new Windows PC, most manufacturers now include a special recovery file/partition on the computers hard drive instead of a DVD. This is fine unless your hard drive fails (and your hard drive will eventually fail). If you do not have any recovery media, you should make some now. We will show you how in lesson 36.

33.3 – Where to backup

If you are still reeling from the cost of buying your new PC, you won't be happy to discover that you are going to need to spend a little more money on a backup solution. However, backing up to the same hard drive is just not an option. If your hard drive fails then so does your backup. The Windows 10 File History backup gives you two main options for backup media, namely secondary hard drives and network drives. Let's take a look at each option.

Secondary hard drives:- These can be either internal hard drives (typically in a desktop computer) or external. External drives usually connect by USB, though some connect via other kinds of interface such as eSATA and (increasingly rarely) Firewire. External drives provide easily expandable storage that is ideal for backup. Most, if not all modern Windows computers have USB connectors. Figure 33.1 shows two USB ports.

Figure 33.1 – Two USB ports on a computer, notice the white USB 'octopus' logo at the top left

When choosing a secondary drive, choose one that is bigger than the system drive in your PC. At least twice as much capacity is desirable, so there is plenty of room for your backups. Remember that we showed you how to determine the capacity of a hard drive attached to your computer in lesson 19.3. Figure 33.2 shows a typical external hard drive that connects to the computer via USB.

Figure 33.2 – A typical external hard drive. Like the vast majority of external drives, this drive connects via USB

Let's look at the advantages and disadvantages of secondary hard drives for backup now.

Advantages:- Fast, affordable high capacity storage. Hard drives continue to increase in capacity and decrease in price.

Disadvantages:- For external hard drives, the user must remember to connect the hard drive prior to the scheduled backup. Fitting an additional internal hard drive requires some technical know how and may not be possible on smaller computers and laptops.

Local network backup:- Once the exclusive realm of businesses, network backup around the home is gaining in popularity. Using network storage can be more convenient than attaching an external hard drive. As long as the network is available any and all computers in your home can access network attached storage. It is usually much easier to remember to leave your Wi-Fi network enabled while you work rather than having to lug in an external drive and attach it. Local network backup uses devices attached to your home network and should not be confused with online or cloud backup which works across the public internet. Figure 33.3 shows a network attached storage device (NAS).

Figure 33.3 – More expensive network storage solutions like this Netgear ReadyNAS can hold multiple hard drives which copy or mirror each other, providing some protection against random hard drive failure

Network backup solutions can be expensive however and they often require technical configuration to get the best out of them. If you are unable to start your operating system and you need to recover from an image backup, you may find that your computer cannot connect to the network and thus your backup is inaccessible.

Let's sum up the advantages and disadvantages of network backup.

Advantages:- Convenient, can be used by several computers in the house. Backups are fast and can be configured to work automatically with little or no user intervention.

Disadvantages:- Relatively expensive, may require expert configuration, restoring image backups from the network is sometimes not possible.

Cloud backup:- The cloud is basically a buzz-word that means "Someone else's computer on the internet". When you backup to the cloud, you send your files to a data centre across the public internet. Cloud backup is growing in popularity thanks to the proliferation of fast broadband internet. In lesson 32 we demonstrated how you could use OneDrive to synchronise and backup files from your PC.

Let's sum up the advantages and disadvantages of cloud backup.

Advantages:- Convenient, available anywhere you have an internet connection. Storing data off-site provides protection from fire, theft and natural disaster in your own home/office (see 33.4 – A note about storing your backups).

Disadvantages:- Can be slow and expensive, especially if you have large amounts of files to store. Files stored in the cloud are more vulnerable to hackers.

In this guide, we will be showing you how to backup using an external USB hard drive, as that is the configuration that we recommend for the majority of home users. We will also show you how to create rescue media so that you can repair your operating system in the event of a hard drive or operating system failure. Users with a small number of non-sensitive files may prefer to use OneDrive to back them up. Small business owners who have data they need to protect against fire and theft may want to look at pre-encrypting their data before uploading it to the cloud using a service like BoxCryptor.

33.4 – *A note about storing your backups*

Remember that hard drive failure and system crashes are not the only disaster you may encounter. Fire, theft, natural disaster and other unfortunate accidents could see both your computer and your backup copy wiped out in one go. To mitigate this danger, you might want to store backup copies at a friends house (you could store his or her backups in exchange) or perhaps in a locked drawer at the office. Since Cloud backups are stored remotely across the internet, they do not suffer from this problem. While the Windows 10 file history backup does not directly support online backup, you can use the OneDrive service to backup your most important files to your OneDrive account, as shown in lesson 32.

That concludes this lesson on preparing your backup strategy. Once you have purchased your external hard drive or backup solution of choice, you can enable automatic backup in Windows 10 easily, we will show you how in the next lesson.

Lesson 34 – Configuring File History backup

In Windows 10, backup is called "File History". File History was introduced in Windows 8 and is virtually unchanged in Windows 10. File History is a fantastic backup solution that protects your files from accidental deletion and accidental changes too.

34.1 – Choosing a File History drive

Just like in previous versions of Windows, we need to set up this feature in order to start using it. Search for "file history" on the search bar and click the first icon that appears. The window shown in figure 34.1 will then appear.

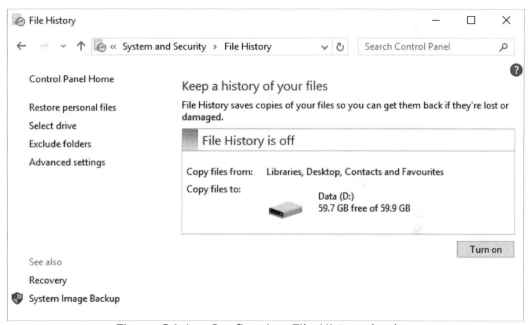

Figure 34.1 – Configuring File History backup

Figure 34.1 shows the initial setup window for File History. File History saves versions of your files, so that for instance if you accidentally delete or change a file, you can always recover it from the File History vault. To setup this feature, you will need a secondary hard drive, either internal or external, or a home network storage location. In the example shown in figure 34.1, we are using a secondary hard drive. By modern standards this drive is relatively small. In reality this device might not have enough storage space to backup a modern sized file collection and if you have a large media library on your PC you may need to invest in something with a bigger capacity.

To get started configuring File History, click on the "Select drive" option. It's the third option down from the top on the left of the window shown in figure 34.1. When you click this link, the window shown in figure 34.2 will appear.

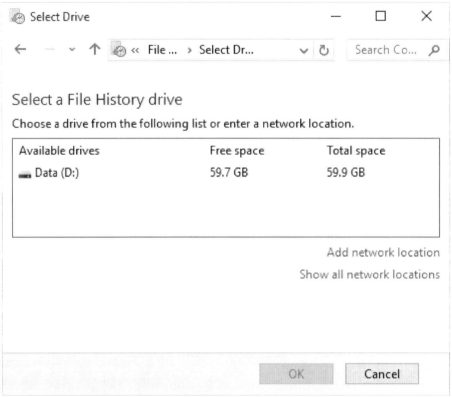

Figure 34.2 – Choosing a drive for File History

The window shown in figure 34.2 lists all the File History compatible drives in your system. Choose a drive, either internal or external, or click the "Add network location" link to add a location on another computer or a network storage device such as a NAS or home server. To choose a drive, click on it from the list and then click "OK". You will then be returned to the window shown in figure 34.1, which will now show your target drive in the "Copy files to:" section.

34.2 – Starting the backup

Click on the "Turn on" button shown in figure 34.1 to start backing up. If you have configured a homegroup already (see lesson 55) you may see a window similar to the one shown in figure 34.3 appear.

Figure 34.3 – You can make your backup drive available to other users on the homegroup

If you choose "Yes" to the option shown in figure 34.3 then other users on your homegroup will be able to use this drive across the network for their File History backups. If you prefer to keep the space all to yourself, choose "No". Once you have made your decision (or if you're not connected to a homegroup) the window will change to the one shown in figure 34.4.

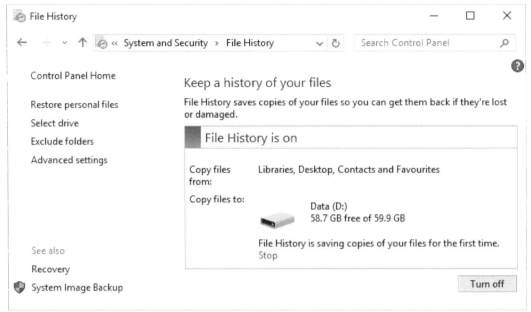
Figure 34.4 – File History is now enabled

Notice in figure 34.4 Windows tells us we are copying files from "Libraries, Desktop, Contacts and Favourites". These are the areas on your PC where you typically store information, so these are the areas that File History will protect. You can exclude certain folders from the backup by clicking "Exclude folders" from the options on the left of the window, then, just click "Add" and browse to the folder you want to exclude. If you want to include a folder that's not currently being backed up, you simply need to add it to your libraries, as shown in lesson 15.2, or place it in your personal folders.

File History is now configured and Windows will save copies of your files to the drive. By default, files will be backed up every hour. When you change any files or folders it will save a new version to the backup. That's all you need to do to set up File History. Before we wrap up this lesson, there are some advanced settings you may want to change.

34.3 – Advanced settings

To access the advanced settings for File History, click on "Advanced settings" from the options on the left. Figure 34.5 shows the Advanced settings window.

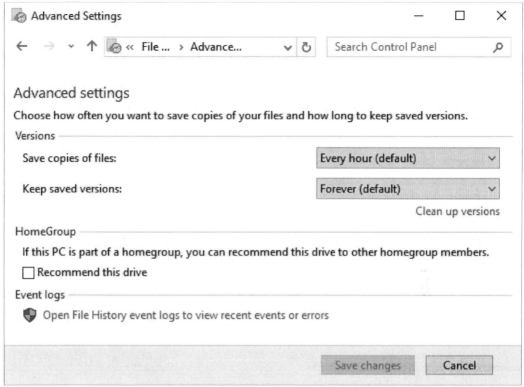

Figure 34.5 – Advanced settings for File History

There are a couple of settings you may want to consider changing here. Firstly, you can make backups more or less frequently than every hour by changing the top most option. The most frequent backup window is "Every 10 minutes". Increasing the frequency of the backups will put more workload on your computer but, of course, provides more security for files you are working with.

The "Keep saved versions" option can be changed to automatically delete files that are older than several months or a year, or to automatically delete old versions when drive space is needed.

Remember to click on "Save changes" if you change any of the options available here.

That is all you need to know to use File History backup, in the next lesson we will look at how to restore files and also discuss some of the limitations of File History.

Lesson 35 – Restoring Files from File History

Backup copies of any kind are useless if you cannot easily restore data from them. In this lesson we will show you how to restore files from your File History backups.

35.1 – Restoring a file

To demonstrate the power of File History, consider the graphics file shown in figure 35.1.

Figure 35.1 – A photograph that's been 'creatively altered'

In figure 35.1 you can see that someone or some-thing has damaged the picture, by adding some scribbles over the top of it. These weren't in the original photograph. Using File History, we can restore a copy and repair the damage. Start File History from the search bar as shown in the previous lesson (see figure 34.1). This time, choose "Restore personal files" from the options on the left. The window shown in figure 35.2 will then appear.

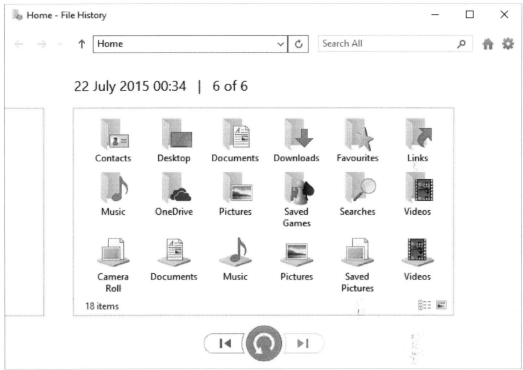

Figure 35.2 – Browsing File History backups

To restore a file or files from File History, simply browse to the files in the File History browser. For instance, the picture file shown in figure 35.1 was stored in the pictures folder. Figure 35.3 shows the pictures folder open in the File History explorer.

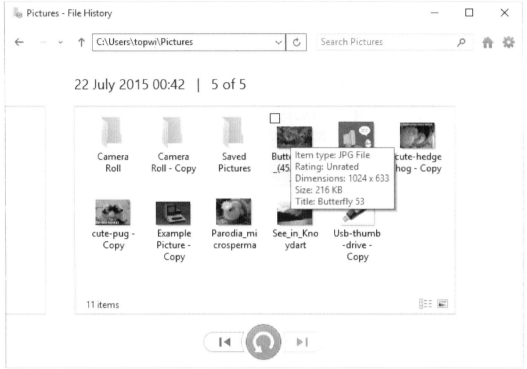

Figure 35.3 – Browsing the pictures library in File History

In figure 35.3 the user has identified the latest version of the picture we saw at the start of the lesson. Double clicking on this file will open it in the File History explorer. Figure 35.4 shows this.

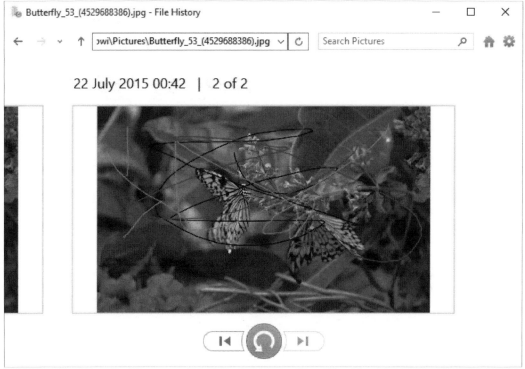

Figure 35.4 – The current version of the file in File History

Notice at the bottom of the windows shown in figures 35.3 and 35.4 that there is a button pointing to the left (next to the large round green button). Click on the button pointing left to go back in time to a previous backup. In the example shown in figure 35.4, when the user clicks on the button, the File History will move back in time to show the image displayed in figure 35.5.

Figure 35.5 – Going back in time to a different version of the file

Once the desired version of the file is located in the backup, it can be restored by clicking the big green button at the bottom of the window. Windows will warn you that there's already a file at that location. In our example, we know for sure that the current file is damaged so it would be perfectly fine to click on "Replace the file in the destination" and then the picture would be restored.

35.2 – Other ways of working with File History

Notice the item check box above the selected file in figure 35.3. You can work with several files while using the File History explorer, not just individual ones. Just like with File Explorer, you can use the forward, back and up controls near the top left of the File History window to navigate around. Note that you cannot drag and drop files between File History and File Explorer, however.

To restore several files from within the File History explorer, you can select them using any of the multiple file selection methods we discussed in lesson 14. For instance you could lasso the files using the mouse or your finger, or use the Control (Ctrl) key to select specific files. Once the files are selected, you can use the green button to restore them to their original directories. Of course, by doing this you may overwrite the current versions of the files. To restore the files to a different directory, click the gear shaped icon in the top right of the window. A menu will appear, from this menu choose "Restore to". Figure 35.6 shows an example of this.

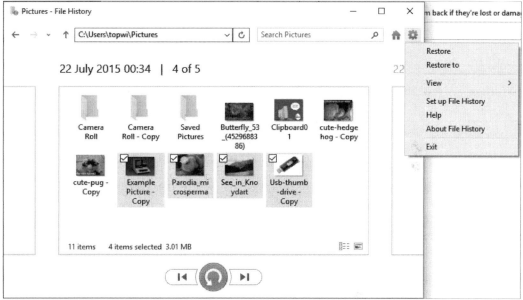

Figure 35.6 – Restoring several files at once to an alternative folder

Using this technique we can put the files anywhere on the PC, without having to overwrite the existing version.

That's all you need to know to use File History to protect your files. As you can see, backup in Windows 10 is now both extremely flexible and extremely easy. Before we round off this lesson, we'll take a quick look at some of the limitations of File History backup.

35.3 – Limitations of File History

To use any backup tool effectively you need to know about its limitations and File History is no exception. While File History might be an ideal solution for many users, it does have a number of shortcomings.

Does not back up program files:- File History backs up data stored in your libraries or personal folders only, it does not backup program files.

When your computers hard drive eventually fails or if your operating system needs to be refreshed or reinstalled, any programs you use will need to be reinstalled as well. All Trusted Windows Store apps are linked to your Microsoft account and can be reinstalled automatically from the Windows store. Desktop software will need to be reinstalled from its original media or original download file.

Beware of older, legacy software designed for Windows XP and earlier. Some of this software stores data within its installation directory and not within your libraries or personal folders. Since File History doesn't back up the program files directory, this data will not be backed up either.

Cannot recover your operating system:– You should make sure you have some way of reinstalling your operating system. This could be your original Windows 10 installation DVD or other media or a system image backup. Hard drives will eventually fail and if you don't have means to reinstall your OS, you may be stuck with a drive full of File History backups you cannot access.

You can use tools such as System Restore (see lesson 62) and Reset my PC (see lesson 63) to repair your operating system, but if you are a power user who installs dozens of applications and makes lots of modifications to the OS, you may wish to investigate system image backups. System image backups take a 'snapshot' of your entire computer, allowing you to restore it in full at any time. System image backup is not covered in this guide but it is still included in Windows 10 under "System Image Backup" which you can reach from the main File History window. There are also dozens of third-party backup tools for Windows that can manage system image backups in various ways.

Cannot backup using online/cloud services:– Windows File History does not directly support backup to an online service such as OneDrive. If, for instance, you store your backups at home and fire, theft or other disaster strikes your house, you will lose both your backups and your working copies in one go. Consider other backup strategies if you have particularly valuable data.

Backups are not encrypted:– If you require a greater level of security for your PC and your backups, you may need to consider third party backup tools that offer encryption, or use File History in conjunction with tools that add encryption to Windows drives.

Lesson 36 – Creating System Repair Media

In this lesson, we are going to look at how to create bootable recovery media in Windows 10. A recovery drive can start your PC even if Windows is damaged, allowing you to start repair options such as System Restore (see lesson 62) or Reset (see lesson 63). Since Windows 10 is designed to run on a wide range of PCs, Microsoft changed the default rescue media from CD-ROM to USB device back in Windows 8. As of Windows 8.1, you can no longer create system repair CDs, you can only use USB devices. To complete this process, you will need a USB drive that is at least 256mb in size and we recommend one that is at least 8GB in size (though on most machines you should be able to get away with 4GB) so that you can include system files. Including system files will allow you to repair your computer in the event of a complete hard drive failure, as we will see in a moment.

36.1 – System repair USB device

To begin creating system repair media using a USB storage device, insert your USB device into the computer. Figure 36.1 shows "This PC" (see lesson 19) with a USB drive attached (Removable Disk F:).

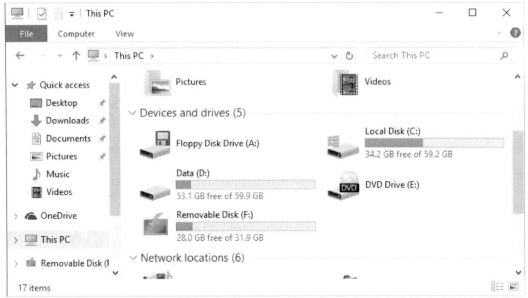

Figure 36.1 – A USB pen/thumb drive attached to the PC will show up under "This PC" like this

To start the process of creating the recovery media, search for "Create a recovery drive" on the search bar and click the icon that appears. Enter your password and/or click on "Yes" when the User Account Control prompt appears. The window in figure 36.2 will then be shown.

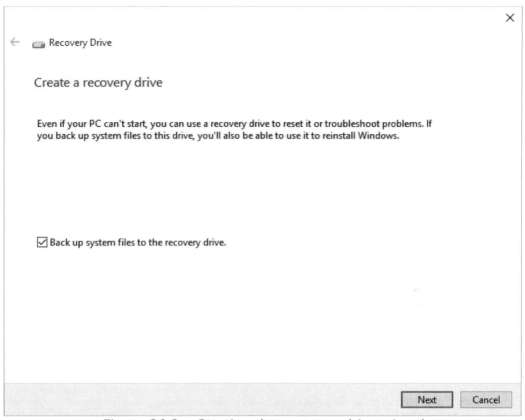

Figure 36.2 – Starting the recovery drive wizard

In figure 36.2 we can see one very useful and important feature, the option to copy system files to the USB drive. What does this mean exactly? Many PCs have a hidden area on their hard drives which can reset the PC back to factory fresh settings. This is great if the operating system fails completely and you cannot start your PC. However, this is no help at all if the hard drive itself fails and needs to be replaced. With this option you can back up the Windows 10 system files to your USB device, this will then allow you to restore your PC to a factory fresh state, even if you have to replace your computers hard drive. You should choose this option if it is available, it could definitely save you time and money in repair bills in the future (be sure to give your recovery drive to the technician if you ever need your PC serviced).

If this option is not available, it may be that your USB device doesn't have enough capacity. If you proceed with creating the recovery drive now, you should make sure you have some other way of reinstalling your OS completely, as you won't be able to do it from the recovery media in this case.

Click on "Next" to get started, the window shown in figure 36.3 will then be displayed after a short delay.

Figure 36.3 – Choosing a drive to use as a recovery drive

In figure 36.3 the recovery drive wizard has found the F: drive, so we can use that. Note that all the information currently on the drive you select will be erased, so make sure you make a backup copy of anything you want to keep. Furthermore, make sure that you have definitely selected the correct drive to use. Cross check using This PC like we did at the start of the lesson if you are in any doubt.

With the correct drive checked and selected, click on "Next". The window shown in figure 36.4 will then appear.

Figure 36.4 – Last chance before your USB drive is re-purposed as a recovery drive

Windows gives us one last chance to copy any information from the USB device. Click on "Create" to begin the process of creating the recovery drive. Windows will then copy and configure the necessary files, this will take a moment, especially if you are copying the system files too. When the process is complete, the window shown in figure 36.5 will be displayed.

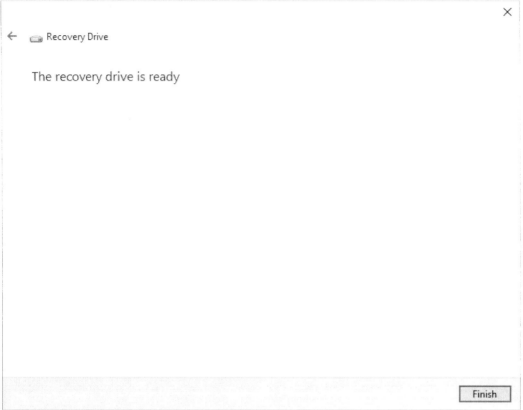

Figure 36.5 – The recovery media is now ready for use

The repair media has now been created. You should reboot your PC and test that it works immediately, then store the media away somewhere safe. If you have trouble starting from the repair media, you may need to change the BIOS or early startup settings on your PC, the details of this vary between PCs. Consult the instructions that came with your PC or motherboard for more information on how to do this.

Lesson 37 – Creating and Modifying User Accounts

Windows 10 lets several users share a computer by creating separate user accounts for them. Each user will have their own personal folders on the computer and their own settings and preferences. Creating separate user accounts for all your family members is highly recommended. By creating limited accounts for your children, for example, you can prevent them changing important settings on the computer while exploring. In the media, we've seen how many families have been shocked when they received large credit card bills after their children borrowed their iPad or iPhone devices. Without the parents permission, the child has purchased in-game items when using their parents devices. This happens on Apple devices as they lack the robust user account system that Windows has.

Even if you are the only user of your computer, if you want to take advantage of the added security benefits of running as a standard user rather than an administrator then you should create two accounts for yourself. A standard, limited account for day to day use and an administrator account for those times when you do need to change system settings. We will explain more about this later in this lesson (section 37.4).

37.1 – Adding a user

In Windows 10, new user accounts are added through the Settings app. Open the Start menu or Start screen and click on the Settings icon, or swipe your finger in from the right of the screen on a touch screen system and tap on the "All settings" button in the Action Centre. The window shown in figure 37.1 should then appear.

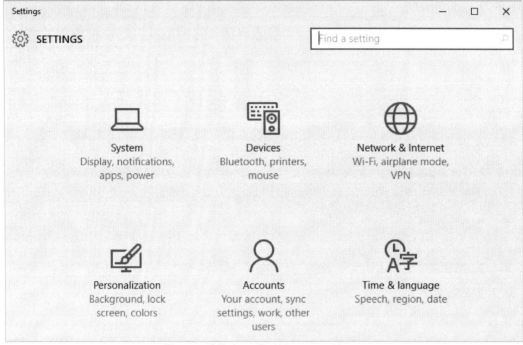

Figure 37.1 – Settings options

If the window that appears on your PC doesn't look like the one shown in figure 37.1, click or tap on the gear shaped icon at the top left of the window, this will immediately return you to the settings window as shown in figure 37.1.

Now, click or tap on "Accounts", the window shown in figure 37.2 will then appear.

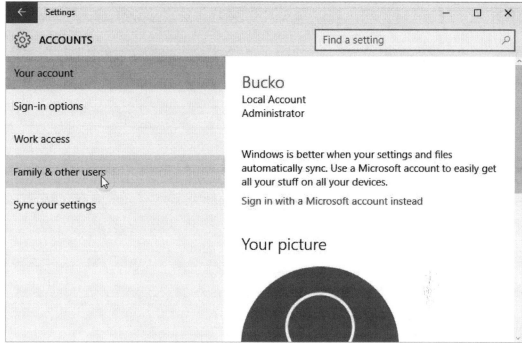

Figure 37.2 – Managing user accounts

To add a new user to the PC, firstly select "Family & other users". The window will then change to the one shown in figure 37.3.

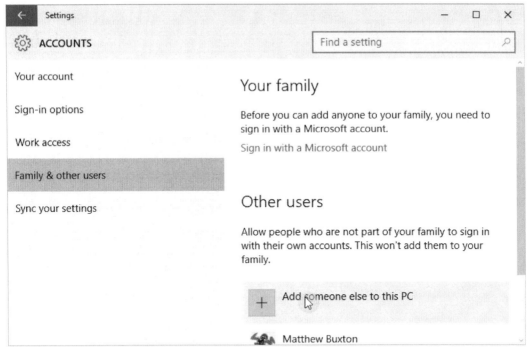

Figure 37.3 – Managing family and other users

Note:- If you don't see the "Family & other users" option, then you are not signed into your PC with an administrator account. In this instance, someone else has set up your user account for you and you will need to ask them for permission to add another user. Sign out and then sign in again using the administrators account to complete this lesson.

To add a new user, click on "Add someone else to this PC". When you click this button, the screen shown in figure 37.4 will appear.

Figure 37.4 – Configuring account types

37.2 – Microsoft accounts vs local accounts

As we discussed way back in lesson 1.2, accounts on a Windows 10 machine can be linked to your Microsoft account if desired. If you do this, your account is tied to Microsoft's other online services on the web, such as Hotmail, Xbox Live and OneDrive. Using a Microsoft account will synchronise your settings between all the PCs you use, as well as sign you in automatically to services like the Windows store and OneDrive.

There are also standard Windows accounts (or local accounts), which aren't linked to Microsoft accounts and act the same as they did in previous versions of Windows. If you are heavily into your home networking for instance, you may have set up your home network with user names and passwords on your shared devices that match the user names and passwords on the PCs in your home. In this case you might want to carry on using the traditional Windows user account. Maybe you don't want to log in with a Microsoft account because you prefer to store your Microsoft account credentials in a password manager app, an app you can't access unless you are logged in. If this is the case, you may be interested to know that you can now create a log in PIN for your device. We will look at this in more detail later in the lesson.

Remember that with a local account you may need to manually sign into the App Store and other online features with your Microsoft account credentials and a small number of features (such as Cortana) are not available.

37.3 – Adding a Microsoft account

For this example we will use a Microsoft account to add a new user to the PC. Fill in the users e-mail address on the screen shown in figure 37.4, this will usually be the users Hotmail or Outlook.com address. If the user is using any Microsoft services online already, be sure to enter the address associated with their Microsoft account. If your new user doesn't have a Microsoft account yet, he or she can get one by clicking the "Sign up for a new e-mail address" link underneath the e-mail address box.

Once you have entered the users e-mail address, click on "Next". The screen shown in figure 37.5 will then appear.

Figure 37.5 – Adding a user with a Microsoft account

Now our new user is set up. The first time the new user signs into this PC, the computer will need to be connected to the internet. They will, of course, also need their Microsoft account password. Click on "Finish" to complete the account creation process. You will then be returned to the screen shown in figure 37.3. You can now add more users or simply continue to use your PC. When you are done using your PC, don't forget to log out (we showed you how in lesson 3.4) so that your new user can log in with his or her account. We show you what happens the first time you log in with a new Microsoft account at the end of the lesson (lesson 37.7).

37.4 – Standard users and Administrators

In Windows 10 we can also configure the accounts security level without needing to dig into the Control Panel. All new accounts added to the PC will default to standard user accounts. This is of course, usually the correct behaviour. Because Administrators can perform system wide changes, gain access to other users files and documents and completely reconfigure the PC, most users should not have administrator rights. To change account security levels, you will need to be logged in with an administrator account. Since one account on your PC always has to be an administrator, if you only have your initial account, it will be an administrator account.

Open the accounts settings window and navigate to "Family & other users", just like when adding a new user. This time however, you should click or tap on an existing user (use the scroll control to scroll down if necessary) and then click "change account type". Figure 37.6 shows an example of this.

Figure 37.6 – Changing an accounts security level

From the drop-down box control that now appears, we can reconfigure the accounts type or security level. The current setting for the account shown in figure 37.6 is "Standard User". It is important to understand the difference between these two security levels that an account can have.

Administrators:- These users have full access to everything on the computer (including potentially the personal folders of other users) and can change any and all settings on the computer. This includes installing new software, changing networking and internet settings or storage configurations. Administrators can basically do whatever they choose.

Standard users:- These users can run and use programs but usually have to ask permission from an administrator before they can change global system settings or install new software. Note that in Windows 10, standard users are free to install Trusted Windows Store apps but not most desktop apps.

Normally, a family computer would only have one administrator, typically this would be the parent or head of the house, or the adult with the most computer experience. Everyone else, especially younger members of the family, should have standard accounts.

Note – Windows will use the term "Account type" to refer to standard user accounts and administrator accounts. Account type can also refer to Microsoft accounts and local accounts. Usually it's pretty easy to know which one is being referred to by context.

37.5 – Creating local accounts

We created a local account way back in lesson 1 when we set up a factory fresh Windows 10 PC. To add a local account to an existing Windows 10 PC, just use the following steps.

Start by following lesson 37.1 up until the point Windows asks you "How will this person sign in?". Now, click "Sign in without a Microsoft account (not recommended)". Don't worry about the "not recommended" part, Microsoft likes to discourage local account use largely because it puts another obstacle between your wallet and the Windows store.

You will now be taken to the local account creation window. Jump all the way back to lesson 1, figure 1.6 and simply follow the instructions from there.

37.6 – Running as a standard user

As discussed previously, all new accounts created using the settings app are created as standard user accounts by default. When you first set up your PC (as in lesson 1) the user account you initially configure will always be an administrator account, since there always needs to be at least one administrator account.

Here is a technique you can use to boost your PCs security. If you are the one responsible for maintaining the PC, create yourself two accounts, one with administrator privileges and one without. To do this, just follow the account creation steps we've covered in this lesson. Your accounts can be either Microsoft or local accounts, whichever you prefer. When creating a separate administrator account, you might want to use your regular user name with the "-administrator" part tacked onto the end.

When you are finished adding your new standard user account, you will need to log out of your administrator account and log back in again with your newly created account. Now, use this newly created standard account as your day to day account. Alternatively, create a new administrator account and then change your existing account to a standard user account, whichever is more convenient for you.

By using a standard account for your day to day computing tasks, you make your PC much more secure against viruses, malware and hackers.

37.7 – Microsoft accounts and sign-on options

To wrap up this lesson, we'll take a look at what happens when you first sign on to a Windows 10 PC with a Microsoft account. Once you have added a Microsoft account to the PC, you can log into it using the techniques we demonstrated in lesson 2.1. Select your account and enter your Microsoft password (the same one you use to log in to any of your Microsoft services on the web). Windows will set up the account and after a short delay, the screen shown in figure 37.7 will appear.

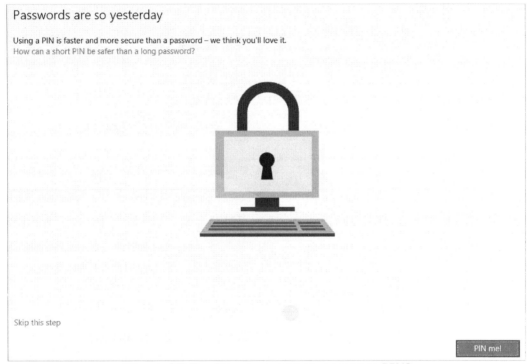

Figure 37.7 – Do you want to create a PIN?

Windows gives you the option of setting a sign-in PIN. Using a PIN is more convenient than using your Microsoft log-in each time and potentially more secure, since the PIN only works with the PC you're currently using, rather than anywhere on the web. If you want to set up a pin, click or tap on the "PIN me!" button in the bottom right. The window shown in figure 37.8 will then appear.

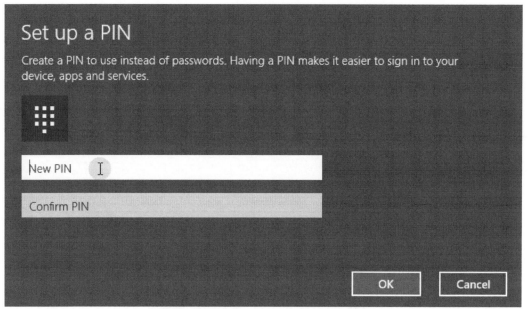

Figure 37.8 – Setting up a PIN

Type your PIN in the top box then confirm it again in the second box. Currently, sign in PINs can only contain numbers (0 to 9) and not letters. Click on "OK" when you are done.

Windows will then give you a little information about OneDrive, we cover OneDrive extensively in lesson 32. Click on "Next" and you will be returned to the desktop, ready to use your new account.

So, now you know how to configure user accounts on your Windows 10 PC and you understand the distinction between administrators and standard users as well as local accounts and Microsoft accounts. The next lesson will look at User Account Controls and how this helpful feature can make using standard user accounts much easier than it was back in the Windows XP days.

Lesson 38 – User Account Controls

In the previous lesson we looked at how to create user accounts and discussed the security advantages of running a standard account rather than an administrator account. In this lesson we will show you how User Account Controls (UAC) work to make running as a standard user more convenient. Firstly, we will discuss in more detail why Microsoft implemented User Account Controls. In Vista, many users did not appreciate that UAC is attempting to fix a fundamental problem in the Windows security model. Instead, they berated the persistent annoying prompts that never appeared in Windows XP. In order to understand why UAC is not your enemy, we need to look at how Windows XP handled account security and why for the most part it was a failure for home users.

38.1 – Halt! Who goes there?

In the last lesson we learned that there are two different security settings for users on a Windows 10 machine, namely standard users and administrators. Generally, administrators can make changes to the computers configuration and install new software. Standard users, on the other hand, are forbidden from making system wide changes and are only cleared to run software already installed. In Windows 10, standard users are free to add new Trusted Windows Store apps to their accounts through the App Store, since each users trusted apps are unique to his or her account. This security model seems fine at first glance, but what about when a standard user wants to install some new desktop software? Certainly if you are running a family PC, it's likely that other users in the house will want to run their own software and not just software from the Windows store. Children might want to install games, for example, which often run in desktop mode.

In Windows XP and Windows 2000, if you wanted to install some new software for a standard user account, you would need to switch to an administrator account, install the software (making sure to make it available to all users), log out of your administrator account and switch back to the standard account. This process was long winded and unfortunately it gets worse.

Lots of older, or simply badly written software just doesn't run under a standard account at all. Because of the fact that most Windows XP machines were pre-configured to run as administrator and because of the frustrations and headaches associated with running as a standard user, most Windows XP users ran administrator accounts all the time.

What is the big deal with running as an administrator? It's my computer, I can change it however I want, right? Unfortunately, running as an administrator also means that your system is wide open to attack from viruses and spyware. If you have full access to your computer, so does any program you run (or accidentally run) while using it, meaning that viruses can very easily propagate, hijack and sabotage key parts of your computer, often without you even knowing about it. With the new Trusted Windows Store applications in Windows 10, Microsoft have taken additional steps to safeguard users. By making every app pass a special vetting process before it is available in the store and restricting what these apps can do, Microsoft hope to mitigate the risk of malware even further. Nevertheless the vast majority of Windows users are still going to want to run desktop software. Even with antivirus and other security software running, running as an administrator is a security risk, but running as a standard user is too inconvenient for most people, or at least it was until User Account Control was introduced.

38.2 – User Account Controls to the rescue

User Account Controls (UAC) work in two ways, when running an administrator account, UAC prompts you to grant permission to make changes to the system. When running as a standard user, it allows you to temporarily elevate to administrator by entering your administrator password, thus saving you the hassle of switching accounts. Figure 38.1 shows a typical User Account Control prompt.

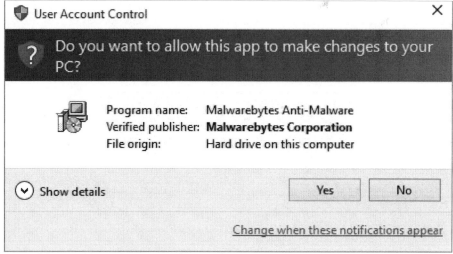

Figure 38.1 – User Account Control prompt on an administrator account

In figure 38.1, Windows has detected that a program we started wants to make changes to the computer. If this alert popped up out of the blue, you would certainly have cause for alarm. In this case it appeared because we started an installation file for a desktop application. Installation files are used to add new programs and features to Windows. Clicking on "Show details" will show where the program is located (the address or path of the file).

You might have noticed the shield icon, like the one on the left here, as you worked through this guide or experimented with your computer. Wherever you see this shield icon next to a task or program it indicates a task which makes changes to your computer and so may generate a UAC prompt. You may have also noticed (especially if you were a Windows Vista user) that clicking on most tasks on the Control Panel no longer results in a UAC prompt window appearing. Why is this? Microsoft scaled back the amount of alerts you typically see by default with Windows 7, and Windows 10 works the same way. If you are running an administrator account then UAC prompts will not appear by default when you change Windows settings. This decision upset some security experts[1] who rightly pointed out that by doing this you are actually making Windows less secure, seems like you can't please everyone.

38.3 – Changing User Account Control settings

To open the UAC settings window, search for "uac" in the search bar and then click on the "Change User Account Control settings" icon that then appears. The window shown in figure 38.3 will then be shown.

---

1   See http://www.osnews.com/story/21499/Why_Windows_7_s_Default_UAC_Is_Insecure

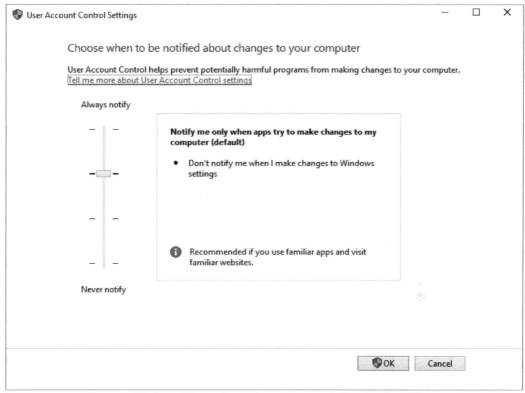

Figure 38.3 – Changing User Account Control settings

On the UAC settings window we can choose from four different settings. The settings are as follows.

Always notify me:- This is the highest security setting and the same behaviour as was seen in Windows Vista. With this setting, UAC asks for your permission every time a program or a Windows system setting is changed. **To get the very best security however, you must create and use a standard user account as discussed in lesson 37.6.**

Notify me only when apps try to make changes to my computer:- This is the default setting. A UAC prompt will appear when you install a new program or run a program which requires administrator access (such as a backup utility). Changing Windows settings will not generate a UAC prompt. This setting aims to balance security with convenience but some more security conscious users have speculated that malware might find a way to impersonate a Windows setting and thus bypass the UAC notification process.

Notify me only when apps try to make changes to my computer (do

not dim my desktop):- This is exactly the same as the previous setting, except without the screen dimming effect seen when a UAC prompt is displayed. This effect is part of a mechanism which stops malware from hijacking the UAC notification and answering for you. If your PC struggles to display the screen dimming effect, choose this setting instead of the default setting.

Never notify me:- This setting disables UAC altogether. This is strongly **not** recommended.

38.4 – User Account Controls and standard accounts

As discussed at the start of this lesson, UAC really comes into its own when used with standard accounts. Windows users can finally stop using administrator accounts for day to day computing tasks and enjoy the improved security of a standard account.

Figure 38.4 shows a UAC prompt window on a standard user account.

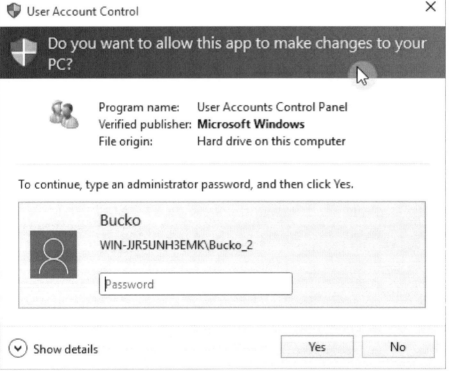

Figure 38.4 – User Account Control prompt on a standard user account

Notice in figure 38.4, we are asked for the administrator's password, why is this? This user account is only a standard account and therefore does not have the necessary rights to make system changes. With UAC we can temporarily activate another account which DOES have these rights. Under Windows XP or Windows 2000, we would have to switch user accounts to make the changes and switch back again. As you can imagine, being able to immediately switch to an administrator account thanks to UAC is much more convenient.

Running as a standard user rather than an administrator is one of the best ways to improve security on your PC. Thanks to UAC, this is now possible and convenient.

You might be interested to know that it is a popular myth (perpetrated by Apple during their old "I'm a Mac and I'm a PC adverts") that other types of computer do not have UAC prompts. On Mac and Linux computers the mechanism is called Sudo. In many ways, UAC works better than Sudo particularly when using graphical user interface programs, though most system administrators will agree Sudo works better when using the command prompt. UAC has also been shown to be more secure than Sudo in many instances.

That concludes this lesson on User Account Controls. This was a complicated lesson with a lot of theory and so give yourself a pat on the back for getting through it. We hope that you understand the advantages of limited accounts now and that you won't curse at UAC prompts quite so much in the future. The next lesson looks at how you can use standard user accounts and Microsoft accounts to manage family safety features to help keep your children safe as they use your Windows 10 PCs and explore the internet.

Lesson 39 – Family Safety

Family safety features in Windows 10 have seen some significant changes. Using the power of the cloud and the convenience of Microsoft accounts, you can now manage your children's use of all your Microsoft devices. In this lesson, we will show you how to use the family safety features. How you use these features is up to you, we're here to advise you on Windows 10, not parenting, so nothing in this lesson should necessarily be considered a recommendation.

39.1 – Family Safety requirements and initial setup

In order to use the Family Safety features in Windows 10 you will need to have a Microsoft account for each child you want to manage and a Microsoft account for the parent too. The parent's account will need to be logged in and configured as an administrator, at least while completing this tutorial. If you need to add or reconfigure user accounts, see lesson 37.

Start by setting up the family safety component on the web and adding the first child account. Visit the link shown here:-

https://account.microsoft.com/family#/add/child

Click on the link if you are using an e-book or carefully type it into your browsers address bar. Once you visit the page, you will need to sign in with your Microsoft account (your account, NOT your child's). If you're not familiar with using a web browser just yet, see lesson 53, where we take an introductory tour of the Microsoft Edge web browser.

Once you visit the link and sign in, the page shown in figure 39.1 should be displayed.

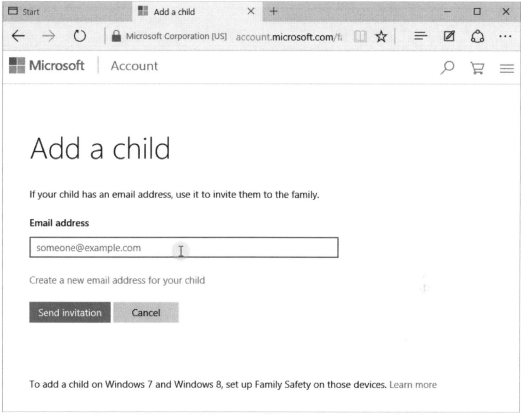

Figure 39.1 – Adding a child account to your family

Enter your child's e-mail address then click on "Send invitation". If your child doesn't have an e-mail address yet, you can set one up for them by using the "Create a new email address for your child" link. When writing this tutorial, we had difficulty using the account creation tool on the page here, so you may need to go to Outlook.com instead and sign your child up there.

Once you invite your child to the family, they will need to accept your invitation to join the family. They do this by logging into their e-mail account and clicking on a link in an invitation e-mail. Typically the older the child the more difficult this process can be. For a younger child, you may have their e-mail account credentials already and can accept the invitation for them. Teenagers typically demand better privacy and will have to complete the process themselves. Of course, if you're the only administrator on your family PC, you can deny your children access to the PC until they have completed this step if you want to.

Figure 39.2 shows the family safety invitation e-mail open in Outlook.com on the web.

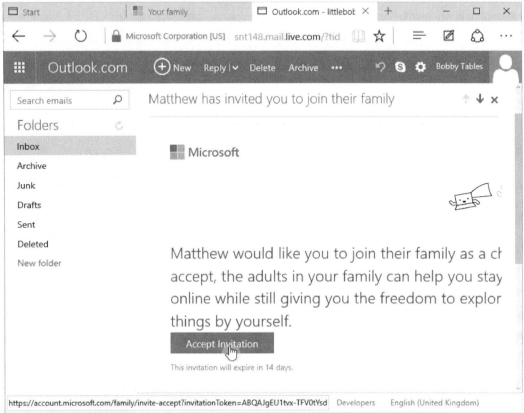

Figure 39.2 – Accepting a family invitation via e-mail

Click on "Accept invitation" and then "Sign in or sign up". If your childs e-mail account is not with Microsoft, you may need to sign them up for a Microsoft account too at this point. If they use an Outlook.com or Hotmail e-mail address, this is already done and you should see a page with information similar to that shown in figure 39.3.

Figure 39.3 – Welcome to the family

39.2 – Activating a child account

With the web setup step complete, we need to go back to user settings in Windows 10. First close or minimise your web browser, if necessary. Now, open the Family & other users settings, just like we did in lesson 37.1 when we added a new user.

You should now see your child's account under "Your family". You will also see a message saying they "Can't sign in". Click on the account and a button labelled "Allow" should appear. Figure 39.4 shows an example.

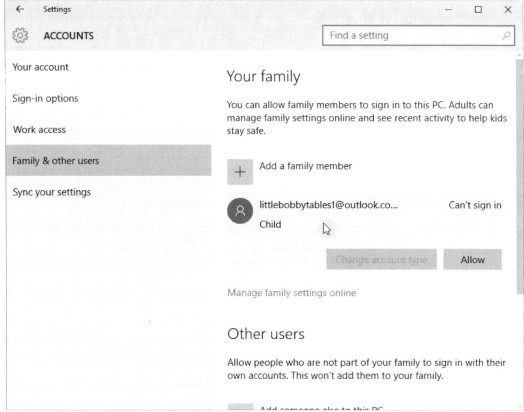

Figure 39.4 – Allowing a child to log onto your PC

Click on "Allow" and then "Allow" again in the window that then appears. The message should then change to "Can sign in".

This child can now sign in to this PC. If you have multiple Windows 10 devices in your home and you want to let your child use them, you will need to repeat this process (from 39.2) on each PC.

39.3 – Family safety settings

To manage settings for your children, click on the "Manage family settings online" link as seen in figure 39.4. This will open up a web browser and take you to the settings page. Click on the child's account you want to manage and you will be taken to the page shown in figure 39.5.

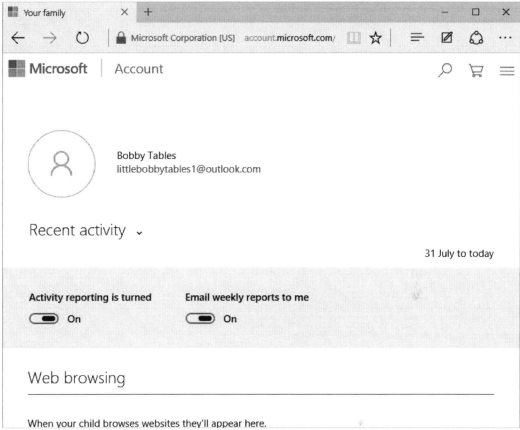

Figure 39.5 – Family safety settings are configured on the web

Use the drop-down box at the top of the screen to choose the different sections within the family safety settings. The sections are as follows.

Recent activity:– Use this section to manage activity reporting. You can see websites your child has visited, which apps and games he or she has been using and how long they have been using a PC. If you leave the "Email weekly reports to me" feature turned on, you will be sent a summary of this activity each week.

Use these options at your discretion. For younger children they can be ideal, but older teenagers may be upset at you knowing every single website they visit and may be discouraged from seeking valuable advice on topics like drugs or sexual health.

Note that these settings are not perfect. If your child somehow manages to install a third party web browser, their activity may not appear in this section. Likewise if they use an older game or a game that isn't downloaded from the Windows store, it may not register on the "Apps and games" section at all.

Web browsing:- Figure 39.6 shows some of the options available in the Web browsing section.

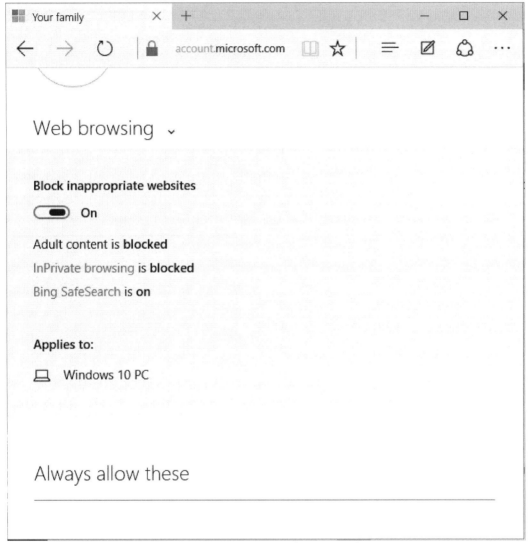

Figure 39.6 – Web browsing family safety options

The first option in this section lets you "Block inappropriate websites". Turn this setting on to block adult content while your child surfs the web. You can also block the "InPrivate browsing" option, which supposedly allows you to surf the web without leaving any traces (though, studies have shown this is somewhat misleading!).

If you use the web filter option here, please remember that no web filter is perfect. While rare, adult sites can slip through the filter. More commonly, especially as children get older and lives get less black and white, web filters struggle to distinguish between genuine information sites and those that any reasonable parent would want blocked. For instance, it's easy for a human to tell the difference between a drug advice service like http://www.talktofrank.com/ and a site that's offering to sell drugs, but it's not so easy for a dumb machine.

Below the filter settings there's the option to manually block a website or manually allow one through the filter. To add a site, copy and paste its web address in full from your browser into the appropriate box, then click "Allow" or "Block" respectively.

Apps & games:- Figure 39.7 shows the Apps & games section.

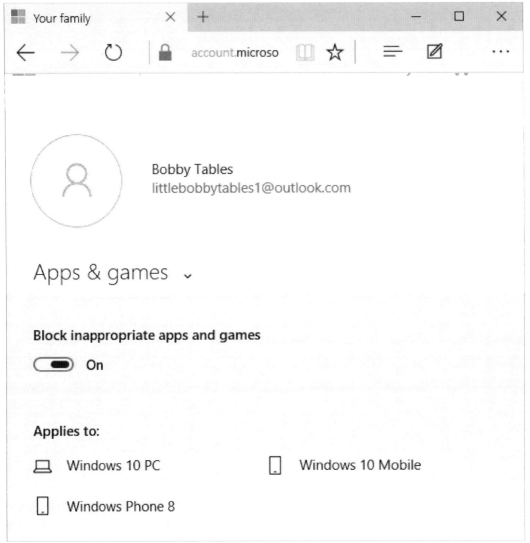

Figure 39.7 – Restricting apps and games

The Apps & games section lets you block any apps or games that are rated as age-inappropriate for your child. Turn on this feature by using the switch at the top of the page. As you can see, this setting works across Windows 10 PCs as well as Windows phones.

By scrolling down you can manually set the age limit for this account, regardless of the age of your child. So for instance if you choose games age appropriate for 7 year olds, your child's account will only be able to download and play games rated for children aged seven and under.

Like all Family safety settings, these restrictions are not infallible. Games obtained outside the Windows store may ignore these restrictions, for instance.

Screen time:- Screen time is a great feature to make sure your children are getting the appropriate sleep and not sneaking an extra go on their PCs behind your back. Using this feature you can limit total screen time as well as control when your child is allowed to use your Windows 10 device. Figure 39.8 shows the screen time settings.

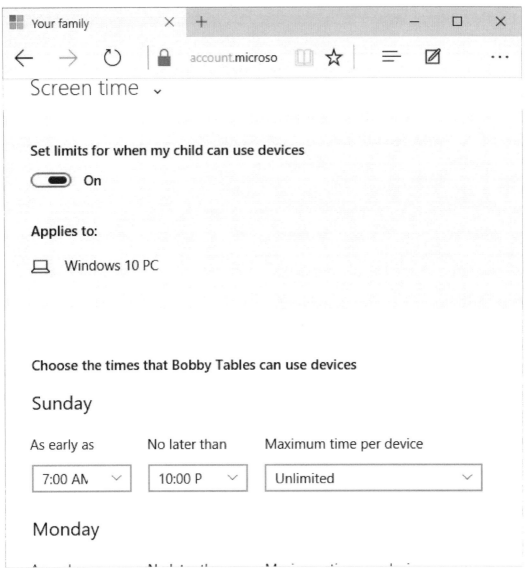

Figure 39.8 – Setting screen time restrictions

Turn on screen time limits by using the switch at the top of the page. You can then set limits for each day. For instance you could stipulate that your child cannot use the PC after 10PM Sunday to Thursday, but give them an extra hour on Friday and Saturday. By using the Maximum time per device setting you can also prevent them from clocking up too many hours on their favourite video games.

That's all you need to know to set up and use Family safety on your Windows 10 PC. As with any parental control tool, Family safety can only do so much to protect your children online. For younger children especially, there really is no substitute for personally supervising their use of your computers and devices.

Lesson 40 – Updating your PC

Keeping your Windows 10 PC up to date is essential if you want to stay ahead of hackers and security threats. New updates improve the security and stability of your operating system and should be applied as soon as they are available. Updates in Windows 10 have gone through some quite radical changes, not all for the better in our opinion, but the updating process is easier than ever.

40.1 – Manually checking for updates

Windows 10 downloads and installs updates for you automatically. To manually check for updates or to configure updates on a Windows 10 PC, open the Start menu or Start screen and click on "Settings", or swipe your finger in from the right on a touch screen and tap on "All settings". The window shown in figure 40.1 should then appear.

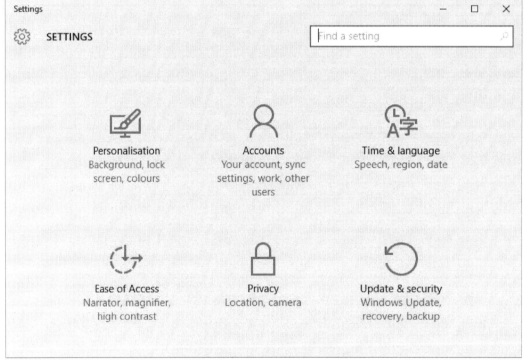

Figure 40.1 – Settings app

If the window that appears on your PC doesn't look like the one shown in figure 40.1, click or tap on the gear shaped icon at the top left of the window, this will immediately return you to the settings window as shown in figure 40.1.

From the options presented in the window, navigate to "Update & security". If you can't see Update & security, you may need to scroll the window down. Once you select Update & security, make sure that "Windows Update" is selected from the options on the left of the window. A window similar to the one shown in figure 40.2 will then be displayed.

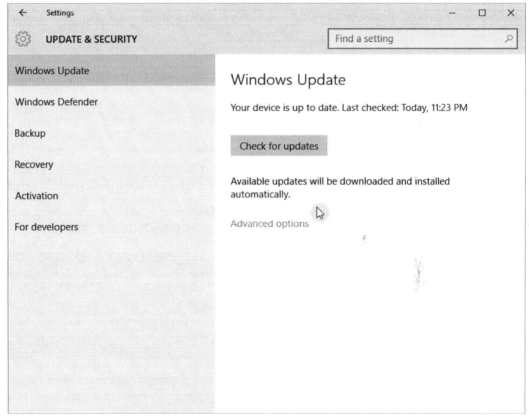

Figure 40.2 – Manually checking for updates

Since Windows automatically downloads updates for you, you may find that the window that appears on your PC looks more like the one shown in figure 40.4. If so, skip ahead and complete installation of your updates, then come back here to learn how to manually check for updates.

To check for updates, click on the "Check for updates" button.

If Windows finds any updates it will start to download and install them automatically. Unlike previous versions of Windows, there's no opportunity to select just the updates you want to install. While it's rare that you need to do this, it can help with troubleshooting, so it's disappointing that this option was removed. Figure 40.3 shows an update being installed.

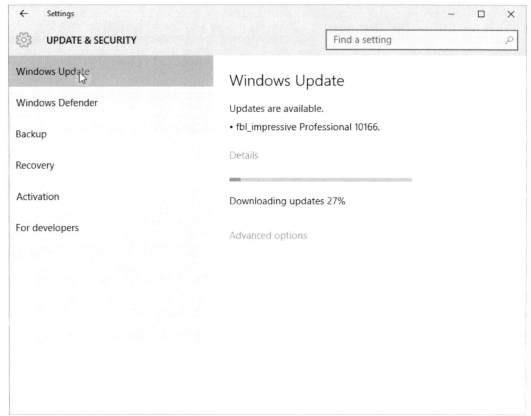

Figure 40.3 – Downloading an update

When an update has downloaded and installed, you will occasionally be required to restart your PC to finish installation. Figure 40.4 shows an example of this.

Figure 40.4 – Scheduling a restart

Windows will then help you schedule a convenient time to reboot your PC. As you can see in figure 40.4, Windows will suggest a time. By scrolling down in the window you can set your own schedule or simply click the "Restart now" button to complete the update process immediately.

40.2 – Advanced update options

In figures 40.2 and 40.3 we can see the "Advanced options" link. Click on this link to access the advanced options for Windows 10 updates. Figure 40.5 shows these options.

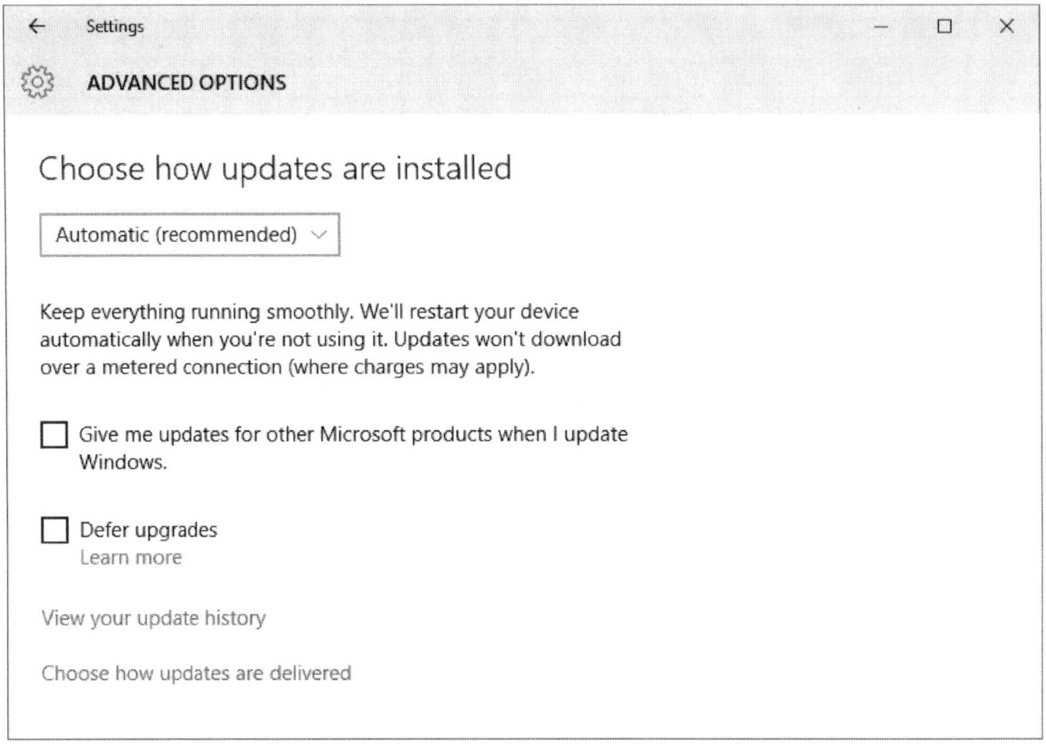

Figure 40.5 – Advanced update options

At the top of the window we can choose how updates are installed. In Windows 10, we can only choose between "Automatic" and "Notify to schedule restart". The only difference between the two options is that Automatic will automatically schedule a time and restart your PC, while "Notify to schedule restart" will pop up a notification and ask you to manually schedule a restart instead.

This option "Give me updates for other Microsoft products when I update Windows" is recommended. This keeps your other Microsoft software, such as office, up to date too.

If you're running Windows 10 professional or enterprise, you will also see the option "Defer upgrades". This option was added by Microsoft so that corporate users could hold off on new upgraded builds until they had chance to test their business critical software. This option is not available for home users and does NOT defer security updates.

You can view the history of the updates that have been installed on your PC by clicking the "View your update history" link.

Finally the "Choose how updates are delivered" option is new in Windows 10. This setting has some interesting options, figure 40.6 shows what happens when you click on it.

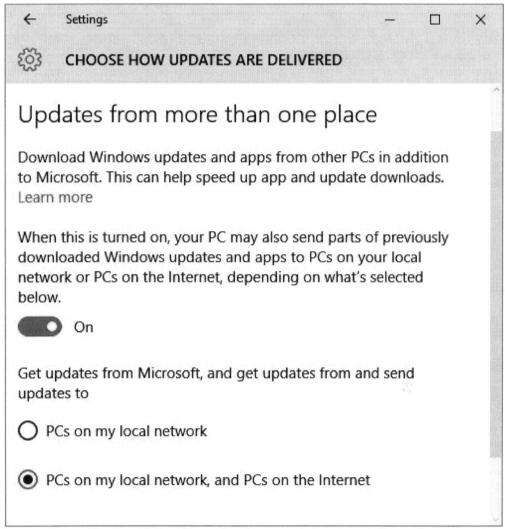

Figure 40.6 – Choosing how updates are delivered

In the past, all your Windows updates came directly from Microsoft servers on the internet, but in Windows 10, Microsoft are trying something new. To speed up the process, you can now download updates not only from Microsoft directly, but also from other PCs in your home or even on the internet. So for example, if someone geographically near to you has already patched their PC, Windows could download some of the updates from them, rather than having to get them from Microsoft.

What's to stop hackers hijacking this process and loading updates with malware? Sophisticated file verification and hashing software will ensure that the updates have not been tampered with, nevertheless you can opt out of this system if you're concerned, or limit it to just PCs in your house (PCs on my local network), it's up to you.

That's all there is to updates in Windows 10. There's some positive changes to be sure, but we're not looking forward to troubleshooting problematic updates now that we can't select which ones to install individually. Just three more lessons in our Windows system and security chapter now, then it is on to some more fun topics.

Lesson 41 – Privacy Options

Even more so than Windows 8, Windows 10 has been designed to work with Microsoft's various online and cloud based services. This has had the side effect of making the privacy options in the operating system even more complicated than before. While services like OneDrive and Cortana are convenient, you should carefully consider exactly what information you and your family put into your PCs. You should also keep in mind where you let that information end up and who you trust to safeguard it. In this lesson, we are going to take a brief look at the Windows 10 privacy options and discuss some of the most important ones.

41.1 – Accessing privacy options

To access the privacy options in Windows 10, we need to open the Settings app. Just like when we checked for updates in lesson 40.1, open the Start menu or Start screen and click on "Settings", or swipe your finger in from the right on a touch screen and tap on "All settings". If the window that now appears on your PC doesn't look like the one shown in figure 40.1, click or tap on the gear shaped icon at the top left of the window, this will immediately return you to the settings window as shown in figure 40.1.

This time however, instead of selecting "Update & security" choose "Privacy". Again, you may need to scroll the window down to find the setting. Figure 41.1 shows the privacy settings window.

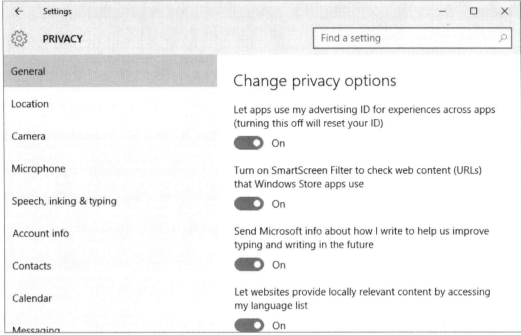

Figure 41.1 – There are now thirteen different categories of privacy options

There are now no less than thirteen different sections that all contain options relating to your privacy. We will start at the beginning with the options contained under the "General" category.

41.2 – General privacy settings

Click or tap on the "General" option to access the general privacy options for a Windows 10 machine. Figure 41.2 shows the resulting options.

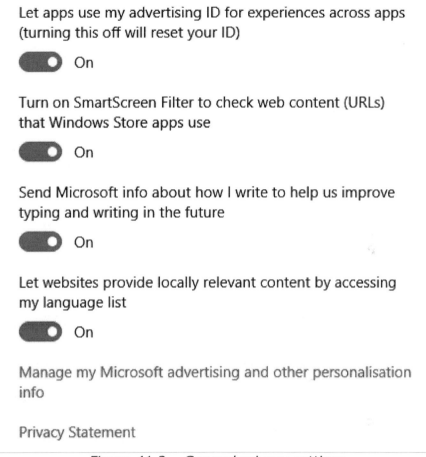

Figure 41.2 – General privacy settings

There are four options available under general privacy settings.

Let apps use my advertising ID for experiences across apps:- Many apps in Windows 10 are supported by ads. By leaving this setting on, you let advertisers tailor the adverts more specifically to you, based on what you do with your Microsoft account. If you play Xbox games often, for instance, you may see more adverts for other games. This data is supposedly anonymous, but if you consider this to be an invasion of your privacy, turn this setting off. You will still see ads in apps with this setting off, but they won't use this extra data to tailor them to you.

Turn on SmartScreen Filter to check web content (URL's) that Windows Store apps use:- This option extends Microsoft Edge's smart screen filter to also inspect any download content that might appear in a Trusted Windows Store app. Usually this is a good idea, since it can stop an app from downloading data from some malicious internet sites. This does mean, however, anonymously submitting to Microsoft for analysis all pages the app is visiting.

Send Microsoft info about how I write to help us improve typing and writing in the future:- With this option on, Windows will send some information back to Microsoft based on what you type or write (on a suitable touch screen with a stylus) into the PC and use it to improve text completion suggestions. This could mean sending Microsoft significant chunks of text that you type into the PC and of course you have no real idea what is transmitted and what isn't.

Let websites provide locally relevant content by accessing my language list:- This is, in basic terms, a long winded way of saying "can a website look at my language list to see what country I am in?". Even with this option off, websites you visit have other ways of determining a rough geographic location for their visitors.

Finally, you can view your Microsoft advertising preferences (these affect all the Microsoft services you use with your account) and view Microsoft's privacy policy in full by using the links at the bottom of the screen.

41.3 – Location privacy settings

Select "Location" from the menu shown in figure 41.1 to view the location privacy settings. Figure 41.3 shows some of these options.

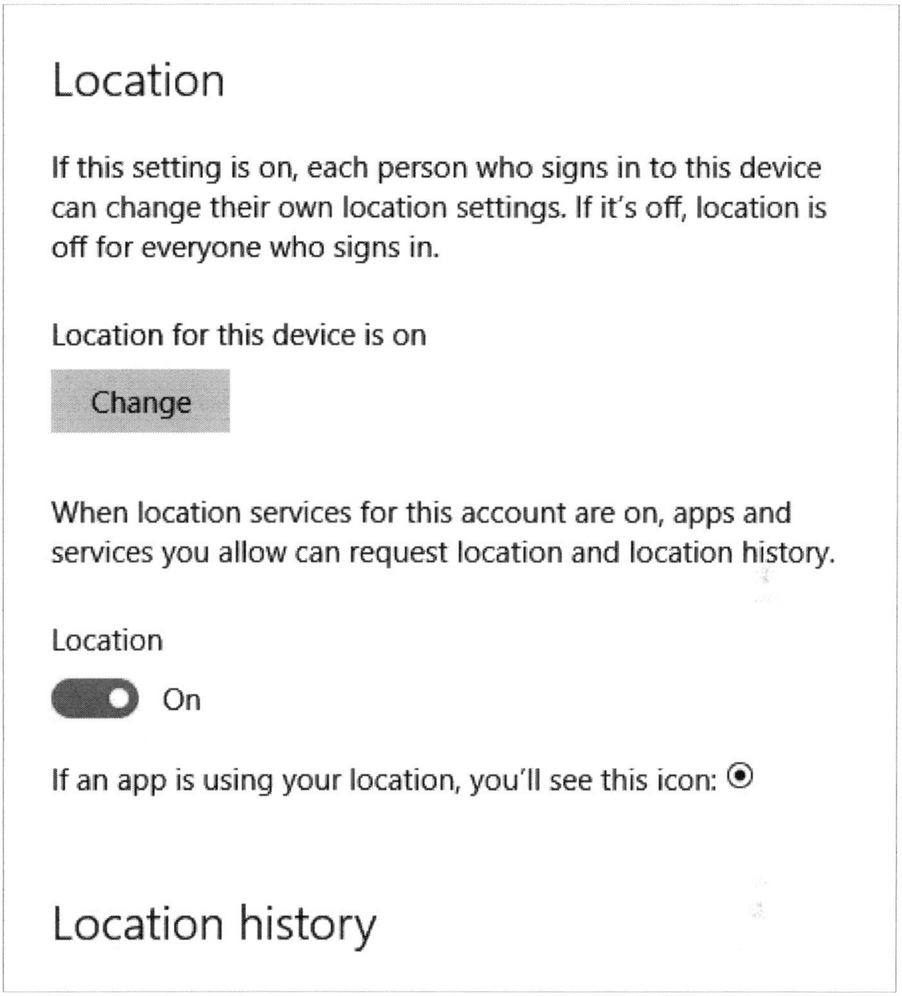

Figure 41.3 – Location privacy options

Location privacy options have got a little more complex in Windows 10. These settings mainly effect portable PCs, but remember, even without a GPS device, you can establish a rough but often surprisingly accurate geographic location by checking the devices internet connection or the cellular network connection.

Location tracking can be a controversial feature. It can feel a little Orwellian having your laptop or tablet track where you are, but if it does, it can use that information to tailor search results, weather forecasts and other data.

At the top of the options you can use the button to toggle all location services on or off for all users of this PC. To do this you will need to be signed in with an administrator account.

The "Location" switch below turns location services off or on for the current user account. Under "Location History" you can click the "Clear" button to clear the list of recently visited locations from your computer.

As with Windows 8, you can enable or disable location information on a per-app basis. So for instance if you had downloaded an app that requested to know your location for no good reason, you could deny the app while still allowing the apps you trust to use your location.

Under "Choose apps that can use my location", you can see which apps are allowed to use your location. To access these settings, simply scroll down in the location privacy options. Figure 41.4 shows an example.

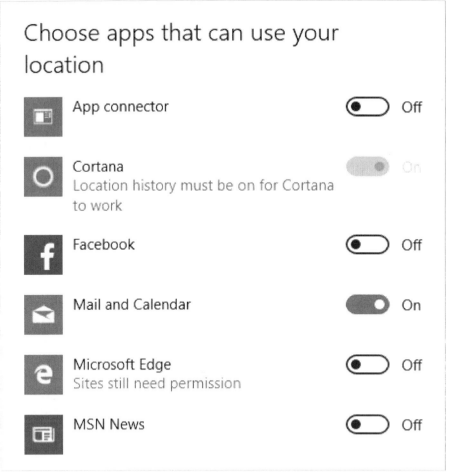

Figure 41.4 – Managing app permissions for location services

When a new app is installed, this setting will be set to "Off" automatically. The first time an app wants to use your location, Windows will ask you for permission. If you deny an application permission and later change your mind, you will need to access these settings to change the permissions.

Notice that some apps (e.g Cortana) cannot function without these permissions, so the only way to disable location services in these apps is to stop using them.

You can also temporarily disable location services at any time by opening the Action Centre and clicking or tapping the "Location" button.

41.4 – Camera and Microphone

The next two options, camera and microphone, allow you to mange which apps can access these devices. An app that can access your microphone for instance can listen to what you say and therefore could be a privacy concern. These options let you control which, if any, apps can access these devices. Each section works in the same way. You can turn off access to the peripheral entirely, or manage which apps have permission, in exactly the same way as managing which apps can use the location services.

41.5 – Speech, inking and typing

Figure 41.5 shows the options available in the speech, inking and typing section.

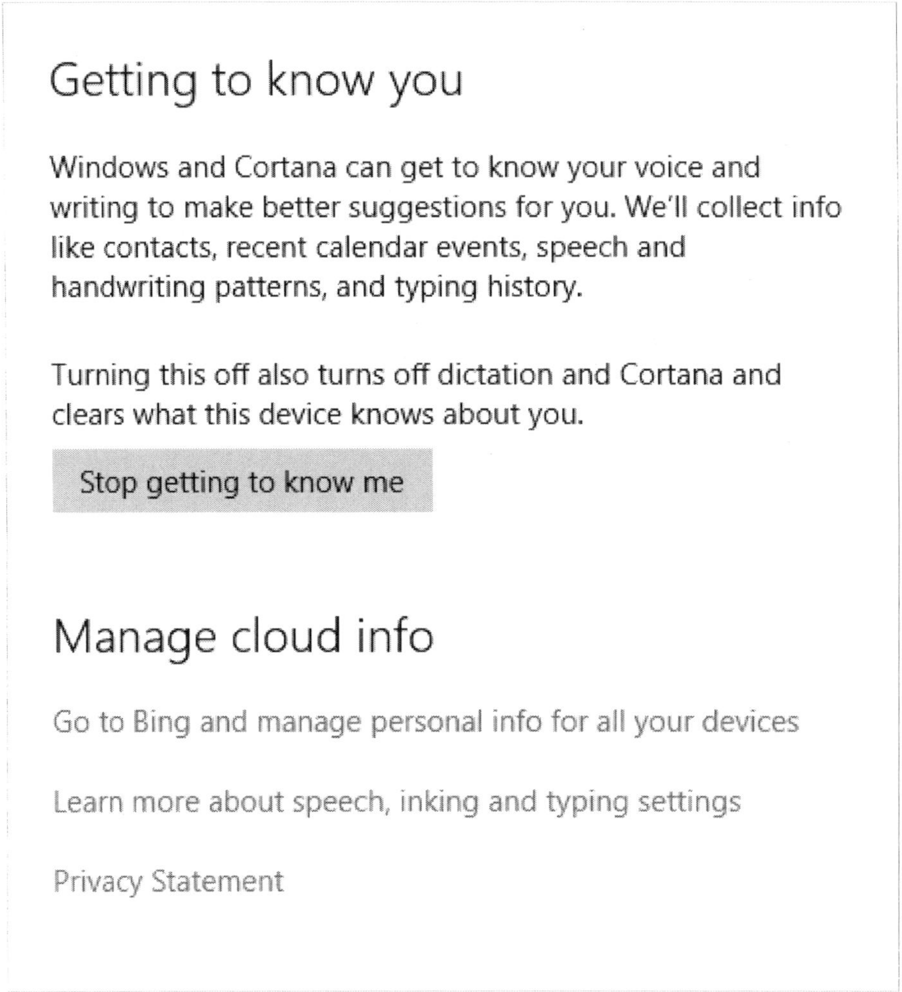

Getting to know you

Windows and Cortana can get to know your voice and writing to make better suggestions for you. We'll collect info like contacts, recent calendar events, speech and handwriting patterns, and typing history.

Turning this off also turns off dictation and Cortana and clears what this device knows about you.

Stop getting to know me

Manage cloud info

Go to Bing and manage personal info for all your devices

Learn more about speech, inking and typing settings

Privacy Statement

Figure 41.5 – Microsoft wants to get to know you

New in Windows 10 is this "Getting to know you" system, which aims to improve search results based on your online activities, speech and handwriting patterns and other data. It does sound a little creepy, but you could simply consider it similar to what a real life personal assistant would do (though if your PA decided to store this data in a big database in the cloud, like Windows does, you might be tempted to fire him).

You can turn this off by clicking the "Stop getting to know me" button. Don't worry, Windows 10 doesn't have feelings, so you can't hurt them. Similarly, if you want to check what Microsoft has been logging about you across all your devices, click on the "Go to Bing and manage personal info for all your devices" link.

41.6 – Account Info privacy options

Figure 41.6 shows the options available under "Account Info".

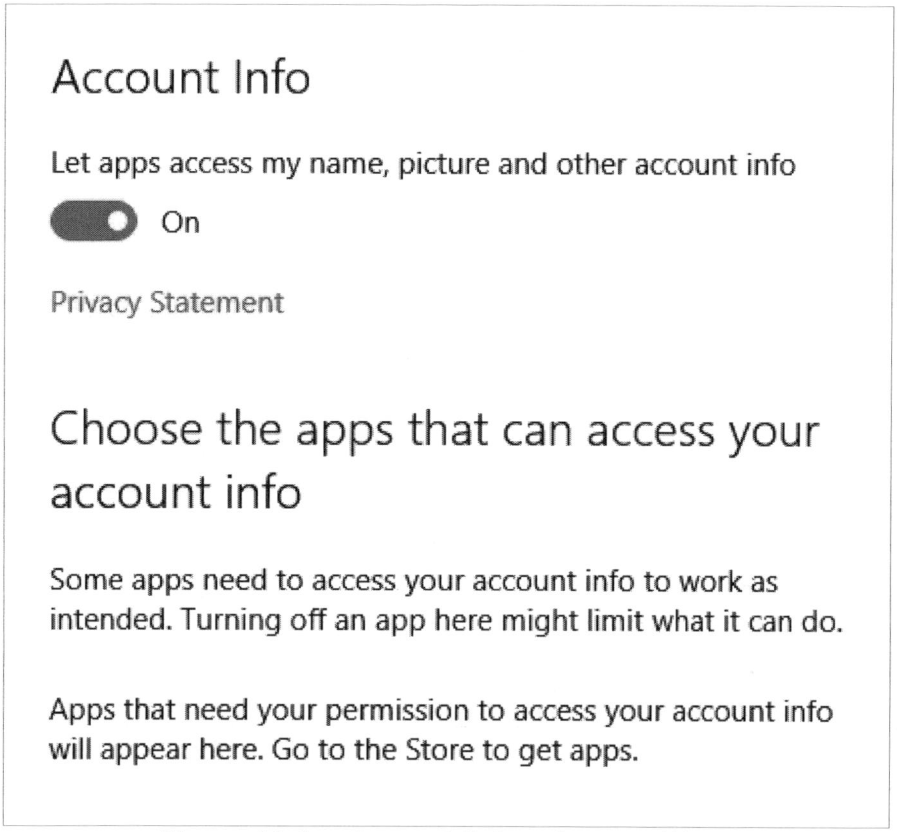

Figure 41.6 – Account Info privacy settings

Typically your account info includes your name, user name and your picture. You can change your account picture at any time by accessing the account settings (see lesson 37.1) and clicking on "Your account".

Apps might want to use this information, for instance a social networking app might use it when posting on your behalf. If you don't want this to happen, ensure this option is turned off. If you have any apps that need to access your account, they will be listed in this section. As with other privacy settings, you can then turn them off or on individually as necessary.

41.7 – Contacts, Calendar, Messaging and Radios

We've grouped the next four sections together because they each work in the same way. Like with location services, for instance, you can turn off access globally to these peripherals or features or you can manage which apps have access. "Contacts" and "Calendar" allow apps to view or manage your contacts list or your calendar and its appointments respectively. "Messaging" controls which apps can access your e-mail or SMS messages. "Radios" controls which apps can access devices such as Bluetooth radios that your Windows PC may have.

41.8 – Other devices

The other devices section contains some settings that let you control how third party devices can interact with your PC. First up we can configure settings for beacons. Figure 41.7 shows these settings.

Figure 41.7 – Settings for beacons and similar devices

So what are beacons exactly? This technology is relatively new. One way it's used is to push information to a device when you're in proximity of something. Perhaps you pass your favourite store and they have an offer on they want to tell you about. If you have the appropriate app on your mobile device and you allow beacons, this information can then be sent to you. Another potential use is for tourism. Perhaps you want to explore the historic quarter of the city. With beacon technology, you could receive alerts about the history of your current location and suggestions for related places to visit.

Further down in the Other devices section we can find the trusted devices section. Figure 41.8 shows these settings.

Figure 41.8 – Managing trusted devices

A trusted device could be a games console like the Xbox One. You can stream video from your PC to your Xbox One console, for instance. When using this device, you set it to trusted so that you don't need your Microsoft account password every time you turn it on and want to play. There are no trusted devices connected to the PC shown in figure 41.8. If there were, we could allow our apps to use them too.

You can also allow certain trusted apps full access to your computers hard drive or other hardware. In this case the Phone Companion app wants full access. Granting this access should be fine, but usually Trusted Windows Store apps only need access to your documents folder, not the entire PC file system. Like the other privacy settings we've seen you can turn off access for all apps with the toggle control here or manage individual apps at the bottom of the window.

41.9 – Feedback and diagnostics

The feedback and diagnostics section lets you control which information is sent to Microsoft in the event that Windows crashes or encounters an unexpected error. You can change how frequently Windows asks for your feedback and enable or disable diagnostic data. Obviously, diagnostic data is very valuable to Microsoft as it helps them track down bugs and other problems in the operating system.

41.10 – Background apps

Certain apps can run in the background on your device. Maybe a social networking app wants to stay running so it can notify you as soon as someone posts a new cat video. You can manage which apps are allowed to run in the background from this page. The settings work exactly like the other sections, simply enable or disable apps as you see fit.

41.11 – Desktop software and privacy

Remember that these settings apply to Trusted Windows Store applications only. Desktop software can ignore these settings and spyware that runs in desktop mode will not pay any attention to how you configure your privacy settings here. To help combat against spyware, we will be looking at the new improved Windows Defender in lesson 43. We also discuss other PC privacy related issues on Top-Windows-Tutorials.com, see http://www.top-windows-tutorials.com/PC-Privacy.html

Phew! That covers the Windows 10 privacy options in a nutshell. Protecting your privacy in this heavily connected digital age is a difficult task that seemingly keeps getting more complex. Even if it's not much fun, Its always worth taking a moment to review the privacy settings for Windows and all the online services you use.

Lesson 42 – Windows Firewall

The job of a firewall is to monitor and restrict the internet traffic flowing in and out of your computer. There are two types of firewall that home users typically use. Software firewalls, like the Windows 10 firewall, are programs that run on your computer. Hardware firewalls are physical items that plug between your internet connection and your PC. Typically home users will buy a router with an inbuilt firewall. We discuss this in lesson 52.3.

42.1 – About the Windows 10 firewall

The Windows 10 firewall provides a basic level of protection against hackers and malware. To access the firewall settings, search for "windows firewall" on the search bar and click on the "Windows Firewall" icon that then appears. Figure 42.1 shows the window that will then be displayed.

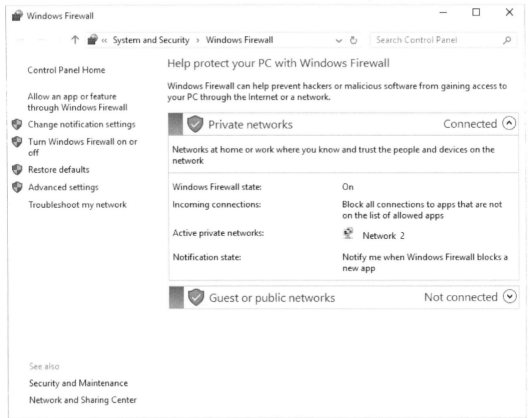

Figure 42.1 – The basic configuration window for the Windows Firewall

In Windows 10, there are two types of network configuration you might typically connect to. Private networks and Guest or public networks. Private networks are networks like your network at home, where you can reasonably trust most people and devices using the network, as long as you have secured your internet connection of course.

Guest networks are networks where you cannot be certain of security, for instance a public Wi-Fi access point, including access points where you need a password, such as at a hotel. Using Guest networks is more risky, since they are open to attack or interception from other users in range or could be controlled by hackers or malicious users themselves.

In figure 40.1 we can see that for "Private networks", Windows Firewall is on (Windows Firewall state: On). We can also see that incoming connections will be blocked unless the program is on the list of allowed programs.

Our wired network, called "Network 2" is listed next to "Active private networks". Looking below to "Notification state" we can see that if Windows Firewall blocks a program it will notify us.

To view settings for Guest or public networks, click on the downward pointing arrow button next to "Guest or public networks". Figure 42.2 shows the resulting window.

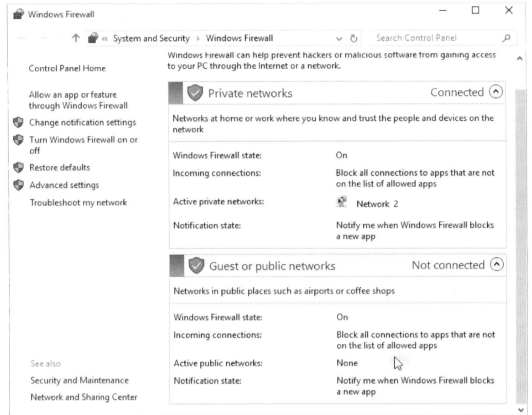

Figure 42.2 – Viewing the public network settings for Windows Firewall

By default, the basic settings for public networks are exactly the same as for private networks. One of the advantages of the Windows 10 firewall for power users is the fact that the firewall can be configured for different network connections. So, if you connect while you're out at a coffee shop, but you have a network at home, you are not restricted to one firewall configuration for them both.

42.2 – Changing firewall settings

To change firewall settings, click on "Change notification settings" from the options on the left. Figure 42.3 shows the window which now appears.

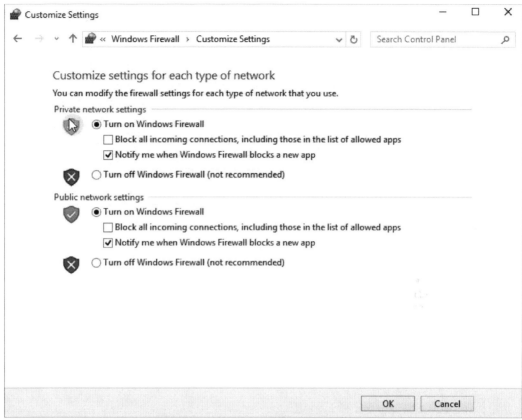

Figure 42.3 – Customising basic firewall settings for each type of network

From this window we can tweak the firewall settings for each connection type. We might decide to block all incoming connections when we are on a public network and doing so does not affect our settings for our private network.

It is also possible to turn the Windows Firewall off entirely, by selecting the option next to the red shield icon. We do not recommend turning the firewall off unless you have a third party firewall to use instead, but it might occasionally be necessary for troubleshooting purposes.

When you are done changing settings, click on "OK". You will then be returned to the previous window.

42.3 – Windows Firewall with Advanced Security

You may notice another icon while working with your PC or following this tutorial for something called **"Windows Firewall with Advanced**

Security". Clicking on this item will open up some advanced settings for the Windows Firewall. We can also access these same advanced firewall settings simply by clicking "Advanced settings" from the options on the left in figure 42.1. The advanced settings are really only for IT experts and so we won't be covering them in this Superguide.

42.4 – Third party firewalls

The Windows 10 firewall lacks many of the features of the more advanced third party firewalls. Firewalls such as ESET Personal Firewall or Zone Alarm contain all the functionality of the Windows firewall and include advanced network packet filtering and intrusion detection mechanisms. Is this extra protection necessary? It is debatable, but many users prefer a third party firewall over the Windows Firewall, even in Windows 10. Figure 42.4 shows a typical third party firewall alert.

Figure 42.4 – A typical third party firewall alert message

In the picture, we can see that individual programs need to ask for access to the internet. This is true in the Windows firewall and in most third party firewalls. In this system, a malicious program should be intercepted before it could send out any information from your computer. You will see similar alerts from Windows Firewall under certain circumstances too. If you are considering a third party firewall, be sure to visit Top-Windows-Tutorials.com for information on our recommended firewall software packages.

That concludes our lesson on the Windows Firewall. You are becoming quite the security expert now. Next lesson we will finish our chapter on system security by discussing the Windows Defender program.

Lesson 43 – Windows Defender

Windows 8 was the first version of Windows to come with an antivirus solution pre-installed. While Windows Defender was present in previous versions of Windows, in Windows 8 and Windows 10, Windows Defender includes anti-virus capabilities too, while the older versions simply focused on anti-spyware. In this lesson we will take a brief tour of Windows Defender.

43.1 – What is antivirus software?

Computer viruses are computer programs (just like everything else that runs on your PC). What makes computer viruses different however is the fact that they are designed to copy themselves throughout your computer's memory or hard drive, or even across the internet. Many computer viruses have malicious components too and may try to cause all sorts of mischief from slowing down your computer to allowing hackers to gain entry and steal confidential data.

Antivirus software is designed to watch for these particular rogue programs and stop them from running and causing whatever brand of mischief they were written for. Historically, Windows has not had the best track record when it comes to security, though this reputation is slowly changing thanks to Microsoft's hard work in this area. Windows is also the most commonly used operating system around the world and this has established it as the favourite target of computer virus designers.

43.2 – Starting Windows Defender

Windows Defender is automatically enabled and doesn't generally need any reconfiguration. It will start with your PC and work in the background. If you need to access the programs interface for any reason, simply search for "windows defender" from the search bar and then click the icon that appears. Figure 43.1 shows the main Windows Defender window.

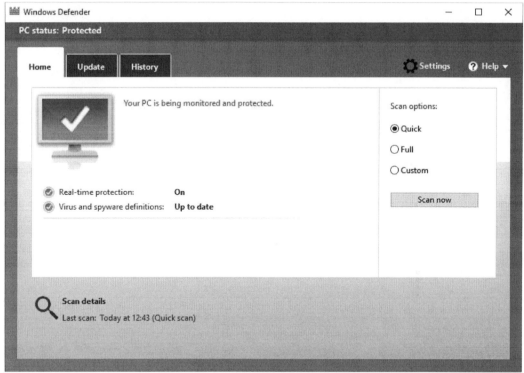

Figure 43.1 – Windows Defender

Figure 43.1 shows Windows Defender running normally. We can see that real time protection is enabled and virus and spyware definitions are up to date. New virus definition updates, which contain updated information about new malware, will download with Windows Update (see lesson 40). To change settings for the program, click on the "Settings" icon near the top right of the window. Figure 43.2 shows the options that will now appear.

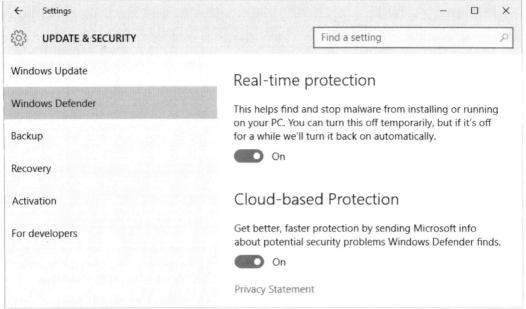

Figure 43.2 – Windows Defender options

43.3 – Windows Defender Options

There are only a few settings you need to be aware of in Windows Defender. In figure 43.2 we can see toggle controls for "Real-time protection" and "Cloud-based protection". With real time protection turned on, files will be scanned as soon as they enter your computer. There's always a small performance penalty with this option, but on a modern PC it's really not noticeable, so we strongly recommend leaving this option on.

When "Cloud-based protection" is turned on, Windows Defender will send data to Microsoft about potential security threats it finds. This data is then used to help improve Windows Defender for everyone. This service was called "The Microsoft Active Protection Service" or "MAPS" in Windows 8.

There are several other settings you can access by scrolling down the list shown in figure 43.2. A related setting to "Cloud-based protection" that's just out of sight in figure 43.2 is the "Sample submission" setting. When this setting is turned on, malware samples can be automatically uploaded to Microsoft so that their security team can analyse them.

There is always a slim chance that some information may be leaked along with the virus samples submitted with the two options detailed here, so keep this in mind when choosing the options.

Finally in this list, we can access the "Exclusions" setting. Occasionally antivirus programs will falsely identify a program as malicious when it is not. In this case, you can add an exception by going to the Exclusions section and clicking on "Add an exclusion". Figure 43.3 illustrates this option.

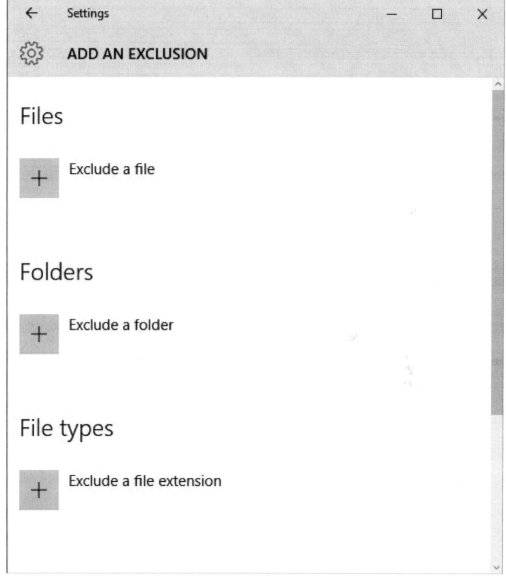

Figure 43.3 – Adding exclusions

In Windows 10 we can add Files, Folders, File types and even Processes (programs that are running) to our exclusion list. To add a file or folder, click on the Plus icon and then simply browse to the directory where your file or folder is stored.

Be careful when adding exclusions, any files you exclude will not be checked for any kind of malware. Do not assume a detected file is a false positive unless you're absolutely certain.

43.4 – Manually scanning your computer

Windows Defender can run a manual scan of your system at any time, just as with most other antivirus packages. Scans are started from the Home tab. In figure 43.1 you may be able to make out the scanning options on the right, they are "Quick", "Full", and "Custom". Quick scan scans the areas on your PC most likely to be targeted by malware, "Full" scans all areas on your PC, except removable devices and "Custom" allows you to choose exactly where to scan. Custom scan can be useful if you want to scan some media that a friend or colleague gave to you, for instance.

To begin a scan, simply choose a scan type and then click on "Scan now". If you choose Custom scan you will then be required to choose the drives or locations you want to scan. Otherwise, you will be sent straight to the window shown in figure 43.4.

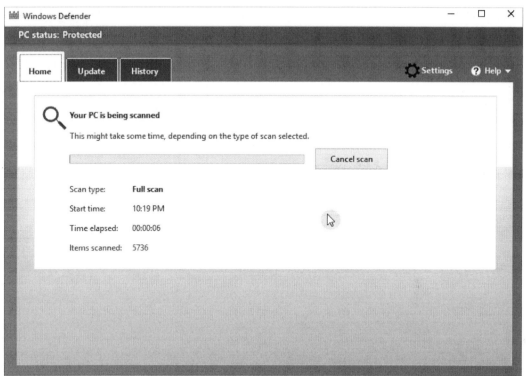

Figure 43.4 – Manually scanning your computer with Windows Defender

The scanning process may take some time, particularly for a full scan. When the scan is complete, you will see the window shown in figure 43.5 if any malware was found.

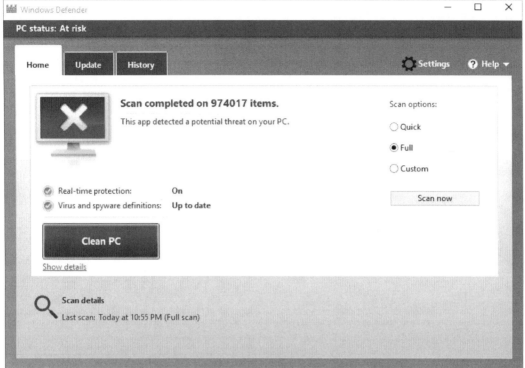

Figure 43.5 – A threat was detected on the PC

Notice how the Windows Defender window in figure 43.5 has turned red, to indicate an active threat on your PC. The program has found a malware sample we placed on the PC as an example. To clean the infection automatically, click on the large "Clean PC" button. Below the button there is a link labelled "Show details". Figure 43.6 shows the window that appears when this is clicked.

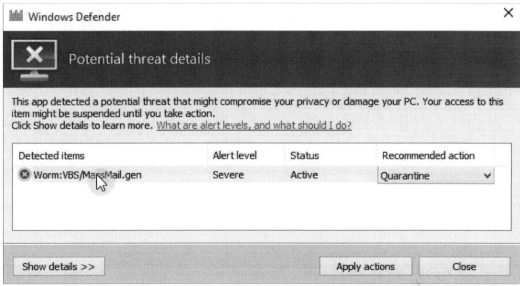

Figure 43.6 – Viewing detected threats

From the window shown in figure 43.6 we can see each individual threat and the recommended action to take to remove it. By clicking one of the detected threats in the list and then clicking on "Show details >>" you can see exactly where the threat was found on your PC. By changing the option under the "Recommended action" column, you can choose either "Remove" or "Quarantine". If you quarantine an infection, it is removed from your PC and stored in a special virus vault where it cannot do any more harm to your system, but you can inspect it. Quarantine is useful for any files you suspect might be false positives, or if you are an expert user and you want to preserve the file for further investigation without risking the security of your PC. You can view any quarantined items by going to the History tab on the main Windows Defender window.

Click on "Apply actions" to remove or quarantine the detected threats from the Window shown in figure 43.6, or simply close the window and use the "Clean PC" button shown in figure 43.5.

43.5 – Automatic scanning

Of course, you don't need to run a scan to detect malware, Windows Defender can detect it in real time. When Windows Defender detects an intrusion, it will notify you immediately. Figure 43.7 shows the notification that will appear.

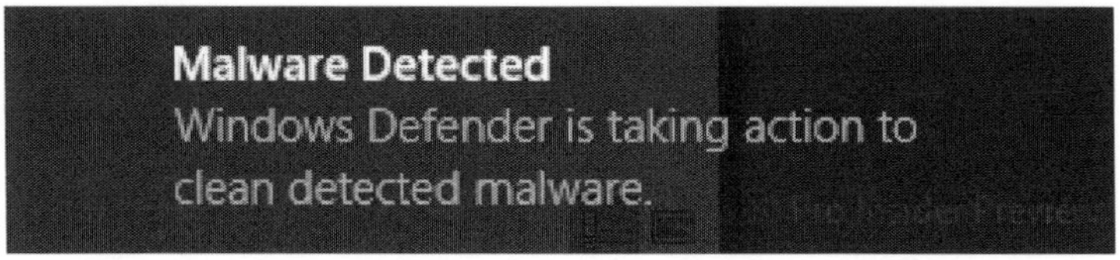

Figure 43.7 – A Windows Defender notification

If you see this notification, don't panic, you don't have a virus, Windows Defender has protected you against one. You can open the programs interface and go to the History tab to get more details about what was detected and removed.

43.6 – Third party antivirus packages

It is great that Windows 10 comes with antivirus software right out of the box, but many users still prefer to use a third-party solution. Third party solutions may integrate other security features too, such as advanced firewalls, web content filtering or e-mail protection. There are dozens of third party antivirus packages available on the market. Some are free, others require a yearly subscription. Traditionally the free antivirus packages have provided a reasonable level of protection, whereas the better paid-for solutions have had better detection rates and less of an impact on system performance. Of course, results vary widely. You can find tutorials for several recommended antivirus packages on our website at http://www.top-windows-tutorials.com/Computer-Viruses-Tutorials.html. AV Comparatives regularly test several anti virus packages, you can find their website at http://www.av-comparatives.org/

Here are a couple of pointers to keep in mind when choosing an antivirus solution.

Avoid little known antivirus packages that use flashy advertising:- There are dozens of fake antivirus packages available through the internet. These packages claim to clear viruses from your computer but actually are a huge security risk in themselves and are often exceptionally difficult to remove. Do not install antivirus software unless you are sure it is legitimate.

Expensive and popular does not always mean the best:- Two of the most popular antivirus solutions, Norton Antivirus and Mcafee have in the past been outperformed by free alternatives such as Avast.

Free is not necessarily bad:- Free antivirus packages like Avast can provide good protection and additional features above and beyond what Windows Defender offers.

That concludes this lesson and also this chapter on computer security. Now that your bits and bytes are secure, we can move on to more exciting topics like customising your PC and installing new software.

Chapter 8 – Your PC Your Way

It will not be long before you want to add your own personal touch to your computer, be it adding some new software or changing the look of the desktop or the lock screen. This chapter is all about making your computer uniquely yours. Yes, it is finally time to leave boring old security behind and have some fun with your new Windows 10 machine!

Lesson 44 – Customising the Mouse

If you have been experiencing difficulty using a mouse (or touch-pad) with your Windows 10 PC, this lesson shows you some ways that you can change the behaviour of the electronic rodent in order to make it easier to use.

In Windows 10, there are actually two places you can tweak mouse settings. If you search for "Mouse" on the search bar and click the "change your mouse settings" result, you will be taken to the Mouse configuration settings within the settings app. However, there is a more in-depth mouse configuration tool we can access. To get to it, search for "mouse" again, but this time choose the "Mouse – Control panel" result. The window shown in figure 44.1 will then appear.

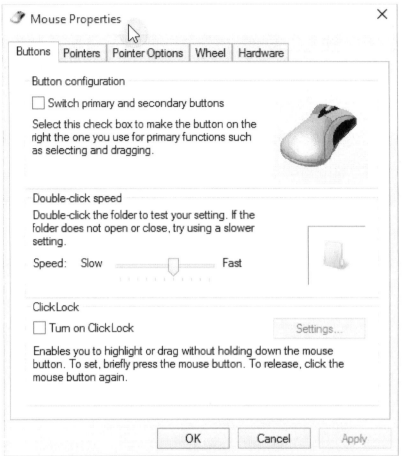

Figure 44.1 – The Mouse Properties window

44.1 – Left handed use and other button options

If you are left handed and place the mouse at the left of the keyboard, you may find it easier to switch the primary and secondary mouse buttons. This makes the mouse much easier and more natural to use if you are a left handed user. Just remember that when this guide talks about 'right clicking', it is referring to the mouse in the default configuration.

To switch primary and secondary (left and right) mouse buttons, select the box labelled "Switch primary and secondary buttons".

If you have issues with double clicking, you can change the double click speed using the sliding control in the middle of the window. If you make the double click speed too slow you may end up double clicking by accident, so be sure to try out your new setting on the practice folder on the right.

If you find dragging icons difficult, you can use "ClickLock". With this setting, you only need to hold down your mouse button for a second to "lock" it down, then hold it for a second again to release it.

Don't forget to click "Apply" when you are done changing the options.

44.2 – Pointers and pointer options

If you have difficulty seeing the mouse pointer, it is possible to choose a larger pointer scheme. Firstly, click on the "Pointers" tab at the top of the Mouse Properties window. Figure 44.2 shows the window which will then open.

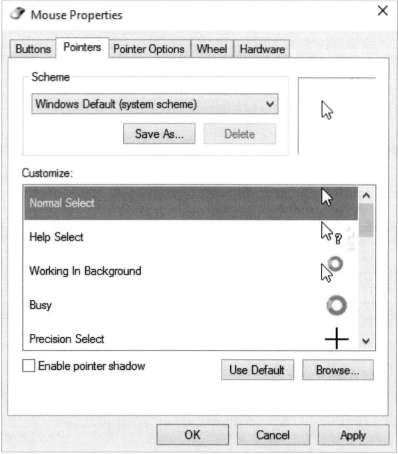

Figure 44.2 – Changing mouse pointers

Using the drop down box at the top of the window, you can choose from a range of Windows pointer schemes. Some, such as the extra large ones, are useful for people who have difficulty seeing smaller pointers.

If you like, you can customise each individual pointer by using the "Customise" box in the middle of the window. Click on a pointer type you want to change and then click "Browse…" to choose a new pointer or "Use Default" to reset the selection back to default.

Once you have chosen a pointer scheme, don't forget to click "Apply" to start using it. There are more pointer options you can configure on the "Pointer Options" tab. Figure 44.3 shows this tab.

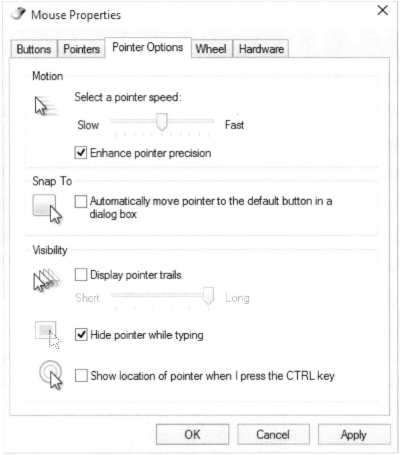

Figure 44.3 – Pointer options

If you find the mouse pointer moves across the screen too quickly, you can adjust its speed using the sliding control under "Motion" at the top of the window. Changes you make on this control take effect immediately, so you can see for yourself if the new speed is more suitable.

The "Snap To" option below the Motion control makes the mouse pointer automatically jump to buttons in windows. This can save some time but beginners usually find this confusing, so we do not recommend this.

Under "Visibility", there are three options. Choosing "Display pointer trails" makes a trail follow your mouse pointer as you move it around the screen. The trail looks like a gang of other mouse pointers relentlessly pursuing the pointer as it cruises around the screen. This makes it easier for some users to spot the mouse pointer as it moves. You can also change the length of the trail by using the sliding control underneath the tick/check box.

Below the pointer trails option is the "Hide pointer while typing" option, this is fairly self explanatory, if you do not want the pointer distracting you while typing, make sure this option is enabled.

If you still have trouble spotting the mouse pointer, select the option "Show location of pointer when I press the CTRL key." The CTRL or Control key is the key in the bottom left and bottom right of the keyboard. It does not matter which one you use. When this option is enabled, a circle will appear around your mouse pointer when you press Control, helping you locate it on the screen.

44.3 – Mouse wheel options

Some mice have a wheel between their two buttons. If you are using a laptop with a touch pad or a mouse without a wheel this will not be relevant to you. If your mouse has a wheel, you can alter the behaviour of the mouse wheel on the Wheel tab. Figure 44.4 shows the Wheel tab.

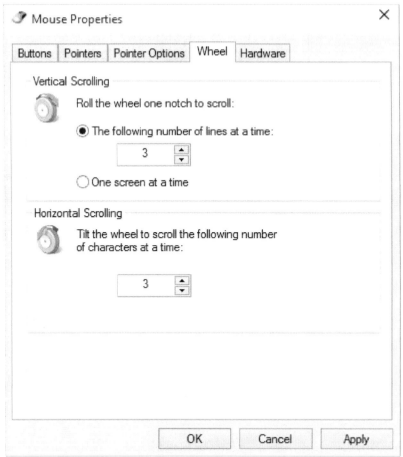

Figure 44.4 – Setting options for the mouse wheel

If your mouse has a wheel, you can use the wheel to scroll up and down text in a document or web page. By default, one click of the wheel will scroll down three lines of text.

Some mouse wheels move left to right too, though these are rare and most only go up and down. If your wheel moves left and right, you can set the amount of characters to scroll with each click by changing the value in the bottom half of the window.

That concludes our lesson on mouse properties. Hopefully, if you have been struggling to master the mouse, this lesson will have made things a little easier for you. In the next lesson, we will discuss customisation options for tiles and other elements on the Start menu or screen.

Lesson 45 – Customising Start

Do you prefer a Start menu or a Start screen? In Windows 10 you can have either and there are lots of customisations you can perform too. In this lesson we are going to look at several ways you can customise the Start menu or Start screen.

45.1 – Resizing the Start menu

We will start with the basics and look at the Start menu running in Desktop mode. When you open the Start menu in Windows 10, you can resize it just like resizing a window (see lesson 5.2). The Start menu can be resized both horizontally and vertically. Figure 45.1 shows a Start menu that has been resized horizontally.

Figure 45.1 – A resized Start menu

45.2 – Adding and removing tiles

On the right of the Windows 10 Start menu we can find the tiles. You can customise these tiles by moving them and pinning and unpinning them. To move a tile, first click on it with your mouse and hold the mouse button down, or press and hold your finger over it on a touch screen. Now, move your mouse pointer or your finger and you will drag the tile. Simply drag the selected tile anywhere you want it and let go, it will then snap into place.

If you no longer want a tile on your Start menu, you can remove it by right clicking on it and choosing "Unpin from Start" (we'll show you how to do this on a touch screen at the end of the lesson, section 45.6). This does not delete the app from your PC, you could still launch it by searching for it, it just removes the tile from the Start screen. Figure 45.2 shows an example of this.

Figure 45.2 – Unpin from Start and other right click options

If you want to add a tile to your Start menu, first search for the app you want to add using the search bar. Then, right click the search result (or tap and hold with your finger on a touch screen) and choose "Pin to Start". The tile for that app will then appear on the right of the Start menu. You can add any kind of app in this manner, but only Trusted Windows Store apps can have live tiles with the constantly changing pictures or information.

45.3 – Resizing and grouping tiles

Have you noticed how some tiles are bigger than others? For Trusted Windows Store apps you can change the size of the app tile. In figure 45.2 we can see the "Resize" option on the right click menu. Move your mouse pointer over this option and a sub-menu will open. You can then choose between "Small", "Medium", "Wide" and for some tiles "Large". Figure 45.3 shows these different sizes.

Figure 45.3 – Tile sizes

On the top row in figure 45.3 we can see the small and medium sizes. Below that, the Microsoft Edge tile is set to "Wide" size. Finally, on the bottom row, the weather app tile is set to "Large" size. Not all apps support large size.

You may have noticed that some groups of tiles on your Start menu have names. For instance in figure 45.2 we can see that the group of tiles is labelled as "Play and explore". You can name or rename any group of tiles by hovering your mouse over the name and then clicking the icon that looks like two horizontal lines. Figure 45.4 shows an example.

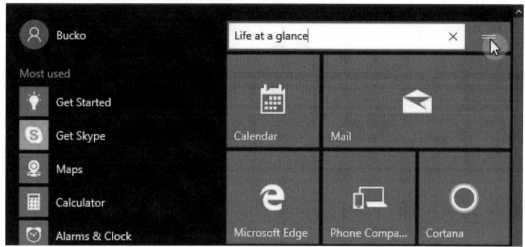

Figure 45.4 – Click the icon shown here under the pointer to rename a group

Simply click the icon shown in figure 45.4 and then type any name you like. Press enter when you are done and the new name will be set.

45.4 – Further Start menu customisations

There are some further customisations we can make to the Start menu. To access these settings, search for "start settings" on the search bar and then click the icon that appears in the results under "Settings". The window shown in figure 45.5 will then be displayed.

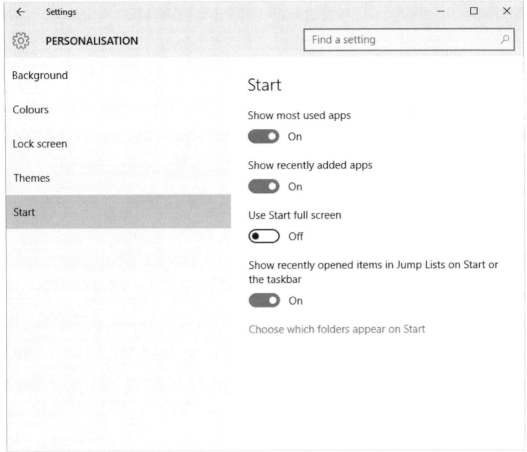

Figure 45.5 – Start menu personalisation options

In the window shown in figure 45.5 you can see various options relating to the Start menu. The top-most options allow you to toggle most used and recently added apps on or off. These sections appear on the left of the Start menu. You can see "Most used" near the top left in figure 45.2.

You can also turn off jump lists. We talked about jump lists on the taskbar in lesson 20 but they appear on the Start menu too. Notice the little arrow (>) next to File Explorer in figure 45.2. That arrow indicates that you can open a jump list and these typically work just like they do on the taskbar.

If you want to, you can go back to a Windows 8 style Start screen by using the "Use Start full screen" option. This is the default setting for Tablet mode, but by enabling this option you will switch to a Start screen in desktop mode too. There are a few key differences between the Start screen and the Start menu, so refer to lesson 8.2 if you want to use the Start screen.

Near the bottom of the window shown in figure 45.5 you can see the option "Choose which folders appear on Start". By clicking this option you can add additional folders to the left hand part of the Start menu. Figure 45.6 shows some of the available options.

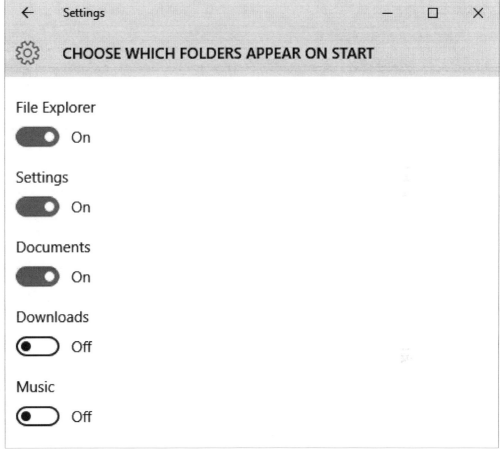

Figure 45.6 – Adding folders to Start

In figure 45.6 the user has turned on the "Documents" folder. When the Start menu is next opened, it will appear like the one shown in figure 45.7. As you can see, the Documents folder is under the mouse pointer.

Figure 45.7 – Start menu with added Documents folder.

45.5 – Start colour and appearance

If you navigate back to the window shown in figure 45.5 and then click on the "Colours" option from the menu on the left, you can access some settings that change the appearance of the Start menu or screen. You will need to scroll to the very bottom of this window. Figure 45.8 shows the options you will then find.

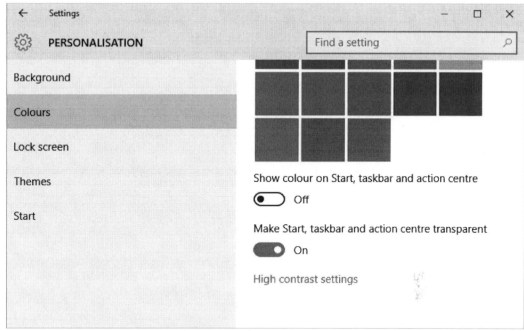

Figure 45.8 – Colour and appearance options for Start

In figure 45.8 you should be able to make out a selection of colours. If you turn on "Show colour on Start, taskbar and action centre", you can pick a colour here and the Start menu, taskbar and Action Centre will change colour to match.

Below that option is the option to "Make start, taskbar and action centre transparent". Notice in figure 45.7 particularly, you may be able to make out the blurred image of a window underneath the Start menu. If you turn this option off, the Start menu will be a solid colour instead and you will not be able to see the desktop or any windows through it.

45.6 – Touch screen differences

When using a touch screen, customising the Start screen or menu works for the most part in the same way, but there are a few key differences. When you tap and hold on a tile, for instance, you can drag it and reposition it just like with the mouse. However, on a touch screen two extra icons will appear when you tap and hold on a tile. Figure 45.9 shows these new icons.

Figure 45.9 – Customising tiles on a touch screen

By using the push-pin icon in the top right hand corner of the tile, you can unpin the tile from the Start screen.

By tapping the "..." icon in the bottom right hand corner, you will open a menu that will allow you to resize the tile or turn the live tile (that is the constantly changing images or information), on or off.

Tap any empty space on the Start screen when you're done working with a tile and these icons will then disappear again.

To rename a group of tiles on the Start screen when using a touch screen, just tap once on the group name or the empty space above a group if it doesn't have a name. You will then be able to enter a new name using the on-screen keyboard.

Apart from these small differences, working with the Start screen on a touch screen PC is exactly the same as when using a mouse.

That concludes our little tour of Start menu and Start screen personalisations. Like every version of Windows, there will almost certainly be several third party tools that allow you to customise the look and feel of the OS even further, or replace the new Start menu entirely with one more to your liking. Look out for tutorials on Top-Windows-Tutorials.com for the best skinning and theming software.

Lesson 46 – Action Centre and Notifications

In this lesson we're going to look at the Action Centre, notifications and notification options.

46.1 – Notifications

If you have been working with Windows 10, you've probably seen notifications pop up on your screen already. Figure 46.1 shows an example of a typical notification.

Figure 46.1 – Notifications appear near the bottom right of your screen

Notifications have been overhauled in Windows 10 and now appear in the Action Centre as well as on the desktop. There are two ways to open the Action Centre. Firstly, you can click or tap on the speech bubble icon in the notification area (the icon is circled in figure 46.1). The other way is to swipe in from the right with a finger on a touch screen. Whichever method you use, the Action Centre will then open. Figure 46.2 shows the Action Centre window.

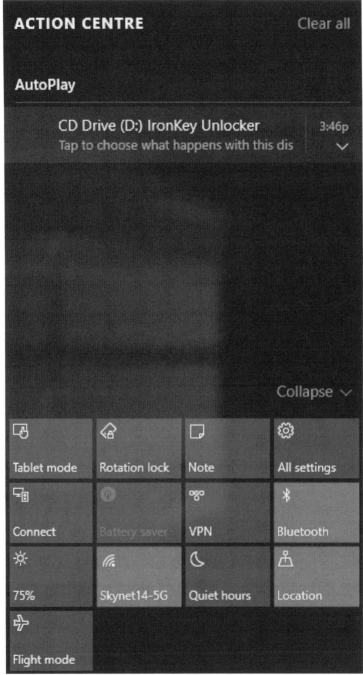

Figure 46.2 – The Action Centre

In the top part of the Action Centre window we can see previous notifications. If there is a down pointing arrow icon, as with the notification shown in figure 46.2, you can click on this to read the notification in full. If a notification was relating to an app or program we can click on the notification to open the associated program. In previous versions of Windows it was very easy to miss a notification, but now most notifications can be reviewed here so you will never miss an important message.

To dismiss all the notifications currently shown in the Action Centre, click on the "Clear all" link in the top right of the window.

46.2 – Quick access buttons

The Action Centre also gives you some quick access buttons that allow you to toggle several common settings or access commonly used features. On a typical PC you will find the following buttons. You may see more or less depending on the hardware in your particular machine. If you only see a row of four buttons in your Action Centre, click on the "Expand" link to reveal more.

Tablet mode - Puts the PC into Tablet mode, optimised for touch screens. We cover Tablet mode extensively in Chapter 2.

Rotation lock - Prevents the screen rotating if you rotate your device. Not all tablets support automatic rotation but for those that do, this setting will prevent it.

Note - Opens Microsoft OneNote, a note taking program/service.

All settings - Opens the settings app where most PC settings can be configured. We've seen the settings app in several lessons including lessons 40 and 41.

Windows 10 Superguide   Top-Windows-Tutorials.com

Connect - Tap this if you want to connect wirelessly to a compatible display or audio device.

Battery Saver - Dims the screen and puts other settings into a lower power mode to conserve the devices battery. If you are running on mains power, this button will be greyed out and unavailable.

VPN - Stands for virtual private network. VPN's are a means of connecting securely to another network or sometimes across the internet. We don't cover VPNs in this guide.

Bluetooth - Turns your devices Bluetooth radio off or on. Bluetooth is often used for wirelessly connecting peripherals like keyboards or headsets.

Brightness - Press the button to cycle through different brightness settings for your screen.

Wi-Fi - Quickly enable or disable your devices Wi-Fi controller. Turning off Wi-Fi significantly improves battery time. If you're already connected to Wi-Fi this button will show the name of the access point.

Quiet Hours - Turns on the Quiet Hours option. Use this option when you don't want to be disturbed. During quiet hours, notification sounds will be muted, for instance.

Location - Tap this button to enable or disable location services. This temporarily overrides any location privacy settings you may have configured using the privacy settings. We discussed location services in lesson 41.3.

Flight mode - Turns off Bluetooth, Wi-Fi, Cellular and any other communication devices. Most airlines will demand you do this when using your device on an aircraft.

When a button or feature is deactivated, its button will be coloured grey. The Flight mode button above, for instance, is turned off. When a feature is active the button will be coloured blue, or whatever accent colour you selected in the colour preferences (see lesson 45.5).

46.3 – Notification options

There are several options we can configure that affect notifications. To access the settings, use the search bar to search for "notifications actions settings" and then click the icon that appears. You will need to scroll down a little in the window that then appears to access the notification options. Figure 46.3 shows the available options.

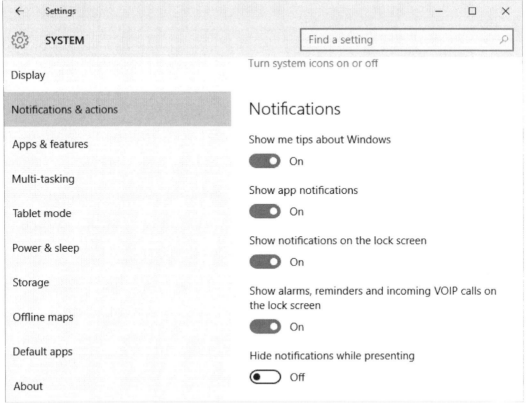

Figure 46.3 – Notification options

The options in figure 46.3 are fairly straightforward. We'll go over them now.

Show me tips about Windows:- Displays usage tips about Windows as you work with your PC. The tips aren't frequent enough to become annoying for most users so this setting is recommended, especially for beginners.

Show app notifications:- Toggles notifications from apps on or off entirely. Usually you would leave this setting on, as an app may have an important notification for you.

Show notifications on the lock screen:- If you show notifications on your lock screen you can see at a glance when a new e-mail comes in, for example, but of course so can anyone else who happens to glance at your computer screen when it is locked.

Show alarms, reminders and incoming VOIP calls on the lock screen:- Even if you turn off notifications on the lock screen you can still opt to have these more urgent notifications appear.

Hide notifications while presenting:- If you use your PC to give presentations, this option will prevent any notifications appearing over your presentation, so that your important business pitch isn't ruined by a reminded to buy a bottle of milk on the way home, for instance.

If you scroll down to the very bottom of the window shown in figure 46.3 you can access notification options for individual apps. Figure 46.4 shows an example.

Figure 46.4 – Notification settings for individual apps

For apps that you have used on your PC and that support this functionality, you can turn notifications on or off on a per-app basis.

46.4 – Notification sounds

You may have noticed that notifications play a sound whenever they are displayed on your PC. It is possible to change or disable this sound, though it isn't very obvious where this setting is. If you want to change or disable notification sounds, follow the steps in this section.

First, use the search bar and search for "change system sounds" and then click on the Control Panel icon that appears. The window shown in figure 46.5 will then appear.

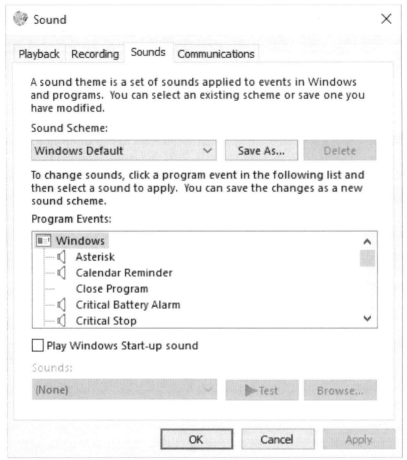

Figure 46.5 – Changing system sounds

Using the scroll control in the middle part of the window, scroll down until you find "Notification" and then click on it once. The box near the bottom of the window, labelled "Sounds:" should change to read "Windows Notify System Generic". Click on the box now and Windows will show you a list of sounds you can use. Choose any sound or scroll to the top and choose "(None)" to disable the notification sound. Figure 46.6 shows an example of this.

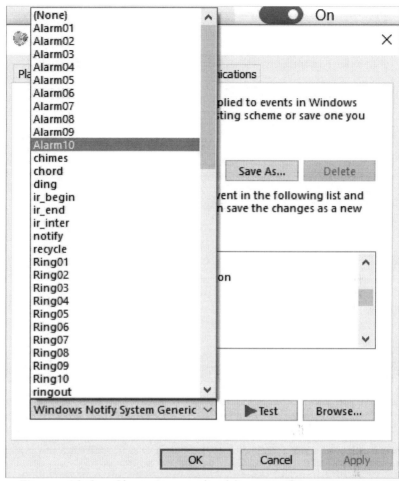

Figure 46.6 – Changing or disabling notification sounds

You can also change the notification sound or any other system sound to any sound you like by clicking on the "Browse..." button and selecting a sample. The sample must be in wave or wav format, not MP3 format.

Click on "OK" when you are done making changes to system sounds.

That's all there is to using and customising the Action Centre, program notifications and sounds. We think that the new notification system in Windows 10 is really great and it finally puts an end to all those missed notifications.

Lesson 47 – Installing new Desktop Software

Windows 10 is compatible with a huge amount of software. Whatever you want to do on your computer, chances are there is an application out there to do it. Typically there are three ways you might purchase or acquire new software. You can use the Windows Store app to purchase (or download for free) Microsoft approved "Trusted Windows Store" software directly to your PC. We cover the Store in lesson 31. You can also purchase desktop software on a CD or DVD disc from a retail store, or as a download from an internet website. All the methods have advantages and disadvantages. The Windows store offers a good selection of pre-approved software for your Windows 10 PC, but this software is limited to what Microsoft approves. Many developers are unwilling to work directly with Microsoft to have their applications officially certified, preferring the more open nature of the traditional Windows desktop. Digital downloads from the internet can be very convenient, but owning a physical disc gives you a backup copy of your software and license. Many industry analysts expect digital distribution to grow and physical distribution to continue to decline, but it may be several years before we see the end of physical software sales entirely.

This lesson will concentrate on choosing and installing desktop software. While Trusted Windows Store apps can be useful, it is desktop software that often has the greatest power and flexibility. Desktop software is also usually optimised for traditional PCs with a keyboard and pointing device such as a mouse or trackpad.

47.1 – Choosing software

When choosing software for your Windows 10 PC, look carefully at the packaging or the website you are buying/downloading from. Look especially for the compatibility information on the packaging/website.

Software labelled as compatible with Windows 10 is guaranteed to work on your Windows 10 PC as long as your system meets the minimum hardware requirements as specified. Check the packaging or the website for details of this.

Almost all software that is labelled as compatible with Windows 8 will work with Windows 10. There are very few exceptions to this.

Almost all software that is labelled as compatible with Windows 7 will work with Windows 10. There are a small number of exceptions, particularly with games software that shipped on optical media.

Almost all software that is labelled as compatible with Windows Vista will work with Windows 10 though there are a number of exceptions, particularly with games software. It's worth checking on the website or asking in store before purchasing.

Software which is labelled as compatible with Windows XP may work with Windows 10, but a significant number of titles will not work correctly or will need a compatibility update from the publisher, or special compatibility tools. You may also need to use the compatibility options which we discuss in the next lesson.

Windows 10 is even compatible with *some* software designed for versions of Windows that pre-date Windows XP, though to take full advantage of Windows 10 features you should always look for a more recent version of the software if you are able to do so.

47.2 – Free software versus paid

There are a lot of fantastic free programs available on the internet, from Office applications to instant messengers and games. Many new computer users eye these freebies with suspicion. "There's no such thing as free!" or "There must be a catch!" they think. Well, a good deal of free software is both free and high quality. There are bad apples of course, software which installs spyware or other less welcome components is common. With a little research on the web you can eliminate these rogue applications and enjoy some really high quality free software. Don't forget to check Top-Windows-Tutorials.com for some great free software recommendations too.

47.3 – Starting installation from optical media

Installing most desktop software you buy pre-packaged from a store is just a matter of inserting the disc into a compatible drive. If your PC didn't come with an optical drive, you can buy one which connects to any spare USB port. When you insert a CD or DVD with a Windows program on it, a notification like the one shown in figure 47.1 will usually appear.

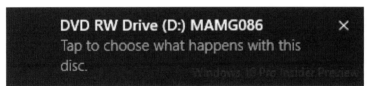

Figure 47.1 – Click or tap this notification to install software from a CD or DVD disc

By clicking on the notification, the window shown in figure 47.2 will appear.

Figure 47.2 – An autorun prompt for CD/DVD software

Choose the option under "Install or run program from your media". In most cases the programs installation routine will then start. Some titles will run directly from the CD or DVD, but most will require installation to your computers hard drive. See your products accompanying documentation for more details.

If you miss the notification shown in figure 47.2, you can either eject and then re-insert your media or open the Action Centre and look for it there (see lesson 46). If you still can't find the notification or it never appears, open This PC and locate the CD/DVD drives icon, then right click on it and choose "Install or run program from your media".

47.4 – Installation examples

Software you download from the internet can usually be installed simply by opening your download folder in File Explorer and then double clicking on the downloaded program file. You need to be running an administrators account or have your administrator password available in order to install new desktop software. Usually, a User Account Control prompt (see lesson 38) will appear when you start installation asking you to grant permission for the program to install, though in some instances it won't appear until part way through the installation process.

Care must be taken when installing new software from the internet, as less reputable sites often lace their downloads with spyware or viruses. Files you download from the internet are stored in your downloads folder, inside your personal folder. If you are not familiar with downloading files from the internet, we cover that in the next chapter, specifically lesson 54.4.

Every program you download or install from a disc will have a slightly different installation process, though there are a couple of elements that are common throughout most software. Firstly, the end user license agreement (EULA). This is a wordy, legal document which explains your legal rights when running the software. For CD/DVD software this may be in the packaging, though usually it is displayed during the installation process.

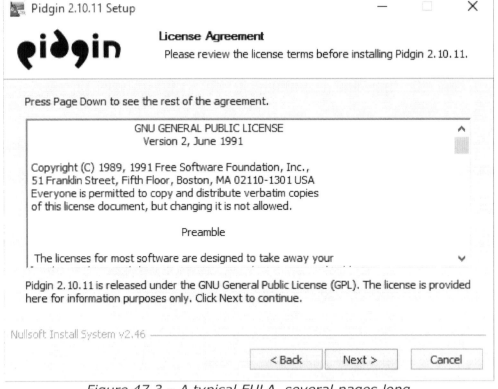

Figure 47.3 – A typical EULA, several pages long

An EULA is like the small print on a contract, we all know that we should read it but few of us do. However, you will not be able to proceed and install the software without indicating that you accept the terms and conditions in the EULA.

Most installers will also give you the option of changing the default installation directory. By default, programs will install to the program files (or program files (x86)) folder on the C drive. However you can change this to be any folder on your computer if you wish. If you have used up all the space on your primary hard drive, you could install to a secondary drive for example. Usually, however, the default location is fine.

Many programs will ask you if you want to make desktop or Start menu shortcuts too. Finally, some software will offer to run as soon as your computer starts up. Remember that this will increase the amount of time it takes for your PC to start, so think carefully before allowing a program to do this.

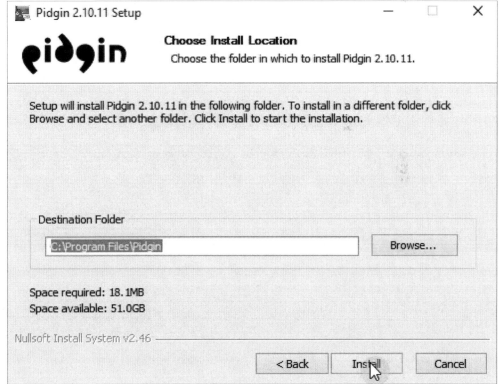

Figure 47.4 – Most software will allow you to change the default installation directory

Often, software will ask you if you want to install for all users. If you have multiple user accounts on your system and you want to make sure that all users have access to the software, select this option.

Pay careful attention as you click through the pages on an installer. Increasingly, software you download from the internet may bundle additional components such as toolbars or other software. In figure 47.5, the installer for the program "DAEMON Tools Lite", a popular CD/DVD emulator tool, is offering to install an additional program called "TuneUp Utilities".

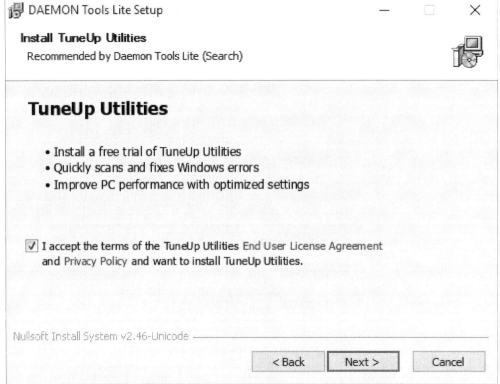

Figure 47.5 – Think carefully before installing additional components like this

While new browser toolbars and programs like this can be useful in some instances, usually they are unnecessary. You do not need to install the program offered in figure 47.5 in order to continue installing DAEMON Tools, though at first glance you might assume that if you deselect the tick/check box presented here, you won't be able to use the software you were installing. In actual fact you can simply deselect the "I accept" box and click on "Next >" to continue installing the software.

When the installation process is finished, the installer will let you know. Beginners are often caught out by the progress bars or meters in installers. Frequently they indicate that the installation is 100% complete before the installation is actually finished. Do not be tempted to close the installer if it stops on 100%, wait for it to complete and close on its own. You can then start to use your new software.

You now know how to add new desktop software to your Windows 10 machine! There are thousands, maybe even millions of useful programs for Windows machines for you to discover that go far beyond what is offered in the Windows store.

In the next lesson we will take a look at the Windows 10 compatibility options that can help run some older software.

Lesson 48 – Legacy Software and Compatibility

Operating systems, like everything else in the world of technology, keep evolving and improving. The unfortunate consequence of this is that certain older software will no longer work on more modern systems. To help with compatibility, Windows 10 has several compatibility mode options you can set for applications. This can often help older software to run on your new operating system.

Note – If you aren't having any compatibility problems with older software, you can skip this lesson.

48.1 – Windows 10 - 64-bit edition

Are you running a 64-bit version of your operating system? Most new Windows 10 computers come pre-installed with the 64 bit version of Windows 10. The 64-bit version of the OS has better performance and can use more memory than is possible in the 32-bit version. The 32 bit version of Windows 10 is slightly more memory efficient, so can still be found on some budget systems.

64-bit versions bring about a whole new range of compatibility problems however. Early versions of Windows ran software for 16-bit processors. This refers to the largest value the processor can work with in one go. On a 16-bit machine, that number is 65535. Clearly this was not going to be adequate for long, so way back in Windows 3.11, Microsoft began to move to 32-bit. In order to maintain compatibility with the programs designed for older processors, a special compatibility layer was added.

However, when running a 64-bit version of Windows, a new compatibility layer works to ensure that 32-bit applications can run and 16-bit applications are no longer supported. Although few users need to run 16-bit Windows applications from the pre-Windows 95 days any more, unfortunately lots of installers for older games and applications were actually 16-bit executables. This means that installing legacy software on 64-bit systems can be somewhat hit and miss.

Figure 48.1 – 16-bit applications will not run on 64-bit versions of Windows

If you ever see the window shown in figure 48.1, you have tried to run a 16-bit application on a 64-bit operating system. No amount of setting compatibility options will help you this time.

48.2 – Using compatibility options

If you are installing software from a CD or DVD and the installation process itself is failing, you might need to configure the programs installer to run in compatibility mode. To do this, insert the CD or DVD into your computer, but don't click on the notification. Now, go to "This PC" in File Explorer and locate your CD/DVD drives icon. Right click on this icon and choose "Open". Figure 48.2 shows an example.

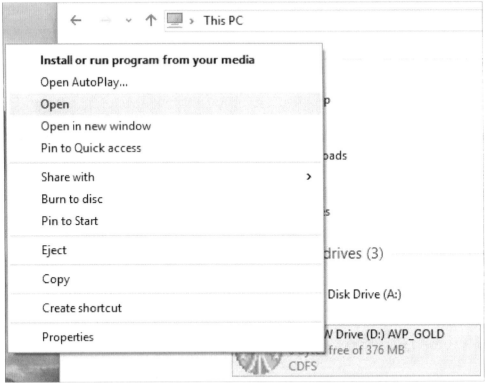
Figure 48.2 - Opening a CD/DVD to investigate the contents

File Explorer will now show the contents of the CD or DVD. In order to determine which file loads when the CD is started, we need to open a file called autorun.inf (which may appear as autorun). Locate this file in the File Explorer window and then right click on it. Choose "Open With..." from the context menu which then appears and then choose "Notepad" from the list of recommended programs. A Notepad window will then open showing the contents of the file. Figure 48.3 shows an example.

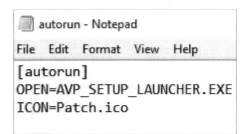

Figure 48.3 – The Autorun file shows us which file the computer opens when the CD or DVD is installed

In the example shown in figure 48.3, we can see that the file we need to work with is called "AVP_SETUP_LAUNCHER.EXE". Find this file in the File Explorer window and right click on it and choose "Properties" from the context menu (just like we did when we looked at folder properties in lesson 16).

The file properties window will then appear, choose the "Compatibility" tab, figure 48.4 shows an example.

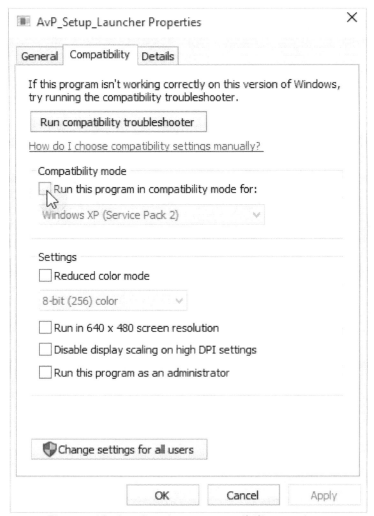

Figure 48.4 – Setting compatibility options

There are several options on this window. The "Run compatibility troubleshooter" option was introduced in Windows 8. Using this option, Windows will try to determine the best compatibility settings for this program. You may want to try this first, before moving on to setting the compatibility options manually.

The most important compatibility settings are the "Run this program in compatibility mode for:" and the "Run this program as an administrator" options.

When you select the box labelled "Run this program in compatibility mode for:" you can then choose the operating system the software was designed for. Check the programs packaging or instructions on the web for details of which option to choose.

Many older or badly programmed Windows programs also require that they be run as administrator. There are two ways to do this, the first way is to select the "Run this program as an administrator" option on this window. The other is to right click (or tap and hold) on the program icon and choose "Run as administrator" from the context menu. Keep in mind that when you run a program as administrator, it gives the software full control over your PC. Never run a program as administrator unless you fully trust it. If you are running a program like this from a standard user account, you will need your administrator password every time you start it.

There are several other compatibility settings that you can try in the middle of the window, although in our experience they rarely make any difference. The "Reduced colour mode" and the "Run in 640x480 screen resolution" options can be helpful for some very old (Windows 95/98 or even earlier) games software. If your old application appears wrong or distorted or has incorrect colours when it is running then choosing some of these options may help, but experimentation is required on a case by case basis.

You can set compatibility options for any desktop program you run or install on your PC. Sometimes software will install correctly but fail to run. To set compatibility options for software you have already installed, simply search for the program and then right click on the icon and choose "Open file location". You will then be taken to a File Explorer window. Figure 48.5 shows an example.

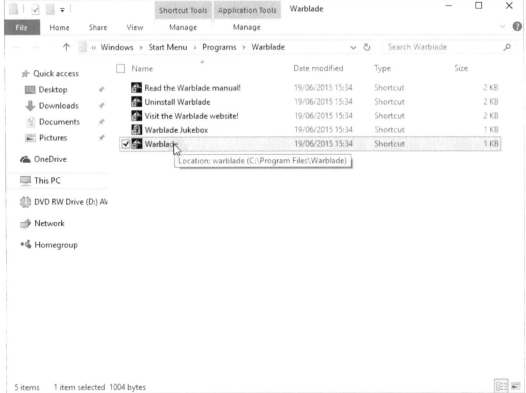

Figure 48.5 – Open file location has taken us to this folder, where we can work with the programs shortcut

Rather than take us directly to the programs folder, Windows has actually taken us to the location of the shortcut instead, but we can work just fine with the programs shortcut in this case. Select compatibility options by right clicking on the programs icon and choosing Properties, then selecting the Compatibility tab just like in 48.2 previously.

48.3 – My software still won't run

Setting compatibility mode options will not help in every case. Some programs simply won't run on Windows 10. There are several other things you can try when faced with a program like this. Firstly, check the publisher or developers web site, if you can find it. They may have issued an update or they may sell a new, improved and fully compatible version.

If that is not an option, you may be able to use virtualization software to install an older version of Windows, such as Windows XP. When you use this kind of software, a window appears on your desktop with an entire copy of

Windows XP inside it, running just as it would do on a normal XP PC. However, virtualization is usually not suitable for multimedia or games software. We don't cover virtualization software in this guide.

There are more hints on running your legacy software on Top-Windows-Tutorials.com, visit http://www.top-windows-tutorials.com/windows-vista-compatibility.html to learn more. If you have an older game title you are struggling to get running, check out our new site http://www.play-old-pc-games.com, where you can find step-by-step instructions for running several popular old PC games, with more games added all the time.

That concludes this lesson on application compatibility options. In the next lesson we will show you how to personalise the look and feel of your desktop by changing your desktop backgrounds.

Lesson 49 – Desktop Backgrounds

If you are bored with the default background on your desktop then it's time to change your desktop background (also called desktop wallpaper). This fun little modification has always been popular and in Windows 10 it's really easy to do.

49.1 – Getting started with desktop backgrounds

To get started, open the desktop and then right click on a blank space on the desktop and choose "Personalise".

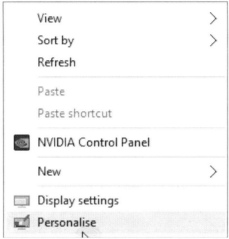

Figure 49.1 – The Personalise option is at the bottom of the context menu

This will open the personalisation settings. Make sure "Background" is selected from the options on the left and then Scroll to the bottom of the options on the right of the window to see the desktop background options, as shown in figure 49.2. If you're on a touch only machine you will probably find it easier to open the Personalisation options by swiping your finger in from the right of the screen to open the Action Centre. Then, tap on the "All settings" button and then choose "Personalisation".

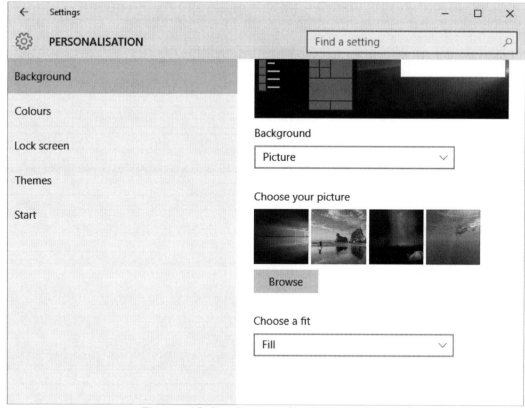

Figure 49.2 – Personalisation settings

At the top of the window we can see a preview of the currently selected desktop background. Click on any picture below "Choose your picture" to change your desktop background instantly. To see what the new picture looks like, refer to the preview at the top or simply minimise this window so you can see your desktop.

49.2 – Using your own pictures on the desktop

It is possible to use any picture stored on your computer as the desktop background. Under the "Choose your picture" section is a button labelled "Browse". Click on this button, then browse to where your picture is stored on your PC. Typically that will be in your Pictures folder or the Pictures library. Click on your chosen picture once and then click "Choose picture". The picture will then instantly be set as your desktop background.

49.3 – Picture positioning options

Since both pictures and desktops come in a variety of sizes, most pictures will not fit exactly into the dimensions of a desktop. To compensate for this, we can choose how the picture is displayed. There are now six different ways to adjust desktop pictures. These adjustments only affect the desktop background as it is displayed, they do not change the actual image file on your computer. You can change the picture positioning options by using the "Choose a fit:" drop down box, which is near the bottom of the window. The picture positioning options are as follows.

Fill:- Expands the image and crops the edges if necessary, so that it fits to the current screen resolution (desktop size).

Fit:- Keeps the pictures aspect ratio (the aspect ratio of an image is its width divided by its height, if this value is ignored when resizing a picture it can become stretched or distorted). Blank space or bars are placed at the top and bottom of the image, if necessary.

Stretch:- Expands the image to cover all of your desktop. Does not always maintain aspect ratio and can make photographs look distorted or out of proportion.

Tile:- Repeats the image across your desktop in a tile pattern, this only works with images smaller than your current desktop.

Centre:- Places the image in the middle of your desktop with blank space around it.

Span:- If you have two or more monitors connected, you will see this option. This will cause the current image to span across all of your monitors. This can look very impressive with panoramic pictures, for instance.

49.4 – Slideshow backgrounds

Just like in Windows 7 and 8, Windows 10 has a desktop background slideshow feature. To use this feature in Windows 10, first click on the drop-down box labelled "Background". Three options will then appear, "Picture", "Solid Colour" and "Slideshow". Select "Slideshow". The options shown in figure 49.3 will then be displayed.

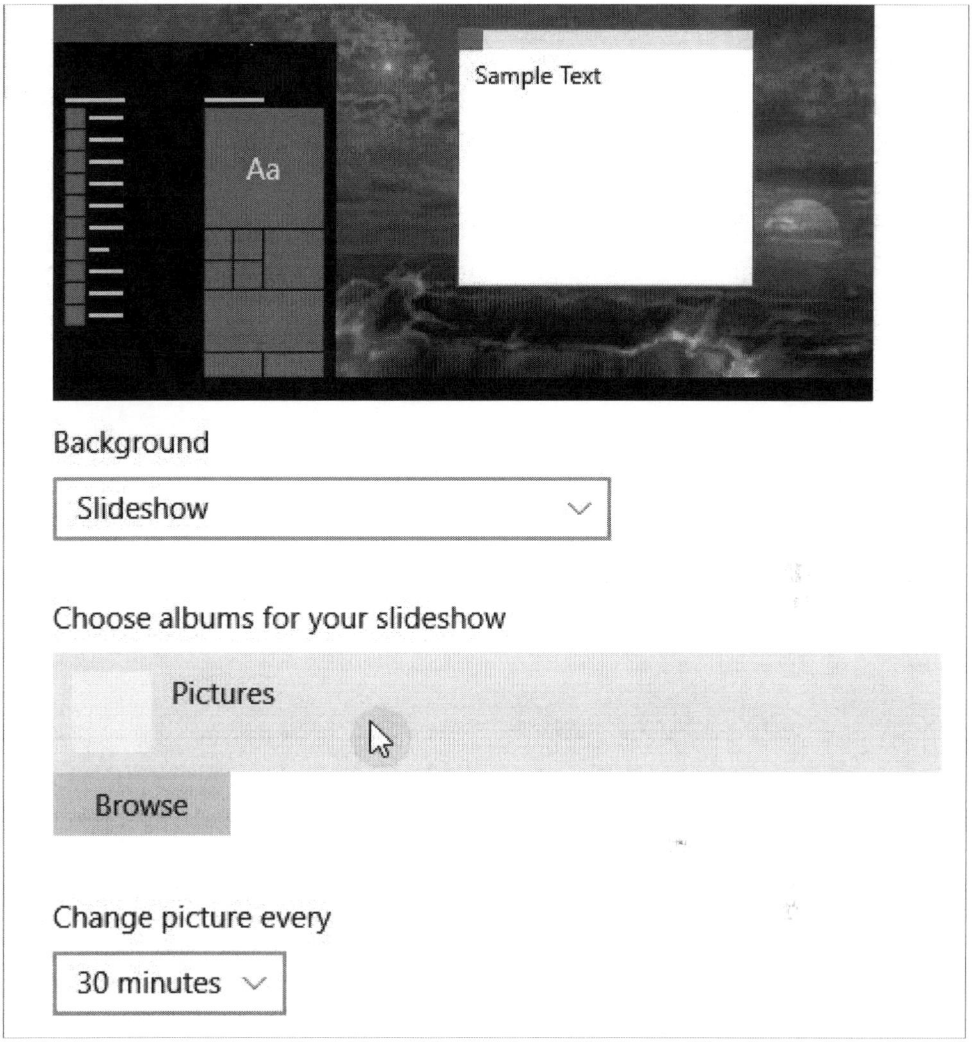

Figure 49.3 – Using the Slideshow background feature

Windows will ask you to "Choose albums for your slideshow". By albums, it actually means folders. Click on the Browse button and browse to any folder that contains pictures. Alternatively, create a new folder yourself and populate it with pictures that you want to use, using the techniques we covered in our File Explorer tutorials in Chapter 3 (we covered creating folders in lesson 13.2 for instance).

By using the drop-down box under "Change picture every" we can specify how long it takes before one image transitions to another, while selecting "Shuffle" will make the pictures appear in a random order.

49.5 – Desktop backgrounds from the internet

We cover connecting to the internet and using a web browser in the next chapter, but if you are already connected then you may want to try this next technique. Lots of sites on the internet offer desktop wallpaper or desktop backgrounds for you to use. For this example we visited this page

http://www.inihdwallpaper.com/bbc-nature-desktop-backgrounds/

This page offers an attractive desktop background image in a choice of resolutions. If a desktop background you want to use is available in a choice of resolutions, you should choose the one that is closest to your monitors native screen resolution. You can find your current screen resolution by right clicking on the desktop, choosing "Display settings" and then clicking advanced display settings (scroll the options window to the bottom if you don't see the link). You don't need your desktop background to match your screen resolution exactly, since you can use one of the "fit" options to compensate.

Figure 49.4 shows the picture open in the Microsoft Edge web browser.

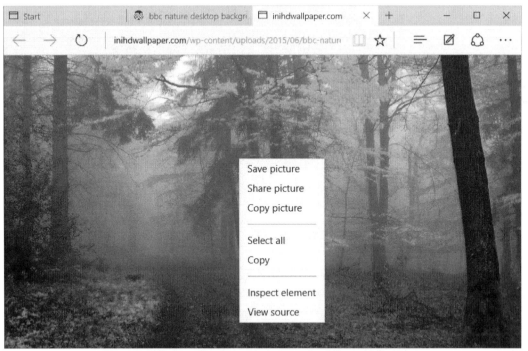

Figure 49.4 – Saving a picture in Microsoft Edge

In Internet Explorer and other popular browsers, you can right click on any picture you find on the web and choose "Set as background" or "Set as desktop background" to automatically set the image as your desktop background. In figure 49.4 the user has right clicked on the image and as you can see, Microsoft Edge doesn't have the capability to set a picture as the desktop background just yet. Instead, choose "Save picture" and place the picture into your pictures folder or any convenient location.

With the picture saved from the web, we could go back to the personalisation options and set the picture as the background. We can also go into File Explorer and find the picture, right click on it and choose "Set as desktop background" from the context menu.

49.6 – Colour settings

Like Windows 8, Windows 10 can automatically set your systems colours based on the desktop background you are currently using. To enable or disable this feature, navigate back to the Personalisation options (figure 49.2) but this time, click on the "Colours" option on the left. Figure 49.5 shows the resulting window.

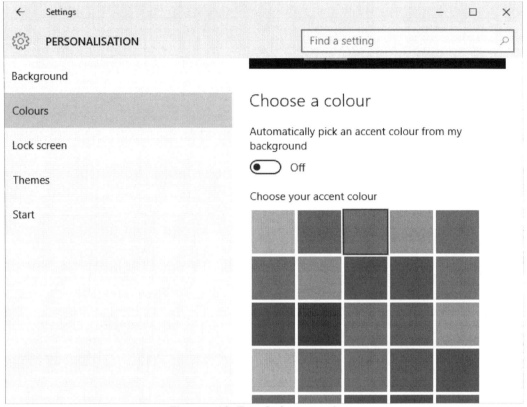

Figure 49.5 – Colour options

To have Windows pick the accent colour based on your current desktop background, turn the "Automatically pick an accent colour from my background" option on. If you have a slideshow background, the accent colour will change each time the desktop background changes too.

Of course, if you'd rather pick your own colour simply turn this option off and click any colour in the window. Be as garish as you like, it's your PC after all!

That's all there is to changing desktop backgrounds on Windows 10. Give it a go yourself, it's a great, fun way to add a personal touch to your device. In the next lesson we will take a look at the customisation options for the lock screen.

Lesson 50 – Customising the Lock Screen

In this lesson we will take a look at customising the lock screen. The lock screen is the screen you see when you first power on your PC or whenever you lock it. In Windows 10 the lock screen can show pictures too.

The quickest way to access the lock screen settings is to use the search bar and search for "lock screen settings". Click or tap the icon that appears. The window shown in figure 50.1 will then appear.

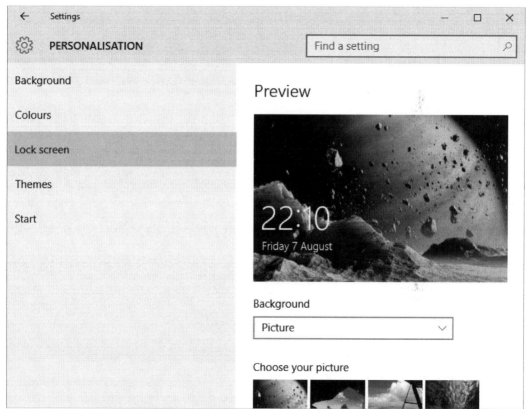

Figure 50.1 – Lock screen personalisation settings

50.1 – Lock screen pictures

To add or change the picture on the lock screen, use the options on the right of the window shown in figure 50.1. The picture options work in exactly the same way as when setting a desktop background, so refer back to lesson 49 if you need a refresher. You can choose pictures or slideshows for your lock screen, just like you can with desktop backgrounds.

50.2 – Lock screen app settings

If you scroll the right hand part of the window shown in figure 50.1 down to the bottom, you will find the lock screen app settings. Figure 50.2 shows these options.

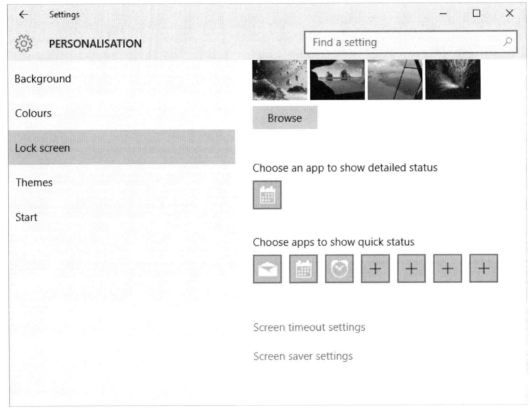

Figure 50.2 – Lock screen app settings

Certain apps can show a quick status icon on your lock screen. This could be useful if, for instance, you wanted to see at a glance if you had received an e-mail while you were away from your PC. Click or tap on the plus shaped icon to see a list of apps that can display this information on the lock screen.

You can also choose one app to show a "detailed status", which as you might expect shows significantly more information than when set to quick status mode. Only certain apps are compatible with detailed status mode.

Near the bottom of the window is a link to the "Screen timeout settings". Figure 50.3 shows what happens if you click on this link.

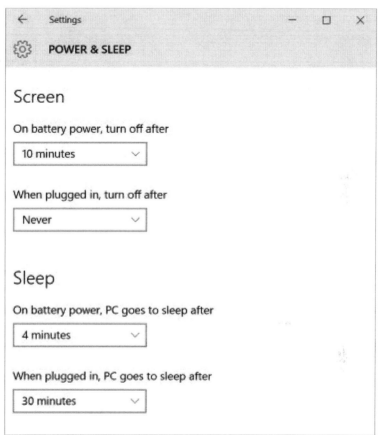

Figure 50.3 – Power & Sleep options

On the Power & Sleep options window you can change how long it is before the screen turns off or the PC automatically goes to sleep. This can be useful for maximising your battery life but of course if your screen turns off too frequently it can be inconvenient.

At the very bottom of the window shown in figure 50.2 we can access the old Windows settings. A screen saver is a pattern or animation that can be displayed on your screen after a period of inactivity. They were originally designed to protect PC monitors from damage due to burn in, where static text or images could become permanently burned into the display if it was left on screen too long. Screen savers aren't used so much these days, as users prefer to switch their displays off to save energy or battery life, so we won't cover them in this guide.

If you've been using a Windows 8 tablet you might be wondering where the lock screen camera settings have got to. Strangely, the option to enable access to the camera from the lock screen, for taking those quick opportune snaps, seems to have disappeared in Windows 10. Hopefully Microsoft will add this back in an update.

That concludes this short lesson on customising the lock screen in Windows 10. Now you know how to change both lock screen and desktop backgrounds, you can really add that personal touch to your device.

Lesson 51 – Devices and Printers

As well as great support for a huge range of software, Windows also supports a massive range of hardware too. When choosing new hardware to use with your Windows 10 PC, look for the "Certified for Windows 10" logo to ensure compatibility.

51.1 – Delving into Devices and Printers

In this lesson, we are going to take a look at the "Devices and Printers" Control Panel section. This is a feature first introduced in Windows 7 that aims to make it easier for users to manage hardware devices on their computers, such as printers, game controllers and monitors. To get started, use the search bar to search for "devices and printers", then click on the icon that appears. Figure 51.1 shows the resulting window.

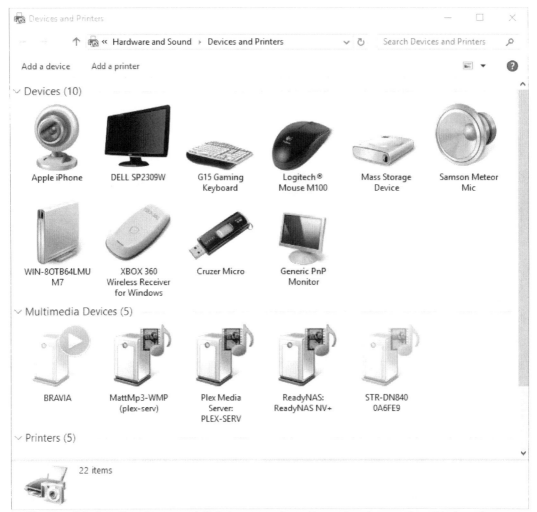

Figure 51.1 – Devices and Printers makes it easier to work with hardware

Devices and Printers gives us a very user friendly way of viewing our hardware. Your window will look different to this unless you have exactly the same hardware in your computer.

For hardware that Windows knows all about, you even get a custom icon that looks like the actual hardware device, such as the icon for the Cruzer Micro USB drive on the second row. In figure 51.1 we can also see two monitors, a keyboard, a mouse, an external hard drive, a USB microphone and various other hardware too. The first icon on the second row down represents the actual computer.

By scrolling the window down, we can see even more hardware, see figure 51.2 for an example.

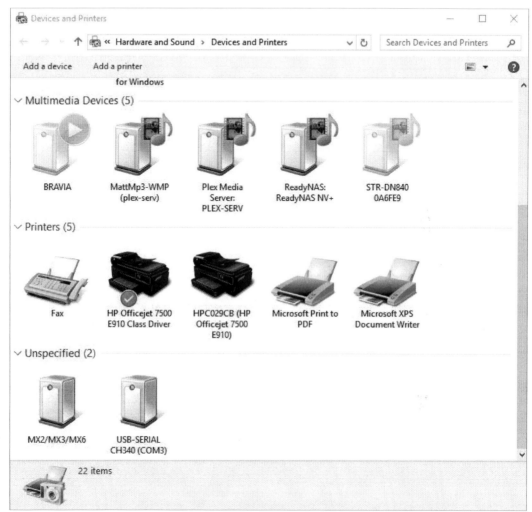

Figure 51.2 – More hardware in Devices and Printers

In figure 51.2 we can see "Multimedia Devices" and "Printers". The Multimedia Devices section lists various devices on our home network. These could be smart TVs or network attached storage devices like the ReadyNAS, or even other PCs with media or file sharing services enabled.

Printers are listed on the next row. In figure 51.2 we can see the generic Windows fax machine, which requires an old fashioned telephone modem to work. The next icon represents an HP Officejet printer. The last two icons are the Microsoft Print to PDF and the XPS Document Writer. Windows 10 comes with these two pseudo-printers. These devices are not real physical printers but they can act like one. Any program which can print documents can use these pseudo printers to save documents to either XPS or PDF format rather than physically printing them. Save paper by using the PDF printer to print and then e-mail a PDF copy of any document, for instance.

The green tick or check mark next to a printer means that this is the default printer. If you want to change the default printer, right click on any printer in Devices and Printers and choose "Set as default printer".

Devices that Windows recognises but does not have detailed information on are shown at the bottom of the list under "Unspecified", with a generic white box icon.

51.2 – Using Devices and Printers

The Devices and Printers window is great for performing common tasks with your hardware and troubleshooting hardware problems. If we right click on a device, there is a list of actions we can take. For the Cruzer Micro USB drive for example, we can browse files or eject the device. For a monitor, we can change screen resolution.

Any devices which appear in Devices and Printers with a warning icon over them potentially have a problem. If a hardware device has a problem you can attempt to troubleshoot it from this window. Right click on a device and choose "troubleshoot". The Windows hardware troubleshooter will then attempt to fix the problem, usually by reinstalling the drivers (drivers are software components that allow Windows to 'talk' to hardware devices). If the troubleshooter fails, you might want to check with the manufacturers for an updated driver.

That concludes our tour of the Devices and Printers section of the Control Panel and concludes this chapter. You now know how to add hardware, software and how to personalise the look of the operating system. In the next chapter we will take you into the world of the internet and home networking.

Chapter 9 – Networking and the Internet

When the first version of Windows launched way back in the mid eighties, there were relatively few computers connected to the internet, or networks of any kind. Home computers usually sat in isolation, never talking to the outside world.

Flash forward to the modern day and millions of homes now have internet connections. Computers now talk to one another across small home networks and the web is part of many peoples daily routine. Windows 10 is well equipped to traverse the information superhighway. You already know about its beefed up security software and its new cloud computing capabilities. In this chapter we will show you how to get your PC online, how to surf the internet and also how to share files and resources in your home with some basic networking tutorials.

Lesson 52 – Choosing an ISP and Getting Connected

Before you can take your Windows 10 PC online, you will need an internet service provider (ISP) and some hardware. Choosing an ISP depends a great deal on where you are located geographically. Deals vary widely and shopping around can often save you money. We will discuss some of the things to look for in an ISP in this lesson to help you make your decision.

52.1 – Types of internet connection

There are lots of technologies used to deliver internet connections, each with their own particular advantages and disadvantages. For domestic internet, there are five technologies that are most common. We will look at each of these technologies now and discuss the advantages and disadvantages of each.

Cable broadband:- Cable internet connections are usually considered the best way to get online. A dedicated wire which provides internet access is connected to your home and a cable modem connects between the incoming wire and your PC or your router (we discuss routers later in this lesson). Fast and reliable, cable connections are highly recommended if they are available where you live.

ADSL:- ADSL is a technology which lets phone companies provide fast internet access through regular telephone lines. ADSL connections can be as fast as dedicated cable connections in some areas. The technology is not as robust as cable but for most users it is more than adequate.

Satellite:- Satellite internet connections are available in regions where no cable or ADSL connection is available. Satellite connections can have good download speeds but have very high latency. Latency is the measure of time between sending information (such as a page request) across the internet and the request arriving at the destination. Because of their high latencies, satellite connections are not suitable for online gaming for example.

Cellular or mobile broadband:- Cellular connections use the now ubiquitous cellular telephone network to connect you to the internet. If you're frequently out on the road, why trust potentially expensive or even dangerous public Wi-Fi access points when you can purchase internet access from your mobile phone service provider? Modern cellular data connections can be almost as fast as cable and ADSL connections, though they are often subject to more stringent download limits and may be charged per amount used rather than simply as a flat fee each month.

Windows 10 has full support for cellular data connections, when you insert a supported and fully activated mobile broadband adapter, you can connect instantly to your provider by opening the Action Centre, clicking on the network icon and then clicking or tapping the name of your mobile broadband network.

Windows is smart enough to know that mobile broadband can be expensive. To combat this, you will always be automatically connected to your Wi-Fi or wired internet connection in preference to the mobile broadband connection. Windows will also defer the downloading of any updates except critical security updates while you are connected using your mobile broadband.

Dial up:- Dial up connections use the existing phone lines to transmit data. They are typically used where no alternative is available or the user is only a light internet user. Dial up connections are very slow and have high latency but are relatively easy to set up. Because of the affordability of faster internet connections, the number of companies offering dial-up access is diminishing quickly.

52.2 – Choosing an ISP

To get the most out of the internet, we recommend choosing an ISP (internet service provider) that provides either a cable or ADSL internet connection where possible. When choosing an ISP, do not just look for a provider who gives you the fastest speeds. Many ISP's now limit the amount of information you can access on the internet in a month or even in a day. Before signing a contract be sure to ask about download limits. On a broadband connection, it is not hard to use several gigabytes of bandwidth a month just surfing the web and watching online videos.

It is also worth checking what hardware the ISP provides with the package. If you have more than one PC in the house then you will need a router to share the internet connection between the computers (or other connected devices like games consoles or smartphones). Read on to find out more about networking hardware.

52.3 – Types of internet hardware

There are lots of devices that can attach to a domestic broadband connection. Your ISP should be able to advise you on what hardware you need. We will give you a few pointers here so that you don't get confused with the techno-babble when dealing with your ISP. Some terms you will need to know about are now listed.

Modem:- A modem is actually a technical anachronism for the old style telephone modems that dialled up to the internet through a phone line. However, the term has been adopted to mean any device which connects to the incoming cable (or satellite). The modem then connects either to your computer, or to a router. Increasingly, cable or ADSL modems and routers are being built into the same box. This is great for saving clutter, but if you have a busy, highly connected house with lots of devices, you may find the basic router/modem box your ISP provides simply isn't adequate for your high-tech family.

Router:- A router is a device that plugs into your modem (or sometimes is built into your modem). Routers share access to the internet amongst all the computers and connected devices in your home. Routers also help to keep hackers out by providing a hardware firewall, so they are recommended even for users with just one computer in the house. Generally, routers come in two types, wired and wireless.

Wired:- When we talk about networking equipment being wired, it refers to the connection used between the equipment. Wired routers connect to computers or other devices by a standard cable called an ethernet cable. Wired networks are faster, more robust, easier to configure and more secure than wireless networks. However, it is not always convenient to use wires to connect.

Wireless:- Wireless networking equipment (also known as Wi-Fi networking equipment) works without the need for cables. This makes it very convenient to use with laptop, tablet or other portable computers or devices, or simply where running a wire is inconvenient. Care must be taken however to ensure that proper security measures are put into place to avoid unauthorised users stealing your internet connection or even snooping around on your computer. Almost all modern routers offer the option of connecting both wired and wireless equipment, meaning you can use the more robust wired connection where it is possible to do so and then connect other devices through Wi-Fi.

52.4 – *Connecting it all up*

Actually connecting all your chosen networking equipment should be straightforward, but there are so many variations and variables that it is simply not possible to go into details here. Your chosen ISP should provide you with the instructions and technical support required to get connected. Remember that when you connect Wi-Fi equipment, you should set the security mode to WPA or WPA2 wherever possible. Do not be tempted to run your wireless connection without any security as this can leave you vulnerable to hackers and free loaders who may abuse your internet connection and even land you in legal troubles.

Windows 10 will connect to wired networks automatically as soon as you insert an ethernet cable. For wireless networks, Windows 10 will scan for networks in range and connect you to any network that you have previously authenticated. To see a list of Wi-Fi networks in range, connect to a new network or disconnect from your current network, click or tap on the Wi-Fi icon in the notification area. Figure 52.1 shows the icon and an example of a typical wireless network list you could see when you clicked on it.

Figure 52.1 – A list of wireless networks in range. Beware of connecting to an unsecured wireless network

To connect to a network, simply select it from the list by clicking or tapping on it and then enter your network key. You only need to enter the key the first time you connect, Windows will remember it for future sessions. Remember that connecting to an unsecured network, one that doesn't need a key (your own or someone else's, even at a coffee shop or internet café) represents a significant security risk as all your web traffic can easily be intercepted by a third party.

You can access some advanced Wi-Fi and networking settings by searching for "wifi settings" on the search bar and then clicking or tapping the icon that appears. Figure 52.2 shows the window that will then appear.

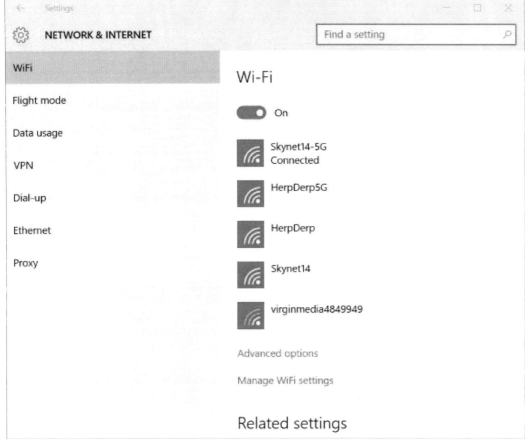

Figure 52.2 – Wi-Fi settings

From the Wi-Fi settings options you can connect and disconnect from a Wi-Fi network. You can also see your data usage history (by clicking on "Data usage") and access advanced Wi-Fi settings. To manage advanced Wi-Fi settings, click on the "Manage WiFi settings" link. The window shown in figure 52.3 will then appear.

Figure 52.3 – Advanced Wi-Fi settings

The top most option "Random Hardware Address" was only recently added to Windows 10, so recently in fact that if you follow our video tutorial for this lesson you will notice it's not even there. If you turn this option on, then every time you connect, Windows 10 will spoof your computers unique MAC address. This makes it much harder for hotspots to identify and track you, since you remove a unique fingerprint from your connection data.

At the bottom of figure 52.3 you can see the option to connect to open hotspots. Open hotspots don't require a password and are a major security risk as anything you access while using them can potentially be seen by a third party or the person controlling the hotspot. Even secured public hotspots represent more of a risk than the connection at your home, but are generally much safer than open hotspots. For best security turn this option off and connect only to secured hotspots.

Then there's the somewhat controversial WiFi Sense options. WiFi Sense is Microsoft's attempt to make sharing access point passwords quicker and easier between friends. Basically, this feature will automatically share access to your Wi-Fi with friends and family in your People app. When your friends are in range of your Wi-Fi access point and you have WiFi Sense turned on, they will automatically be authenticated onto the network.

WiFi Sense does not actually share your Wi-Fi password or your network admin password for your router. When you use this feature and decide to share a network, you will be asked to provide a separate shared password that will be encrypted and then passed between devices by WiFi Sense servers. The person and device you're sharing your network access with will not actually see any password at all.

While this feature may be convenient, who can honestly say they carefully prune their address book and make sure that everyone in there would be welcome on their home broadband? Call us cynical but for now we're going to advise against using this feature.

That concludes this brief lesson on connecting your Windows 10 PC to the internet. Windows 10 PCs are built and designed for constant internet connection, so to get the most out of your machine you should pair it with the best internet connection possible.

Lesson 53 – The Microsoft Edge Browser

Windows 10 comes with not one but two different web browsers. The old faithful Internet Explorer 11 is still included, but it has been usurped by the new kid on the block, Microsoft Edge. Microsoft Edge has been designed to work well on both touch and desktop systems and replaces the touch version of Internet Explorer that Windows 8 tablet users may have been familiar with. In this lesson, we will show you the basics of using Microsoft Edge to surf the web. Once you have an internet connection, the first thing most users do is try out the World Wide Web and Edge is a convenient way to access the web on a Windows 10 machine.

53.1 – Starting Microsoft Edge

You can start Microsoft Edge like any other app by searching for it on the search bar, clicking its Start menu icon or tile or by clicking its pinned shortcut on the taskbar. Edge will then open on the default page, as shown in figure 53.1.

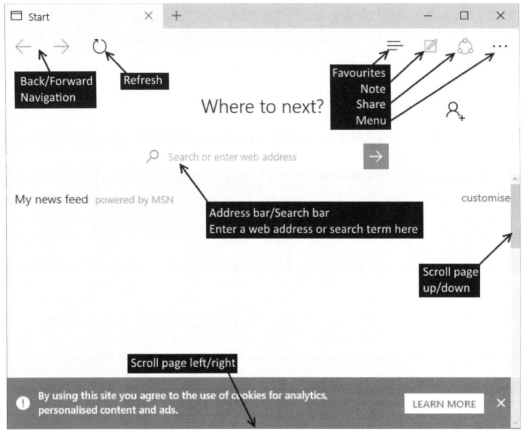

Figure 53.1 – Microsoft Edge's default page

53.2 – Your first Microsoft Edge session

The first thing you will want to do with your browser is visit a web page. Unless you have a specific web address that you want to visit, you will probably want to search the internet to find what you are looking for. Fortunately, searching is really easy. In the box labelled "Search or enter web address", click once with the mouse or tap with your finger. Now, enter your search query. You can enter one word (e.g. "Pizza") or multiple words (e.g. "Pizza recipes with ham"). Once you have typed your search, either click the right pointing arrow icon at the far right of the box or simply press the Enter key on your keyboard. You will then be taken to a results page. Figure 53.2 shows an example of this.

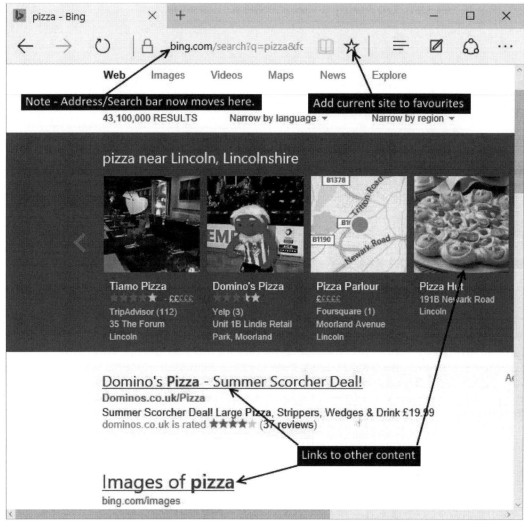

Figure 53.2 – Search results in Microsoft Edge

Search results are ranked by the search engines own special criteria and do not necessarily reflect the pages accuracy or relevancy.

Now we've navigated to an actual web-page, we can see that the address/search bar moves to the top of the browser window. To perform another search or to visit a website, you now type your query into the box here.

When navigating around a web page, use the scroll control on the right of the window to move up and down the page and the scroll control at the bottom of the window to move the page left and right. These controls auto-hide, if you don't see them, move your mouse to the right or bottom edge of the browser window. If the page is small enough to fit in the browser window entirely, these controls will not be available.

If you're using a touch screen the scroll controls won't be visible at all. Instead, simply swipe your finger across the page to navigate around.

Links on a web page take you to another page, links are coloured blue on some web pages but not all. If you suspect that some text may be a link, hover your mouse over it. Your mouse pointer will become finger shaped if the text is indeed a link. Clicking on a link will take you to another page. Images on a page can also be links.

When you click a link, the back/forward navigation controls (see figure 53.1) will become active. To go back to the previous page, use the back button (the arrow pointing to the left). Clicking on the forward button will return you to the page you just went back from.

Finally, if you get a web address, perhaps from the TV or from a magazine article, you can into the address/search bar. Click on the bar once with your mouse and then use the Delete or Backspace key to delete the current address, if necessary. Now, type the new address (also known as a URL) and press Enter. You need to enter the address exactly as given (although it doesn't matter if you use upper or lower case, www.WinDows.com is exactly the same web address as www.windows.com).

If you entered the address accurately, you will be taken directly to that page on the internet, rather than a page of search results.

That concludes this lesson. You now know enough to start using Microsoft Edge and exploring the internet. In the next lesson we will look at a few other features to help make your web browsing more productive.

Lesson 54 – Microsoft Edge Part 2

In this lesson we will finish our introductory tour of Microsoft Edge by looking at some other useful things you can do in the browser as you explore the web.

Figure 54.1 shows a Microsoft Edge window and the features we will be looking at in this lesson.

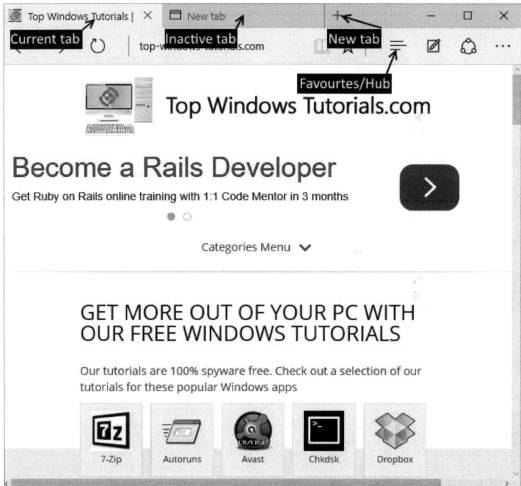

Figure 54.1 – More Microsoft Edge features

54.1 – Tabs

Tabbed browsing is one of the most useful features to be added to modern web browsers. Tabs are useful when you want to work with two or more web pages at once, to compare prices for example. In figure 54.1 you can see two tabs currently open. To open a new tab, click on the plus shaped icon marked "New tab" in figure 54.1. To switch between tabs, simply click on them.

In any open tab it is possible to enter a web address or search query into the address bar. Navigating or searching for pages in one tab will not change the web content displayed in another, which means you can refer back to the content in another tab at any time just by clicking on the desired tab.

You can have as many tabs open as you like, just click to the right of your last tab to open a new one. Of course, having too many open tabs at once can become confusing!

54.2 – Favourites

When you find a website you want to revisit, you do not need to remember the address, you can add it to your Favourites (Favorites in the USA) list instead. This is often called "bookmarking" in other browsers. To add a site to your Favourites, open the page in the active tab and then click on the small star shaped icon labelled "add current site to favourites" that you can see clearly in figure 53.2. The window shown in figure 54.2 will then open.

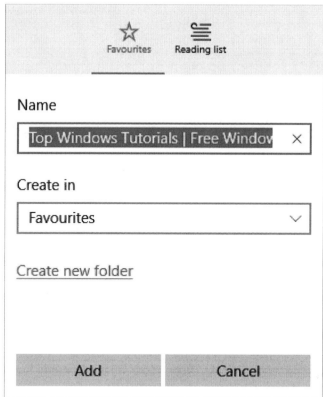

Figure 54.2 – Adding a site to Favourites

In the top box you can enter a name for your favourite, if you don't like the default. You can then create the favourite by clicking on "Add" or create a new folder to store it in by clicking on "Create new folder". Perhaps you want to file all the computer help sites you find in a folder called "Computer help". Simply click on "Create new folder" and then enter a name for the folder.

The next time you add a favourite, you can add it to an existing folder by using the "Create in" drop down box. Figure 54.3 shows an example of this.

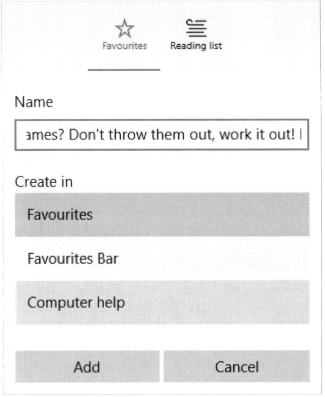
Figure 54.3 – Adding a new favourite to a folder

To view and visit your favourites, you need to use the button labelled "Favourites/Hub" in figure 54.1. Click on this button and then click on the star-shaped icon that appears. Figure 54.4 shows an example of this.

Figure 54.4 – Browsing favourites in Microsoft Edge

Using the hub you can browse all your favourites. In figure 54.4 the user has navigated to the "Computer help" folder that they created and inside there are two favourite sites that have been saved. To visit a site, just click on it once from the list and it will instantly open. If you want to remove a site from your Favourites, right click on the site in the list and choose "Remove" from the menu that then appears. Favourites that you delete like this are sent to the Recycle Bin and can be recovered from there if accidentally deleted.

You can also make your Favourites appear as a sidebar on the right of the Microsoft Edge window. To do this, click on the push-pin icon that you can see in the top right hand corner of figure 54.4. Having your favourite sites show up as a sidebar can be convenient, if you are using a smaller screen however it may take up too much room on your monitor while you browse the web.

54.3 – Advanced Microsoft Edge options

There are some advanced settings we can change in Microsoft Edge. To access these settings, click on the "…" icon in the top right of the browser window. The icon is marked as "Menu" in figure 53.1. When you click on the icon, the menu shown in figure 54.5 will open.

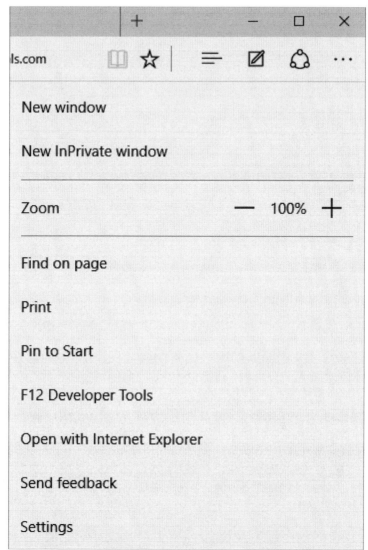

Figure 54.5 – Microsoft Edge options menu

From this menu you can access various tools such as zoom controls for the web page and developer tools. For this lesson, we're interested in the Settings menu item. Clicking this item brings up the menu shown in figure 54.6.

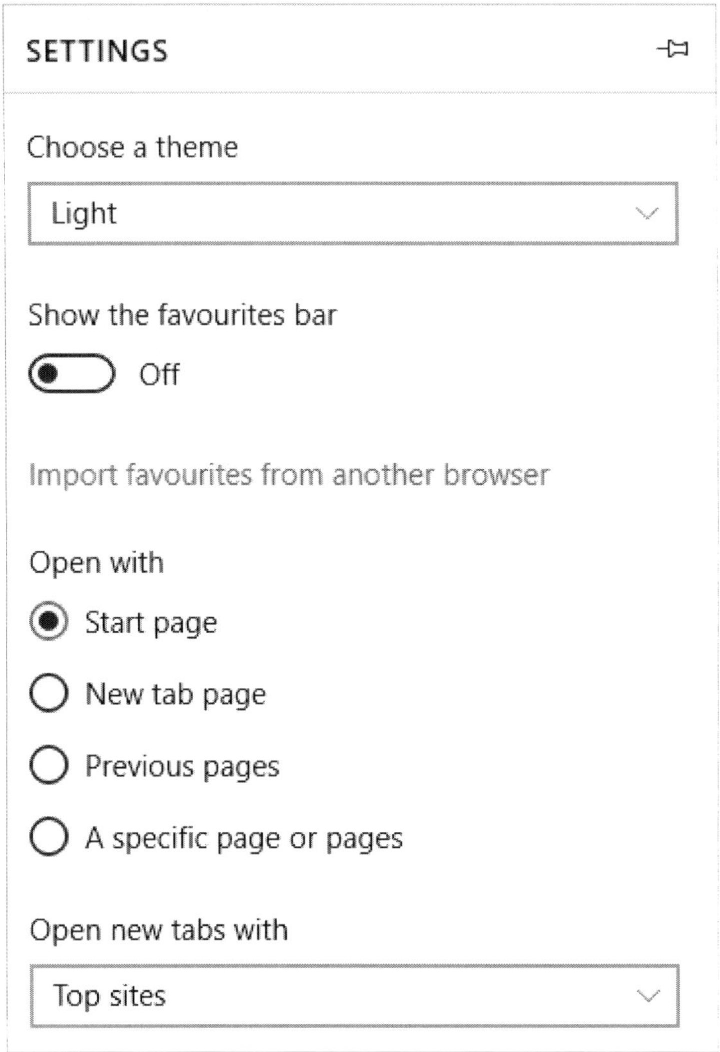

Figure 54.6 – Microsoft Edge settings

You will need to scroll down this list to see all the available options. We won't be covering these options in great detail in this guide, but there are some things we want to make you aware of. If you scroll to the bottom part of the list you can find the "Clear browsing data" section. Content from pages you visit on the internet is cached to your computer, along with search history and other potentially private information. If anyone else uses your PC and has access to your account, they can see which sites you have been visiting. If you don't want anyone to know about the sites you recently visited, click on the "Choose what to clear" button and then select the types of information you want to remove. Of course, if you do share your PC, you should create separate accounts for everyone that uses it and we covered how to do that in lesson 37.

54.4 – Download manager

At some point during your internet use, you will probably want to download a file to your computer. To start a download, all you need to do is click on the download link on a web page. To manage your downloads, Microsoft Edge has an in-built download manager. To access it, click on the icon labelled Favourites/Hub in figure 54.1 and then click on the down pointing arrow icon. Figure 54.7 shows an example.

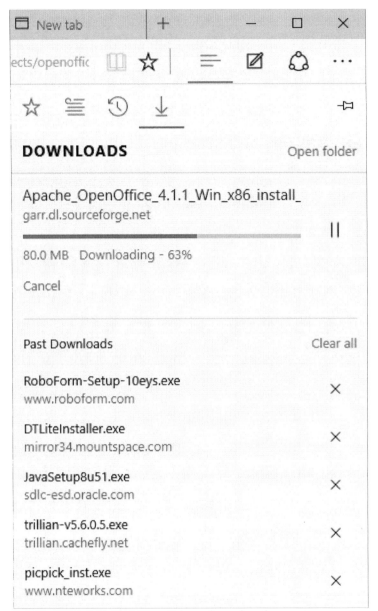

Figure 54.7 – The Edge download manager

Any active downloads are shown at the top of the download manager. The blue bar shows the progress of the download.

Any files that have downloaded will appear in the bottom part of the download manager under "Past Downloads". When a download is complete, you can click on the blue text link that says "Open folder" to open the download folder in File Explorer and access your file(s). Alternatively, just click or tap on the download to open it directly from the download manager.

Remember that files you download from the internet can contain malware. To minimise the risks, always make sure that your antivirus program or Windows Defender is running and is up to date and only download from reputable sites.

That concludes our tour of Microsoft Edge. We have barely scratched the surface of what you can do with the web and with Edge, in fact we could probably make a whole new Superguide about this new browser alone! Don't forget that Microsoft Edge isn't the only way to browse, alternative browsers such as Firefox and Google Chrome have been increasing in popularity over recent years. Check them out when you become more confident, you may find you prefer them.

In the next lesson, we will round off our guide to networking in Windows 10 by looking at how Homegroups make it easy to share files and resources with PCs throughout your home.

Lesson 55 – Homegroups

These days it is not uncommon to find two or more computers in one household. Many homes have one computer per family member. Even though the price of powerful hardware has tumbled in recent years, a computer, printer or storage device is still a significant investment for most people. Luckily, Windows now includes software that makes it really easy to share files and printers on your home network. Don't have a home network, are you sure? If you have a router that shares your internet connection between PCs in your home, either wired or wireless, then you already have a home network and you can begin this lesson. You can skip this lesson if you only have one PC in your home.

55.1 – Creating a homegroup

To get started making a homegroup, make sure all the family computers you want to share resources with are turned on and connected to the network (if they can access a web page then everything is good to go). Now, search for "homegroup" on the search bar, and click on the Control Panel icon that appears. The window shown in figure 55.1 will then appear.

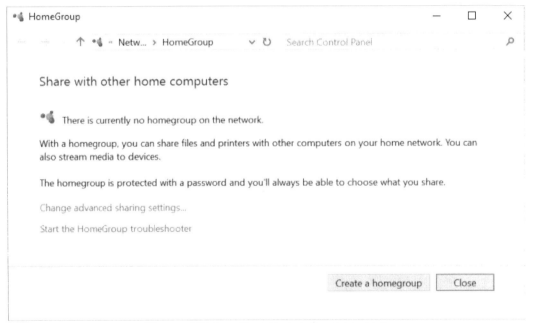

Figure 55.1 – Creating a homegroup

If you have never configured a homegroup on your network, Windows will now give you the option of creating one. This only needs to be done once, on one PC in your home. Click on "Create a homegroup" to begin the process, then click on "Next" on the introductory window which then appears. There will be a short pause and then the options shown in figure 55.2 will appear.

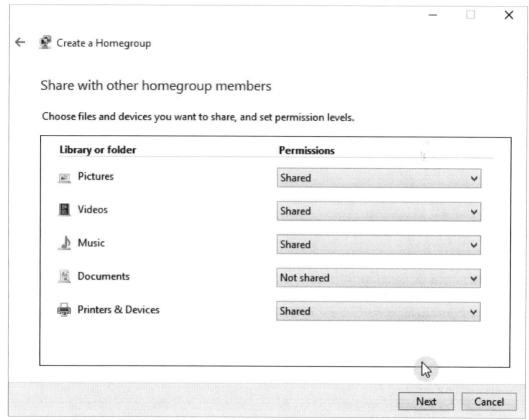

Figure 55.2 – Choosing file types to share on a homegroup

Choose the file types you want to share on your homegroup. You can share pictures, videos, music, documents and printers and devices. The first four options relate to the library or personal folders on your PC, so if you turn on music and picture sharing for instance, the content of these two libraries or folders will be available on the home network.

Sharing a folder on the homegroup like this opens up your files to other people on your home network. Keep this in mind when selecting what to share. You may have video content that isn't suitable for younger members of the family, for instance. By default, other users on the homegroup will be able to view and open your files but will not be able to change them. We will show you how you can limit which files and folders you share, later in this lesson.

Click on "Next" when you have decided which folders and resources to share. The window shown in figure 55.3 will then appear.

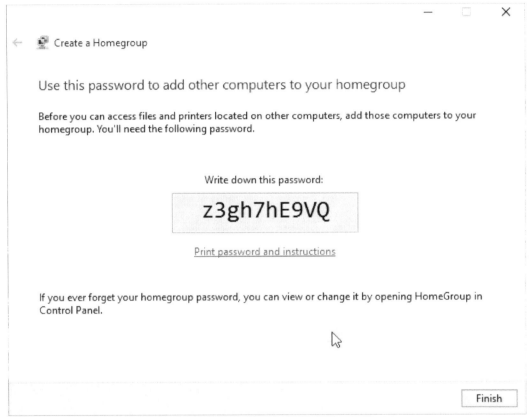

Figure 55.3 – Homegroup password

The window that now appears shows you the homegroup password. Write this down exactly as it is shown on the screen. The password is 'case sensitive' which means that upper case and lower case letters are different ('A' is not the same as 'a'). Any computer joining your homegroup will require this password. Click on Finish when you are done. The homegroup is now set up. Before we set about adding other computers to the homegroup, we will look at how you can restrict access to certain folders or files.

55.2 – Restricting access to files or folders

When you share files on the homegroup, all the files in your libraries or personal folders are shared. What if, for example, you had some video content that was not suitable for children? You could simply opt not to share videos at all, but then the children would miss out on everything. You could take the unsuitable content out of your video library and store it elsewhere, but then it won't show up when you use your video library. Fortunately there is a better solution.

Firstly, open up File Explorer and browse to the content you want to restrict. When you have located the file or folder you want to keep private, right click on it and choose "Share with → Specific people". Figure 55.4 shows the correct context menu option.

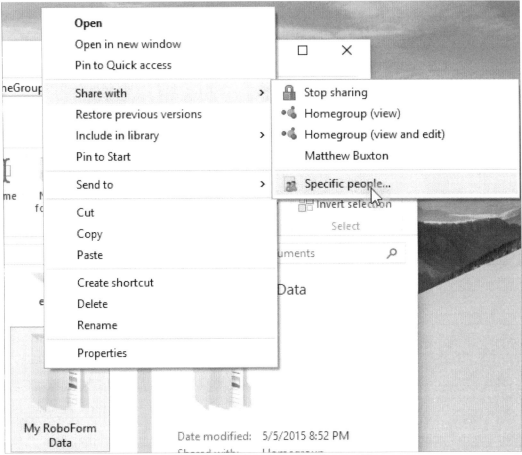

Figure 55.4 – Selecting sharing options

When you select this option, the window shown in figure 55.5 will appear.

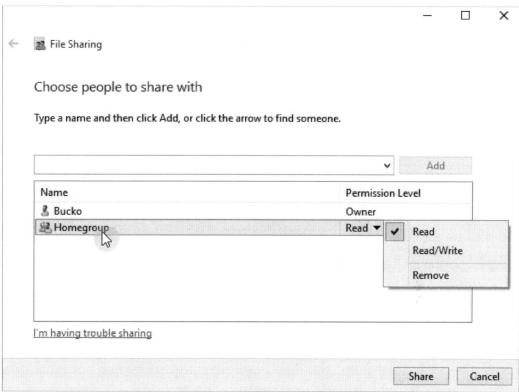

Figure 55.5 – Setting sharing options

In figure 55.5 we can see that the permissions for "Homegroup" are set to "Read". We can exclude a file from sharing completely (without deleting it from the local PC) by clicking the little arrow next to "Read" and then choosing "Remove", or we can give read (only) or read/write access to other users on the homegroup from the same menu. By default, other users on the homegroup can see your files but not change them. If you need to change files from another computer choose "Read/Write", but make sure you have a backup in case someone else in the house accidentally deletes your files. When you're done making changes, click on "Share" to close the window and activate the new permissions.

55.3 – Joining an existing homegroup

Connecting another computer to an existing homegroup is done in exactly the same way as setting up a homegroup in the first place. On the computer you wish to include in the homegroup, open the HomeGroup settings, exactly like we did at the start of the lesson. Instead of seeing the "Create a homegroup" button, this time you should see the "Join now" button as shown in figure 55.6.

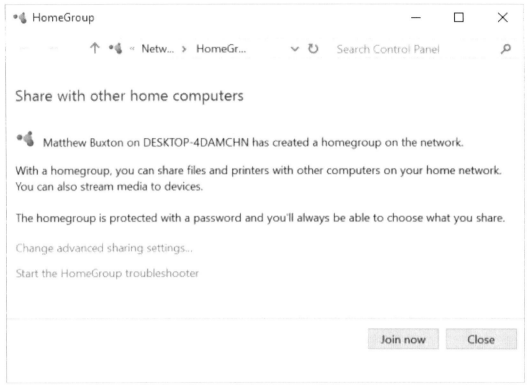

Figure 55.6 – Connecting to an existing homegroup

This time, Windows has detected an existing homegroup on the network. To join in and share files and printers, click on the "Join now" button, then click "Next" on the introductory window that will then appear. Just like when you set the homegroup up initially, the window shown in figure 55.2 will appear. Choose which of the libraries or folders you want to share from this computers hard drive, just like before, then click on "Next".

You will then need to enter the homegroup password you wrote down earlier in the lesson. Enter it exactly as you wrote it down then click on "Next". and then click on "Join". You will then see the options shown in figure 56.2. If you entered the password correctly, your PC will join the homegroup after a short delay.

Note - If you are running a third party security package that includes a firewall, you may have trouble connecting to a homegroup. Temporarily disable your firewall and try to connect again. If you can connect with your firewall turned off, contact the vendor of your firewall product for technical support and advice or to obtain an upgrade.

55.4 – Browsing a homegroup

You can browse a homegroup through File Explorer. Simply open up a File Explorer window and you will see the homegroup icon in the Navigation pane on the left of the window. Click on it and you will then see the other users PCs in your homegroup. Figure 55.7 shows an example of this.

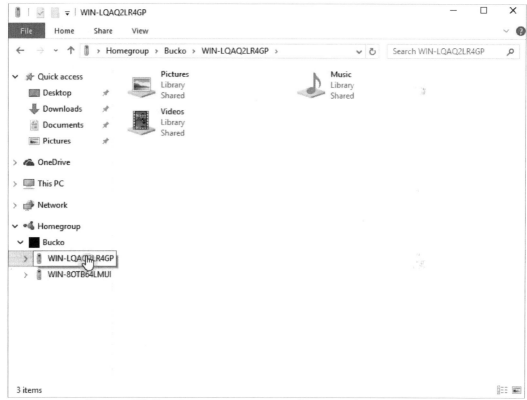

Figure 55.7 – Browsing a users files on the homegroup

When browsing the homegroup, the hierarchy works like this. The individuals user-name is shown at the top level. Below that, each device they use on the home network is shown. Below each device are the folders and files on that device. In figure 55.7 we can see that the user "Bucko" has two Windows PCs that he has connected to the homegroup.

If a computer in your home has more than one user, each user will have to log on, join the homegroup and authorise their files to be shared before they will show up under "Homegroup" in File Explorer.

If you want to leave a homegroup at any time, simply go to the homegroup settings window again (as in lesson 55.1) then click on the "Leave the homegroup" link.

55.5 – *Renaming computers*

Notice in figure 55.7 that the user Bucko has two computers connected to the homegroup. The top computer is called "WIN-LQAO2LR4GP". That may be enough for Windows to tell which machine it is, but it's not terribly helpful for a human being. Luckily we can change this computer name to something more friendly, like "Study PC" or "Rachel's Room" for example. To rename the computer you are currently working on, search for "rename computer" on the search bar and then click on the icon that appears. The window shown in figure 55.8 will then appear.

Figure 55.8 – Computer name settings

You can enter a description in the box at the top of this window, but if you want to change the name that appears when you browse the homegroup in File Explorer, you need to click on the "Change..." button near the bottom of the window. The window shown in figure 55.9 will then appear.

Figure 55.9 – Renaming a computer

Delete the existing name under "Computer name:" and type any name you like, then click "OK" (leave all the other settings alone). You will need to restart the PC to finalise this change. Once you do, it will appear with your more user-friendly name when you access it in File Explorer.

You have now completed this lesson on homegroups and also this chapter on networking and the internet! In the next chapter we take a look at Windows Media Player. This program is, for many users, the preferred way to play and organise music on the Windows desktop.

Chapter 10 – Windows Media Player

In this chapter, we are going to focus on Windows Media Player. Windows Media Player is pretty much unchanged from Windows 7, but that's not necessarily a bad thing, since it was a very competent piece of software when launched. If you're using a big-screen desktop PC with a keyboard and mouse, Windows Media Player is still one of the best ways to both organise and play your media files.

Lesson 56 – Introducing Windows Media Player 12

In this lesson we will look at running Windows Media Player 12 for the first time. We will also show you how to play back both music and video. To get started, load Windows Media Player by searching for "windows media player" on the search bar, then click on the icon that appears.

56.1 – Running Media Player for the first time

The very first time you run the program, you will see the window shown in figure 56.1.

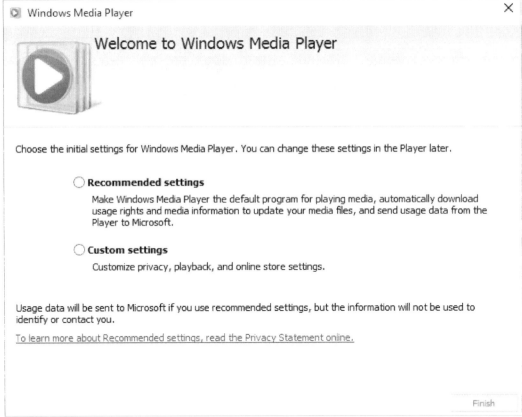

Figure 56.1 – First time setup of Windows Media Player

Windows Media Player uses your internet connection, if available, to download information about the media you are playing. Choose "Recommended settings" to get started right away or "Custom settings" if you want to analyse the settings and privacy policy in detail. For this example, we will choose the "Recommended settings" button, then click "Finish". You will then be taken to the main Windows Media Player window as shown in figure 56.2.

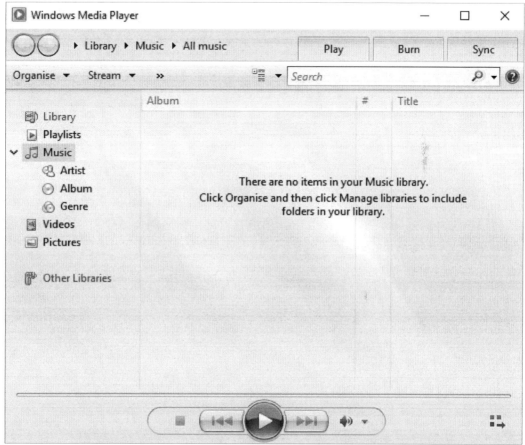

Figure 56.2 – The main Windows Media Player window

Unlike Windows 7, Windows 10 doesn't come with any sample music to get you started. Before continuing with this lesson you may wish to copy some media files into your libraries or music folder. If you purchased the Windows 10 Superguide DVD or download, you can use the Sample Media installer to install a simple music file called "A Hundred Pipers". Alternatively, go to lesson 57 where we add music from an audio CD.

Playing music and video with Windows Media Player is really easy. There are two ways to start playing a file that we will demonstrate in this lesson.

Firstly, we can drag and drop media files from File Explorer onto the Windows Media Player window. To do this, make sure the "Play" tab is selected, then open File Explorer and navigate to the folder where the media file you want to play is stored. To play a file, drag it, as if you were moving it, over from the File Explorer window onto the right hand side of the Windows Media Player window. The file will then play right away. Figure 56.3 illustrates this.

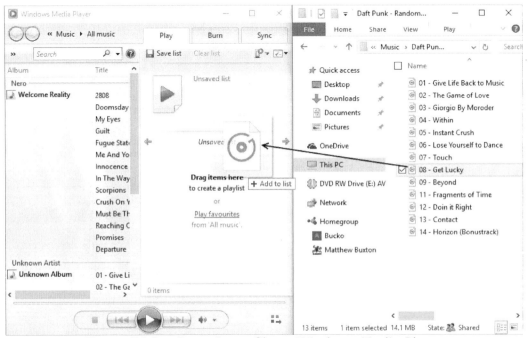

Figure 56.3 – Dragging a file to Windows Media Player

The first file you drag to Windows Media Player will start playing instantly. You can keep dragging files onto the window to create a playlist. Files on a playlist will play one after the other.

You can add video files to your playlist too, in exactly the same way. If you want to jump directly to an item on your playlist (to play it immediately), just double click on it.

56.2 – Playing video

Figure 56.4 shows Windows Media Player playing a video file.

Figure 56.4 – Playing a video in Windows Media Player 12

Figure 56.4 shows the buttons available in video playback. The controls are the same when playing music (apart from the full screen control). If you can't see all the buttons illustrated here, you may need to make your playback window a little wider. We will take a look at each button now.

Shuffle:- This changes the order in which files are played from your playlist. When shuffle is on, files are played in a random order.

Repeat:- Repeats the current playlist (rather than just the file you are currently playing). When this option is disabled, playback will stop when the end of the playlist is reached. Otherwise it will resume from the beginning again (or a random point if shuffle is enabled).

Stop:- Stops playback of the current media file. You are then given the option of returning to the media library or resuming playback.

Previous:- Go to the previous file on your playlist.

Play:- When a file is playing, this button will pause playback. When a file is paused, pressing this button will resume playback.

Next:- Go to the next item on your playlist.

Mute:- Turns off all sound.

Volume:- Adjusts the level of the volume by moving the slide control.

Fullscreen:- Make the video play back in full screen mode, taking up all the space on your monitor. Not applicable for audio files.

Back to library:- Takes you back from the media file and returns you to your media library.

56.3 – The media library

Earlier in the lesson we showed you how to drag and drop media on to Windows Media Player in order to start playing it. This is handy for playing music on removable media, for example. Normally however, you would use the music library to play files from your computer. Any media files you add into your libraries or personal folders will automatically be available in Windows Media Player. The media library navigation pane is shown on the left of the Media Player window (see figure 56.2).

You can browse the library by file type, using the Navigation pane or search for media either by name or metadata by typing into the search box near the top right of the window. Enter a search query then press Enter or click the magnifying glass icon at the right of the search box to start the search.

To play an item from your media library just double click it. To add it to your playlist, drag it across to the right and drop it in the same area we dropped the files from File Explorer.

To save a playlist, click on "Save list" (you can see this button in figure 56.3) then enter a name for your list. Saved playlists appear in the library under "Playlists". You could create playlists ready for a house party for example, or just to match your mood. To start playing a playlist, just double click it.

That concludes this lesson on Windows Media Player. Now you know how to play audio and video media files. In the next lesson we will look at how to copy your CD collection to your computer and create a digital jukebox of all your favourite tunes.

Lesson 57 – Ripping CDs

Have you ever wanted to create your own jukebox? By ripping your CDs to your computers hard drive you can do just that. Ripping a CD means taking a copy of the music on the CD and storing it in your computer. The copyright law in most countries allows you to do this, as long as you own a copy of the original CD. This means that you can access all your music without having to have the original CD in the CD drive or player!

To rip a CD, you will of course need an optical drive in your PC. If your PC didn't come with one, most computer stores sell external DVD drives that will do the job just fine. DVD and even Blu-ray drives are backwards compatible with CD, so any such drive will work with the techniques shown in this lesson.

57.1 – Setting ripping options

Before we get started ripping CDs, let us take a look at some options. On the main Windows Media Player window, click on the "Organise" menu and then choose "Options". Now, choose the "Rip music" tab. Figure 57.1 shows you how to do this.

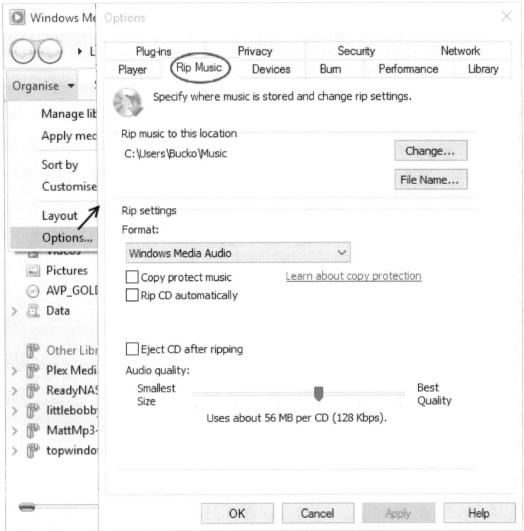

Figure 57.1 – Accessing ripping options

By default, music that you rip will be stored in Windows Media Audio format. If you are planning to use the music on a generic MP3 player, it might not be compatible with Windows Media Audio format. Choose "MP3" in that case.

You can change formats by using the drop down box under "Format:". In Windows 10 you can even encode in the highest quality FLAC (free lossless audio codec) and ALAC (Apple lossless audio codec) formats. These formats generally result in larger file sizes, but copy your music files from your CDs in the very highest quality, with no loss of information. If you are playing the music files back on high quality audio equipment, you may also want to up the quality of the copy, though doing so increases the file size. You can change quality settings by using the slide control at the bottom of the window. There is no right or wrong setting, experiment and find out what sounds best to you. Note that there are no quality adjustments possible for FLAC or ALAC formats as they are always encoded at the highest possible quality.

When you are done setting ripping options, click on "Apply" then on "OK". You will then be taken back to the main Media Player window.

57.2 – Ripping a CD

To rip a CD using Windows Media Player 12, firstly insert your audio CD. It should then show up in the Navigation pane, under "Music". Click on it once. Figure 57.2 shows a Media Player Window with an Audio CD ready to play.

Figure 57.2 – An audio CD in Windows Media Player

Just like regular media, you can double click on CD audio tracks to play them. You can also drag them over to the right (as long as the Play tab is selected) and make a playlist.

We could start ripping the CD right away, but first, check that the track names are set correctly. To save the hassle of renaming them later, you can look up the track names in the online CD database. Windows Media Player will usually do this automatically. If you need to override this behaviour or look up a CD manually, right click on the CDs icon in the media library (on the navigation pane on the left) then choose "Find album info" on the context menu that appears. Media Player will then connect to the internet and look up the track names and information about the album. This saves you entering them manually later. Of course, you will need an internet connection for this to work. Figure 57.3 shows the "find album information" window.

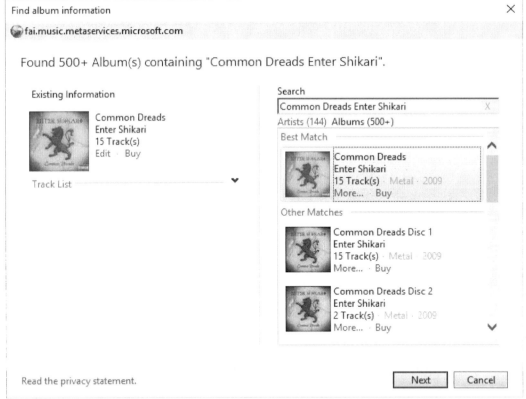

Figure 57.3 – Looking up an album online

Sometimes Windows Media Player will find the album information automatically, other times you will need to search for it yourself by entering the artist and album name into the search box. When you find a match for the album, click on it from the list and then click "Next". You will be able to confirm that the details are correct before clicking on "Finish".

The track listing will then be automatically filled out, just like in figure 57.4.

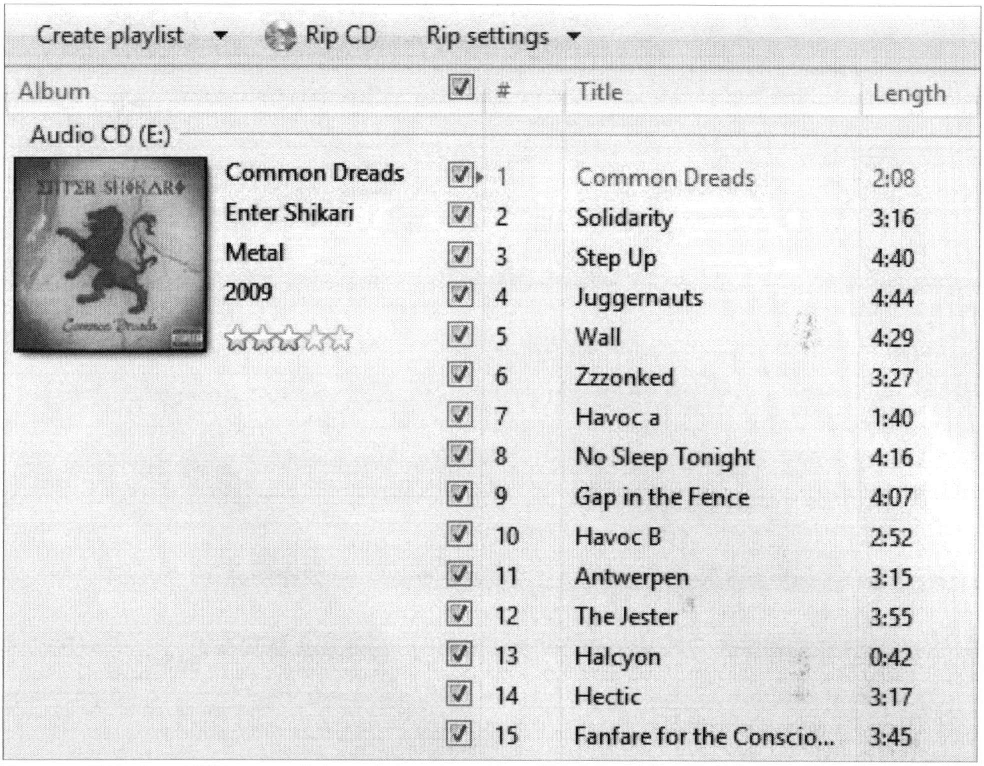
Create playlist
Rip CD
Rip settings
Album
#
Title
Length
Audio CD (E:)
Common Dreads
Enter Shikari
Metal
2009
1 Common Dreads 2:08
2 Solidarity 3:16
3 Step Up 4:40
4 Juggernauts 4:44
5 Wall 4:29
6 Zzzonked 3:27
7 Havoc a 1:40
8 No Sleep Tonight 4:16
9 Gap in the Fence 4:07
10 Havoc B 2:52
11 Antwerpen 3:15
12 The Jester 3:55
13 Halcyon 0:42
14 Hectic 3:17
15 Fanfare for the Conscio... 3:45

Figure 57.4 – Filling out track names by looking them up on the internet is much quicker than typing them yourself

We are now ready to start ripping some music. You can rip the entire CD or individual tracks, just deselect the ones you don't want. When you are ready to start ripping the disc, right click on the disc icon in the library Navigation pane (it will now be correctly named if you looked it up online) and choose "Rip CD to library".

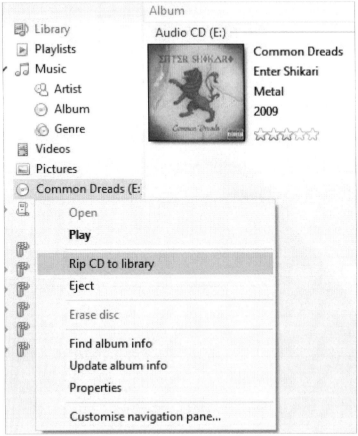

Figure 57.5 – Starting the CD ripping process

57.3 – Copy protection options

If this is the first time you have ripped a CD, the window shown in figure 57.6 may appear.

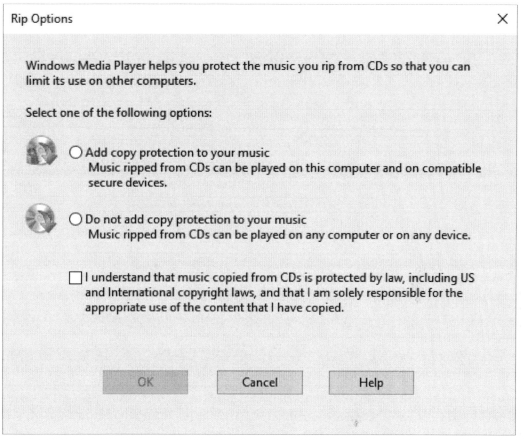

Figure 57.6 – Setting copy protection options

When ripping music from CDs, you can choose to add protection to your ripped audio files. Adding protection can help you use the media within copyright law, but it can also cause problems with some types of media players, so we recommend that you do not. You must also tick/check the box at the bottom of the window that states that you understand most music CDs are protected by copyright law. Please use the files you copy/rip from your CDs for your own personal use and do not share them with friends or on the internet.

Click on "OK" when you have selected an option and ticked/checked the box. Ripping will then begin. This window will only appear the first time you rip a CD, Media Player will remember your preferences for next time.

Media Player will then begin ripping the CD. You can continue to use the program while this takes place. When the ripping process is complete, the music files will be added to the library automatically. You can now remove the CD and enjoy your music at any time just by accessing it through the library. Since the music library is used by the Groove Music app too (see lesson 27), you will find that if you use the Groove Music app, your newly ripped album will be available there too.

That concludes this lesson on ripping audio tracks in Media Player 12. In the next lesson we will round up our introductory tour of Media Player 12 as we look at a few other useful features of the software.

Lesson 58 – Wrapping up Media Player

In this lesson we will be going over some of the features we briefly mentioned in the other lessons, especially the media library and playlists.

58.1 – Browsing libraries

As we mentioned in lesson 56, the libraries in Windows Media Player 12 and your music library (or music folder) are linked, meaning you can browse your music collection from File Explorer or through Media Player. The media libraries also link with the Groove Music app. Browsing in Media Player can be more convenient if you want to play and browse music and video.

Just like in File Explorer, there are different views you can choose for browsing your media. If you do not like how the data is laid out in your media library, you have several options. Use the drop down box next to the search box to change views. Figure 58.1 shows where this control is.

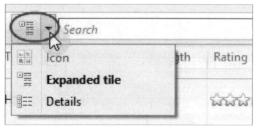

Figure 58.1 – The view options control

Depending on what type of media you are viewing, you will have several choices. Details view is useful for working with lots of tracks at once. In this view, you can set ratings by simply clicking on the stars next to the song title. Figure 58.2 shows a media library in details view.

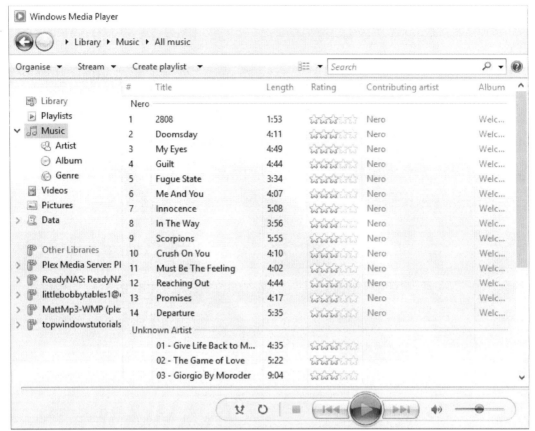

Figure 58.2 – Media library in details view

Use the scroll control near the bottom of the window to see other columns which contain various information about your music or media files. If you don't see a scroll control here, then all the available columns are already displayed. To sort by a column, click the column once.

By right clicking on a column and choosing "Choose columns" it is possible to see a list of all the different types of information that can be displayed about the media files. Figure 58.3 shows this list.

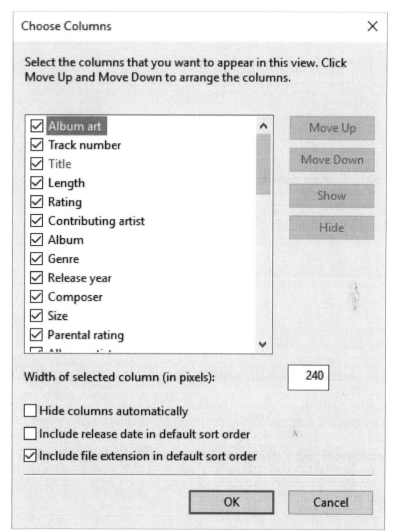

Figure 58.3 – Choosing columns to display in the media library

Of course, some categories will not be relevant to all types of media. To display a column, simply select it then click "OK", it will then appear. You can also automatically hide empty columns by making sure the "Hide columns automatically" option is selected in this window.

You can also resize columns by dragging them, or reorder columns by dragging them to a new place. As you can see, working with Media Player is a lot like working with File Explorer. Don't forget there is also a very handy "Search" box, where you can search by artist, album, song title or any other relevant criteria. This is very useful for quickly finding things in your media library.

58.2 – Viewing pictures

We have talked about video and music files in Media Player but we did not mention picture files until now. Media Player 12 can view picture files too. Figure 58.4 shows the picture section of the media library.

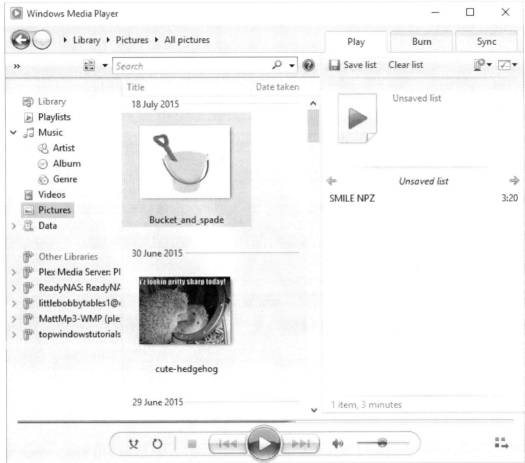

Figure 58.4 – Browsing pictures in Windows Media Player

To view pictures, just double click on them, Windows Media Player will play them as a slideshow. You can queue pictures up in a playlist just like other media, making it easy to create a custom slideshow.

That concludes our tour of Windows Media Player 12 and this chapter. We have barely scratched the surface of the power of Windows Media Player in these lessons, do not be afraid to dive in and experiment, it is the best way to learn.

The next chapter focuses on routine PC maintenance and troubleshooting, to help keep your new PC running in tip-top condition.

Chapter 11 – Troubleshooting and Maintenance

Your PC is almost certainly the most versatile gadget you have in your home. No normal television, toaster or microwave oven could ever come close to performing as many tasks as even the most humble Windows 10 PC. This is great of course, but the downside is that PCs typically need more maintenance than regular household gadgets. Don't worry if that sounds like hard work, if you followed our advice on PC security then hopefully you won't encounter too many problems. In this chapter we will show you some simple things you can do to keep your Windows 10 machine running like new.

Lesson 59 – Uninstalling Software

If you no longer use a program, it is a good idea to uninstall it. Uninstalling software frees up disk space and can free up computer resources too, if the software in question was running all the time. Sometimes it is necessary to uninstall an old program to make way for a new one. This is true in the case of most security software (i.e. firewall and antivirus packages). It is also a good idea to uninstall and reinstall a program if you are experiencing technical problems with it.

59.1 – Uninstalling Windows Store software

To uninstall a Trusted Windows Store app that you downloaded from the store or that came bundled with Windows 10, simply locate the program on your Start menu or Start screen or search for it on the search bar. Once you have located the app, right click on its tile or icon (or press and hold with your finger) A menu will then appear, choose "Uninstall". Figure 59.1 shows an example.

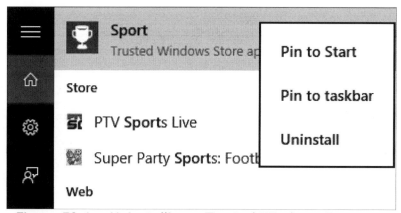

Figure 59.1 – Uninstalling a Trusted Windows Store app

That's all there is to uninstalling Trusted Windows Store apps. Note that a number of Windows 10 apps that come bundled with the OS (such as Store and Cortana) cannot be uninstalled.

If you want to reinstall a Trusted Windows Store application you will need to re-download it from the store. For paid apps, as long as you use the same Microsoft account you won't need to pay for the program again. Alternatively, if an app appears on your Start menu, you can simply unpin it and then just find it again by searching if you do ever need it.

59.2 – Uninstalling desktop software

In this example, we are going to look at how we uninstall a typical desktop program. The actual uninstallation process will be different for every piece of software but the basic steps are usually the same.

Before you begin uninstalling any software, it is a good idea to make sure it is not running. Although a properly written uninstall script should take care of this, it never hurts to check yourself. If you do not see a window for your program, check the notification area (see lesson 21) for the programs icon. If you can see an icon, right click on it and choose "quit", "close" or "shutdown" if the option is available.

To start the uninstallation process, you will need to be logged in as an administrator, or have your administrator password ready. Search for "Uninstall a program" on the search bar and then click the icon that appears (it may read "Change or remove a program"). The Control Panel will now open and show you a list of all the desktop programs installed on your PC. You may need to scroll down until you find the program you want to uninstall. When you find the desired program, click on it and choose "uninstall" if the option is available or "change" if it is not. Figure 59.2 shows an example of this.

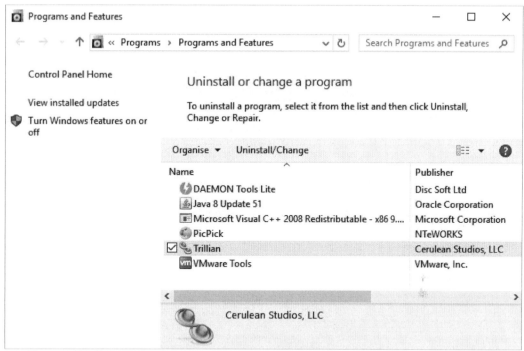

Figure 59.2 – Choosing a program to uninstall. Some software must be uninstalled by selecting "Change" while other software will have an "Uninstall" option in the same place

Once you click on "Uninstall" or "Change" the uninstallation process will begin, you should then follow the on screen prompts to remove your software. These prompts will be slightly different for every program you uninstall, but they are usually straightforward. Normally you will need to confirm that you want to remove the software when User Account Control prompts you.

Sometimes you will have to restart your PC to finish the uninstallation process. The uninstaller should offer to do this for you if it is necessary. Once your computer restarts, the uninstallation process is complete.

That concludes this short lesson on uninstalling software. In the next lesson we will take a look at how to remove temporary files and other clutter using the Disk Cleanup utility.

Lesson 60 – The Disk Cleanup Utility

In Windows 10 you can reclaim disk space and clean up temporary files by using the Disk Cleanup Tool. This tool was improved in Windows 7 and in Windows 10 it works in much the same way.

60.1 – Starting a disk cleanup

To start the tool, search for "disk cleanup" on the search bar, then click on the icon that appears.

Once you click on the icon, The window shown in figure 60.1 will appear if you have more than one hard drive in your system.

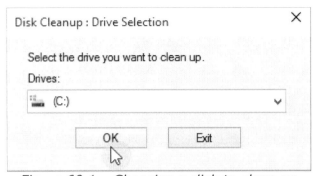

Figure 60.1 – Choosing a disk to clean up

Choose a drive to clean up by using the drop-down box control. Some computers will only have the C: drive, in which case you won't be prompted to choose a drive to clean. In this lesson we will show you how to clean the C: drive, which is usually the drive or partition that Windows is installed to. Choose the C: drive (it should be selected by default) then click "OK".

60.2 – Choosing cleaning options

The Disk Cleanup utility will then scan for temporary files. When this process is complete, the window shown in figure 60.2 will appear.

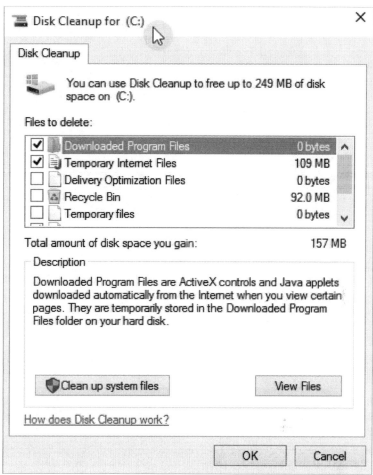

Figure 60.2 – Choosing temporary files to remove

Figure 60.2 shows the Disk Cleanup utility presenting us with a list of all the temporary files that can be deleted from the computer. If you scroll down the list and click on an item, you can see a description of the files that this cleanup option removes. In figure 60.2, the "Downloaded Program Files" option is selected, in the description we can see that this includes ActiveX and Java applets downloaded automatically. Selecting this option will not delete files you have downloaded into your downloads folder. Generally, since each option only cleans temporary files, it is safe to select them all.

Notice the button near the bottom of the window that says "Clean up system files". If you click this button, which requires you to have administrator rights on the computer, the Disk Cleanup utility will re-scan and include temporary system files too.

For this example, we will choose every item on the list, then click on "OK". The Disk Cleanup utility will then ask us to confirm that we want to delete the files, figure 60.3 shows the window which will appear.

Figure 60.3 – Confirm the removal of temporary files to start the cleanup process

This is your last chance before the items are deleted. Unless there is something you really wanted to recover from the Recycle Bin or from the temporary files or error logs on your PC, it is safe to click "Delete Files". Note that if you are cleaning up system files, this can include your previous version of Windows, so make sure that you definitely don't want to roll-back to Windows 7 or 8 before you proceed.

Once you click on "Delete Files" the cleanup process will then begin. When the process is complete, the utility will exit automatically. You have now cleaned the temporary files from your computer and reclaimed the disk space.

That concludes this lesson on the Disk Cleanup utility. PC maintenance really isn't as difficult as you imagined is it? In the next lesson we take a look at how we can improve system performance with the disk defragmenter tool.

Lesson 61 – Disk Defragmentation

As you go about your daily computing routine, adding files, removing files and rearranging files, the hard disk in your computer becomes more and more fragmented. File system fragmentation slows down access to files because the pieces of a file may be scattered across the disk, rather than stored together neatly. To combat this problem, the Optimise Drives tool can automatically rearrange your hard disk. The tool is easy to use and completely safe and will even run automatically. In fact, many users will not need to change the programs settings at all.

61.1 – The Optimise Drives window

To start disk defragmention manually or to change settings, search for "defragment" on the search bar, then click on the "Defragment and Optimise Drives (Desktop app)" icon to load the program. The window shown in figure 61.1 will then appear.

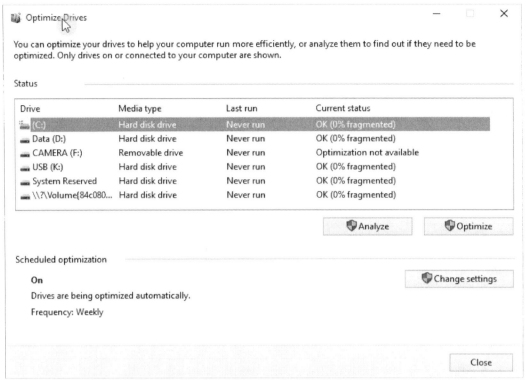

Figure 61.1 – The Optimise Drives tool

Figure 61.1 shows the main Optimise Drives tool window. From this window we can schedule regular defragmentation or manually optimise any hard disks in our computer. We will take a look at scheduled defragmentation first. Click on the "Change settings" button near the bottom of the window. The window shown in figure 61.2 will then open.

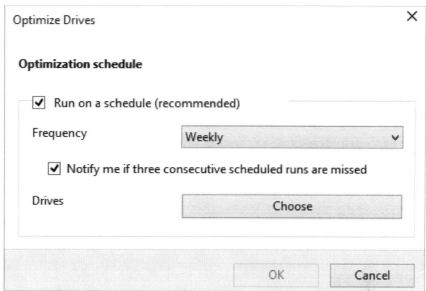
Figure 61.2 – Scheduling a defragmentation

61.2 – Setting a schedule

In this window we can choose a schedule for automatic "set it and forget it" disk optimisation. When the "Run on a schedule (recommended)" option is selected, defragmentation will be automatic. By changing the "Frequency:" control, you can also choose between daily, weekly or monthly optimisation. Daily is a little excessive but monthly might be suitable for a computer that isn't used frequently. Weekly will be the best option for most users.

Enabling the second tick/check box in the window will cause Windows to notify you if three consecutive scheduled runs are missed. If you have more than one hard drive or hard drive partition, click on "Choose" to choose which disks will be optimised as part of the schedule. Figure 61.3 shows the drive selection window.

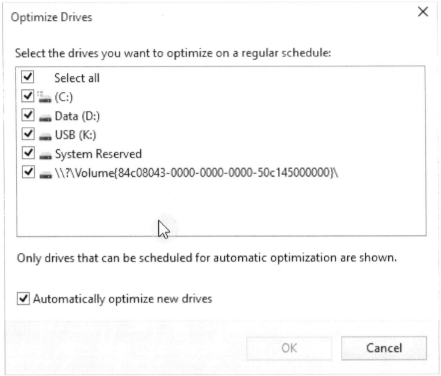

Figure 61.3 – Selecting drives to automatically optimise

In most instances you should simply select every drive available so that all your hard drives are defragmented and optimised, though you might want to deselect any removable drives. Click on "OK" when you are done making changes or "Cancel" if no changes were necessary. The window will then close and return you to the window shown in figure 61.2. Click on "OK" again to finish setting the optimisation schedule. You will then be returned to the main Optimise Drives window as shown in figure 61.1.

61.3 – Manual defragmentation

Once you have set a schedule for disk optimisation, that is really all you need to do to keep your disk defragmented and working at peak performance. If for any reason you want to do a manual disk defragment then simply choose the disk to defragment from the list near the top of the window shown in figure 61.1. Choose a disk by clicking on it and then click on the "Analyse" button.

Windows will then analyse the disk and tell you what the percentage of fragmented files is. If this value is high, you might want to go ahead and manually defragment the disk. To start a manual defragmentation, simply click on "Optimise".

Optimisation will take a while, but you can use your computer for other tasks while it takes place. When the process is complete the utility will simply stop, you will not even be notified that it is done!

That is all there is to keeping your disks defragmented with the Disk Defragmenter utility.

In our next lesson, we will look at the System Restore utility. This utility can help solve serious computer problems by restoring your system settings to an earlier time.

Lesson 62 – System Restore

The System Restore utility was introduced with Windows XP and has been refined in Windows Vista, Windows 7 and Windows 8. In Windows 10, it works just like it did in Windows 8. If you have a serious problem with your PC after installing a new program or piece of hardware, the System Restore utility can "roll back" to an earlier time when your PC was working correctly.

62.1 – Enabling System Restore

To check if system restore is enabled, search for "restore point" on the search bar and then click on the "Create a restore point" icon that appears. The System Properties window will then appear, as shown in figure 62.1.

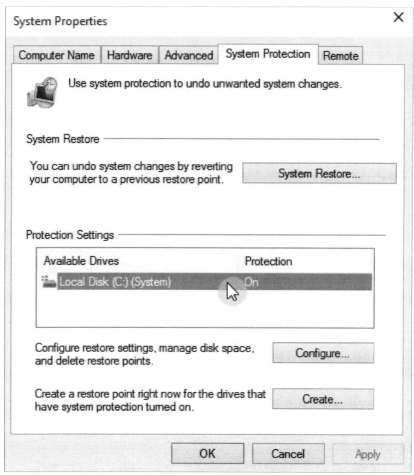

Figure 62.1 – System restore is enabled for this drive

In figure 62.1 we can see that System Restore (protection) is turned "On" for "Local Disc (C:) (System)". System Restore works on a per-drive basis. The computer in figure 62.1 has only one hard drive, if there was a secondary hard drive then system restore would need to be enabled for that drive too, if desired. Usually, it's only necessary to turn on System Restore for your C: drive, as that is where Windows is installed.

To change system restore settings for a drive, click on the desired drive in the list and then click on the "Configure..." button. The window shown in figure 62.2 will then appear.

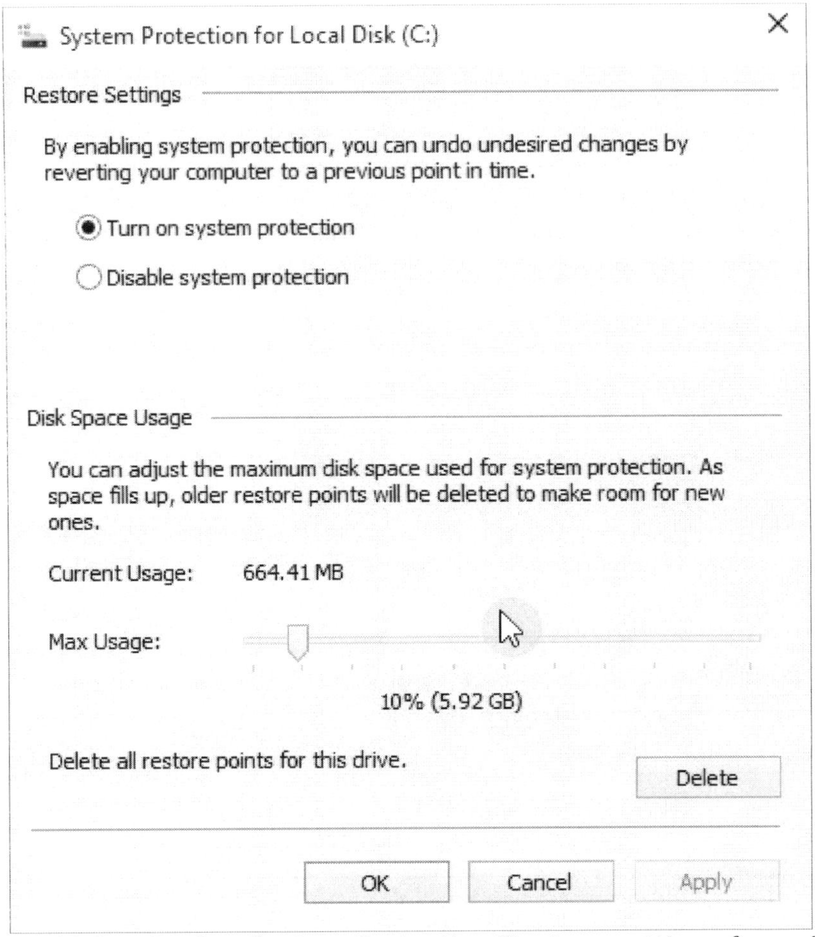

Figure 62.2 – Setting System Protection/Restore settings for a drive

From the window shown in figure 62.2 you can turn system protection on or off for the selected drive. You can also change the amount of disk space reserved for system protection and system restore points by moving the slider control in the bottom half of the window. Typically you would reserve between 5 and 10% of the drives space.

62.2 – Creating your own system restore point

Windows will often create system restore points automatically. Some Windows programs also create them when they are installed or before they perform certain tasks. Users can also easily create their own manual system restore points at any time. To do this, use the "Create…" button near the bottom of the window shown in figure 62.1. Windows will prompt you to name your restore point. Enter any name you like and then click "Create" again. Wait a moment until Windows tells you that the restore point was created.

Once you create a system restore point (or one is created automatically), you can roll back to it at any time. To start the process, click on the "System Restore..." button near the top of the window shown in figure 62.1. The System Restore 'wizard' window will now open. Figure 62.3 shows this window.

Figure 62.3 – Beginning a system restore

The System Restore tool will now guide you through the process of selecting and restoring a system restore point. System Restore only affects system settings. Files such as pictures, videos and e-mails will not be altered. Because of this it is often more convenient to use System Restore than it is to restore from a backup when troubleshooting computer problems.

62.3 – Choosing a restore point

The System Restore utility has two options on the first window. "Recommended restore:" or "Choose a different restore point". The recommended restore option will restore from the most recent restore point. If you restore from the recommended restore point and your system still malfunctions, you can choose a different, earlier restore point. Figure 62.4 shows the window that appears if you select "Choose a different restore point".

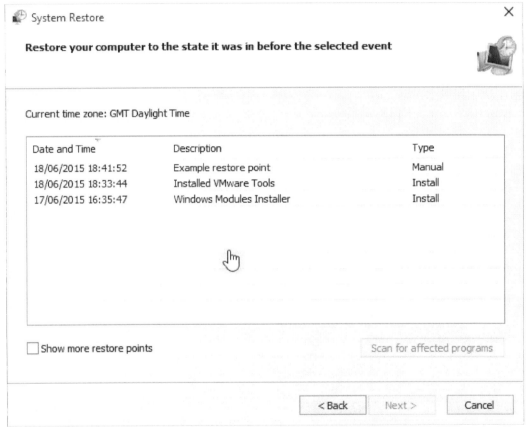

Figure 62.4 – Choosing a restore point

To choose a restore point, simply select it from the list and then click on "Next >". You can see a description of why the restore point was created, along with the date and time it was made. If you suspect that the problems you are having are down to a specific program or update you installed, you can restore to a specific restore point to test your theory.

62.3 – Restoring from a restore point

Once you choose a system restore point, you will need to confirm your selection, figure 62.5 shows the window that appears.

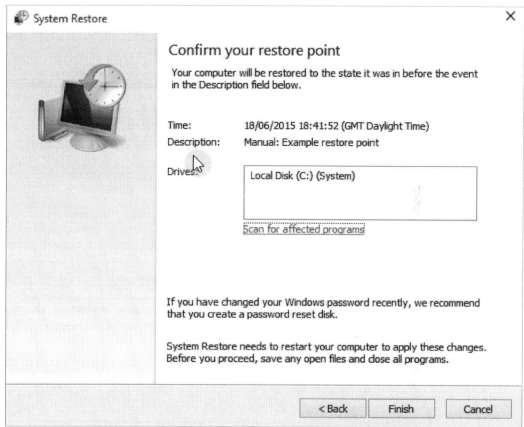

Figure 62.5 – Confirming a system restore point

This window gives us some pointers to note before we begin with the system restore process. We can "Scan for affected programs" to see if any of the programs on our computer are likely to need reinstalling after this process is completed. If you have recently changed your password, using System Restore might revert back to the old password, so make sure you can remember them both or create a password reset disk.

Since the restore process will restart your PC, you also need to close down any running programs and save your work. Click on "Finish" when you are ready to proceed.

You will receive one final warning not to interrupt the system restore process, click on "Yes" and the process will then begin. It will take several minutes to complete.

When the process is complete, the system will restart and return you to the Lock screen. You should now log back into your computer and check to see if the problems you were having are resolved. If they are not, you can start System Restore again and either undo the system restore or choose another restore point.

62.4 – Undoing a System Restore

Before the System Restore utility rolls back to a restore point, it creates a restore point containing your current configuration. That means you can easily undo a System Restore. Start the system restore process again and the window shown in figure 62.6 should appear.

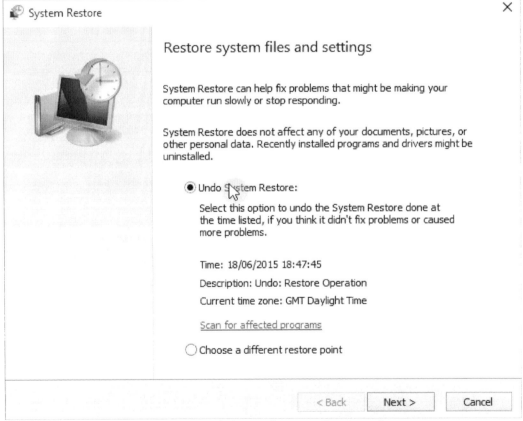

Figure 62.6 – Undoing a System Restore is easy

When you choose "Undo System Restore:" the process works in exactly the same way as when you use System Restore normally. You are in actual fact restoring from a restore point that was created before you ran System Restore the first time!

That's all you need to know to use System Restore on your Windows 10 PC. In the next lesson we will be taking a look at the Reset your PC feature. This is a maintenance tool that was introduced in Windows 8 that makes repairing troublesome PCs much easier.

Lesson 63 – Reset your PC

In this lesson we are going to look at the "Reset your PC" feature. This feature was named "Refresh your PC" in Windows 8. The feature serves two purposes. Firstly, it can be used to remove all your programs and data from your PC if, for instance, you want to sell your computer or give it away. Secondly, it can reinstall your operating system without affecting the files stored in your personal folders. This is useful if you think your operating system files have become corrupt, for instance.

63.1 – Beginning a system reset

To use this feature you will need to be logged in with an administrator account (you can't simply use UAC to activate this feature). To access the feature, open the Start menu and click on "Settings", or open the Action Centre (e.g by swiping your finger in from the right of the screen) and tap on "All settings". Now, in the Settings app, navigate to Update & Security and make sure "Recovery" is selected from the options on the left. You should then be looking at a window like the one shown in figure 63.1.

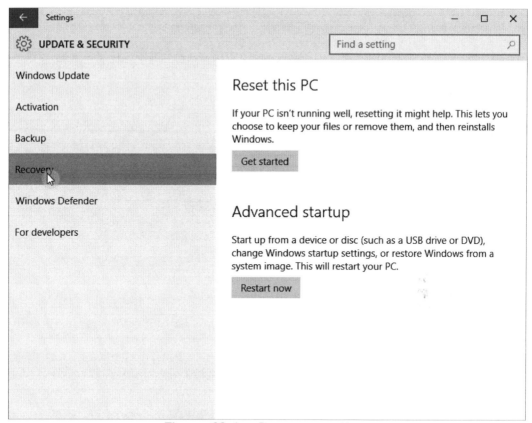

Figure 63.1 – Recovery options

63.2 – Reset options

In figure 63.1 we can see the "Reset this PC" option. Click on the "Get Started" button and the message shown in figure 63.2 will appear.

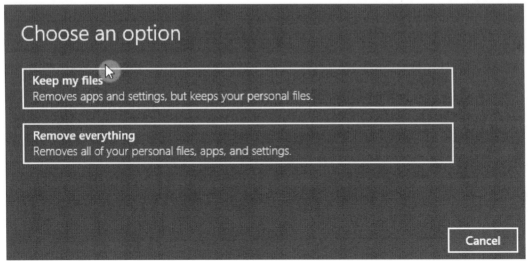

Figure 63.2 – Choosing a reset option

You now have two options; "Keep my files" and "Remove everything". If you want to completely start from fresh, you would choose the bottom option. Before you choose this option, make sure that you have backed up anything and everything in your personal folders or anywhere else on your PC.

If you just want to factory reset your PC without affecting your personal files, choose the top option. By using either of these options, you will lose any desktop programs you have installed. Many of your PC settings and customisations will also be reset to default. After the procedure is complete you can, of course, reinstall any desktop software you need. Before you resort to the Reset feature, you should try the System Restore utility we covered in lesson 62 to undo recent changes to your PC.

Even when using the "Keep my files" option to reset your PC, it's certainly not a bad idea to make sure that any important files on your PC are safely backed up before proceeding.

If you are sure you want to proceed with a Reset, simply choose the appropriate option by clicking on it. If you choose to keep your files, a message similar to the one shown in figure 63.3 will appear.

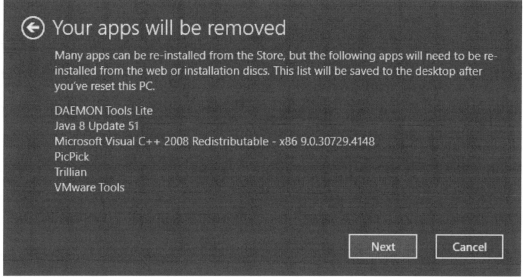

Figure 63.3 – Be prepared to reinstall your apps after the process

Windows will list the apps on your PC that will be removed during the process and will therefore require reinstallation. This list will also be placed in a file on your desktop after the reset process is complete.

If you select the "Remove everything" option, the message shown in figure 63.4 will appear.

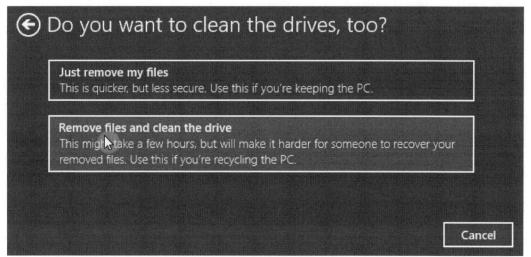

Figure 63.4 – Cleaning a drive can remove traces of personal files

Rather than just reinstalling Windows, you're now given the option of cleaning your drive. If you are selling or giving away your PC, you should choose the "Remove files and clean the drive" option to make sure that your personal files cannot be recovered by whoever receives the PC. As we explained in our Recycle Bin tutorial (lesson 18), files that are deleted from your PC aren't really gone, at least until another file overwrites the free space, and can be recovered with special software.

After choosing a cleaning method above (if necessary), you should be ready to reset the PC. The message shown in figure 63.5 should be displayed.

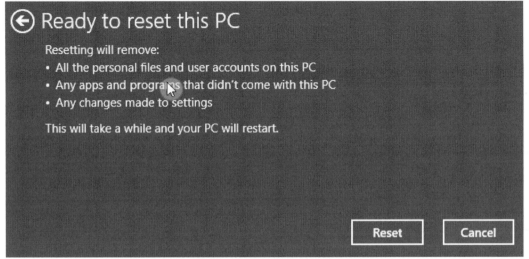

Figure 63.5 – Ready to reset the PC

If you upgraded from Windows 7 or 8, You may see a warning that resetting the PC will make it impossible to go back to your previous version of Windows. If you installed Windows 10 from a DVD or other media, you should make sure you have that media to hand too.

This is the last chance to change your mind. Click on "Reset" now to start the process or "Cancel" to abort.

63.3 – Finalising and resetting

Once you click on "Reset", the computer will restart. Rather than the regular Windows startup, you will see the screen shown in figure 63.6.

Figure 63.6 – Wait while Windows resets your PC

The resetting process will take some time, when it is completed, your computer will reboot automatically. If you chose the "Keep my files" option, you can now log back in as normal. You will see straight away that some of your preferences have been reset and you may need to reconfigure networking settings. You should now reinstall any desktop software that you use. If you go to the desktop you will find a file called "Removed Apps". Double click on it to see a list of the programs that were uninstalled.

If you used the "Remove Everything" option however, you will need to set your computer up again from scratch. All of your files and folders will have been removed. All user accounts will be deleted and all software, apart from the default apps that come with Windows 10, must now be reinstalled. Your

PC has effectively been reset to a factory fresh state. Refer to lesson 1 if you need help setting up your PC again.

That concludes this lesson on System Reset. Hopefully this isn't a feature you will need to use very often, but when problems do occur, it can be a good last resort to get your PC into a fully working state again. In the next lesson we look at the Windows Task Manager, a tool that is designed to manage and close troublesome programs.

Lesson 64 – Task Manager

Sometimes when you work with your computer, an application will stop responding to the mouse or keyboard. When this happens, it will not be possible to close the program because the window will freeze, preventing you from doing anything with it. For (hopefully rare) situations like these, you can use the Task Manager to force the application to close. The Task Manager in Windows 10 is the same as in Windows 8 and it shows significantly more information than in the task manager in Windows 7 and previous versions of Windows.

64.1 – Starting the Task Manager

There are several ways to start the Task Manager. One way is to search for "task manager" or "taskmgr" in the search bar and click on the icon that appears at the top, Task Manager will then open.

If your computer is not responding normally, you may not be able to use the search bar. In that case, use the following keyboard shortcut. Press and hold the Control, Alt and Delete keys together. You don't need to press them all at the same time, you can press them one after the other as long as you end up pressing all three at once.

When you press these three keys together, the screen shown in figure 64.1 will appear.

Figure 64.1 – Summon this screen by pressing the Control, Alt and Delete keys together

Choose "Task Manager" from the menu to load Task Manger.

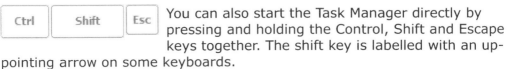 You can also start the Task Manager directly by pressing and holding the Control, Shift and Escape keys together. The shift key is labelled with an up-pointing arrow on some keyboards.

What if you don't have a keyboard attached to your Windows 10 PC? In that case you can press and hold the Windows button on your device (the physical button that opens the Start menu or Start screen) and then quickly press and release the power button. The menu shown in figure 64.1 should then open, allowing you to select Task Manager.

Figure 64.2 shows Windows 10 Task Manager open in basic view mode.

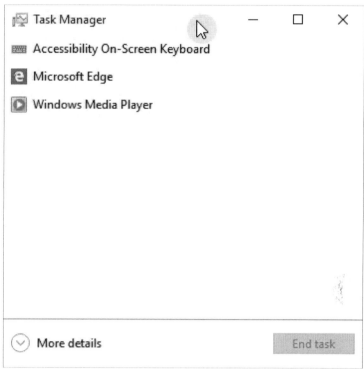

Figure 64.2 – Windows Task Manager

64.2 – Managing tasks

Task Manager shows us a list of programs that are currently running. In figure 64.2 we can see Microsoft Edge and Windows Media Player, as well as the on-screen keyboard. These programs are running and behaving normally. Occasionally a program will freeze or stop responding to input. When this happens you may need to start the Task Manager to end the program.

A program/task which has stopped responding will be marked as "Not responding". If you cannot end the program normally, select it from the list of tasks in Task Manager and then click the "End Task" button. Windows will then attempt to force the program to exit. You may see a window appear telling you that the application is not responding and that you might lose data if you proceed to force it to close. Any information you were working on in your program that was not saved will probably be lost, but if the application is no longer responding this may be the only course of action you can take.

64.3 – Processes

To access the Processes tab, firstly click on the "More details" button near the bottom of the window. This will change Task Manager into advanced mode. Now you can select the Processes tab from the top of the programs window. Figure 64.3 shows the Task Manager open on the Processes tab.

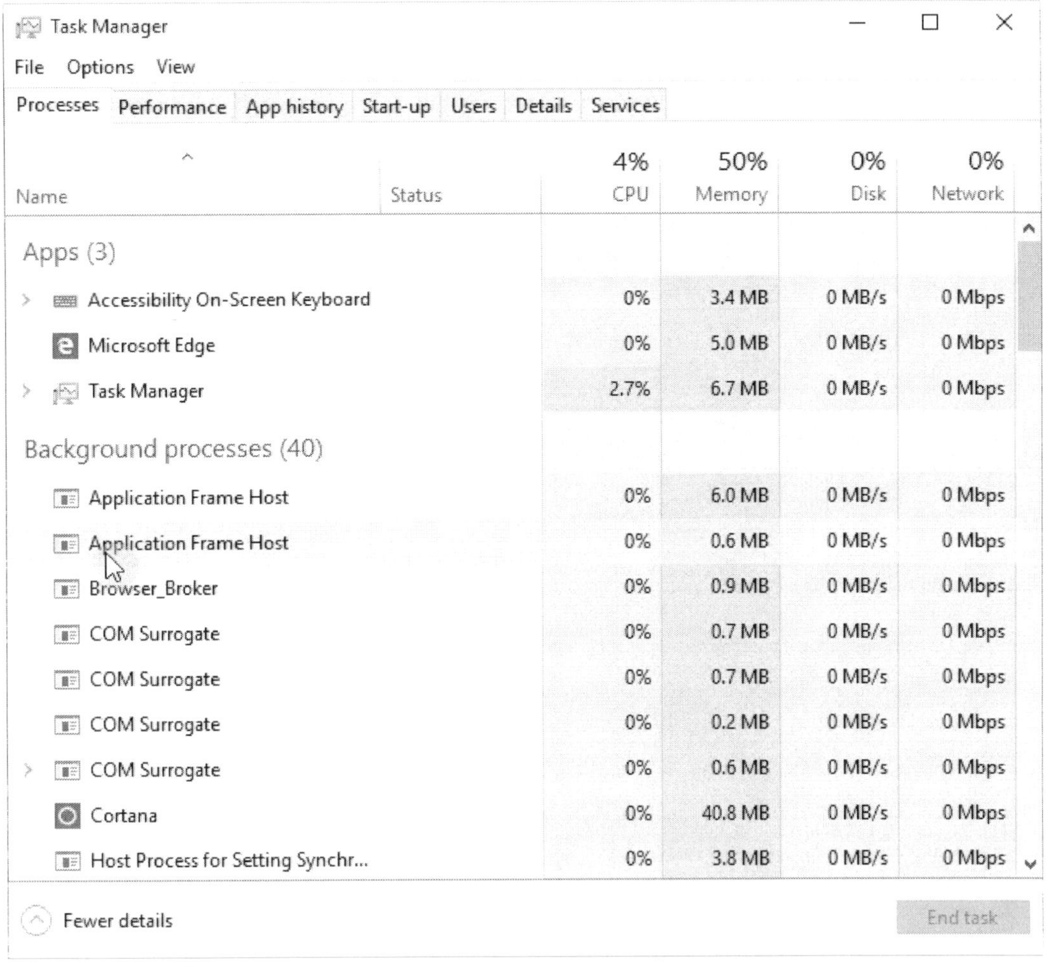
Task Manager
File Options View
Processes Performance App history Start-up Users Details Services
Name
Status
4% CPU
50% Memory
0% Disk
0% Network
Apps (3)
Accessibility On-Screen Keyboard 0% 3.4 MB 0 MB/s 0 Mbps
Microsoft Edge 0% 5.0 MB 0 MB/s 0 Mbps
Task Manager 2.7% 6.7 MB 0 MB/s 0 Mbps
Background processes (40)
Application Frame Host 0% 6.0 MB 0 MB/s 0 Mbps
Application Frame Host 0% 0.6 MB 0 MB/s 0 Mbps
Browser_Broker 0% 0.9 MB 0 MB/s 0 Mbps
COM Surrogate 0% 0.7 MB 0 MB/s 0 Mbps
COM Surrogate 0% 0.7 MB 0 MB/s 0 Mbps
COM Surrogate 0% 0.2 MB 0 MB/s 0 Mbps
COM Surrogate 0% 0.6 MB 0 MB/s 0 Mbps
Cortana 0% 40.8 MB 0 MB/s 0 Mbps
Host Process for Setting Synchr... 0% 3.8 MB 0 MB/s 0 Mbps
Fewer details
End task

Figure 64.3 – The Processes tab lists all running processes

In this view, Task Manager gives you more details about the CPU (basically your computers brain), Memory, Disk and Network usage of all the running processes. A process might be an application, either one that is running with a window or hidden in the notification area, or a subsystem or service managed by the operating system.

Just like in the basic view, you can end a process by clicking on it from the list and then clicking "End task". Be careful when ending processes, you will lose any unsaved data in the program. If you end a system process, you might make your computer unstable, forcing you to restart it.

64.4 – Other Task Manager tabs

The other tabs available in the Task Manager can occasionally be useful too, so we will take a quick tour of them now.

The Performance tab shows a graphical representation of computer resource use on your PC. Figure 64.4 shows the Task Manager open on the Performance tab.

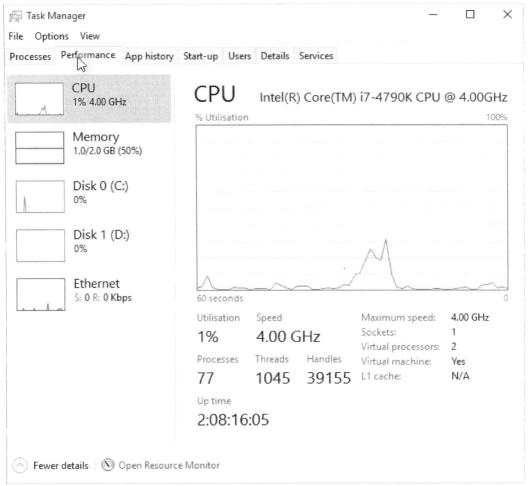

Figure 64.4 – The Performance tab of the Task Manager

You do not need to understand all the technical jargon shown in figure 64.4. The important things to note are CPU Usage and Memory. You can click on any of the small graphs on the left of the window to get a bigger view over in the right.

The CPU usage gauge is an indicator of how much computing work your PC is doing. When your computer is idle on the desktop, you should see around 0% to 3% CPU usage. If there is always some CPU activity going on pushing the meter higher, you may have some spyware or other software running in the background.

The Memory gauge is a measure of how much data the computer is working on at the moment. If this gauge is nearly full, your computer is running out of resources. Try closing some programs to free up some memory.

The Disk gauge shows how frequently your computer is writing to disk. Again, this should be low when you're not running any software.

The Ethernet gauge shows any network activity that is currently going on in the background. If you aren't running any networking or internet software, this should generally be at 0%.

The "App history" tab was introduced in Windows 8. Figure 64.5 shows the Task Manager open on this tab.

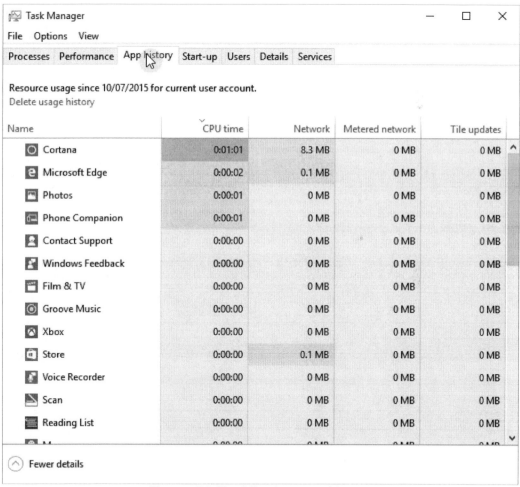

Figure 64.5 – Viewing app history

The App history tab is quite useful, as it shows CPU usage by a program over a period of time. So for instance in the Processes tab you might see spikes of CPU usage, in this tab you can see what has really been gobbling up the computing time on your PC. In figure 64.5 we can see that Cortana has used the most CPU time. If you suspect a program of periodically slowing down your PC, check here to see if its CPU time count is high. Sadly, the App history tab only works with Trusted Windows Store apps and not regular desktop apps.

Also introduced in Windows 8 was the Startup tab. Here we can see programs that start up with the PC, along with their "Startup impact". Programs listed with a high startup impact cause your PC to start slower. To disable them from starting when your PC starts, right click on them and choose "disable". If disable is greyed out for a specific program, you may need to restart Task Manager with administrator rights (run as administrator).

Next there is the Users tab. On this tab you can see which users are logged in or connected to your PC, along with a summary of how many CPU resources their programs are using. On a home PC this is usually limited to just your account.

The Details tab was also first introduced in Windows 8. Figure 64.6 shows this tab open in Task Manager in Windows 10.

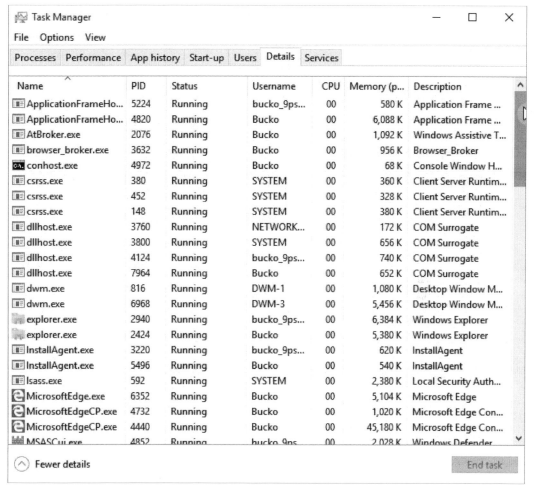

Figure 64.6 – Details view in Task Manager

This tab shows information about running processes rather like the old Task Manager did in previous versions of Windows. Again, simply click on a task and then click "End task" if you want to terminate it.

Finally, the Services tab shows which services are available on your PC. Services add extra functionality to Windows such as networking or DVD recording. From this tab you can start and stop services by right clicking on them. We do not recommend doing this unless you are an advanced user and know exactly what you are doing.

64.5 – Running a program from the Task Manager

It is possible to run a program from the Task Manager. To do this, open the File menu and choose "Run new task". You will need to know where the program file is located on your computer however. In some rare instances this can be useful, if you find yourself troubleshooting a serious PC problem the Task Manager may be the only way to run a program if the Start menu wont open, for example. If you ever find the taskbar has disappeared from the desktop, you can usually restore it by starting Task Manager and opening the Run new task option and typing in "Explorer".

This is the last lesson in our PC maintenance section and it marks the end of the lessons for Windows 10! You have not finished learning about Windows 10 though, no-one ever has. Don't forget to visit Top-Windows-Tutorials.com regularly to keep up with the latest tips, techniques and tutorials for getting the most out of your Windows 10 PC.

In the last chapter we take a brief look at some popular Windows software that is compatible with Windows 10.

Chapter 12 – And Finally...

You now know all about Windows 10, but the real purpose of an operating system is to help you run software. In this last chapter we will discuss some popular software packages that let you accomplish various computing tasks. While Windows 10 comes bundled with lots of software, there are a colossal number of third party apps, games and other programs to discover both online and in the Windows store. Remember that there are always plenty of other software recommendations on Top-Windows-Tutorials.com too.

Popular Windows Software

You will always be spoilt for choice when looking for software to run on your Windows 10 machine. As the most popular operating system for home computer users, Windows has a software package to suit almost every need. In this final section, we will explore some common home computing tasks and look at some popular software packages that help you with them.

65.1 – Software recommendations

E-mail

The mail tile is great for tablet PCs and light usage but really doesn't have the flexibility that power users demand. Fortunately, there are several alternatives.

Mozilla Thunderbird (Free, see http://www.mozillamessaging.com/en-US/thunderbird/)

Reclaim your inbox with this powerful free e-mail program which includes anti-spam technologies and is extendible through plug-ins.

Microsoft Outlook (from $99.95 or $9.99 per month with a Microsoft Office suite, see http://office.microsoft.com/en-us/outlook/)

Microsoft's powerful Outlook package is part of the ever popular Office suite and includes a professional e-mail package as well as a personal organiser and calendar application. It is the standard PIM (personal information manager) in many businesses.

Games

There are thousands of game titles available for Windows machines, from easy pick up and play titles to complex and in-depth simulation games. You can find games in the Windows store or why not check out our favourite third party games marketplace, GOG.com ?

Image and photograph editing

The Photo app is fun for viewing your photos on a touch device, but when you want to get serious with your photographs you should check out these programs.

Adobe Photoshop / Photoshop Elements (from $99, see http://www.adobe.com/products/photoshop-elements.html)

Photoshop remains the image editing program of choice for professional photographers and artists around the world. The Elements version is an excellent choice for home photographers.

Google Picasa (free – see http://picasa.google.com/)

Enhance, catalogue and display your pictures on the desktop with this popular tool from the search engine giant Google.

Paint (bundled with Windows 10)

Windows 10 includes a basic desktop graphics utility called Paint, which can be used for simple image editing.

Paint.net (free – see http://www.getpaint.net/)

An amazing free graphics package with a feature set that rivals those found in commercially available alternatives.

Instant messaging, video and voice chat

There are lots of great IM apps for both desktop and touch users.

Skype (free – see www.skype.com/)

Skype has been the market leader in internet telephony and voice over IP (VOIP) communications for several years now. What that means is, you can use your internet connection to call your friends on Skype for free. You can also use Skype to call normal telephones at rates which are often far cheaper than other services. If you have a webcam, you can also video chat with your Skype friends too!

Jitsi (free – see https://jitsi.org/)

Jitsi is the ideal video conferencing application for the privacy conscious user. Featuring strong encryption and privacy safeguards that Skype and other closed-source software cannot match.

Pidgin (free – see https://pidgin.im/)

There are several popular instant messaging services in use on the internet today. If you have friends on several services, Pidgin can connect to them all through one handy interface.

Music and Multimedia

Windows Media Player and the Film and TV apps are not the only ways your Windows 10 PC can sing and dance. There are plenty of great software packages out there that can help you discover your media in new and exciting ways.

Plex (basic version is free, see https://plex.tv/ and the Windows store)

Plex organises your video, music, and photo collections and streams them to all of your screens. Use Plex as a media player on your PC or as a media server for your whole home, streaming media to dozens of compatible devices such as smart TVs and games consoles.

VLC (free – see www.videolan.org/vlc/ and the Windows store)

VLC is a popular media player with a low memory and processor overhead that is renowned for its high compatibility with a wide range of media files. VLC can also play DVD movies, a capability sadly removed in Windows 10 due to licensing costs.

Music creation

Want to make sweet music with your PC? There are plenty of software packages that can help with that too.

Cakewalk SONAR Platinum (from £39 per month – see http://www.store.cakewalk.com/)

SONAR Platinum is the easiest way to turn your PC into a fully-fledged music production studio. Fuelled by over 25 years in the relentless pursuit of innovation, SONAR is re-inventing the modern recording studio. With SONAR you can record live instruments, vocals, or any audio source (compatible hardware permitting).

Sound Forge (from $59.95 – see http://www.sonycreativesoftware.com/soundforgesoftware)

Sound Forge Audio Studio software is the easiest way to record, edit, encode, and master audio on your PC. Includes vinyl recording and restoration tools to help you convert those precious old records (compatible hardware permitting).

Online safety

Children love to explore the internet, but not everything and everyone they encounter is suitable for them. Windows 10 includes a family safety module that we cover in lesson 39, but there are other good alternatives too.

Optenet (From $39.95 – See http://www.optenetpc.com/)

Optenet PC is a highly effective internet filter which can filter adult and unsuitable content with minimal false positives and without making your internet run slowly.

Password Management

If you use a wide range of websites and online services then a password manager tool is essential. Most people cannot remember more than 3 or 4 unique passwords and recycling the same password over several sites is extremely bad for your online security.

KeePass (Free, see http://keepass.info/)

If you want a free password manager but don't want to store your passwords in the cloud, look no further than the light-weight, open source password manager KeyPass.

Roboform (free for up to 10 passwords, $29.95 for unlimited, see http://www.roboform.com/)

Roboform has long been one of our favourite password managers. It is preferred by many users because it offers an offline storage mode, meaning your passwords never have to be stored online.

StickyPassword (Basic version is free, see https://www.stickypassword.com)

A new upcoming password manager that works across PCs and mobile devices and can sync via the cloud or local network connections.

Social networking

While most users check their social networking sites on the web, it can be easier, faster and more fun to use a dedicated app to do so. There are dedicated apps for most of the popular social networks in the Windows store, but here are some often overlooked gems that can power up your social networking on your Windows 10 device.

Instapic (free – search the Windows store)

Keep up with your friends on the popular photo sharing service Instagram with this free app which works fantastically on both tablet and desktop PCs.

MobyPicture (free – see http://www.mobypicture.com/)

MobyPicture gives you a desktop widget that allows you to instantly drag and drop photographs and upload them to Facebook, Twitter or Flickr.

Tweetdeck (free – see http://www.tweetdeck.com/)

Monitor your Twitter accounts from one handy app with Tweetdeck. Supports multiple Twitter accounts and all for free.

Web browsing

Microsoft Edge is not the only way to get around the web!

Mozilla Firefox (free – see http://www.mozilla.com/firefox/)

Firefox is a popular alternative to Internet Explorer. Faster, safer, and smarter, Firefox also has a huge range of plug-ins that can be used to extend and customise the browser.

Google Chrome (free – see http://www.google.com/chrome)

Google Chrome is another very popular alternative browser. It is known for its super fast browsing speeds and simple, uncluttered interface.

Word processing and office

Microsoft Office (from $9.99 per month – see http://office.microsoft.com/)

The de-facto standard Office suite for many businesses, colleges and universities. Includes the industry standard word processor, Microsoft Word and probably the most powerful spreadsheet package in the world, Microsoft Excel.

LibreOffice.org (free – see https://www.libreoffice.org/)

A fantastic Microsoft Office compatible productivity suite that is completely free! While the spreadsheet component can't quite compete with Microsoft Excel, the word processor component is a very worthy competitor to Microsoft Word. This book was written using LibreOffice.org Writer!

Appendix – Using Touch PCs

Touch screen PCs are becoming more common, but are still something of a rarity compared with PCs equipped with a keyboard and mouse or trackpad. Because of this, most of the lessons in this guide were written and recorded using the traditional keyboard and mouse setup. Following the lessons on a touch only machine simply means translating the mouse commands into the touch gestures shown in the table.

For details of all the touch gestures Windows 10 recognises, see lesson 7.

Mouse:– The basic gestures are the same or similar on a touch screen as they are on a mouse.

Mouse Action	Touch Equivalent
Left (or primary mouse button) click	Tap
Right click	Press and hold with your finger
Control + Mousewheel (to zoom)	Make a pinching gesture on the screen

Most operations will work the same way with touch, for instance to drag windows, you press and hold your finger to the screen, rather than clicking and holding your mouse button.

Keyboard:– When using a Windows 10 PC in Tablet mode, Windows should automatically display the touch keyboard whenever you tap on a text entry area. If it does not, press and hold your finger on the taskbar and choose "Show touch keyboard button". The touch keyboard button will then appear in the notification area (see lesson 21), allowing you to activate it manually.

You can show and hide the touch keyboard button while working in desktop mode by following our notification area tutorial, lesson 21.2.

Index

16-bit..429
32-bit...18, 20, 23, 428
   vs. 64-bit..20
64-bit..18, 20p., 23, 428p.
   16-bit applications...429
   vs. 32-bit...428
Accent colour..442
Action Centre....43, 73, 75, 85, 192, 329, 371, 409, 411pp., 419, 423, 436, 453, 524
Address bar..95
Administrator..329, 335, 340
   Risks...340
   Run this program as...432
Adobe Photoshop..250, 542
ADSL..452
ALAC..492
All settings..413
Antivirus software..384
   Third party..392
Apple iPad...329
Apple iPhone...180, 329
Apps...
   All..47p.
   Background..376
   Default..31
Autorun...430
Back button..76, 81
Backup...
   File History..305
   Image..305
   Media..307
      Cloud...309
      Local network...308
      Secondary hard drive...307
   Storing your backups...310
Battery Saver..414
Beacons...374
BIOS...328
Bitlocker...18p., 201
Bluetooth...116, 374, 414p.
BoxCryptor..310
Breadcrumbs...96p.
Brightness (button)..414
Cable broadband..452
Cakewalk SONAR Platinum..544
Calendar app..234
   Add an event..236
   Multiple calendars..235
   Reminder...235

```
    Views..................................................................................................235
Camera................................................................................................371
    Privacy.............................................................................................371
CD......................................................................................................179
    Database.........................................................................................494
    Ripping....................................................................................491, 495
        Options......................................................................................491p.
    Software..........................................................................................422
Certified for Windows 10........................................................................447
Change or remove a program................................................................506
Change the size of text, apps and other items........................................86
Click....................................................................................................15
    Right................................................................................................15
ClickLock............................................................................................397
Cloud..........................................................................................291, 309
    Hackers...........................................................................................298
    Storage...........................................................................................291
Compatibility options...................................................................429, 432pp.
Compatibility troubleshooter................................................................432
Compressed (zipped) folder see Zip file
Computer viruses................................................................................384
    False positive..................................................................................388
Connect (button)................................................................................414
Contacts see People app
Content view.....................................................................................103
Context menu. 114pp., 119, 121, 129, 142pp., 168p., 178, 430p., 433, 436, 477, 494
Copy..................................................................................................116p.
    vs. Cut............................................................................................117
Cortana.........................13, 38, 51, 53, 58, 207pp., 235, 334, 365, 371, 505, 538
    Activate..........................................................................................207
    Add a category...............................................................................218
    Add a topic.....................................................................................218
    Halo................................................................................................210
    Hey Cortana.............................................................................216, 218
    Notebook.................................................................................216, 218
    Open apps......................................................................................222
    Play music......................................................................................222
    Privacy....................................................................................209, 212
    Reminders......................................................................................220
    Send e-mail....................................................................................222
    Talking to.......................................................................................215
    Tell a joke......................................................................................222
    Troubleshoot..................................................................................222
    Turning Cortana off.................................................................51, 212
    Typing to........................................................................................212
CPU...................................................................................................534
Cruzer Micro USB........................................................................448, 450
Cut....................................................................................................116p.
Data..................................................................................................306
```

Date and time..
    Adjust..43
Desktop...18, 38pp., 43, 61, 126, 186
    Background..44, 249, 436p.
        Choose picture...437
        Colour settings...441
        From the internet...440
        Positioning options...438
        Slideshow...438
    Computer..22, 176
    Create shortcut..116
    Dim (UAC)...344
    Peek..61, 189
    Shake..62
    Show...43
    Snap...61
    Software...336, 340, 420
        Additional components..426
        Choosing..420
        Free vs. paid...422
        Installation directory..425
        Installing...422p.
        Privacy..376
        Shortcut..425
        Spyware or viruses...424
        Tablet mode..77
        Uninstalling..506
        vs. Trusted Windows Store app..420
    Wallpaper...436
Details pane..106p., 142, 168, 198
Details view...98, 104
Devices and drives..177
Devices and Printers..447pp.
Diacritics..202
Dial up..453
DirectX..13, 22p.
Disk Cleanup..178, 508pp.
    System files..509
Documents folder..92
Double click...396
Drag...73
Driver..450
DVD...176, 179
    Rewriter..179
    Software..422
    Video...179
E-mail...116, 224
    Accounts..226
    Attachments...232

Cc/Bcc..232
Delete...231
Forward..231
New message...231
Reply..230
Subject...232
  See also Mail app
Ethernet cable...454
EULA *see* License agreement
Express settings..30, 35
Facebook..545
  App...288
Family & other users..331
Family safety...346
  Add a child..347
  Apps & games..353
  Child account...349
  Invitation..347p.
  Manually block website...353
  Recent activity..351
  Screen time..355
  Settings...350
  Web filter..353
  Website..346
  Your family...349
Fax..116
File..
  Delete..119, 168
  Extensions..111, 162pp.
  Name collision...118
  Rename..119
File Explorer 16, 41p., 47, 55, 71, 77p., 85, 88p., 91pp., 97, 99, 103pp., 108pp., 114, 117, 125pp., 134, 137pp., 143, 149p., 152pp., 162p., 167, 169, 175, 177, 189, 198, 204, 251, 296, 320, 423, 429pp., 433, 439, 481, 488, 490, 499
  Column..104p.
  Libraries...133
  Navigation controls...95
  Search tool...95
  Sorting..108
  See also Details pane, Preview pane
File History..311p.
  Advanced settings...314
  Backup frequency...315
  Configuring..311
  Exclude folder..314
  Explorer..317p.
  Homegroup...313
  Keep saved versions...315
  Limitations...321

Restore from..316, 320
    To a different directory..321
Select drive..312
Turn on...313
Film & TV app..262p.
  Aspect Ratio..266
  Buying media...267
  Cast to Device...266
  Choose where we look for videos..267
  Full Screen...267
  Menu...264
  Pause..267
  Play...267
  Repeat..267
  Size...263
  Videos...265
  Volume...267
Firewall...377
  Third party...382
  See also Windows Firewall
FLAC..492
Flickr...545
Flight mode..415
Floppy disk..116, 179
Folder..
  Advanced Settings..156
  Attributes...145
  Automatically expand to current...156, 158
  Click items...154
  Create new..112pp.
  Customise..148
  Default location..147
  Delete..119
  Documents...91
  Hidden..158
  Icons...149p.
  Merge...118
  Nest..113
  Open...94
  Open in new window..154
  Optimise this folder for..149
  Options..132, 152
      General...153
  Personal...91, 112, 177
  Pictures..149
  Privacy...154
  Properties...144p.
  Rename..119
  Reset Folders..156

Size 145
Views 97, 155
Games 542
Getting to know you 372
    Privacy 372
Google Chrome 31, 473, 546
Google Picasa 543
GPS 279
GPU 22
Graphics card/Processor *see* GPU
Groove Music app .... 83, 138, 253pp., 261pp., 266p., 498p.
    Albums view 256
    Browse music 256
    Buttons 254
    Choose where we look for music 261
    Current Track 259
    Play a track 258
    Playlist 259
        Add track 260
    Previous/Next Track 259
    Repeat 259
    Search bar 256
    Seek 259
    Shuffle 259
    Sign In 261
    Size 254
    Volume 259
Group by 109, 139
Hard drive .... 21, 176p.
    Capacity 21
    Compress 179
    Defragmentation 511
    Failure 305
    Properties 178
    Solid state 21
    Space 177
    vs. RAM 20
Hardware troubleshooter 450
Hidden ....
    File 158
        Show 159
    Folder ....
        Show 159
    Items 111
Hide app icons 78
Hide empty drives 180
Hide protected operating system files 161
Home theatre receiver 181
Homegroup 93, 111, 146, 474pp., 479, 482

Browse	481
Create	475
Hierarchy	481
Joining	479
Leave	482
Password	476
Permissions	479
Rename computer	482
Restricting access	477
Icons view	99p.
Indexing	
Diacritics	202
Encrypted files	201
File types	202
Add your own	203
Location	200, 202
Options	199
Rebuild	202
Information apps	269
Instagram	545
Instapic	545
Internet Explorer 11	459
Internet Service Provider *see* ISP	
ISP	452p.
Item check boxes	110
Jitsi	543
Jump list	183p.
Start menu	406
KeePass	545
Language list	368
Laptop	22
Let apps use my advertising ID	367
Libraries	130, 132pp., 138pp., 147, 156, 200, 490, 499
Add a location to	136
Default save location	138
Folders true location	143
Manage	134
Music	138, 261
Pictures	141
Public save location	138
Show	133
Videos	267
LibreOffice.org	546
License agreement	28, 34, 424
Limited accounts	329
See also User accounts - Standard user	
List view	101
Local account	37p., 228, 333p., 337
Create	38, 337

Location...
    Button..414
    Choose apps that can use my location..370
    History...370
    Privacy...370
    Tracking...369
    See also Privacy - Location
Lock..48p.
Lock screen...39p., 443
    App settings..444
    Camera settings..446
    Pictures..443
    Settings..443
MAC address..457
Mail app..224, 228
    Add e-mail accounts...227, 233
    Formatting..232
    Inbox..228
    Mailbox sync settings..229
    Move messages..234
    New message...231
    Options..232
Manchester..276
Map network drive..181
Maps app...274
    3D Cities..281
    Directions..277p.
    Favourites...279, 281
    Layouts..274
    Map views...275
    Navigation mode..278p.
    Rotate map..275
    Route planning...276
    Search bar...276
    Show Location..275
    Tilt map...275
    Zoom in/Out...275
Media player..180p.
Memory..21
Memory/storage card reader..180
Metadata...105, 107p., 197pp., 204, 490
    Edit...198
    JPG picture..198
Metro Commander..**88p.**
Microphone...215, 371
    Privacy...371
Microsoft account. 23, 36pp., 207, 226, 228, 290, 296, 299, 322, 333pp., 337p., 346, 348, 367, 375, 505
    Adding...334

PIN..338
  Sign-on options...338
  vs. Local account..37, 333
Microsoft Edge.......13, 31, 41p., 73, 81pp., 154, 216, 299, 368, 404, 440p., 459pp., 467pp., 473, 546
  Clear browsing data..470
  Download a file...471
    Risks...473
  Enter address directly...462
  Favourite...464, 466
    Add a site..464
    Browsing..467
    Sidebar..468
  Links..462
  Navigation controls..461p.
  Search..460
    Results..461
  Settings menu...469
  Tabs...464
  Zoom controls..469
Microsoft Office...546
Microsoft Outlook..542
Microsoft Print to PDF...450
Mobile broadband..452p.
MobyPicture..545
Modem..453
Modern app *see* Trusted Windows Store app
Mouse...395
  Configuration settings...395
  Control panel...395
  Double click..396
  Left handed...396
  Pointer..
    Hide while typing..399
    Motion...399
    Schemes...398
    Show location...399
    Snap To..399
    Speed..399
    Trails...399
    Visibility..399
  Properties..396
  Wheel...399p.
Mozilla Firefox...546
Mozilla Thunderbird...542
Multi-monitor...189
  Taskbar..189
Multimedia Devices...449
Music Tools...96

Navigation pane............................92pp., 111, 133, 156pp., 175, 481, 490, 493, 495
    Expand..93
    Libraries..132
Netbook..22
Network..43, 93, 474
    Data usage..456
    Guest or public..378
    Home..474
    Icon..192
    Locations..181
    Private..378
    Wired..454
    Wireless..454
News app..268
    Buttons...270
    Category...269
    Interests...270
    Local news..270
    Read...269
    Search bar..269
Notebook *see* Laptop
Note (button)...413
Notification area...24, 41, 43, 191pp., 296, 301, 411, 455
    Customising...192, 194
    Icons...196
    Menu..192
    New vs. old..191
    System icons..195
Notifications..43, 411, 413, 416p.
    Dismiss...413
    Hide while presenting...417
    On the lock screen...416
    Options...415
    Settings for individual apps..417
    Sounds...417
Office 365...298
OneDrive.....37, 55, 93, 111, 134, 137, 192, 233, 246, 291pp., 309p., 322, 333, 339, 365
    Change location..293
    Fetch..296
    File Explorer...293, 296p.
    Icon..301
    Manage storage..301
    On the web..299
    Settings..301
    Sign in..292
    Sync settings..294, 302
    Touch app..302
Operating system recovery media..306

Optenet..544
Optimise Drives tool...511p.
    Manual...514
        Schedule..512
Paint..543
Paint.net...543
Parent directory..95
Password...30, 37p., 40, 296
    Hint..38
    Manager..334
Paste...116p.
People app..232, 237
    Add contact...240
    Adding an account...237p., 244
    Browsing..239
    Edit contact..240p.
    Linking contacts...242p.
    Search..239
    Unlink contact..243
Personal Digital Assistant (PDA)..181
Phone Companion..180
Photos app..245
    Additional options...248
    Browsing..246
    Copy..249
    Delete...248
    Edit..248
    Effects..251
    Enhance...247
    Filters...250
    Picture editing tools..249
    Print..249
    Rotate..248
    Selective focus tool...251
    Share..247
    Slideshow..247
    Viewing photos..246
Picture..
    Set as background...249
    Set as lock screen..249
Pidgin...543
Pinch...74, 547
Play-old-PC-Games.com..435
Playlist...260
Plex...544
PNG file...107
Pointer...397
Power button..76
Power options..49

Press and hold..547
Preview pane...105p., 142
Previous Versions..146
Printer...449p.
    Default..450
    Pseudo...450
Privacy..
    Account Info...373
    Contacts..374
    Location..368
    Options...365p.
ProgramData...161
Programs...305
Quick access...93, 111, 153p., 413
    Pin to...111
Quiet Hours..414
RAM..20p., 23
Rayman Jungle Run...286
Recording device...223
    Set Default..223
Recovery media *see* Operating system recovery media
Recycle Bin..44, 116, 119, 164, 166pp., 248, 467, 510
    Disable..173
    Empty..167
    Folders...171
    Large file...169
    Network storage..170
    Properties..171p.
    Restore..167
    Ribbon...167
    Size..172
Reduced colour mode..433
Region & Language settings..222
Regular account *see* Local account
Reset your PC..524p.
    Keep my files..526
    Remove everything...527
    Remove files and clean the drive..528
    Removed Apps..529
Restart..49p.
Ribbon..95
    Hide..96
    Music Tools..96
    Open...96
    Show..96
Roboform..545
Rotation lock..413
Route planning...274, 276
Router...453p., 474

SanDisk Cruzer...179
Satellite internet...452
Screen resolution..433
    640x480...433
Screen saver..445
Search...
    Index *see* Indexing
    My stuff..55p., 199
    Results..55
    Ribbon..205
    Show..56
    Tags...107
    Tools..204
Search bar.........................42, 51p., 54p., 76, 78, 91, 198, 207, 212, 216, 234, 403
Search index..179
Send to menu..115
Services...539
Settings..
    Accounts..330
    Network & Internet..456
    Notifications & actions..416
    Personalisation..436, 444
    Power & Sleep..445
    Update & Security...359, 365, 525
    Windows update..359
Shield icon..342
Show me tips about Windows..416
Shut down..48pp.
Sign out..48p.
SkyDrive *see* OneDrive
Skype...543
Sleep...49, 445
Smartphone...180p.
SmartScreen Filter...368
Software *see* Desktop – Software, Trusted Windows Store app
Sort by..109, 140
Sound Forge...544
SSD..21, 305
    See also Hard drive – Solid State
Standard users...
    vs. Administrators..335
Start button...**41, 45, 48, 51, 77p., 80**
Start menu. 13, 18, 40p., 45pp., 50p., 75p., 115, 224, 234, 237, 262, 268, 274, 280, 283, 288, 358, 365, 400pp., 524, 540
    Choose which folders appear on Start...407
    Colours...408
    Jump list...406
    Personalisation..406
    Pin folder to..115

Pin to..403
Resize..401
Start screen...13, 40, 45pp., 51, 72p., 75pp., 80p., 86p., 358, 365, 401p., 406, 409p.
StickyPassword..545
Store app..283
    Account menu..289
    App page...286
    Browsing..283
    Download manager..288p.
    Downloads...290
    My Library..290
    Payment options..290
    Purchase (history)...290
    Redeem a code...290
    Reviews and ratings..286
    Search..284
    Settings..289
    View account...290
Sudo..345
Swipe..73
    In...73
System repair media...323
    Choosing a drive...326
    Copy system files...325
    See also Operating system recovery media
System Restore...516
    Enabling..516
    Point..518
        Choosing..520
        Create...518
        Restoring from...521
        Roll back to..519
    Scan for affected programs..521
    Settings..517p.
    Undoing...522
System sounds...417
System tray *see* Notification area
Tablet..22, 71, 74, 80, 84
Tablet mode......................................**15,** 40, **64, 75, 77pp., 84pp., 406, 413, 547**
    Back button...78
    Multitasking..81
    Resizing apps..83
    Taskbar..78
    Turn on or off...**75**
    vs. Desktop mode..**76**
Tags..104, 107p., 197pp., 204
Talktofrank.com...353
Tap...71, 547
    and Hold..71

Double	71
Task Manager	531
App history	537
CPU usage gauge	536
Details	538
Disk gauge	537
End task	533, 535
Ethernet gauge	537
Memory gauge	536
Performance	535p.
Processes	534
Running a program	540
Services	539
Starting	531p.
Startup	538
Users	538
Task view	**42, 64, 66pp., 80p., 83**
Taskbar	41p., 50p., 60p., 76, 78, 87, 183pp., 194p., 197, 406
Auto-hide	87, 187
Buttons	188
Disappeared	540
Hiding	86
Lock/Unlock	185
Moving	185
Properties	186p.
Resizing	185
Toolbars	185
Temporary files	509
The Film & TV app	**262, 265**
This PC	94, 111, 175
Tile	47, 402
Group	405, 410
Live	47
Pin	403
Resize	404, 410
Unpin	402
vs. Icons	47
Tiles view	102
Touch screen	
Gestures	71
Working with	71
Trusted device	375
Trusted Windows Store app	13, 19, 22, 59, 77, 283, 340p., 376, 403
Downloading and installing	287
Purchase	287
Reinstall	505
Tablet mode	77
Uninstalling	505
Update	288

  Vs. Desktop app..288
Tweetdeck..545
Twitter..545
UAC *see* User Account Control
Undelete...167, 170
Upgrade icon...24
USB...192, 307
  Drive..179, 323, 450
  Port..307
  Safely removing...192
User Account Control...**340,** 424
  Administrator accounts..342
  Always notify me...343
  Disable..344
  Myths..345
  Never notify me...344
  Notify me only when apps try to make changes to my computer.....................343
  Prompt...341p.
  Settings...342
  Standard accounts...344
User accounts...
  Adding..329, 332
  Administrator..336
  Security level..335
   Change..335
  Standard user...336
Virtual desktop..42, 63p., 66pp.
  Move to..67
  Switch to...66
Virtualization...434
Virus definition updates...385
VLC..544
Volume icon..43, 192
VPN...414
Wallpaper *see* Desktop background
Weather app...55, 77p., 271p.
  Hourly forecast...272
  Places...273
  Settings..273
Web filter...353
Wi-Fi..454, 456
  Button..414
  Connect...455
  Open hotspot..457
  Security...454
  Sense..458
Window..59
  Close..60
  Dragging...117

    Maximise 60
    Minimise 59
    Move 60
    Name 59
    Network 111
    Resize 60
    Restore 60, 78
Windows 10 Home **18,** 19
Windows 10 Mobile .... **19, 22p.**
Windows 2000 .... 340, 345
Windows 7 13pp., 18, 23, 32, 39, 41, 45pp., 59p., 62, 71, 130, 132, 156, 177, 183p., 191, 204, 342, 421
Windows 8 ..13p., 18pp., 23p., 43, 45, 47, 70, 76, 81, 84pp., 95, 130, 175, 197, 224, 237, 247, 253, 274, 302, 311, 384, 421
Windows 9 18
Windows 95 433
Windows Defender 384
    Clean PC 390
    Cloud-based protection 386
    Exclusion .... 386pp.
    Malware detected 391
    Manual scan 388
    Quarantine 391
    Real-time protection 386
    Sample submission 386
    Settings .... 385p.
Windows Explorer *see* File Explorer
Windows fax machine 449
Windows Firewall 377
    Advanced settings 382
    Configuration 378
    Settings 380
    Turn off 381
Windows Live Photo Gallery 250
Windows Media Audio format 492
Windows Media Player 138, 183p., 253, 262, 486pp., 493p., 499, 502p., 543
    Audio CD 493
    Choose columns .... 500p.
    Copy protection options 497
    Details view 499
    Drag and drop 488
    Find album info 494
    Media library 490
    Mute 490
    Next/Previous 489
    Pictures 502
    Play 489
    Playing media 488
    Playlist 488, 490

Repeat..489
Rip CD to library..495
Running for the first time...486
Search..501
Shuffle...489
Slideshow..502
Stop..489
Video..489
Views...499
Volume...490
Windows Store *see* Store app
Windows Store App *see* Trusted Windows Store app
Windows update..358, 385
    Advanced options...361
    Choose how updates are delivered..363
    History..362
    Manually check for updates..359
    Scheduling a restart...361
Windows Vista...23, 32, 41, 59, 61, 342p., 421
Windows XP............................23, 32, 41, 175, 191, 322, 340, 345, 421, 434p.
Wireless network *see* Network – Wireless, Wi-Fi
Xbox Music app..253
Xbox One...375
Xbox Video app..262
XPS Document Writer...450
Zip file...116

Printed in Poland
by Amazon Fulfillment
Poland Sp. z o.o., Wrocław